ene yo

Apple Pro Training Series

Logic Pro 9
Advanced Music Production

David Dvorin
with Robert Brock

Apple Pro Training Series: Logic Pro 9 Advanced Music Production
David Dvorin with Robert Brock
Copyright © 2010 by David Dvorin

Published by Peachpit Press. For information on Peachpit Press books, contact:

Peachpit Press
1249 Eighth Street
Berkeley, CA 94710
(510) 524-2178
www.peachpit.com
To report errors, please send a note to errata@peachpit.com. Peachpit Press is a division of Pearson Education.

Apple Series Editor: Serena Herr
Project Editor: Nancy Peterson
Development Editor: Eric Schumacher-Rasmussen
Production Coordinator: Kim Wimpsett, Happenstance Type-O-Rama
Technical Editors: Robert Brock, David Dvorin
Technical Reviewers: Raymond Barker, Josh Hinden
Copy Editor: Darren Meiss
Media Reviewer: Jay Payne
Media Producer: Eric Geoffroy
Compositor: Maureen Forys, Happenstance Type-O-Rama
Indexer: Joy Dean Lee
Cover Illustrator: Kent Oberheu
Cover Producer: Happenstance Type-O-Rama

Notice of Rights

Notice of Liability

Trademarks

ISBN 13: 978-0-321-64745-0
ISBN 10: 0-321-64745-9
9 8 7 6 5 4 3 2 1
Printed and bound in the United States of America

Contents at a Glance

Table of Contents

Getting Started

We are lucky to live during one of the most exciting periods in the music production industry. Just a few short years ago, you would need a studio filled with synthesizers, hardware effects processors, mixing consoles, and expensive multitrack tape machines to accomplish what you can now do in a small project-based environment with a computer, an audio interface, and the right software. It's a good time to be a musician.

Apple Pro Training Series: Logic Pro 9 Advanced Music Production is intended to show experienced composers, arrangers, and producers how to enhance their skills by working with real projects in real-world scenarios. You'll learn how to increase the efficiency of your production workflow and accelerate editing tasks. You'll work on refining your mixing techniques, manipulating tempo and pitch, creating notated parts and scores, mixing for surround sound, and working with video and film. You'll unlock the limitless potential of Logic's groundbreaking software instruments by creating your own sounds from scratch.

Whether you're tweaking a song structure, applying effects processing, or editing audio and MIDI tracks, this book will give you the insider tips that will make your time with Logic Pro 9 more productive and more creative.

The Methodology

This book is written for those who already have a working knowledge of Logic Pro. (Beginning or less-experienced Logic users should read *Apple Pro Training Series: Logic Pro 9 and Logic Express 9* by David Nahmani.) Composers, audio engineers, and music producers currently working with Logic Pro will have the most to gain from reading this book.

The book is divided into five sections:

▶ Lesson 1 lays the foundation by helping you customize your Logic workflow. You'll create an environment that will increase your efficiency on your own projects as well as on the exercises in the book. Lesson 2 reveals Logic's deep feature set for manipulating time and pitch, including the new Flex Time feature.

▶ In Lessons 3 through 6, you'll create your own sounds on Logic's most advanced software instruments: ES2, EXS24 mkII, Sculpture, and Ultrabeat. Gaining an understanding of these powerful synthesizers and samplers will bring a wealth of musical resources to your sessions.

▶ In Lessons 7 through 9, you'll shape your tracks into an arrangement. With Logic Studio's MIDI and audio editing tools, you can refine the sound and structure of your composition, correcting production problems and making the most of your best takes.

▶ A composition is only as good as it sounds, which makes mixing and mastering your arrangement an essential part of the creative process. Lessons 10 through 12 guide you in taking your composition to the final level, using Logic Pro's Mixer, automation, control surface support, and effects processing to bring the highest degree of production quality to your creative output.

▶ For many projects, Logic Pro will be an all-inclusive working environment that takes composers and producers from musical idea to final recording. But there are times when you need to get your ideas on paper or when you're using your musical skills to serve a visual image. Lesson 13 provides a foundation for developing your surround sound mixing skills by using Logic's extensive new surround support. In Lesson 14 you'll create objects in the Environment to process MIDI data in all sorts of interesting ways. Lesson 15 shows you how to use Logic Pro's extensive notation capabilities to create musical parts and scores. In Lesson 16 you'll explore Logic Pro's power as a film and video scoring tool. Finally, in Lesson 17 you'll learn how to best transport sessions between Logic and other DAWs, enabling you to freely collaborate with studios running other software applications.

About the Apple Pro Training Series

Apple Pro Training Series: Logic Pro 9 Advanced Music Production is part of the official training series for Apple Pro applications developed by experts in the field. The lessons are designed to let you learn at your own pace. You'll find that this book explores many advanced features and offers tips and techniques for using the latest version of Logic.

Although each lesson provides step-by-step instructions for creating a specific project, there's room for exploration and experimentation. It is recommended that you follow the book from start to finish or at least complete the lessons in each part of the book in order. Each lesson concludes with a review section summarizing what you've covered.

System Requirements

Before beginning to use *Apple Pro Training Series: Logic Pro 9 Advanced Music Production*, you should have a working knowledge of your computer and its operating system. Make sure that you know how to use the mouse, navigate standard menus and commands, and also open, save, and close files. If you need to review these techniques, see the printed or online documentation included with your system.

For the basic system requirements for Logic Pro 9, go to www.apple.com/logicstudio/specs.

> **NOTE** ▶ If your display resolution is less than 1440 x 900, the included lesson files will display differently than shown in the book. Even so, you will be able to follow the lessons as described.

Copying the Logic Lesson Files

The DVD-ROM provided with this book includes folders that contain the lesson files used in this course. Each lesson has its own folder. You must have a standard installation of Logic Pro 9 on your hard disk to perform the exercises in this book.

To install the Logic project files:

1   Insert the *APTS_Advanced Logic 9* DVD into your DVD drive.

2   On your desktop, double-click the APTS_Advanced Logic 9 icon to view the disk contents.

3   Drag the Advanced Logic 9_Files folder from the DVD to the Music folder on your hard disk.

About the Apple Pro Training Series

Apple Pro Training Series: Logic Pro 9 Advanced Music Production is both a self-paced learning tool and the official curriculum of the Apple Pro Training and Certification Program.

Developed by experts in the field and certified by Apple, the series is used by Apple Authorized Training Centers worldwide and offers complete training in all Apple Pro products. The lessons are designed to let you learn at your own pace. Each lesson concludes with review questions and answers summarizing what you've learned, which can be used to help you prepare for the Apple Pro Certification Exam.

For a complete list of Apple Pro Training Series books, see the ad at the back of this book, or visit www.peachpit.com/apts.

Apple Pro Certification Program

The Apple Pro Training and Certification Programs are designed to keep you at the forefront of Apple's digital media technology while giving you a competitive edge in today's ever-changing job market. Whether you're an editor, graphic designer, sound designer, special effects artist, or teacher, these training tools are meant to help you expand your skills.

Upon completing the course material in this book, you can become an Apple Certified Pro by taking the certification exam at an Apple Authorized Training Center. Certification is offered in Final Cut Pro, Motion, Color, Soundtrack Pro, DVD Studio Pro, Shake, and Logic Pro. Certification as an Apple Pro gives you official recognition of your knowledge of Apple's professional applications while allowing you to market yourself to employers and clients as a skilled, pro-level user of Apple products.

For those who prefer to learn in an instructor-led setting, Apple offers training courses at Apple Authorized Training Centers worldwide. These courses, which use the Apple Pro Training Series books as their curriculum, are taught by Apple Certified Trainers and balance concepts and lectures with hands-on labs and exercises. Apple Authorized Training Centers have been carefully selected and have met Apple's highest standards in all areas, including facilities, instructors, course delivery, and infrastructure. The goal of the program is to offer Apple customers, from beginners to the most seasoned professionals, the highest-quality training experience.

For more information, please see the ad at the back of this book, or to find an Authorized Training Center near you, go to training.apple.com.

Resources

Apple Pro Training Series: Logic Pro 9 Advanced Music Production is not intended as a comprehensive reference manual, nor does it replace the documentation that comes with the application. For more information about Apple Logic Pro 9, refer to these sources:

▶ Logic Pro 9 User Manual: Accessed through the Logic Pro 9 Help menu, the User Manual contains a complete description of all the features.

▶ Apple's website: www.apple.com

Acknowledgments

The authors wish to give sincere and humble thanks to all of the talented musicians who provided material for use in this edition of the book:

▶ Tom Langford for his song "I Was Raised"

▶ Grant Levin for his composition "A Blues for Trane"

▶ Rocky Winslow and Randy McKean for playing on "Georgie the Spider"

▶ Composer Joe LoDuca, engineer Scott Davidson, and the folks of Electric Entertainment for the use of the score and footage from the Leverage series

▶ Caesar Filori and Wide Band Network for providing "Anatomy of a Human Bomb"

▶ Brandon Jaehne for use of "Gibsonia"

1

Time   This lesson takes approximately 90 minutes to complete.

Goals   Create and save your own custom template

Customize existing screensets for session needs

Learn the advantages and disadvantages of locking screensets

Assign key commands to speed up a workflow

Access needed tools quickly and efficiently

Back up and share your settings

Speeding Up Your Workflow

Spending a little time up front in preparation saves considerable production time when you are knee deep in a project. The quicker you can get your ideas into Logic, the more time you can spend creating and producing music and audio!

This lesson covers techniques to make your Logic sessions more efficient, going beyond the basics to speed up your workflow. Throughout, you will learn how to quickly access common functions and tools, as well as how to customize Logic to suit your individual needs.

Creating Your Own Template

Although an extensive collection of premade templates comes with Logic Pro, eventually you will want to create custom templates to suit your individual workflow. You can do this by modifying one of the premade templates or making an entirely new one. In the following exercises, you will create a custom template from scratch, then configure the interface for maximum workflow efficiency.

1   Choose File > New.

The Template dialog opens. You may have noticed that the Template pane always contains an Empty Project at the top, no matter which collection you select (Explore, Compose, or Produce).

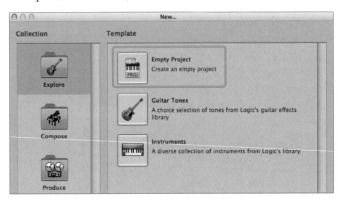

By clicking this button, you can create a project without any preconfigured tracks, routings, or display settings.

2   In the Templates pane, click the Empty Project button.

An empty project is created, and the New Tracks dialog opens, awaiting input.

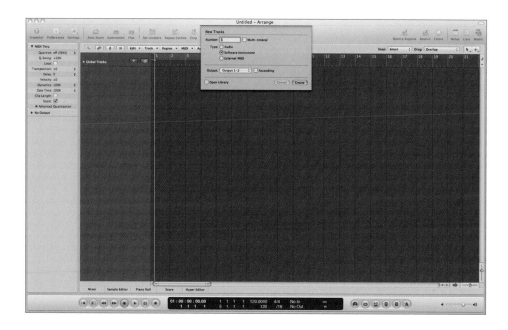

Creating New Tracks

The New Tracks dialog allows the quick creation and configuration of all types of tracks.

1   In the New Tracks dialog, select the Audio option, if it's not already selected.

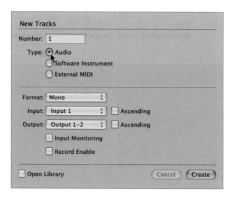

2   In the Number field, enter *8*.

3 In the Format menu, choose Stereo, if it's not already selected.

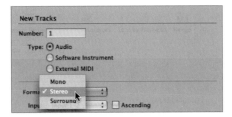

4 Click Create.

NOTE ▶ In the New Tracks dialog, you can assign inputs and outputs automatically (even assigning multiple tracks in ascending order), as well as set them to open with input monitoring turned on and recording enabled. This gets you ready for laying down new tracks immediately.

Eight new stereo audio tracks are created and appear in the Arrange area's track list.

You can create additional groups of tracks at any time by opening the New Tracks dialog.

5   In the Arrange area's local menu bar, choose Track > New.

TIP You can also open the New Tracks dialog by clicking the Create Track (+) button at the top of the track list.

The New Tracks dialog opens.

6   In the Number field, enter *8*.

7   Select the Software Instruments option.

8   Select the Open Library checkbox.

By selecting the Open Library option, you can automatically create new tracks and display the Library in the Media area.

9   Click Create.

The Library opens, and eight software instrument tracks are created and displayed in the Arrange area's track list.

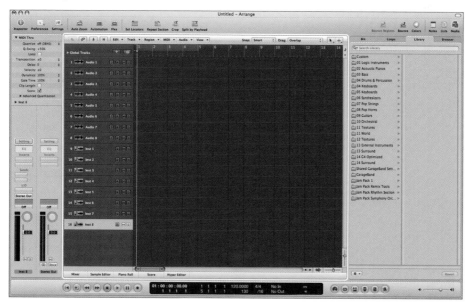

Customizing the Interface

Logic has the reputation of being a highly customizable software application for good reason. Not only can you conform the viewing area to a specific workflow, but you can also customize access to the functions you use the most, keeping them at your fingertips.

The toolbar provides access to common editing functions and often-used areas. The toolbar can also be customized.

1   Control-click the toolbar area and choose Customize Toolbar from the shortcut menu.

The Customize Toolbar dialog appears.

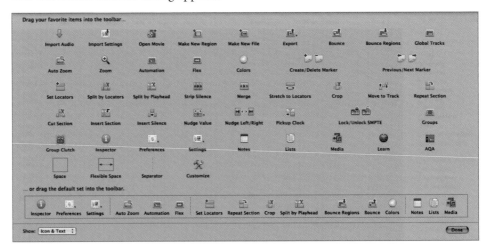

Functions in the Customize Toolbar dialog can be added to the toolbar by dragging their icons to the toolbar.

2   Drag the Import Audio icon to the toolbar, just to the right of the Split by Playhead button.

NOTE ▶ If you drag an icon to a location between two existing buttons, the buttons will move to make space for the new button.

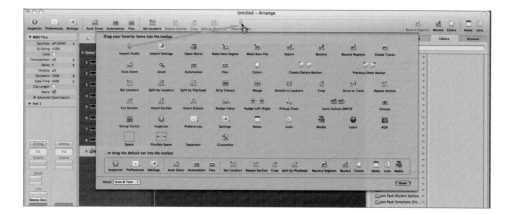

3 Click Done.

The Import Audio button is added to the toolbar.

NOTE ▸ Adding buttons to the toolbar is a user preference and will be present in all project files.

In addition to customizing the toolbar, you can also customize the Transport bar.

4 Control-click the Transport bar and choose Customize Transport Bar from the shortcut menu.

The Customize Transport Bar dialog appears.

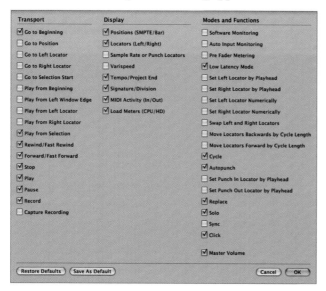

To customize the Transport bar, select the checkbox of each function you want to add.

5 In the Transport column of the dialog, select the Go to Position checkbox.

6 Click OK.

The button is added to the Transport section on the left side of the Transport bar.

NOTE ▶ Adding buttons to the Transport affects only the individual project file and will not be present in all project files. Transport customization can be saved to a template, however, enabling you to create new projects with your preferred Transport setup already in place.

Creating Screensets

Logic Pro allows direct access to all editing and mixing functions from the Arrange area. This single window interface significantly speeds up workflow, but it can also get a little crowded when displaying many items at once.

Screensets enable you to assign area and window combinations (including all zoom settings and view options) to a number key on the computer's keyboard. In the following exercises, you will create a custom screenset for your template.

1 Click the various editor buttons at the bottom of the Arrange window.

It is especially apparent in the Mixer and Media area (Library) that screen real estate only goes so far! Even with a streamlined interface, a separate screenset dedicated to the Mixer could be advantageous.

NOTE ▶ Depending on your display size and resolution, you will have more or less visible screen area. Therefore, your view might differ from the screenshots presented throughout this book.

2   Click the button of the active editor to close the editing area.

By default, new project files have only one screenset. You can create a new screenset customized for mixing that still contains a small Arrange area to provide an overview of the project tracks.

3   Press the 2 key.

A new screenset is created, indicated by *Screenset 2* in Logic's menu bar.

4   Click the Mixer button.

The Mixer appears at the bottom of the Arrange window.

You now have a screenset consisting of the Mixer area and a small Arrange area.

Maximizing Workspace

When you work with larger productions, it is helpful to have as much space as possible to view the musical data. You should set up Screenset 2 for maximum viewable space in both the Arrange area and the Mixer, while making sure that you're still able to access important project information.

Currently, the Arrange area can display only four tracks; you need to scroll down to see additional tracks. If this small Arrange area is to serve as an overview of the project's tracks, you must adjust the view to display as much of the arrangement as possible, both vertically and horizontally.

1   At the far right of the Arrange area, drag the vertical zoom control all the way up.

> **NOTE** ▶ If you are using a smaller screen resolution than 1140 × 900, the vertical zoom control might be hidden from view. If this is the case, use the Zoom Vertical Out key command (Control-Option–Up Arrow) instead.

The Arrange area view shrinks vertically, but it still may not display all 16 tracks you created earlier. To see all the tracks, you need to gain screen space by closing infrequently accessed and redundant areas. Since you are devoting this screenset to mixing, access to the toolbar's editing and viewing functions is not essential.

NOTE ▶ Even when the toolbar is hidden, the editing and viewing commands are still accessible in the Arrange area's local Edit and View menus.

2   At the upper-right corner of the Arrange window, click the Toolbar button.

The window expands slightly, allowing a full display of all 16 tracks in the Arrange area.

Although the Inspector's channel strips and Parameter boxes are vital when you're working in the Arrange area, they are not needed when you're mixing a project.

3   In the Arrange area's local menu bar, choose View > Inspector to hide the Inspector.

The Inspector is now hidden, allowing more channels to appear in the Mixer and more measures in the Arrange area.

In Logic (as in any other application), windows and areas must be in *key focus* for you to make any changes in them. That is, windows need to be active before you can interact with them. A highlighted top bar and thin white border indicates a window is in key focus. For your customized mixing screenset, it makes sense to have the Mixer area receive key focus.

4   Press the Tab key to shift key focus to the Mixer.

The Mixer's top bar will be highlighted to indicate that it has key focus.

NOTE ► Key focus can also be shifted to an area by clicking the area's top bar, or cycled through available windows by hitting the Tab key.

Locking Screensets

At present, your screenset is open to any additional changes, and it will always reflect the last state in which you left it. In Logic terms, the screenset is unlocked and can be continuously altered.

Considering that you just spent a fair amount of time configuring the screenset for mixing purposes, it makes sense to lock the screenset so you can return to this state any time you need to.

1 Choose Screenset 2 > Lock.

A small bullet appears between *Screenset* and the number 2 in the menu bar, signifying that the screenset is locked.

NOTE ► A screenset's menu displays the names of the areas or windows used in that screenset. These can be named anything you like by choosing Rename from the menu.

2 Press the 1 and 2 keys to switch screensets between the Arrange/Library screenset and the Arrange/Mixer screenset you just locked.

Screenset 2 opens, configured as it was when locked.

Comparing Unlocked and Locked Screensets

When you are new to Logic, your tendency is to lock all screensets. However, the unlocked state has distinct advantages, because you can spontaneously tweak a screenset to suit each stage of your production (increasing or decreasing zoom levels, for example). An unlocked screenset is especially valuable during editing. Often you are bouncing between different editors and adjusting specific parts of the project. It is helpful, then, to return to a screenset that's in the same state you left it when you continue work on a specific project area.

However, this takes some getting used to, and unintentional alterations can occur. If you are satisfied with the given configuration of a screenset, it is a good idea to lock it, protecting it from further changes until you unlock it again.

This exercise will help you get a feel for using unlocked and locked screensets.

1 Press 1 to open the Arrange/Library screenset.

2 In the Tool menu, choose the Pencil tool.

3 On the Inst 1 track, click the grid line at bar 9 to create a blank region.

4 Hold down Control-Option while drawing a selection rectangle around the Inst 1 region you just created.

The region will zoom in to a high degree.

5 Press 2 to open Screenset 2, and then open Screenset 1 again.

Notice how recalling Screenset 1 restores the zoomed state in which you left it. Now repeat the same steps with Screenset 1 locked.

6 Control-Option-click the background of the Arrange area to return to the previous zoom state.

The Arrange area appears as it did when you started this exercise.

7   Choose Screenset 1 > Lock.

8   Hold down Control-Option while dragging a selection rectangle around the Inst 1 region, as you did previously.

9   Open Screenset 2, and then open Screenset 1.

This time when you return to Screenset 1, the region is displayed exactly as it was when you locked the screenset. No matter what edits are performed within the screen-set (zooming, in this case), it will return to a normalized state, almost like a template.

10 Delete the region you created by selecting it and pressing Delete.

Using Key Commands

As you become familiar with Logic's feature set, you'll notice that you perform some tasks more often than others. By assigning a command to a specific key on the computer's key-board, you can execute common functions without reaching for the mouse and navigating a hierarchical menu system. Key command assignments are written to a location within the ~/Library/Application Support/Logic folder and are accessible to all Logic projects. Although your key commands act as a preference, they are written to a separate file, enabling you to initialize the main preferences without affecting your key assignments. This differs from the screensets you created in the last exercise, which are saved within each project file.

Logic's Key Commands window is a powerful mapping tool that lets you assign a key (or key combination) to nearly every menu item within Logic and also to some special func-tions that can be accessed only by using a key command.

If you've been working with Logic for some time, you are probably using default key commands and have assigned some custom commands of your own. Let's start by review-ing the basic procedure for key assignments and follow up with additional techniques to maximize the potential of this powerful feature.

Viewing Key Assignments

1   Open Logic's Key Commands window by choosing Logic Pro > Preferences > Key Commands.

The Key Commands window opens.

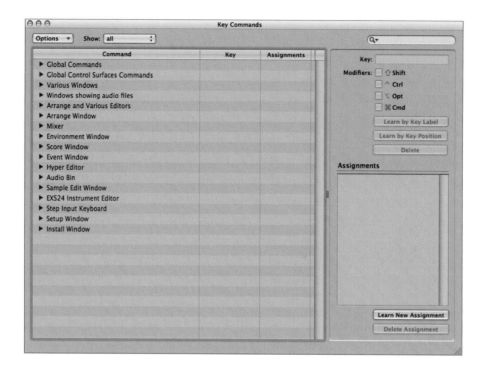

2   In the Key Commands window, from the Options menu, choose Expand All.

The list expands to show all possible key commands. Scroll down using the scroller to the right of the pane to get an idea of the breadth of the assignable functions within Logic. There are a vast number of choices, to be sure!

TIP ▶ Assign key commands only to actions you perform often. This way you will always have your most-used actions at your fingertips but avoid being overwhelmed with having to remember too many commands.

3   In the Key Commands window, from the Options menu, choose Collapse All.

The Commands column now shows only those categories that represent the main application areas, instead of listing every available command. You can view key commands more methodically in this manner.

Topping the list is the Global Commands category, which contains actions that function regardless of the window or editor you are working in at a given time.

4   Click the disclosure triangle to the left of Global Commands.

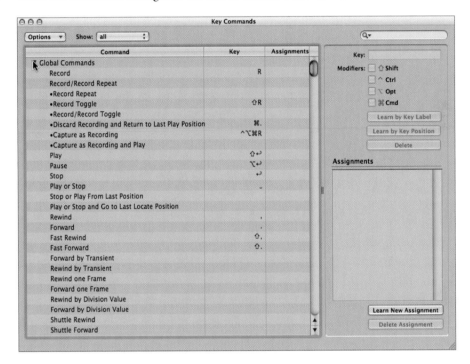

Clicking the disclosure triangle for a given window or category enables you to quickly view all the commands associated with it.

Assigning Keys to Commands

Let's assign a useful key command that doesn't already have a default assignment.

1   Click the Shuttle Rewind command, located near the bottom of the currently visible part of the list (use the scroller, if necessary).

2   Click the Learn by Key Label button, located at the right side of the window.

NOTE ▶ A key label is what is actually imprinted on the individual key. Logic has been localized for many languages, so this becomes important because computers sold internationally have different keyboard layouts. In this way, a function assigned to, say, the Y key will be activated regardless of where the key is on a given keyboard.

3 Press the comma key.

An alert message appears.

This message is Logic's fail-safe to keep you from assigning the same key to multiple commands. It also provides an option for quickly reassigning the key to a new command.

The Key column in the Key Commands window shows the key assignments in use. In the current example, you can clearly see that the comma key is assigned to the Rewind command. However, as you remember from scanning the list, not all functions are easily determined, which is why this alert message is beneficial.

4 Click Cancel.

5 With the Learn by Key Label button still active, press Control-comma.

The key combination you entered is displayed in the Key column next to the Shuttle Rewind command.

NOTE ▸ This combination of key (comma) plus modifier key (Control) is also represented in the area above the Learn by Key Label button.

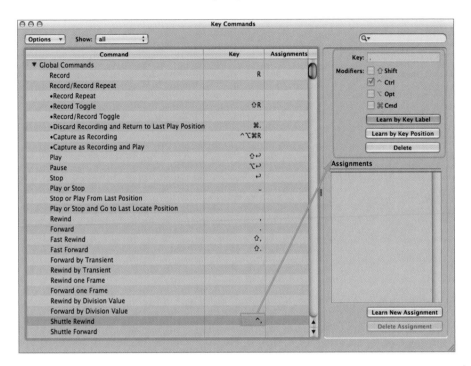

6   Click the Shuttle Forward command (located below Shuttle Rewind).

7   Press Control-period to assign that key combination.

8   Close the Key Commands window.

You have assigned two very useful key commands for getting around in the Arrange area. Try pressing these keys, observing their effect on the playhead. Note how you can increase the winding speed by repeatedly pressing the period or comma while holding down the Control key. Try initiating movement in a single direction, and then "braking" by pressing the key in the opposite direction. This behavior is modeled after analog tape transports and video decks, where each press of the rewind or fast-forward button increases the direction speed.

TIP ▶ For key commands to be useful, you must remember the key assignment. Therefore, choose assignments that provide a clue to their functions. The first letter of a function, or a graphic representation of it, represents a good place to start. (For example, the comma and period keys also have the less-than and greater-than symbols, which visually represent the forward and rewind functions, respectively.) Also try to think about commands as parts of families of similar functionality, then assign related commands to keys with different modifiers. (For example, since comma is the command for Rewind, Control-comma is a logical choice for Shuttle Rewind.)

Using Key-Command-Only Functions

Some functions are accessible only via key commands and not available as menu items. These commands should not be overlooked, however, as they can be quite useful.

In the upper-right corner of the Key Commands window is a search field. This functions like the search in many other Apple software applications. You can, for example, use it to search for Logic's many playback functions.

1   Open the Key Commands window, this time using its own key command, Option-K.

2   Click once in the search field and enter *play*.

   NOTE ▶ You do not need to press Return to initiate the search.

The left pane of the Key Commands window now lists every command that has the word *play* in it, regardless of the category. You'll notice that some of the commands have a bullet (•) in front of them.

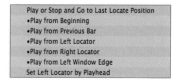

The bullet indicates that this function is accessible only via key command, and it is not available as a menu choice.

3   Scroll down (if necessary), and click "Set Locators and Play."

4   Assign "Set Locators and Play" to Shift-Spacebar.

5   Close the Key Commands window.

> **TIP** ▸ This useful key command packs multiple functions into a single keystroke. Used in the Arrange area or in any editor, it creates a cycle area (setting the locators first) around a selected region or event and then initiates playback. Use this command when you want to quickly audition the section around a given region or event.

Accessing the Tool Menu

Logic's Tool menus offer essential manipulation of data within a variety of windows. These tools are indispensable, changing the Pointer tool to act in a variety of helpful ways. Easy access to these often-used objects is extremely important. Let's take a moment to explore the ways you can gain quick access to the Tool menus.

There are many Tool menus in Logic. The available tools change depending on the functions of a window or editor.

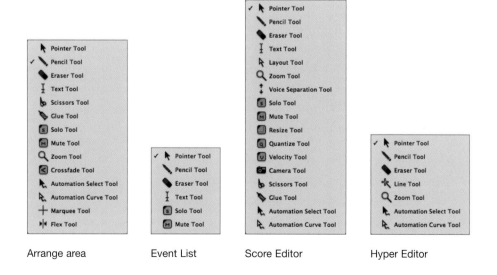

Arrange area   Event List   Score Editor   Hyper Editor

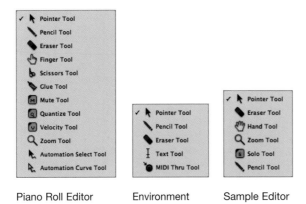

Piano Roll Editor   Environment   Sample Editor

As you can see in the previous figures, the Tool menus vary in number as well as types of tools. Even so, there is a great deal of overlap in frequently used tools (the Pointer tool, for instance).

In all cases, the Tool menus are located on the upper-right side of the screen, usually a distance away from where you wish to use the tool. This distance may seem small the first few times you move your mouse across the screen, but if you find yourself switching tools often while editing (and most of us do), this movement can become tedious and ergonomically harmful. In the following exercises, you will use Logic's shortcuts to gain quick access to a Tool menu, enabling you to work in a more efficient manner.

Using the Alternate Tool

When working with objects in any window, you have two tools always available at the mouse position, represented by the two Tool menus. The left menu option is your default tool, and the right menu option is your alternate tool, made available by pressing the Command key. The ability to switch between these two tools at the place you are actually working (your current pointer position) enables you to more quickly toggle between often-used tools, which speeds workflow.

1   In the Arrange area, choose the Pointer tool from the left (default) Tool menu, if it is not already chosen.

2 From the right (alternate) Tool menu, choose the Pencil tool.

3 Move your pointer over the main part of the Arrange area and press the Command key while watching the pointer.

The pointer changes to the Pencil tool.

The Pencil tool in this case is referred to as the Command-click, or alternate, tool. You can think of the action as a momentary toggle to a tool you've preset.

Saving the Alternate Tool to Your Screenset

Tool assignments can be different for each area or window that has a Tool menu. These assignments are saved with the screenset, so let's add your Command-click assignment to the screenset you created earlier in this lesson.

1 Unlock Screenset 1 by pressing Shift-Command-L.

2 Lock Screenset 1 by pressing Shift-Command-L again.

The Command-click tool designation is saved to the screenset.

> **TIP** ▶ Take some time to think about which tools you use most often in each of the editors, and then assign alternate tools in your screensets using the technique you just learned.

Quickly Accessing the Tool Menu

1 Move your pointer to the middle of the Arrange area.

2 Press the Esc key.

A floating Tool menu appears at the pointer position.

3 Click the Eraser tool.

The Tool menu disappears, and the Pointer tool is now an Eraser tool.

This technique can save many a trip across the screen to select a new tool, because it opens the Tool menu when and where you need it for editing.

4 Press the Esc key again.

Instead of choosing the desired tool using the mouse, try an even quicker key command.

5 Press the 5 key on your keyboard.

The Tool menu disappears, and the Eraser tool changes to the Scissors tool.

NOTE ▸ When the floating Tool menu is open, the number keys that you usually use for screensets are overridden until a selection is made.

6 Press the Esc key twice to return to the Pointer tool.

TIP ▸ Many users assign key commands to their most-used tools. This lets you access common tools that are shared by separate editors (the Pointer tool, for instance). Try searching for the tool names in the Key Commands window to see your options.

Working with Hard-Wired Tool Menu Commands

Just as holding down the Command key lets you momentarily toggle to an alternate tool, you can also carry out common functions by using tools in conjunction with other modifier keys. These "hard-wired" commands aren't listed within menus, so a list of the most useful ones is provided here for easy access:

Key	With Tool	Result
Control	Any tool	Opens a shortcut menu with associated functions when clicking
Control-Option	Any tool	Changes the tool to the Zoom tool
Option	Pointer tool	Creates copy when dragging a region or event
Option-Shift	Pointer tool	Creates alias (MIDI) or clone (audio) when dragging a region
Shift	Pointer tool	Changes multiple selected region or event endpoints to same absolute time when dragging
Option	Pointer tool	Time stretches or compresses region when dragging region endpoint
Option-Shift	Pointer tool	Time stretches or compresses multiple regions when dragging endpoint, sets length to same absolute time
Shift	Pencil tool	Imports audio file at clicked location
Shift	Pointer tool	Selects nodes in automation track
Control-Option	Pointer tool	Adjusts curves in automation track
Control-Shift	Pointer tool	Adjusts the crossfade curve
Option	Fade tool	Deletes crossfade
Option	Solo tool	Solos and plays region from beginning
Option	Marquee tool	Creates marquee selection at region borders
Option-Shift	Marquee tool	Adds selected region to marquee selection

NOTE ▶ These commands are used throughout the lessons in this book. It's a good idea to have a bookmark at this page for future reference.

Using Tool Click Zones

New to Logic Pro 9, tool click zones can dramatically speed up region editing in the Arrange window by automatically selecting a Fade or Marquee tool when the mouse pointer is positioned over specific "hot spots."

These options are set within Logic's preferences.

1   Choose Logic Pro > Preferences > General to view the Preferences window.

From here you can select different preference categories (General, Audio, and so on) by clicking the buttons at the top. Once you select a category, you can access different aspects of preferences by clicking a tab.

2   Click the Editing tab.

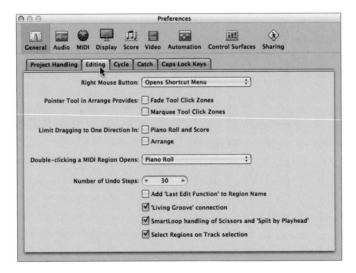

The screen shot shows Logic's Editing preferences, which include the assignment of the Pointer tool click zones.

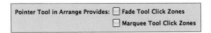

The first checkbox, Fade Tool Click Zones, when selected, will automatically change the Pointer tool to a Fade tool when positioned over the upper-left and upper-right corners of an audio region.

NOTE ▶ This function is not available for MIDI regions, as they do not allow fades to be created with the Fade tool.

The second option, Marquee Tool Click Zones, when selected, will automatically change the Pointer tool to a Marquee tool when positioned over the lower half of any region (audio or MIDI).

NOTE ▶ Both settings for the tool click zones can be utilized in combination, and they do not interfere with the Pointer tool's dynamic region loop or length editing capabilities.

Controlling the Tool Menu with a Two-Button Mouse

When using a two-button mouse with Logic, you gain another way to access the Tool menu. To do this, you must first designate the function of the right mouse button, choosing between four modes of operation.

1   Click the Right Mouse Button pop-up menu to view the options.

The first option, "Is Assignable to a Tool," enables you to assign a tool of your choice to the right mouse button. Once this option is chosen, a third Tool menu appears next to the default and alternate Tool menus, representing the right-click tool. Essentially, this assignment works similarly to the Command-click, or alternate, tool you looked at earlier. However, it functions independently of the Command-click tool, in effect providing three tool choices at your disposal at any given time.

The second option, Opens Tool Menu, works similarly to pressing the Esc key (see "Quickly Accessing the Tool Menu," earlier in this lesson), displaying a Tool menu at your current mouse position.

The third option, Opens Shortcut Menu, works similarly to pressing the Control key (see "Working with Hard-Wired Tool Menu Commands," earlier in this lesson), displaying a shortcut menu with associated functions at the current mouse position.

The fourth option, "Opens Tool and Shortcut Menu," combines the second and third option, providing access to both menus at your current mouse position.

2   Choose Opens Shortcut Menu, if it is not already chosen.

3   Close the Preferences window.

Saving a Project Template

You have spent quite a bit of time customizing this project. Now you can save it as a template for future use.

1 Choose File > Save as Template.

The "Save Template as" window opens, automatically pointing to a save location in the Project Templates folder that was created when you initially installed Logic Pro.

2 Enter the filename *Advanced Logic*.

3 Click Save.

The template is now saved to your hard disk and will appear the next time you create a new project, in the My Templates collection.

Opening and Creating Projects Automatically

Having a selection of templates at your fingertips can be useful in any given situation. However, most of the time you'll want to start your sessions with the same basic configuration. You can configure Logic Pro to automatically launch a given template or empty project by setting a startup action preference.

1 Choose Logic Pro > Preferences > General.

2 Click the Project Handling tab.

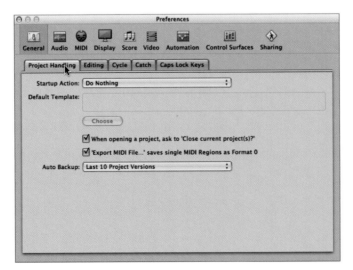

3 Click the Startup Action pop-up menu to view the menu items.

These commands dictate Logic's action on startup, ranging from Do Nothing (no project file is loaded) to Create New Project Using Default Template. Once you have created a general-purpose, or default, template (as you have been doing in this lesson), it is convenient to have Logic automatically base a new project file on it at startup. This will let you get to work as soon as Logic opens.

4 Choose Startup Action > Create New Project Using Default Template.

Now all that's needed is to specify which template Logic will use as the default.

5 Click the Choose button.

The Template dialog opens.

6 In the Collection pane, click My Templates.

7 In the Template pane, click Advanced Logic.

The file path pointing toward the Advanced Logic template is displayed in the Default Template field.

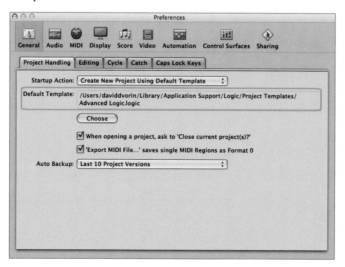

The next time you open Logic, it will automatically create a new project based on the template you created in this lesson.

8   Close the Preferences window.

Backing Up and Transporting Your Setup

After you've spent considerable time customizing your Logic setup, it is a good idea to back up your key commands and project templates for retrieval in the future.

If you work in multiple locations, it is advisable to take these with you when you work on another Logic setup in a different facility. USB flash drives are great for carting around your personal Logic settings. Use the following table to copy files from your main system:

Setting	File Location
Key commands	~/Library/Application Support/Logic/Key Commands
Project templates	~/Library/Application Support/Logic/Project Templates

To benefit from the portability of your Logic settings, you must load them into the host system. The contents of both your Key Commands and Project Templates folders must be copied to the location listed above in the new system to make them available.

> **NOTE** ▶ You can also export and import key commands from within the Key Commands window by choosing the item in the Options menu.

Importing Screensets

Sometimes when you're working on Logic song files from other people, you may wish to import your own screensets so that you can more comfortably navigate through their songs. You can do this as a settings import from one project file to another, and it only requires that you have a copy of one of your project files available.

1   Choose File > Project Settings > Import Project Settings.

The Import Project Settings file selector dialog opens.

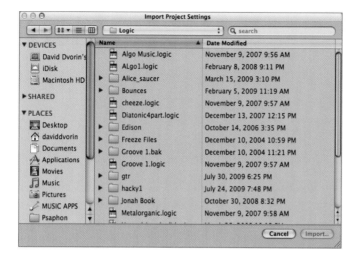

2   In the file selector dialog, go to Music > Advanced Logic 9_Files > Lessons and select the 02_The Only Light Thats On_Start.logic file.

3   Click Import.

The Import Settings dialog opens.

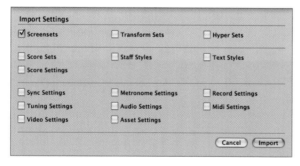

4   Un-check all other selections besides Screensets, if not already done.

5   Click Import.

6   Press the numbers 1 through 4 on your keyboard to view the imported screensets.

Logic copies the screensets to the current project.

Accessing Your Settings over a Network

Logic offers you the ability to back up and share user-created plug-in settings, channel strip settings, and key commands over a network. This makes it convenient to transport your custom settings from machine to machine in a networked facility, or anywhere you have an Internet connection.

1 Choose Logic Pro > Preferences > Sharing.

The Preferences window opens, displaying Sharing preferences.

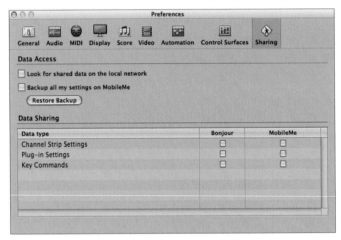

Data can be exchanged over a local network using Apple's Bonjour technology or over the Internet using a MobileMe account.

NOTE ▶ Logic uses settings defined in your System Preferences to access your MobileMe account, so make sure that these settings are configured prior to transfer.

To share your data over a network, first select the data type you are sharing (Channel Strip Settings, Plug-in Settings, or Key Commands), and how you would like to share it (Bonjour or MobileMe).

2 Select the appropriate Channel Strip Settings, Plug-in Settings, and Key Commands checkboxes in the Bonjour and MobileMe columns.

NOTE ▶ Depending on whether or not you've accessed your MobileMe account with Logic before, you may receive a dialog asking permission to use the account information in your keychain. If this is the case, you need to click either Allow Once or Always Allow in order for Logic to gain access.

Backing Up Your Settings Using a MobileMe Account

If you have access to a MobileMe account, you are able to back up and restore channel strip settings, plug-in settings, and key commands to your iDisk. This enables you to efficiently back up precious custom settings without using external hard drives or optical media. It also provides a convenient way to retrieve your settings; all you need is Internet access.

To send data to a MobileMe account, you need to select the "Backup all my settings on MobileMe" checkbox within the Data Access area in the Sharing preferences.

1   In the Preferences window, select "Backup all my settings on MobileMe."

The backup operation starts immediately, indicated by a status message at the bottom of the window.

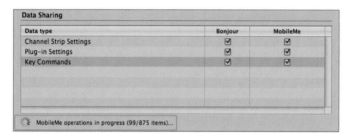

TIP ▸ You can find out the date and time of your last MobileMe backup by placing your pointer over the "Backup all my settings on MobileMe" checkbox.

After you've saved the settings to your MobileMe account, you can retrieve them by clicking the Restore Backup button.

2   Click the Restore Backup button.

A message appears asking if you want to overwrite your local settings with the ones uploaded to the MobileMe account.

3   Click Restore.

The data is restored to your computer.

NOTE ▶ You can access the settings backed up to a given MobileMe account with any computer connected to the Internet by logging on to the iDisk Public folder for the MobileMe account. The files are written to the Public/MusicAudioData directory. You can even access them via a web browser by using the following URL: http://idisk.mac.com/MOBILEMEUSERNAME/Public/MusicAudioData.

Sharing Settings on a Network

In addition to backing up and restoring your own settings, Logic can use an active network connection to gain access to the settings of others. This can be done by connecting to another's MobileMe account (via the Internet) or using Bonjour (in a local network).

1   In the Sharing Preferences window, select "Look for shared data on the local network."

As long as a network connection is detected, you should be able to access any Mac running Logic with data sharing enabled. (See "Accessing Your Settings over a Network" in this lesson.)

NOTE ▶ To access settings via Bonjour, all machines must have Logic Pro open.

When connected, you can access shared key commands via the Options menu in the Key Commands window.

2   Close the Preferences window.

3   Open the Key Commands window by choosing Logic Pro > Preferences > Key Commands.

4   Click the Options menu and choose Presets.

The Presets menu displays a Bonjour submenu containing the key command sets available from other machines on the local network.

5   Close the Key Commands window.

In addition to key commands, Bonjour also allows access to shared plug-in and channel strip settings wherever you normally use them (the Library, channel strips, and plug-in windows).

6   In the Library, click the Bonjour menu at the bottom of the list.

All available accounts are shown.

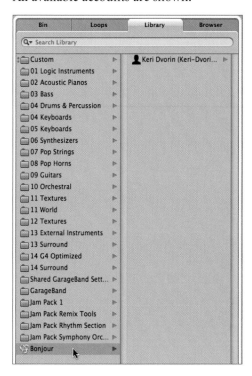

NOTE ▸ A target account must have user-created settings to display the Bonjour menu.

7   In the Bonjour menu, click an account to access the channel strip settings.

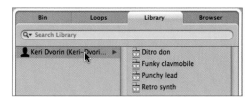

You can also use a MobileMe account to share settings. To do this, you must have an active Internet connection and the appropriate account information to access the MobileMe account.

8   At the bottom of the Library, click the Action pop-up menu and choose Connect to MobileMe.

The Connect to MobileMe dialog appears.

Here you can choose whether you want to connect to your own MobileMe account or the public folder on another's (by entering the account name).

9   Click OK.

Once a connection is established, you can now access the MobileMe account's settings by selecting it within the Library.

NOTE ▶ The MobileMe folder will list all user-created channel strip settings within account folders. If you haven't created any channel strip settings, the user account folder will be dimmed (unable to be selected). When new user channel strip settings are created, you need to disconnect then reconnect to the MobileMe account before they will appear within the Library.

10 Close the project.

NOTE ▶ You can disconnect from the MobileMe account by choosing "Disconnect MobileMe accounts" from the Library's Action menu.

Lesson Review

1. What are project templates?

2. What are some of the ways you can customize a project file?

3. What is the advantage of an unlocked screenset?

4. Identify two strategies for creating key commands that help you remember them.

5. Are all key commands accessible via menus?

6. In what ways can you quickly access the Tool menus?

7. In what ways can you back up and share your settings?

Answers

1. Project templates are premade project files containing various configurations specific to certain session tasks, such as composing and mixing.

2. Project files can be customized by adding buttons to the toolbar and Transport bar and by maximizing various areas of the workspace.

3. An unlocked screenset can be advantageous during the editing stage because it allows a dynamic view of the current data.

4. Assign a key command only if you find yourself performing a menu command often. Assign keys that provide a clue to the function of a command, such as a key with a graphic representation or the first letter of the function.

5. No. Some useful functions are accessible only via key command, indicated by a bullet preceding the name in the Key Commands window.

6. You can access the Tool menus quickly by using alternate tools, using the Esc key to display the Tool menu at the pointer location, and using a two-button mouse.

7. Custom key commands, plug-in settings, and channel strip settings can be backed up to traditional storage media, as well as to a Bonjour account on a local network or a MobileMe account accessed via an Internet connection.

2

Lesson Files
Advanced Logic 9_Files > Lessons > 02_Georgie the Spider_Start.logic

Advanced Logic 9_Files > Lessons > 02_The Only Light Thats On_Start.logic

Media
Advanced Logic 9_Files > Media > Georgie the Spider

Advanced Logic 9_Files > Media > The Only Light Thats On

Time
This lesson takes approximately 90 minutes to complete.

Goals
Use the Apple Loops Utility to create your own Apple Loops

Use the Time and Pitch Machine to create a harmonized part

Use the Pitch Correction effect to intonate an audio track

Manipulate the phrasing and feel of audio tracks using the Flex tool and flex markers

Quantize audio regions with flex time to change the feel or tighten the timing

Conform the timing of one region to that of another by creating custom groove templates

Use speed fades to simulate turntable or tape machine effects

Use varispeed to smoothly change the tempo of the entire project

Match a project's time grid to a freely played recording for further editing and development

Working with Time and Pitch

Music production has finally reached the age where time and pitch are fluid. Not too long ago, it would have been impossible to alter the overall speed of an audio recording without affecting the pitch, not to mention the phrasing and feel. Recent trends in audio production technology have attempted to address this, incorporating features that allow you to manipulate time and pitch.

Logic Pro has a large repertoire of time and pitch manipulating tools to address common problems that arise within a production environment. There are so many options, in fact, that it can be difficult to determine what tool is good for a specific job.

Certain approaches aren't always suitable for a specific piece of material, and unexpected results (desirable or not) can occur. To achieve a better outcome, you need to manipulate the available parameters and help the computer make more appropriate choices.

In this lesson, you will explore Logic Pro's palette of time and pitch manipulation features, learning which technique is best suited for the material at hand. In addition, you will explore Logic's ability to "beat map", or align its time grid to a rubato performance.

Creating Your Own Apple Loops with the Apple Loops Utility

Apple Loops are essentially audio or MIDI regions with additional information written to the file's header. In software such as Logic and GarageBand, the information enables the time stretching and pitch shifting of the region to be done independently of each other in real time.

You might have already created your own Apple Loops by selecting a region and using the Add to Apple Loops Library command. While this is certainly convenient, the process is indiscriminant and lacks the ability for the user to optimize the result for the individual material.

Enter the Apple Loops Utility, an application installed with Logic Studio that allows you to both tag and manually edit how transients, or initial attacks, are detected and used for time stretching.

In this exercise, you will use the Apple Loops Utility to convert a standard audio file to an optimized Apple Loop, adding it to your library for possible future use.

> **NOTE** ▶ The Apple Loops Utility works only with audio regions, and does not allow you to create Software Instrument Apple Loops (SIALs).

1   Choose File > Open, and in the file selector dialog, navigate to Music > Advanced Logic 9_Files > Lessons and open **02_Georgie the Spider_Start.logic**.

The project opens.

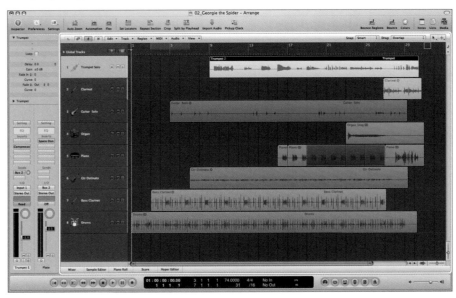

2   Play the project to familiarize yourself with the arrangement.

> **NOTE** ▸ All audio recorded, bounced within, and exported from Logic Pro has the ability to follow the project's tempo (with the Follow Tempo option selected within the Region Parameter box), but only Apple Loops have the distinct advantage of automatic pitch shifting, conforming to the project's key or chord changes that are present in the Chord global track.

Most of the pieces are there, but there are some timing problems in the individual parts, which will be addressed later on in the lesson. For now, you will direct your attention to the Piano Loop region that makes up the majority of the piano part. You will use this region for creating an Apple Loop using the Apple Loops Utility.

3   Select the Piano Loop region located at measure 17.

4   In the Transport, click the Solo button.

A yellow border appears around the Piano Loop region, indicating that it is soloed.

5   Play the project from measure 17 to audition the piano part, stopping the project after you become familiar with the repetitive loop.

6   In the Arrange area's local menu bar, choose Audio > Open in Apple Loops Utility. A dialog appears asking you to identify the length of the audio file.

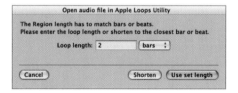

For the Apple Loops Utility to analyze the data, it must discern how the file length relates to music beats and bars. The Apple Loops Utility makes an educated guess based on the region length compared to the Logic's own bar/beat ruler.

7   Click "Use set length." The Apple Loops Utility opens, displaying the filename in the Assets drawer (at the far right), with the Tags tab open.

Tagging Files

Tags are pieces of information used by many applications, including those that support the Apple Loops file format. Adding tags will not directly affect the tempo or pitch prop-

erties of a file, but tags are essential if you plan on adding a file to the Apple Loops library
(accessed by Logic's Loop Browser). These bits of information constitute a database,
enabling you to search for material based on specific criteria. Let's look at these properties
by creating tags for the Piano Loop file that you imported.

The upper-left portion of the Tags tab contains property tags related to the file's musical
content.

The Apple Loops Utility supplies default values for the time signature, number of beats,
key, and tonality. The Piano Loop region you are working with will be looped within the
arrangement, so it is necessary to indicate this within the property tags.

1   If it's not already selected, click the Looping radio button.

Earlier, you specified that the file was 2 bars in length, but in order to match up with
the correct meter, you need to specify the exact number of beats it contains.

2   In the Number of Beats field, enter *8*.

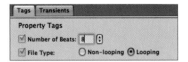

Db minor is the key of the original audio file. In order for this file to appear in searches
of a similar tonality, you need to indicate this within the Key and Scale Type menus.

3   From the Key menu, choose C#/Db.

4   From the Scale Type menu, choose Minor.

Move down to the Search Tags pane, where you can define the music genre and instrument type for the file.

5   In the Instrument list, choose Keyboards > Piano.

6   In the Descriptors pane, look at the list that describes the musical content.

7   Select the radio buttons for the options that best describe the musical characteristics of the Piano Loop part, as shown here:

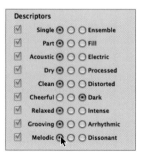

Working with Transients

Now that you've defined the search tags of the audio file, it is time to work with properties that directly relate to time stretching and pitch transposition.

Transients are good indicators of where beats occur in an audio file, and they typically show up as sharp attacks with the highest amplitude (tallest areas of a waveform). The Apple Loops Utility automatically detects transients and applies markers based on their characteristics in conjunction with the bar and beat information you supplied when opening the utility. These transient markers are used as a map, enabling Logic to make decisions about where best to apply time stretching and pitch transposition.

1 Click the Transients tab to display the audio file waveform.

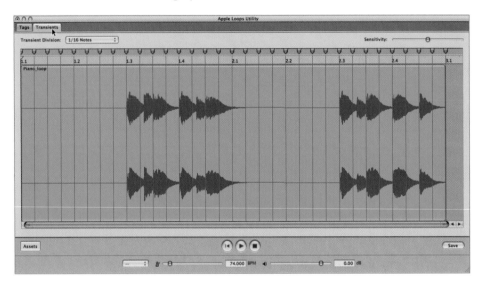

NOTE ▸ You may need to enlarge the window and zoom in to better view the information within this window.

By default, the Apple Loops Utility uses sixteenth-note divisions, but this might not always be appropriate for the given material. It is best to check results by listening to the file played from within the utility, which will immediately apply time stretching and pitch transposition based on the settings.

2 If it is not already done, make sure that the Tempo slider (marked with a metronome symbol) is set to the recording's original tempo (74 bpm, in this case).

TIP ▸ An easy way to enter new tempos in this window is to double-click the value in the BPM field and enter the number with the keyboard.

3   At the bottom of the window, click the Play button.

The file plays, looping over and over. Depending on the settings that were in use the last time the Apple Loops Utility was opened, the file could play back in the wrong key.

4   If necessary, click the Key pop-up menu in the lower part of the window and choose "–" to indicate the original key of the part. The file now plays in its original key (Db minor).

5   While playing the file, try choosing different keys from the Key pop-up menu, listening to them one at a time.

The loop transposes up smoothly via semitones and sounds as expected until it reaches the F#/Gb setting, where the pitch immediately drops down 11 semitones (an octave below what is expected). This still reflects the key accurately but achieves better-sounding results.

NOTE ► This octave transposition is mirrored when Apple Loops are played back in the Arrange area. Although an octave transposition accurately represents the key, it might create surprises when moving from the root to the fifth or in similar progressions.

6   Return to the original key by choosing "–" in the Key pop-up menu.

7   While playing, drag the Tempo slider to a value of 60.000 bpm. The loop plays at a slower tempo.

Listen to the sound that is produced when you adjust the tempo to your target (60 bpm). The sound has a slight tremor that falls at the sixteenth-note divisions. This was not present in the original file, and it will need to be addressed with tighter transient mapping.

8   Click the Stop button.

Look at the numbers displayed above the waveform (1.1, 1.3, 2.1, 2.3, and so on). These correspond to bars and beats, separated by a period. Thus, 1.1 represents the first bar, first beat; 1.3 represents the first bar, third beat. You can use this reference to compare the transients of the audio file with the bar/beat ruler.

By default, the Transient Division menu (at the top left) is set for sixteenth notes. In order to get good results, this setting should reflect the smallest significant note division for the loop. You can tell by comparing the Piano Loop waveform with the transient markers that while notes are struck at a sixteenth-note interval, they also have a swing feel and don't align on the second and fourth sixteenth note of the beat. In order to get a more transparent result when shifting tempo and pitch, you need to specify more accurate placement of the transient markers. A good place to start is by using the Sensitivity slider.

9   Drag the Sensitivity slider all the way to the right. As you do this, notice that the transients match up to the swung sixteenth notes in the audio waveform.

Although this helps adjust the transients to better fit the rhythmic feel of the audio file, it still leaves a few transients located at the tails of sustaining notes.

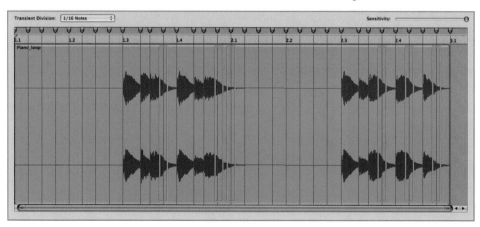

To help eliminate the jittery sound when slowing the loop down, you must eliminate the transient markers located in these sustain areas.

10   Click each of the transient markers that fall on the tails, and press Delete (you can use the preceding illustration as a guide).

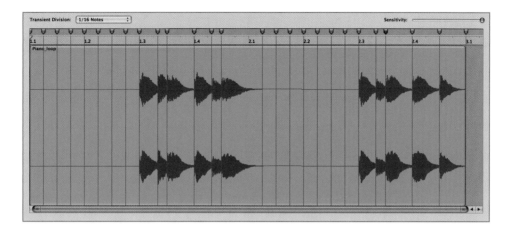

11 Play the file, listening to the result. The playback is now acceptably smooth.

12 If the playback is still looping, click the Stop button.

> **TIP** ▶ You can adjust transients by dragging them to a new location, or create them by clicking in the dark gray area at the top of the window.

Saving Apple Loops to the Library

To take advantage of the adjustments and the information you defined, you have to save the file. When you save the file, the new data is added to the file and made accessible to any application that reads Apple Loops.

1 In the lower-right corner of the interface, click the Save button. The information you provided, both tags and transients, is saved to the file.

2 Choose Apple Loops Utility > Quit Apple Loops Utility.

The easiest way to add the new Apple Loop to your library is to drag it directly from the Finder onto Logic's Loop Bowser.

3 In Logic, click the Media button in the toolbar and, if necessary, select Loops, opening the Loop Browser.

4 In the Finder, navigate to Music > Advanced Logic 9_Files > Media > Georgie the Spider > Audio Files.

5   Drag the Piano Loop file and drop it directly onto Logic's Loops area. Piano Loop
is added to your Apple Loops library and is listed below with the tags you enabled
within the Apple Loops Utility.

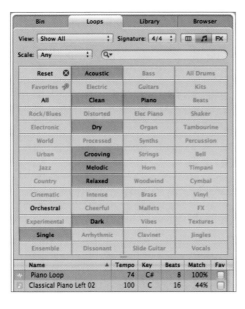

6   Close the Media area.

Using the Time and Pitch Machine

Before Apple Loops were integrated within Logic, all tempo and pitch adjustments to
audio files were done with the Time and Pitch Machine, which functions differently from
Apple Loops. The most obvious difference is that Apple Loops work in real time, dynamically changing pitch and tempo in relation to the project; using the Time and Pitch
Machine is an offline, file-based process that permanently alters a file's pitch and tempo.

Even so, the Time and Pitch Machine has its advantages, especially with regard to control.
Apple Loops offer automatic adaptability, but they are locked to a given project's tempo
or key and are not very useful when you want to shift audio material independently of a
project's tempo, key, or chord track (this includes making pitch adjustments of less than a
semitone).

Let's open another piece of material and use the Time and Pitch Machine to create a pitch-shifted copy, harmonizing with the original.

1 Select the Clarinet track.

2 Play the project from measure 26 to audition the Clarinet region, stopping the project after you become familiar with the material.

3 At the top of the track list, click the New Track with Duplicate Setting button. A new track is created below the selected one, with the same settings.

4 Option-Shift-drag the Clarinet region downward, copying it to the newly created duplicate track at the same position.

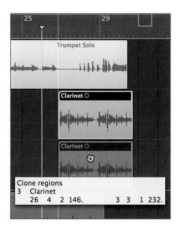

Since you will be transposing this copy of the region, it is recommended to save the region as a unique audio file. This allows you to make changes to the copied file without altering the original audio file.

5 With the newly copied region highlighted, choose Audio > Convert Regions to New Audio Files from the Arrange window's local menu. A file selector dialog opens, asking what you'd like to name the new audio file.

6   In the name field, enter *Clarinet Harmonized*. Click Save.

Now that you've created a new audio file you can work with, it's safe to work with it in the Time and Pitch Machine. You access the Time and Pitch Machine from the Sample Editor.

7   Double-click the new Clarinet Harmonized region, opening the Sample Editor.

8   Resize the window to display the file in its entirety, zooming out horizontally if necessary.

9   At the top of the Sample Editor, click the Prelisten button to hear the Clarinet Harmonized audio file.

TIP The Sample Editor (as well as the Audio Bin, Apple Loops Browser, and Browser) can play the displayed content using either a special Prelisten audio channel strip or the channel strip for the track where the region material lies. This latter mode, called Auto-select Channel Strip, is enabled by default, and allows you to audition through the inserts, volume, and panning of the channel. You can, however, change this behavior by Control-clicking the Prelisten button and choosing Prelisten Channel Strip from the shortcut menu.

10   In the Sample Editor's local menu, choose Factory > Time and Pitch Machine. The Time and Pitch Machine window opens.

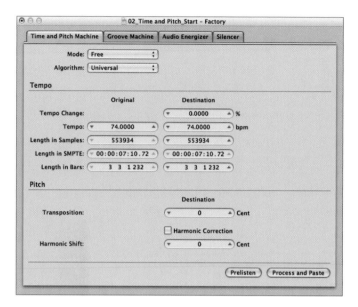

The Time and Pitch Machine offers nine algorithms designed to work with different types of audio material, prioritizing certain musical aspects to better make decisions that affect the time and pitch shifting. These are chosen within the Algorithm menu located at the top of the Time and Pitch Machine window.

11 If it's not already chosen, choose Universal from the Algorithm menu.

Universal is the default algorithm, which is a good, all-around algorithm for most audio material. This works well for the Clarinet Harmonized audio.

Using Harmonic Correction with Pitch Transposition

Pitch transposition usually involves shifting the complete frequency spectrum up or down by a constant value. In effect, everything within the sound source is shifted, including natural resonances (called *formants*). This works well for some material, but it can create unnatural results in material (such as instruments or voices) containing a harmonic structure that is integral to the sound.

A good example is the pitch shifting of a cello note. When all the material is shifted upward (including formants), the pitch changes, and the "body," or timbre, of the instrument changes as well. What results is a higher pitch that sounds as if it were emanating from a smaller instrument (a viola or violin in this case), rather than the original instrument.

If your aim is to change the pitch of a given file while maintaining its resonances, the formants must be left unaltered. The Time and Pitch Machine can be set to use such a process, called *Harmonic Correction*, to achieve natural results when pitch shifting.

Try this out by changing the pitch of the Clarinet Harmonized region using Harmonic Correction. The goal is to transpose the pitch of the file up a minor third while retaining the inherent resonances of the sound.

1   In the Transposition parameter, click the Destination field and enter *300*. Press Return.

This transposes the sound up 300 cents, or three semitones (there are 100 cents in a semitone). Note that the Harmonic Shift parameter value also changes to 300. With Harmonic Correction deselected, Logic will adjust the pitch and the formants together.

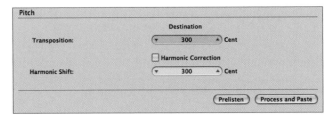

2   Select the Harmonic Correction checkbox.

3   In the Harmonic Shft parameter, click the field and enter *0*, then press Return. This indicates that you wish to retain the original formants of the file, while altering the pitch independently.

4   Click the Process and Paste button.

The operation is performed while Logic Pro displays the progress.

NOTE ▶ Tempo, pitch, and harmonic (formant) changes can be applied simultaneously or independently of each other.

5   Close the Time and Pitch Machine window, and play the file from within the Sample Editor. The Clarinet Harmonized file retains all of its original character, but sounds a minor third higher.

6   Close the Sample Editor by clicking the Sample Editor button.

7   In the Transport, click the Solo button to deactivate solo mode.

8   Play the project to hear the new region within the context of the composition.

TIP ▶ Although operations in the Sample Editor are usually destructive (and thus permanently change the file), settings within the Time and Pitch Machine can be tried on material without destructive results. Logic Pro will cache changes to disk depending on the number of undo steps set within the Sample Editor preferences (Preferences > Audio > Sample Editor). After an operation is completed, you can always undo by choosing Edit > Undo in the Sample Editor or by pressing Command-Z.

Accessing the Time and Pitch Machine in the Arrange Area

Sometimes a small adjustment is needed to conform slightly slower or faster regions to the project's tempo. Although there are many, more sophisticated ways of accomplishing this (as you will investigate later in the lesson), you can use the power of the Time and Pitch Machine to quickly stretch or contract the region within the Arrange area.

1   Click the Media button, opening the Audio Bin tab.

2   Drag the **Organ.aif** file to the Organ track at the beginning of measure 11. The Organ region is imported to measure 11.

3   Play the project to listen to the newly imported region. Notice that the Organ region sounds out of sync and doesn't quite reach all the way to the next bar.

4 Close the Media area.

5 Take a look at the choices on the Audio > Time Stretching Algorithm menu in the Arrange area's local menu bar.

As you probably noticed, the available choices reflect the algorithms presented within the Time and Pitch Machine when accessed in the Sample Editor.

6 From the Arrange area's Audio menu, choose "Time Stretch Region to Nearest Bar."

The region conforms to exactly one bar. You can now loop the region and have it play back in perfect time with the other material.

TIP ▶ The "Time Stretch Region to Locators" command works in an almost identical fashion, using the Time and Pitch Machine's engine to time-stretch or compress the audio region to the region defined via the left and right locators.

7   In the Parameter box, click the Loop parameter checkbox.

The Organ region is looped until it reaches the Organ_long region (at measure 23).

TIP ▷ The time of an audio region can also be manipulated by graphically dragging out its border to line up with a given bar or beat. This can be especially handy for creating a half-time or double-time feel for a given region.

Using Pitch Correction

Logic's Pitch Correction plug-in works in real-time on audio input, dynamically intonating a performance by aligning it to a pitch quantization grid, or scale. This is not unlike doing pitch adjustments within the Time and Pitch Machine, except that it functions in real time. Especially useful when it is not possible to record another take, it can truly salvage an otherwise perfect performance.

In the project you are working with, the trumpet performance exhibits good intonation with the exception of a single note at the beginning of measure 16. In the following exercise, you will apply pitch correction to just this measure so as to not affect the rest of the material.

1   Select the Trumpet track.

2   In the Transport, click the Solo button.

3   Create a Cycle region from 16 1 1 1 to 17 4 1 1.

4   Play the project, stopping after you've had a chance to familiarize yourself with the trumpet phrase.

The first note of the trumpet phrase is flat (it is between C and C#/Db).

5   On the Inspector channel strip for the Trumpet track, click the top insert slot and choose Pitch > Pitch Correction > Mono. The Pitch Correction plug-in opens.

The Pitch Correction plug-in works best on clean, monophonic material within any pitch range. However, you need to specify the pitch range of the input signal to achieve the best possible results. This is done within the Range area, on the left side of the interface.

6 If it's not already enabled, select the normal button in the Range area.

In order to make effective settings within the Pitch Correction plug-in, it helps to visualize the pitches of the input material. The keyboard area, located in the center of the plug-in, indicates the pitches detected by the plug-in. By selecting the Show Input or Show Output buttons below the keyboard, you can display the pitches detected upon input (pre-process) or output (post-process). Show input is selected by default, enabling you to visualize the incoming pitches from the trumpet phrase.

7 Play the project, watching the keyboard area in the middle of the interface, stopping after you have had a chance to observe the detected pitches of the input material.

The phrase starts on C, and ends with a slur descending from G#/Ab.

The main goal of pitch correction is to affect only the material that is out of tune. To aid in doing this, you can select a scale that works with the chosen material. The piece is in Db minor (or its enharmonic key, C# minor), so you need to specify this within the Root and Scale menus, located at the top of the interface. In order to access the Root menu choices, you need to select the scale first.

8   In the Scale menu, choose natural min scale, and in the Root menu, choose C#.

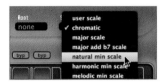 

This conforms the tuning to a C# (Db enharmonic) natural minor scale and will quantize the input to the selected notes. You can monitor the amount of correction applied by observing the Correction Amount display at the bottom.

9   Play the project, watching the Correction Amount display while listening to the results. Stop the project after you've had a chance to monitor the amount of pitch correction.

The C at the beginning of the phrase is pitch-shifted upward by about 80 cents to a C#.

A melodic part may contain different notes than what is dictated by the scale. You can modify the scales provided by the Pitch Correction plug-in to achieve better results in relation to your melody. You add and subtract pitches from the scale by clicking them within the keyboard area.

10   Click the B in the keyboard area to deselect it.

This forces the C and B notes to be tuned up to the root (C#/Db), avoiding the C altogether. You can see these results when switching the display to show the output.

11   Click the Show Output button.

12   Play the project, watching the keyboard area and stopping after you have had a chance to observe the detected pitches of the input material.

You might have noticed that the trumpet player adds a descending glissando at the end of the phrase. These notes are meant to smoothly fall, adding to the bluesy feel of the part. The Pitch Correction plug-in is detecting these notes, as evidenced in the keyboard area, but it is acting too slowly to enact much pitch correction. You can adjust the response of the plug-in by dragging the Response slider at the right.

13 Drag the Response slider down all the way to 0.00 ms.

14 Play the project, stopping after you've had a chance to hear the result.

Each note in the glissando is articulated, adhering tightly to the pitch grid. This is obviously an extreme (and unmusical) setting and should only be used when radical pitch correction (or special effect) is needed.

15 Drag the Response slider upward to about 102.00 ms.

Even with a more reasonable response speed, you still get a slight but unwanted pitch quantization on the glissando. By bypassing the notes individually, you can leave them untouched by pitch correction, leaving only the notes enabled that you want to affect.

16 Click the Bypass (byp) buttons adjacent to the D#, E, F#, and G# keys.

17 Play the project, stopping after you've had a chance to hear the result. The trumpet phrase plays back in tune, without unnatural artifacts.

Automating the Pitch Correction Plug-in

The settings are now dialed in for the phrase you have been working with. These settings, however, may not work so well for other phrases in the track.

1 Turn Cycle off.

2   Play the project from measure 9, listening to the Pitch Correction plug-in on the first trumpet phrase.

3   Stop the project.

As you can hear, the Pitch Correction you specified for the phrase beginning at measure 16 does not work for the first phrase, as it alters the material.

4   Click the Bypass All button to the left of the keyboard area.

5   Play the project from measure 9, listening to the trumpet phrase without Pitch Correction.

The recording sounds much better without pitch correction, preserving the natural inflection of the performer. The solution is to automate the Bypass All button, only having the pitch correction active for the phrase beginning on measure 16.

6   Choose View > Track Automation in the Arrange window's local menus. Automation is displayed for all tracks.

7   Click the Automation Parameter menu and choose PitchCor > Bypass all.

8   Using the Pointer tool, Option-Control-Shift-click and drag around the trumpet phrase you worked on earlier (16 1 1 1 to 17 4 1 1).

Two new sets of nodes are created around the selected area.

9   Click between the two sets of nodes, and then drag downward until the automation track displays "Off."

10   Play the project from around measure 14, stopping it after you've heard the results.

The Pitch Correction is active only for the trumpet phrase.

11   Choose View > Track Automation in the Arrange window's local menus, hiding track automation from view.

12   In the Transport, click the Solo button to deactivate solo mode.

Using Flex Time

New to Logic Pro 9, flex time allows you to manipulate the timing of audio in previously impossible ways, positioning and changing the length of individual notes or phrases as easily as if they were MIDI events. Using flex time's many features, you can change the rhythm, phrasing, and feel of individual audio regions or entire tracks.

In the following exercises, you will try your hand at using flex time to both shape musical phrases and tighten the timing of recorded parts, nondestructively.

1   In the Trumpet track, use the Zoom tool (Control-Option) to drag around the phrase starting at approximately 20 4 1 1 and ending at approximately 23 2 1 1.

2   Create a Cycle region from 20 4 1 1 to 23 2 1 1.

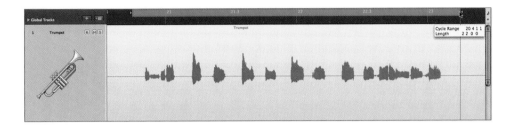

3   Play the project, stopping after you've had a chance to familiarize yourself with the trumpet phrase.

The simplest way to utilize flex time is by using the Flex tool in the Arrange window's toolbox. This allows you to do simple adjustments of audio timing by clicking and dragging on the waveforms.

4   In the Arrange window's toolbox menu, select the Flex tool.

5   With the Flex tool, click the Trumpet region. A dialog window appears, asking you to select the flex mode from a menu.

6   At the bottom of the dialog window, click the disclosure triangle.

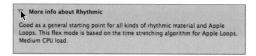

Flex time uses different modes to optimize its time-stretching and compression abilities. Similar to the algorithms used in the Time and Pitch Machine, these modes should suit the audio material with which you wish to work. To help you make a selection, Logic describes the material that works best with each.

7 Select each mode in the Flex Mode menu, reading the displayed description to become familiar with each mode's function.

Considering that you will be using flex time on the solo trumpet phrase, Monophonic is a good choice.

NOTE ► You will investigate the various modes in more depth later on in the lesson.

8 Choose Monophonic from the Flex Mode menu.

9 Click OK.

Logic takes a moment to analyze the Trumpet track.

NOTE ► Flex modes are set for an entire track, and are not region- or selection-based.

Let's start off by using the Flex Tool to reposition a few notes in the phrase a sixteenth note earlier, changing the rhythm.

10 Using the Flex Tool, drag the beginning of the waveform situated at 21 1 4 1 to 21 1 3 1.

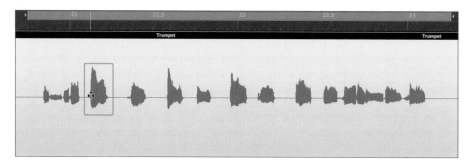

The waveform (note) moves a sixteenth note earlier.

11 Drag the beginning of the waveform situated at 21 3 2 1 to 21 3 1 1.

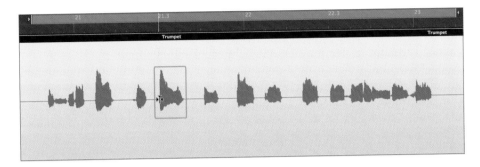

12 Play the project, listening to the trumpet phrase in relation to the beat. Stop the project after you've had a chance to hear the rhythmic change you enacted.

You can also use the Flex tool to lengthen or shorten individual notes, stretching or compressing the audio waveform.

13 Drag the end of the first waveform you repositioned (starting at 21 1 3 1) to 21 2 2 1, making it longer.

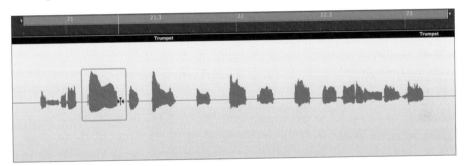

14 Drag the end of the waveform you repositioned to start at 21 3 1 1 to 21 3 4 1, making it longer.

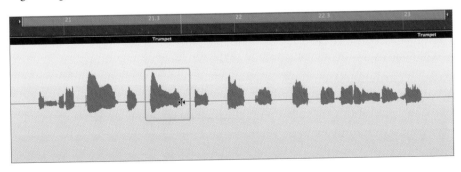

15   Play the project, listening to notes you stretched within the phrase. Stop the project after you've had a chance to hear the result. The rhythm and phrasing of the trumpet phrase is changed, giving it a different feel while retaining the sonic character of the original recording.

Flex time achieves its transparent results by setting transient markers when it first analyzes the track, similar to the transient detection described earlier in this lesson with Apple Loop creation. When you dragged on the audio waveforms, invisible flex markers were created on top of and near these transient locations, allowing you to manually alter the timing of the audio material.

In order to more accurately perform time manipulation, you need to see both the transient markers and the flex markers. These can be viewed by toggling on Flex view.

16   In the Arrange window's local menus, choose View > Flex View.

> **TIP** ▶ Once you've been introduced to Flex view, you will probably be using it quite a bit, toggling back and forth between it and normal view. It is highly suggested, therefore, to use the Hide/Show Flex View key command (Command-F) rather than choosing it from the menu each time.

When Flex view is enabled, transient markers show up as light-gray lines, with the flex markers depicted as white lines with orange handles at the top of the region border.

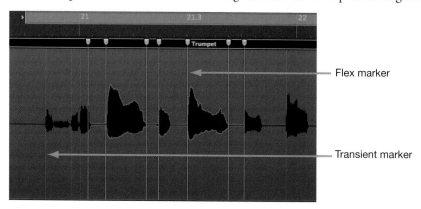

Flex marker

Transient marker

You can now clearly see the edits you performed earlier by looking at the placement of the flex markers and the waveforms themselves. When Flex view is on, time-expanded waveforms have orange borders, and time-compressed waveforms have green borders.

NOTE ▶ A red border appears when time compression reaches a factor of 8 or larger (0.125 of the original length). You are able to perform such high-speed compression, but you'll be presented with a warning before doing so.

Creating Flex Markers in Flex View

When you perform time compression or expansion, flex time uses flex markers as points of reference. When flex markers are dragged, time shifting occurs on either side, affecting material situated within adjacent flex markers (if any). In this way, you can think of flex markers as pins, holding down material until you manually adjust or move through them.

When working in Flex view, the Pointer becomes a multifunction tool, allowing you to insert single or multiple flex markers at specific locations, depending on where your pointer is situated.

In this exercise, you will use these tools to manually create flex markers, making a rhythmic adjustment to the phrase.

1   Click the Trumpet track's Solo button to enable solo mode for the track.

2   Place the cursor at the top of the region area, directly over the transient marker located at 21 4 4 1.

The cursor changes to display a single marker. This is used to create a single flex marker at the transient marker location.

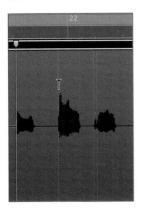

3   Click the transient marker. A single flex marker is created at the selected transient marker.

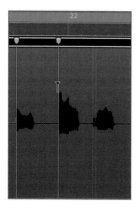

4   Drag the newly created flex marker to the right, aligning it to 22 1 1 1.

The audio event is moved to the right, lining up with the downbeat of bar 22. Note that all audio events occurring after the flex marker are moved equally, putting the entire ending of the phrase out of time. In addition, the audio event prior to the flex marker was time-stretched (it now has an orange border).

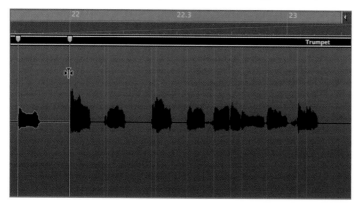

In order for you to shift only the desired audio event, you need to create more flex markers surrounding it, pinning down the adjacent material.

5   Double-click the flex marker you just created, deleting it. The audio returns back to its original state (before you made the adjustment).

6   Place the cursor at the bottom of the region area, directly over the transient marker located at 21 4 4 1.

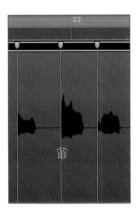

The cursor changes to display three markers. This is used to create three flex markers: one at the selected transient marker location, as well as the two surrounding transient markers.

7 Click the transient marker.

Two new transient markers are created.

NOTE ▶ There was already a flex marker on the left (created in the previous exercise).

8 Drag the newly created flex marker to the right, aligning it to 22 1 1 1.

NOTE ▶ When dragging flex markers, the waveform's surrounding area turns increasing shades of green (compression) or orange (expansion), representing the degree to which the audio is being altered in real time.

This time, the audio event is moved without shifting the material to the right, but the material to the left is still time-stretched (depicted in orange). In order to move the audio event without stretching the previous one, you will need to create one additional flex marker, not at an existing transient marker location but after the tail of the previous audio event.

9   Choose Edit > Undo Drag Flex Marker (or press Command-Z). The audio returns to the previous (preshifted state).

10   Place the cursor in the upper half of the region area, directly after the waveform occurring at 21 4 1 1.

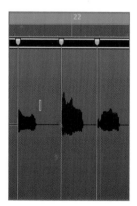

The cursor changes to display a single line. This is used to create a flex marker at a location where there is no transient marker.

> **TIP** ▶ You can also click in the lower half of the region, creating three flex markers: one at the selected location (with no existing transient marker), as well as the two surrounding transient markers.

11 Click the current location (after the tail of the audio event). A flex marker is created between the two existing flex (and transient) markers.

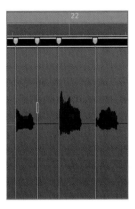

> **TIP** ▶ You can change the position of a flex marker without performing any time compression or expansion by Option-dragging.

12 Drag the flex marker you have been working with to the right, aligning it to 22 1 1 1. The audio event shifts to the right without affecting the surrounding material.

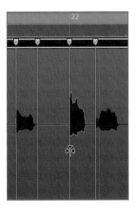

13 Control-Option-click the background to zoom out to the previous level.

> **TIP** ▶ Once you get used to the behavior of creating flex markers, you don't need to first click and then drag the created marker. Instead, you can quickly create and adjust a flex marker in a single action by holding the mouse button down and dragging, achieving the same results.

Shifting and Stretching Audio Using Marquee Selections

You can also use the Marquee tool to make adjustments to an entire phrase at a time without having to manually create flex markers first. Essentially, you can shift a selection forward and backward in time (or both time compress and expand the selection), while automatically time compressing or expanding the surrounding material to make it fit.

In the following exercise, you will use the Marquee tool to quickly select and shift a phrase back by a half a beat, without having to make a single region cut.

1 Click the Trumpet track's Solo button to disable solo mode for the track.

2 In the Trumpet track, use the Zoom tool (Control-Option) to drag around the phrase that starts at approximately 12 1 1 1 and ends at approximately 14 1 1 1.

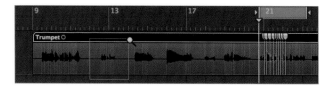

3 Create a Cycle region from 12 1 1 1 to 14 1 1 1.

4 Play the project, stopping after you've had a chance to familiarize yourself with the trumpet phrase.

The phrase is early, and it should be shifted later by an eighth note.

5 Using the Marquee tool, drag to select the entire phrase.

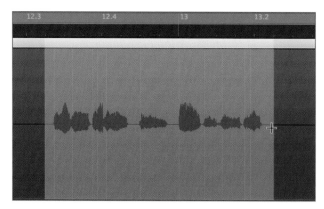

6 Position the cursor at the top part of the selection area.

The cursor turns into a hand. This is used to shift the entire selection backward or forward in time.

7 Drag the marquee selection to the right an eighth note (see the following illustration for a reference).

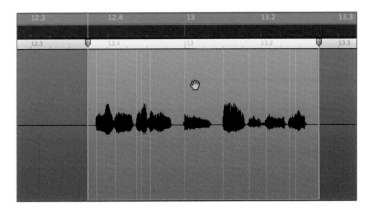

Two flex markers are created at the selection borders (as well as at the surrounding transient markers), and the selected audio material is shifted to the right.

NOTE ▸ The audio on either side of the selection is time-expanded or contracted, as evidenced by the slight green and orange colors to the left and right, respectively. With the current material, this time compression and expansion is slight.

8 Play the project, listening to the results.

9 Turn Cycle off.

10 Control-Option-click the background to zoom out to the previous level.

TIP ▸ An entire marquee selection can be time-stretched or time-compressed by dragging the lower half of the region.

Quantizing Audio with Flex Time

As you discovered in the last few exercises, flex time allows you to edit audio events in the same manner as MIDI events, adjusting length and shifting the timing manually by using the mouse. This also extends to techniques like quantization that are used in tightening the timing of an entire region.

When using quantization with flex time, both flex markers and transient markers are used to adjust the timing in relation to the time grid. This means that you do not need to create flex markers first to do simple, region-based adjustments like quantization.

In this exercise, you will use flex time in conjunction with quantization to change the feel of the Drums track.

1   Select the Drums track.

2   Click the Drum track's Solo button, enabling solo mode for the track.

3   In the Drums track, use the Zoom tool (Control-Option) to drag around the area starting at approximately 1 1 1 1 and ending at approximately 3 1 1 1.

4   Create a Cycle region from 1 1 1 1 to 3 1 1 1.

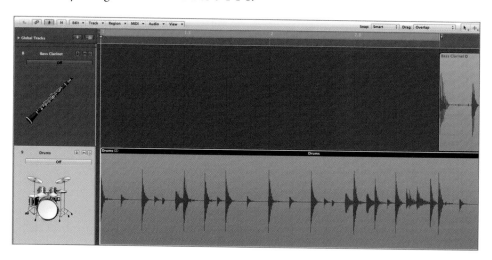

5   Play the project, stopping after you've had a chance to familiarize yourself with the drum groove.

Note that Flex view is still on from the previous exercise. When Flex view is active, you select the mode for the track by choosing from the Flex Mode menu, located in the track header.

6   From the Flex Mode menu, choose Slicing.

NOTE ▸ Slicing mode is unique among the flex modes in that time compression or expansion is not applied. Instead, it makes slices at transient markers, playing each at its original speed. This makes it an excellent choice for drums and percussion.

Logic takes a moment to analyze the track, and then it displays the detected transient markers.

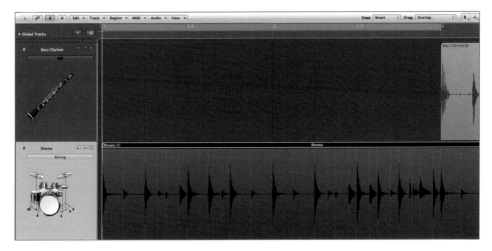

7   In the Region Parameter box, click the Quantize menu and choose 1/16-Note.

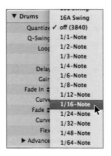

8   Play the project, stopping when you have had a chance to listen to the change in feel. The Drums track now plays back with a straight sixteenth-note feel.

> **TIP** Each flex mode offers associated parameters that are used to fine-tune how flex time works with selected material. These are accessed within the Inspector's Track Parameter box. To find out more about these parameters, see the "Getting to Know the Flex Modes" section in the User Manual.

9   In the Region Parameter box, click the Quantize menu and choose 16F Swing.

10   Play the project, stopping when you have had a chance to listen to the change in feel.

The Drums track now plays back with a swing feel, slightly delaying every other sixteenth note.

11   Click the Drums track's Solo button to disable solo mode for the track.

12   Turn Cycle off.

13   Control-Option-click the background to zoom out to the previous level.

> **TIP** You can align flex markers to the transients of other tracks by creating the flex marker first and then dragging upward or downward to adjacent tracks. A yellow guideline appears that snaps to the transients in the adjacent region, aligning the flex markers to match. This is especially useful for aligning doubled parts or multitracked drums.

Editing Transient Markers in the Sample Editor
Although flex time usually does a good job of creating transient markers at appropriate locations, on occasion you will need to make manual adjustments of your own to better

serve the audio material. This can be of major importance, as processes like quantization rely on the location and number of transient markers to align the material to the time grid.

The Gtr Ostinato audio file could benefit from a bit of tightening up by applying quantization. In this exercise, you will alter flex mode's automatic transient marker placement to best fit the material for quantization.

The deletion, creation, or adjustment of transient markers takes place in the Sample Editor.

1 Select the Gtr Ostinato track.

2 Click the Gtr Ostinato track's Solo button, enabling solo mode for the track.

3 Play the project, stopping after you've had a chance to familiarize yourself with the part.

4 From the Gtr Ostinato track's Flex Mode menu, choose Rhythmic.

> **NOTE ▶** Both Polyphonic and Rhythmic mode are similar in that they both work well on polyphonic material. It is recommended that you use Polyphonic mode for timbrally complex material, including material with reverb or delay tails. Rhythmic mode is best used for drier, rhythmically active material, such as rhythm guitar, keyboard/ piano, and other harmonic parts.

Logic analyzes the track, creating transient markers.

5 In the Region Parameter box, click the Quantize menu and choose 1/16-Note.

6 Play the project, listening to the results of the quantization.

Activating flex time tightens up the timing considerably, but you probably noticed that it also creates audible artifacts, especially within sustaining notes.

To see what might be causing this, let's take a closer look at the transient markers within the Sample Editor.

7 Double-click the top of the Gtr Ostinato region, opening it in the Sample Editor.

8   Using the horizontal zoom slider or key commands (Control-Option–Left Arrow),
zoom out to view approximately two measures.

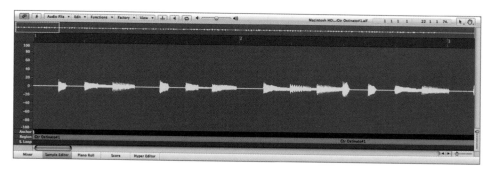

9   Click the Transient Editing Mode button to enable it.

The transient markers detected by flex time are displayed in the Sample Editor.

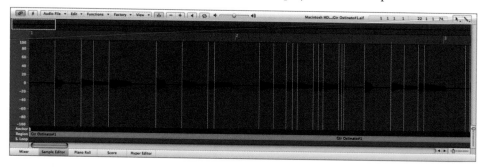

10   Click the Prelisten button to audition the audio file in the Sample Editor, observing
where the transient markers fall in relation to the material. Click the Prelisten button
again to stop playback.

Similar to when you worked with the Apple Loops Utility earlier in the lesson, the
flex time analysis created unneeded transient markers during the sustain portions of
notes. These extra transient markers are causing a problem when applying quantization, producing unwanted artifacts. Fortunately, you can use the Delete (−) and Add
(+) buttons to decrease and increase the amount of detected transients, respectively.

11   Click the Delete (−) button.

Some of the transient markers disappear.

12 Click the Delete (–) button three more times, eliminating the transient markers within the sustain portions of the notes.

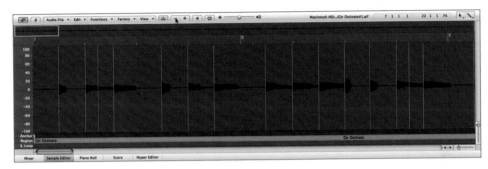

TIP ▸ You can thin out or increase the amount of detected transients within an isolated area by first selecting an area within the Sample Editor and then using the Delete (–) and Add (+) buttons. Single transient markers can also be deleted by double-clicking them.

13 Close the Sample Editor.

14 Play the project, listening to the quantized Gtr Ostinato region again. The audio file plays back without any artifacts.

15 Click the Gtr Ostinato track's Solo button to disable solo mode for the track.

16 Play the project, listening to the quantized track within the context of the composition. Stop the project.

Creating and Using Groove Templates with Flex Time

Groove templates are essentially customized quantization maps taken directly from the timing of the selected region. These are especially useful when you want to apply the rhythmic feel of one region onto another.

In this project, the Bass Clarinet part has a unique feel, purposefully rushing beats 2 and 4. The part needs a little tightening, however, and because of its unique rhythm, it cannot be aligned to the time grid using one of the available quantize settings. The timing could be tightened up manually by inserting and dragging flex markers as before, but repeating this process for the entire track becomes tiresome.

In this exercise, you will create a groove template from a portion of the track with which you performed flex editing and then apply it onto the remaining portion, tightening up the timing for the entire Bass Clarinet part.

1 Select the Bass Clarinet track.

2 Click the Bass Clarinet track's Solo button, enabling solo mode for the track.

3 In the Transport, click the Metronome button to turn on the metronome click.

4 Play the project, stopping after you've had a chance to familiarize yourself with the part in comparison with the metronome click.

The part purposely rushes beats 2 and 4 by approximately a sixteenth note. However, the part is uneven and needs to be tightened up.

5 From the bass Clarinet track's Flex Mode menu, choose Monophonic.

NOTE ▶ As the name suggests, Monophonic mode is good for monophonic instruments and vocals such as melody or bass lines.

Logic analyzes the track, creating transient markers.

6 Using the Scissors tool, separate the Bass Clarinet region at measure 5, creating a two-bar region starting on measure 3.

Similar to the approach you used earlier when quantizing, it's a good idea to prep the audio region by eliminating unneeded transient markers before creating a groove template.

7 Double-click the two-bar Bass Clarinet.1 region to open the Sample Editor.

8 Use the Zoom controls in the Sample Editor to show the entire region's contents.

9 Click the Transient Editing Mode button.

10 Use the Delete (–) button to decrease the number of transient markers, until the only remaining transient markers are the ones situated at the loudest points of amplitude (tallest waveforms).

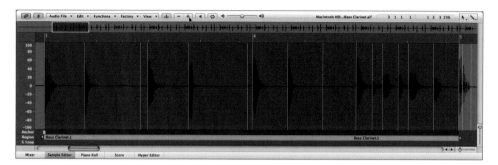

11 Close the Sample Editor.

12 Use the Zoom tool (Control-Option) to drag around the two-bar region, magnifying it.

13 Set a Cycle region from 3 1 1 1 to 5 1 1 1.

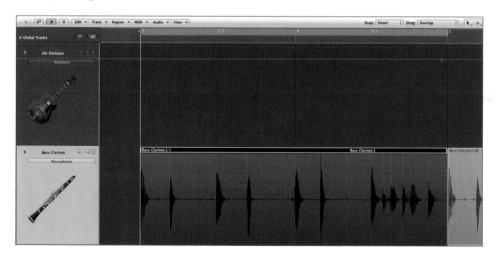

14 Using the method you learned earlier, create and drag a flex marker, lining up the transients occurring near 4 1 4 1 (see the following illustration for reference) to the time grid, placing it exactly a sixteenth note before the beat.

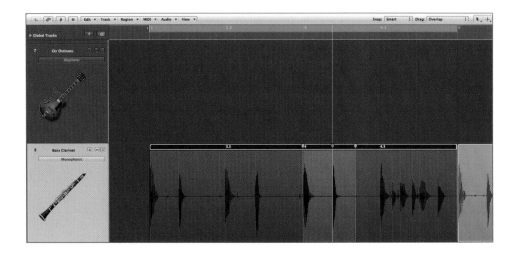

15 Play the project, stopping after you've had a chance to listen to the time-adjusted part in reference to the metronome.

The timing is much tighter now for the selected region. The goal is to have this rhythmic timing be consistent for the entire track. Rather than move through the entire part, eliminating unneeded transient markers in the Sample Editor and then manually creating flex markers, you can simply create a groove template out of the "fixed" region, and then apply the same feel to the rest of the track. Groove templates are created within the Region Parameter box's Quantize menu.

16 Turn the Metronome off.

17 Turn Cycle off.

18 Control-Option-click the background to zoom out to the previous level.

19 In the Region Parameter box, click the Quantize menu and choose Make Groove Template.

20 Select the Bass Clarinet.2 region (remaining part of the track).

21 In the Region Parameter box, click the Quantize menu and choose Bass Clarinet.1.

The Bass Clarinet.2 region takes on the characteristics of the Bass Clarinet.1 region, tightening the timing.

22 Click the Bass Clarinet track's Solo button to disable solo mode for the track.

23 Play the project, listening to the timing of the track within the context of the composition.

> **TIP** ▶ Try experimenting with both Tempophone and Speed flex modes for special effect. Tempophone mode breaks the signal into a stream of tiny grains, whose size can be set in the Track Parameter box. Here, you can also control how these grains overlap each other by adjusting the crossfade parameter. Speed mode works similar to a tape recorder, adjusting speed along with time.

Using Speed Fades

One of the new features added to Logic Pro 9 is the ability to create speed fades, or rapid pitch and rhythmic effects simulating the speeding up or slowing down of turntables and tape machines. These fades are created just like any other and are selectable from within the Region Parameter box.

In this exercise, you will create this special effect on the harmonized clarinet part you created earlier in the lesson.

1 Use the Zoom tool (Control-Option) to drag around the two Clarinet regions, magnifying them.

2 Using the Crossfade tool, drag over the top Clarinet region, creating a fade-out from about 30 2 3 1 to the end of the region.

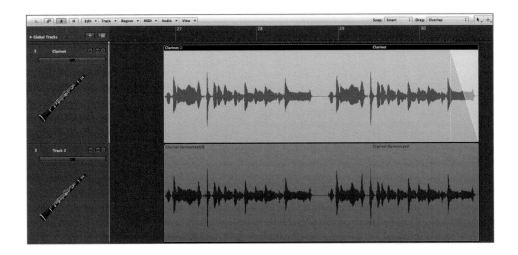

3   In the Region Parameter box, click the Fade menu and choose Slow Down.

Because fades are applied to individual regions one at a time, you will need to create speed fades for both, matching the timing of the fade.

4   Double-click the Out value, to the right of the Fade menu (which now reads "Slow Down"), and press Command-C to copy the value.

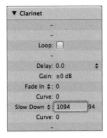

5   Select the bottom Clarinet region.

6   In the Region Parameter box (for the bottom Clarinet region), click the Fade menu and choose Slow Down.

7   Double-click the Out value, to the right of the Fade menu (which now reads Slow Down), and press Command-V to paste the value.

A speed fade appears on the bottom Clarinet region at the same position.

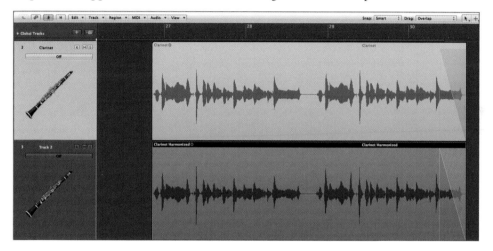

8   Play the project, listening to the result of the speed fades.

The audio slows down, simulating a stopping turntable.

9   Control-Option-click the background to zoom out to the previous level.

Making Tempo Adjustments with Varispeed

Also new to Logic Pro 9, varispeed allows you to speed up or slow down the entire project, keeping all audio and MIDI events in perfect time. This is an extremely handy feature, not just to hear how the song would sound at a slower tempo, but also to give an artist who is having difficulty playing to the original tempo the ability to record their part at a slower speed.

In order to use varispeed, its controls must be displayed within the Transport.

1   Control-click the Transport and choose Customize Transport Bar from the shortcut menu.

2   In the Display column, select Varispeed.

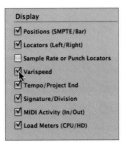

3   Click OK.

In the Transport bar, a new button appears, as does the Varispeed display (currently set for Speed Only mode). The button is used to toggle varispeed on and off, making changes within the display area to the left.

4   Click the Varispeed button to enable it.

5   Double-click the Varispeed value and enter *30*. Press Return.

6   Play the project, listening to the result.

The project plays back smoothly, at 30 percent faster tempo.

NOTE ▶ The results of your varispeed adjustment can also be seen in beats per minute. You can set this by clicking the varispeed readout and choosing Resulting Tempo.

Varispeed is not limited to altering the speed only, and it can emulate the pitch change that occurs when slowing down or speeding up a tape machine or turntable.

7   Click the Varispeed display and choose Varispeed (Speed and Pitch) from the menu.

8 Play the project, listening to the result.

The project plays back not only at a faster tempo but also at a higher pitch.

NOTE ▸ Ordinarily, varispeed does not affect external MIDI instruments, but you can change this behavior by choosing "Varispeed and MIDI" from the menu.

9 Click the Varispeed button to disable it.

10 Choose File > Save As.

11 Name the project *02_Georgie the Spider_Finished* and save to Music > Advanced Logic 9_Files > Lessons > Completed.

12 Close the project.

Working with Rubato Passages

In Logic, you will generally be working with music based on a constant tempo or recorded to a metronome click. In this common situation, Logic's tempo and time-signature settings create a time grid in which you plot events. This enables data to be displayed musically, in relation to bars and beats.

However, sometimes you will want to record without a click, gaining the freedom to vary the tempo and play with rhythmic flexibility (to play with *rubato*, in music parlance). In this situation, the trick is not only to maintain a performer's interpretation, with its deviations in tempo, but also to display the musical data in correct time (bars and beats). You can use beat mapping to align Logic's time grid with these tempo variations.

Once the time grid matches the performance, you can use Logic's compositional and arranging features (quantization, time-based effects, notation, Apple Loops, and so on) to work with data as if it had been recorded to a metronome click.

For this exercise, you will use Logic's Beat Mapping track to create tempo changes for each event that deviates from a constant tempo.

Using the Beat Mapping Track

The Beat Mapping track, one of Logic's global tracks, works hand in hand with related tracks such as the Signature and Tempo tracks. Think of it as working like an adaptive ruler, letting you graphically tie events to particular bars and beats (all derived from the Signature track). When events are defined according to their bar positions in the Beat Mapping track, tempo changes are created in the Tempo track to align the grid.

Both MIDI and audio tracks can form a basis on which to generate a beat map. Let's start by opening the project file used in this exercise, which contains both MIDI and audio versions of a rubato piano piece.

1   Choose Music > Advanced Logic 9_Files > Lessons > **02_The Only Light Thats On_ Start.logic.**

The project contains a single MIDI track being output through the EXS24 mkII instrument (a piano sample), along with a muted audio track of the same material.

2   Play the project to familiarize yourself with the material.

3   In the Transport bar, click the Metronome button to turn on Logic's click.

4   Play the project again, this time listening to the tempo deviations of the piece against the click.

Things start off without too much deviation, but the click is really out of sync by measure 4.

5   At the upper-left corner of the Arrange area, click the Global Tracks disclosure triangle.

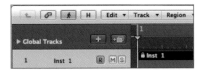

The global tracks appear, displaying only the tracks used for this exercise: Signature, Tempo, and Beat Mapping.

> **TIP** ▶ You can display any or all of the global tracks by choosing View > Configure Global Tracks and choosing whatever you wish to view. This setting will be saved with the screenset and can be hidden or exposed at any time using a key command or menu selection.

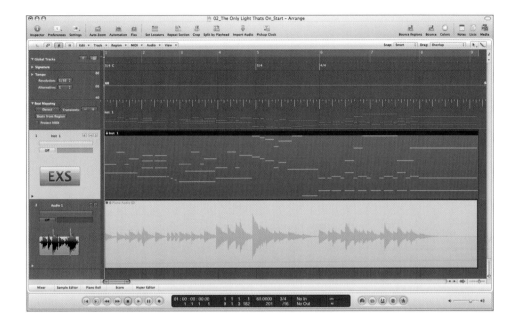

As you can see in the Signature track, the piece starts in 3/4 but also contains bars of 5/4 and 4/4. The time signatures are reflected in the Beat Mapping track, with bars and beats displayed graphically by lines representing the time grid (not unlike the Bar ruler).

If this grid is to be used as a reference, Logic's division value (a freely definable part of a beat) must reflect the smallest rhythmic value within the piece of music. The music you are using has a triplet feel, so it is necessary to select a division of 12 instead of 16 (the default).

6   In the Transport bar, double-click the Division field in the Time Signature display and enter *12*.

The ruler and grid now display triplet divisions instead of sixteenth notes.

Beat Mapping a MIDI Region

To start aligning the grid to the music, you need to select the material you want to work with.

NOTE ▶ The Beat Mapping track works with regions, not tracks (which contain multiple regions).

1   If it is not already selected, select the MIDI region on the Inst 1 track.

Colored lines appear in the Beat Mapping track, indicating each MIDI event (with velocities) in the selected region. You will use both these lines and the bar/beat lines above, "tying" them together to realign the grid.

2   Zoom in horizontally until about four bars are visible in the Arrange area. This enables you to see greater detail when working in the Beat Mapping track.

3   In the top portion of the Beat Mapping track, drag the line representing measure 1, beat 2 (1 2 1 1) downward, connecting it to the light-green event (1 1 3 305) in the bottom portion of the track.

The line turns yellow as you are connecting it, and a help tag (Set Beat To) displays the event's position before alignment.

When you release the mouse button, the points are aligned, and a new tempo event is created (61.0169) in the Tempo track.

NOTE ▶ Logic uses very fine tempo increments (as small as one ten-thousandth of a beat!) for accurate alignment.

4   Using the same technique, connect the line representing measure 1, beat 2, division 3 (1 2 3 1) to the light-green line located below and slightly to the left (1 2 2 294).

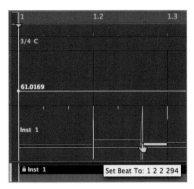

Another tempo event is created in the Tempo track (63.7053).

5   Connect the line representing measure 1, beat 3 (1 3 1 1) to the light-green line located below and slightly to the right (1 3 1 35).

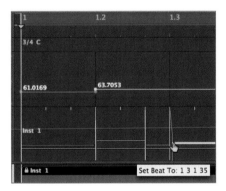

Another tempo event is created in the Tempo track (57.5868).

6   Connect the line representing measure 1, beat 3, division 3 (1 3 3 1) to the light-blue line located below and slightly to the left (1 3 2 292).

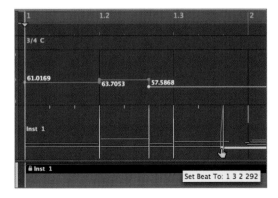

For every note event connected, a new tempo is indicated, creating an accurate depiction of the region's timing. Therefore, the more events that are beat-mapped, the closer Logic's time grid will conform to the music.

For the rest of this exercise, you will finish beat mapping the entire piano part, creating an accurate time map of the piece.

Here are two areas to watch out for:

Position	Situation	Recommendation
2 1 1 1	The slur and slightly staggered chord entries create multiple possibilities to draw connections.	Try experimenting with what works best in representing the downbeat.
3 1 2 1	Deviates from triplet feel to eighth notes for one beat	Change the division to /8 (eighth notes) to work with the grid above the two eighth notes.

7   Continue connecting related lines in the Beat Mapping track, moving from left to right for the entire region.

TIP ▶ If you make a mistake, you can erase any beat allocation by double-clicking it or by using the Eraser tool.

8   When you are finished, check your work by listening to the EXS24 mkII piano part along with the metronome click.

For comparison, a beat-mapped Tempo track has been created for you as a reference. You can access this in the Tempo Alternative menu in the Tempo track.

NOTE ▶ The Tempo Alternative menu allows you to save and recall up to nine tempo "maps" created in the Tempo track.

9   From the Tempo Alternative pop-up menu, choose 2.

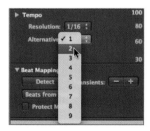

The Tempo track now displays the premade tempo events created from beat mapping.

10 Play the project with the click to compare the premade Tempo track with your results, toggling back and forth between Tempo tracks using the Tempo Alternative menu choices (1 and 2).

Checking Your Results in the Piano Roll Editor

You can check how well you performed beat mapping by viewing the events graphically in the Piano Roll Editor. Here you can clearly see the individual events lined up on the time grid and compare the results achieved with beat mapping to the original, non-beat-mapped track.

1 With the MIDI region selected, click the Piano Roll button to display the MIDI events in detail.

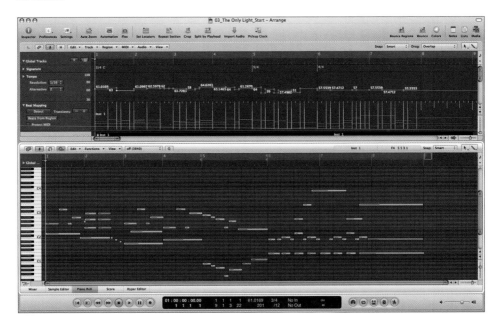

2 In the Tempo Alternative menu, switch among 1 (your beat map), 2 (the premade beat map), and 5 (not beat-mapped) options, comparing how the note events align to the grid.

You can see major discrepancies between the beat-mapped (1 and 2) and non-beat-mapped (5) versions, especially from measure 4 onward.

Beat Mapping an Audio Region

Using an audio region as the source for beat mapping involves a technique similar to using a MIDI region. Instead of using MIDI note events, however, the Beat Mapping track uses audio transients for alignment points. To do this, Logic needs to analyze the source to detect the transients (somewhat like the Apple Loops Utility).

Let's mute the MIDI track and unmute the audio track before we start working with the audio track version.

1 Close the Piano Roll Editor to display the regions in the Arrange area.

2 Use the Mute tool to mute the Inst 1 region.

3 Use the Mute tool to un-mute the Piano Audio region.

4 From the Tempo Alternative pop-up menu, choose 3.

5 Click in the track header of the Beat Mapping track (but do not click the buttons or menus) to select everything in the track, and press Delete.

All beat events are erased, allowing you to continue with a fresh slate.

NOTE ▶ Neither the work you performed with beat mapping nor the premade Tempo track is deleted when you do this, because they were saved to the first two Tempo Alternative slots.

6 Select the Piano Audio region in the Audio 1 track. The audio waveform is displayed in the Beat Mapping track.

7 In the Beat Mapping track, click the Detect button.

A progress bar appears for the transient-detection process. After the analysis of the selected audio is performed, the detected transients are displayed in the Beat Mapping track as vertical white lines.

NOTE ▶ Depending on your settings, Logic may prompt you to confirm whether you want to overwrite all previous transients. For the sake of the exercise, click OK.

8   Zoom out horizontally so that you can see the entire track.

Take a close look at the results displayed in the Beat Mapping track. As you experienced earlier with both the Apple Loops Utility and flex time, there are some unnecessary transients that were detected. You can increase or decrease the detected transients in the Beat Mapping track by clicking the Add (+) or Delete (–) buttons within the track header.

9   In the Beat Mapping track header, click the Delete (–) button a few times to reduce the number of transients detected.

The number of transients is reduced, providing a better picture of the relevant timing events in the audio file.

Now that you have accurate timing events in the Beat Mapping track, you are ready to begin the process of aligning the time grid.

10   Connect related lines in the Beat Mapping track as you did in the previous exercise, moving from left to right for the entire region.

11   When you're finished, play the track with the metronome click to check your results.

NOTE ▶ A premade Tempo track using the audio region as a guide has been provided for comparison in Tempo Alternative slot number 4.

Lesson Review

1. Which important aspect of an audio file determines how the Apple Loops Utility manipulates timing?

2. Which two attributes of a Logic project determine how Apple Loops are conformed?

3. Which offline Logic feature is used to exercise detailed control over an audio file's pitch (in addition to its timing), including the natural resonances (formants) of a given sound?

4. What works on audio input, dynamically intonating a performance in real time by aligning it to a pitch quantization grid?

5. Flex time uses what as a point of reference when time compressing or expanding?

6. When making region-based time adjustments on audio like quantizing, flex time uses what to adjust the timing in relation to the time grid?

7. Flex time transient markers can only be edited where?

8. How are speed fades created?

9. True or false: Varispeed can alter both pitch and time of an entire project.

10. Which global track lets you graphically align Logic's time grid to a rubato part?

11. True or false: Both audio and MIDI regions can be beat-mapped.

Answers

1. Transients. They must be defined accurately through automatic and manual means to achieve the best results when creating Apple Loops.

2. The project's key and tempo determine how Apple Loops are conformed.

3. The Time and Pitch Machine provides detailed control over pitch and time, and it uses pitch shifting to preserve the natural resonances of a given sound.

4. The Pitch Correction plug-in intonates audio input in real time, dynamically intonating a performance by aligning it to a pitch quantization grid.

5. Flex markers are used as points of reference for time manipulation, and they may be created independently of, or on top of transient markers.

6. When making region-based time adjustments like quantizing, flex time uses both flex markers and transient markers as timing references aligning to Logic's time grid.

7. Flex time transient markers can only be edited in the Sample Editor.

8. Speed fades are created with the Fade tool and specified within the Region Parameter box.

9. True. Varispeed can alter both pitch and time of an entire project (including MIDI regions).

10. The Beat Mapping track allows the accurate rescaling of the time grid to a rubato part.

11. True. Both audio and MIDI regions can be used as the basis for beat mapping.

3

Lesson Files	Advanced Logic 9_Files > Lessons > 03_ES2_Start.logic
Media	None
Time	This lesson takes approximately 60 minutes to complete.
Goals	Trace the signal flow through the ES2
	Select, combine, and blend multiple waveforms from all three oscillators to generate interesting sounds
	Shape the generated sound with the filters
	Modulate parameters with low-frequency oscillators and envelopes
	Add additional processing through output parameters

Synthesis with the ES2 Synthesizer

The ES2 Synthesizer is a hybrid synthesizer, inspired by the designs of well-loved analog and digital synthesizers of both past and present. From large-sounding leads to evolving pads, classic analog waveforms to digital waveforms and FM, the ES2 offers a wide array of tools for synthesizer enthusiasts.

With so much available here, starting off creating your own sounds can be overwhelming. In this lesson, you will walk through the various sections of the ES2, learning how to create new sounds from scratch. Even if you are not that interested in creating new sounds, you can also apply these skills to modifying stock presets to better fit your needs.

> **NOTE** ▶ Middle C may be designated as either C4 or C3, depending on the manufacturer of your MIDI keyboard. To accurately follow the directions within this lesson (and others throughout the book), you will need to set the "Display Middle C as" preference to C3 (Yamaha). This command can be found in the Preferences > Display > General tab.

> **TIP** ▶ To learn more about the basic properties of synthesizers and how they generate and modify sound, check out the "Synthesizer Basics" section in the Logic Studio Instruments manual. This serves as an excellent introduction to the synthesis aspects explored within this lesson, and it is highly recommended for beginners.

Understanding the User Interface

Most of Logic's software instruments share interface features that represent how sound is generated and shaped. With synthesizers, it is especially important to trace the signal flow through controls that affect a particular aspect of the sound.

1   Choose File > Open.

2   In the file selector dialog, navigate to Music > Advanced Logic 9_Files > Lessons and open **03_ES2_Start.logic**.

The project opens, displaying the ES2 Synthesizer interface.

Let's take a look at the ES2 interface, tracing the signal flow through the instrument.

Sound generation section   Filter section   Output/processing section

Modulation section

On the upper-left side, you can see the three oscillators that are responsible for the ES2's sound generation. Surrounding each oscillator are controls for tuning and mixing.

Moving to the right, you find the filter section, where the frequency spectrum of the raw sound is shaped.

At the far right is the output section for the ES2, with controls for volume and effects (distortion, chorus, flanger, and phaser).

In the lower half of the interface is the modulation section, comprised of the modulation router and, below that, the modulation sources. Here you can manipulate any of the ES2 controls via any other parameter and real-time input.

In general, signal flow is moving from left to right. This is true for almost all of the Logic software instruments, with few exceptions.

TIP ▶ In order to hear how and what each section contributes to the overall sound, it is advisable to begin with a stripped-down preset using only a single oscillator and no modulation routings. This allows you to construct a sound from the ground up, engaging specific portions of the synthesizer one at a time, as needed.

Exploring the Oscillator Waveforms

The ES2 sound generation section consists of three oscillators capable of producing everything from classic analog waveforms to digital waves. The oscillators' raw signals are sent to the other sections of the synthesizer for further shaping of the sound.

Let's start off by exploring all of the waveforms for each oscillator, and examine the unique potential of each.

1   Play your MIDI keyboard, listening to the sound.

You are currently hearing Oscillator 1 generating a sawtooth wave, as shown in green surrounding the knob.

TIP ▶ When you select a software instrument in the track list for the first time, there might be a slight delay (around 100 milliseconds) at first. This is because Logic does not engage live mode until it receives its first MIDI message. The delay doesn't affect the playback of sequenced material, but it can interfere with live performance and tracking. If you require perfect timing for the first played note, you need to send silent MIDI events in advance (for example, sustain pedal, pitch bend, or modulation wheel).

2   Drag Oscillator 1's wave knob up and down, listening to the various waveforms available (sine, triangle, square, pulse, and so on.).

In addition to dragging the knob with the mouse, you can quickly and precisely select a waveform by clicking it within the ring around the wave knob.

3   Click the sine selection, located at the bottom of the ring around Oscillator 1's wave knob.

In addition to the choices depicted on the ring, all three oscillators offer 100 sampled digital waveforms, called Digiwaves. These are accessed within a scrollable parameter located at the bottom (defaults to sine).

4   Play a key on your MIDI keyboard while slowly dragging upwards on the sine selection (Digiwaves), listening to the result. Settle on a waveform you like.

5   Click the on/off button for Oscillator 2, turning it on.

If you played your MIDI keyboard at this point, you wouldn't hear Oscillator 2 at all. because the Oscillator Mix control is only set to output Oscillator 1. You can set the proportional mix level of each oscillator within the Triangle located to the right. Each point of the Triangle represents one of the three oscillators.

6   Within the Triangle, drag the square icon to the far left (Oscillator 2).

Just like Oscillator 1, Oscillator 2 offers a variety of analog waveforms in addition to the 100 Digiwaves. Although there is some overlap (sawtooth, triangle, square), Oscillator 2 offers some unique functionality, including a variable-width pulse wave.

As you turn the wave knob from the 12 o'clock to the 5 o'clock position, the square wave's pulse width proportions change, creating different timbres.

7   Play a key on your MIDI keyboard while slowly dragging Oscillator 2's wave knob from the 12 o'clock to the 5 o'clock position, listening to the result.

8   Click the on/off button for Oscillator 3, turning it on.

Oscillator 3 has similar waveforms with a slight variation: a noise generator that can be used for nonpitched percussive sounds or to blend in with other waveforms.

9   Within the ring around Oscillator 3's wave knob, click Noise.

10   Within the Triangle, drag the square icon to the bottom (Oscillator 3).

11   Play a key on your MIDI keyboard while dragging the square icon in the Triangle towards the center, blending the output of the three oscillators to taste.

Just like Oscillator 2, Oscillator 3 offers a pulse wave with variable pulse width.

12   Click the square wave located at the 12 o'clock position on the ring around Oscillator 3's wave knob.

13   Play a key on your MIDI keyboard, listening to the result.

14   Move the square in the oscillator mix Triangle until you hear the output of Oscillator 1 and 2 roughly equally.

Each oscillator has dedicated tuning controls, located immediately to its left. These Frequency knobs allow you to set the pitch offset of the oscillators within a three-octave range. This allows for harmonization, octave doubling, and the introduction of slight tuning variances to fatten up your sounds.

15 While holding down a key on your MIDI keyboard, drag Oscillator 2's Frequency knob counter-clockwise down to –12 (semitones), listening to the results.

Oscillator 2 sounds an octave below Oscillator 1.

Just as you can click the settings in the ring around the wave knob, you can click the octave settings (12, 24, 36) on the outside of the Frequency knob to quickly change the setting.

16 On Oscillator 2's Frequency knob, click the 0 setting to negate the tuning offset.

The tuning change you just imparted to Oscillator 2 was in semitones. Tuning can also be set by cent intervals (100 cents/semitone) for subtle detuning of one oscillator against the other. You can do this by dragging the cents setting (indicated with the letter *c*) within the Frequency value field.

17 Play a key on your MIDI keyboard while dragging the cents setting in Oscillator 2's Frequency field downwards to –3.

The slight, 3-cent detuning between Oscillator 1 and 2 creates a bigger, more lush sound, similar to a chorusing effect.

18 In the Frequency field, Option-click the cents setting to return it to 0.

Using Oscillator Modulation to Create Interesting Sounds

You may have noticed that there were specific waveform settings on each oscillator that we didn't explore. These options do not specifically produce sound on their own, but instead are dependent upon the settings of the other oscillators to produce a sound.

Using Frequency Modulation

Frequency Modulation, or FM, synthesis has been around since the late '60s and provides a unique way to create interesting harmonic timbres using two audio-range oscillators. Using even simple sine waves, you can modulate, or modify, the frequency of one oscillator (called the carrier), by another (called the modulator) to produce complex results. You can think of FM simply as fast vibrato, wherein the rate of pitch change is in the audible range (20 Hz to 20 kHz).

With the ES2, Oscillator 1 acts as the carrier, whose frequency can be modulated by the frequency of Oscillator 2. In order to best hear the effect of the modulation source upon the carrier, it is necessary to only hear Oscillator 1's output in the mix.

1   Use the Triangle to set the mix output to Oscillator 1 only (all the way to the top right).

2   At the top of the ring around Oscillator 1's wave knob, click the sine wave shape.

Note that when you select this waveform, FM also becomes selected, which indicates that Oscillator 1 is set to FM mode.

3   Hold down a key on your MIDI keyboard while dragging Oscillator 1's wave knob upwards, increasing the intensity of FM from Oscillator 2.

The sound becomes increasingly complex with new harmonics called sidebands.

NOTE ▶ It is normal to hear only the carrier's output (and not the modulator) in FM synthesizers, but you can certainly hear both outputs with the ES2 by positioning the square within the mix Triangle between Oscillator 1 and 2).

With FM synthesis, the tuning relationship between the carrier and modulator oscillators directly affects the sidebands that are produced. This is accomplished on the ES2 by changing the tuning of Oscillator 2 with the frequency knob.

4   Hold down a key on your MIDI keyboard while dragging Oscillator 2's frequency knob upwards.

The sound becomes more inharmonic and metallic.

5   Option-click the frequency knob for Oscillator 2, returning it to 0.

TIP ▶ You can generate even more complex sounds by using complex source waveforms for the modulator (Oscillator 2). Try the Digiwaves for interesting modulation sources.

Using Ring Modulation

Ring modulation differs from frequency modulation in that instead of modulating the frequency of one oscillator by another, it modulates amplitude instead. You can simply think of this as fast tremolo (instead of vibrato).

An interesting effect of ring modulation is that you only hear the sidebands it creates, which are made up of the sum and differences between the frequency of the carrier and modulator oscillator. This creates inharmonic frequencies, which results in a metallic sound. While ring modulation doesn't always produce sounds useful for melodic pitched instruments, it is an excellent sound design tool for creating otherworldly timbres and textures.

With the ES2, Oscillator 2 both outputs the sound and supplies a simple square wave signal that is modulated with the output of Oscillator 1.

1   Use the Triangle to set the mix output to Oscillator 2 only (all the way to the left).

2   At the bottom of the ring around Oscillator 1's wave knob (about the 7 o'clock position), click the triangle wave shape.

This will be the modulation source.

3   At the bottom of the ring around Oscillator 2's wave knob (about the 7 o'clock position), click the Ring.

This will be the carrier source.

Just like with frequency modulation, the tuning relationship between the carrier and modulator oscillators directly affects the sidebands that are produced. This is accomplished on the ES2 by changing the tuning of *either* Oscillator 1 or 2 with the frequency knob.

4   Hold down a key on your MIDI keyboard while dragging Oscillator 1's frequency knob upwards, listening to the result.

As you can hear, a complex metallic sound is produced that changes in relation to the tuning of Oscillator 1.

5   Option-click the frequency knob for Oscillator 1, returning it to 0.

Using Oscillator Synchronization

With oscillator synchronization, the start time (phase) of one oscillator is slaved to another. If the synced oscillators are set to the same frequency, you simply get a doubled waveform. However, if the oscillators are set to different frequencies, the slaved oscillator is forced to reset before it finishes a complete cycle, the result of which are not harmonized oscillators (separate pitches) but instead an interesting timbre change.

With the ES2, oscillator synchronization can be set for both Oscillator 2 and Oscillator 3, slaving to the frequency of Oscillator 1. On both oscillators, you have a choice of either synchronizing a generated sawtooth or square wave to the chosen waveform of Oscillator 1.

1   In the ring around Oscillator 2's wave knob (about the 8 o'clock position), click the sawtooth sync setting.

2   Hold down a key on your MIDI keyboard while dragging Oscillator 2's frequency knob upwards, listening to the result.

The sound changes in timbre as you adjust the frequency of the slaved oscillator (Oscillator 2) in relation to the triangle wave being generated by Oscillator 1.

3   Within the mix Triangle, click somewhere close to the middle.

Sculpting Your Sound Using the Filters

A synthesizer's filter section allows you to carve out only the frequencies generated by the oscillators you want to hear. Of utmost importance to the quality of sound is the character and flexibility of the filter or filters.

The ES2 provides two independent filters that can be set in series or parallel for flexible routing and sculpting of the sound generated by the oscillators. With the stripped-down preset we are using, the two filters are set in series by default, the signal feeding from one filter to another.

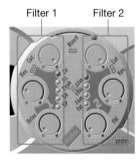

In order to gain an understanding of what each filter can do to the generated sound, you need to listen to them one at a time. When in series, the Blend slider at the top of the filter section acts as a cross-fader between Filter 1 and Filter 2. As you can see, the Blend control is set all the way to the right (above Filter 2), so only Filter 2 will affect the sound from the oscillators.

Typical of subtractive synthesis, Filter 2 is a dedicated low-pass filter with variable cutoff, slope, and resonance. Let's take a listen to its effect on the sound.

1   Hold down a key on your MIDI keyboard while dragging Filter 2's Cutoff knob downwards to about halfway, listening to the result.

As you decrease the cutoff frequency, high frequencies are reduced, allowing only low frequencies to pass (hence the name, "low-pass filter"). You set the way frequencies past the cutoff frequency are attenuated by selecting different slope settings (12 db, 18 db, or 24 db).

2   Press a key on your MIDI keyboard while selecting the different slope settings (12 db, 18 db, and 24 db) one at a time, listening to the differences.

NOTE ▶ Slope is measured in decibels per octave. A higher number generates a steeper slope, attenuating more frequencies higher than the cutoff frequency.

You can boost the gain at the cutoff frequency with the Resonance knob, which will emphasize the filter's cutoff point and even self-oscillate when boosted at high levels.

3   Hold down a key on your MIDI keyboard while dragging Filter 2's Resonance knob upwards to about the 2 o'clock position, listening to the result.

You can really hear the effect resonance offers by sweeping the filter cutoff when resonance is boosted.

4   While holding down a key on your MIDI keyboard, drag Filter 2's Cutoff knob down and up, listening to the result.

5   Set the filter's cutoff frequency back to about the 2 o'clock position.

You might have heard a drop in low frequencies when you boosted the resonance of the filter. This behavior mimics the original circuits in vintage synthesizers. If you'd like, you can add the low frequencies back in while using high resonance by selecting the Fat setting.

NOTE ▸ The Fat setting has little or no effect with low resonance settings.

6   Click the Fat setting, then play a key on your MIDI keyboard to hear the result.

The low frequencies are restored, giving more weight to the sound.

Filter 2's cutoff frequency can be modulated in a similar manner to the FM setting we looked at earlier in the "Using Frequency Modulation" section. In this case, the cutoff frequency is the carrier, while the modulator source is Oscillator 1. The amount of frequency modulation is set by Filter 2's FM knob.

7   While holding down a key on your MIDI keyboard, drag Filter 2's FM knob upwards, listening to the result.

This is a different sound than the oscillator frequency modulation explored earlier, but it offers a unique way to create interesting timbres.

8   Option-click Filter 2's FM knob to return it to 0.

Now that you've explored what Filter 2 has to offer, let's direct our attention to Filter 1.

9   Drag the Blend control to the far left, over Filter 1.

Filter 1 is a multimode filter, providing not only low-pass (Lo), but high-pass (Hi), peak, band reject (BR), and band pass (BP) modes. Adjusting cutoff frequency can have a different effect depending on the mode selected.

10 Drag Filter 1's Cutoff knob to about the 2 o'clock position.

11 On the right side of Filter 1, try clicking the filter mode buttons one a time while holding a key on your MIDI keyboard to see how they affect the sound.

Low pass only lets through frequencies *below* and around the cutoff frequency (as we saw with Filter 2); high pass only lets through frequencies *above* and around the cutoff frequency. Band pass only lets through a narrow band around the cutoff frequency; band reject does the opposite, cutting out the frequencies around the cutoff frequency. Peak mode simply boosts frequencies around the cutoff frequency, acting similar to parametric equalizers.

NOTE ▶ Filter 1's high-pass and low-pass filter modes have a fixed slope of 12 db.

12 Select high-pass mode for Filter 1 by clicking its mode button.

Below Filter 1 is a Drive knob, which distorts the signal before it is fed into the filter section (both Filter 1 and 2). Boosting this knob adds pleasant harmonic distortion that can add grit or fatten up a sound considerably.

13 While holding down a key on your MIDI keyboard, drag the Drive knob upwards, listening to the result.

So far you've only been listening to a single filter at a time. You can blend the output of Filter 1 and 2 by sliding towards the middle of the Blend control.

14 While holding down a key on your MIDI keyboard, drag the Blend control to about midway between the two filters, listening to the result.

As you can hear from the dip in volume, the high-pass and low-pass filter settings for Filter 1 and 2, respectively, are almost canceling each other out. This is because the two filters are in series, wherein the low frequencies are first cut out by Filter 1's high pass, and then some of remaining low frequencies are cut out by Filter 2's low pass. You can hear the effect of both filters equally by putting them in parallel, in effect splitting the sound generated by the oscillators to feed both filters at once, combining the result.

15 At the lower right of the filter section, click the Series/Parallel button.

The filters change orientation to illustrate parallel processing.

16 Play a key on your MIDI keyboard to hear the result of the filters working in parallel.

Now you can blend the output of the split signal passing through the separate filters by using the Blend control.

17 While holding down a key on your MIDI keyboard, drag the Blend control to about 0.54 (three-quarters of the way towards Filter 2), listening to the result.

Using Modulation

Now that you've shaped the raw sound using the oscillators and filters, it's time to have some fun changing the sound dynamically by using the modulation section. Our sound so far, while interesting in timbre, is quite static, and it doesn't respond to performance input (velocity and so on.). By using modulation, you can, in effect, have the ES2 change its settings dynamically, creating evolving sounds that respond to touch and gesture.

The heart of the modulation section is the modulation router. It is here that all modulation is routed, like a virtual patch bay, from source to target. The modulation router contains ten slots where you can assign individual routings to affect the sound.

To better explain how it works, let's start by taking a look at one of the pre-existing routings that is standard on almost all synthesizers.

1   Look at the second slot in the modulation router.

Each slot in the modulation router has an assignable Target, Source, Intensity, and Via parameter. The Target parameter represents what will be changed dynamically. Here, the target is the tuning of all three of the oscillators (Pitch123). The Source parameter represents what will generate the change, in this case, one of the two low-frequency oscillators (LFO1) offered by the ES2.

NOTE ▶ An LFO is just like one of the oscillators we looked at earlier, except that the frequencies it affects are slow, well below the frequency of human hearing. As such, the LFOs are perfect for invoking gradual change over a parameter.

The arrows immediately to the right of the slot represent the intensity of the effect (how much the LFO will change the pitch.)

The Via parameter assigns a source to control the modulation intensity. In this routing, the mod wheel (Controller 1) is assigned.

In effect, the pitch of all three oscillators is being gradually changed back and forth by the LFO, with the mod wheel giving user control as to the depth of the pitch change. This all translates to vibrato.

2   Hold a key while turning the mod wheel up and down on your MIDI keyboard.

The intensity of the vibrato effect changes as you adjust the mod wheel.

In this instance, intensity is given a range, represented by the split arrows showing minimum and maximum values. You can change the range by dragging the top or bottom arrow, or even move the whole range up and down by dragging between the arrows. When dragging, pay attention to the help tags to better position the intensity slider.

3   Drag the top arrow (the orange one) of the intensity range upwards to 1.00.

4   Hold a key while turning up the mod wheel on your MIDI keyboard all the way.

The pitch change is more significant (and extreme) at the top of the range.

You can return to an intensity of 0 quickly by clicking the little zero symbol immediately to the left of the intensity slider.

5   Click the zero symbol.

6   Drag the top arrow (the orange one) of the intensity range upwards to around 0.25.

Using the Low-Frequency Oscillators

The speed and shape of the routed vibrato can be modified by working with the source (LFO1) settings, which is displayed below the modulation router.

1   While holding down a key on your MIDI keyboard, drag LFO 1's Rate slider downwards, listening to the result.

The rate of vibrato slows down.

2   Set LFO 1's rate back to about three-quarters of the way up (5.500 Hz).

Just like the oscillators in the sound generation section, the ES2 LFOs can have different waveforms, which dictate how the Target parameter will change during the LFO cycle. You can select waveforms by clicking the column of buttons adjacent to LFO 1 and 2, respectively.

3 While holding down a key on your MIDI keyboard, select LFO 1's Wave buttons one at a time, listening to the result.

The effect on oscillator pitch changes shape, depending on the waveform selected.

TIP ▶ The bottom two waveforms output random values. The top of the two steps from value to value, and the bottom choice smoothly transitions between the values. These are excellent for assigning subtle, unpredictable variations to a parameter.

4 Select the triangle wave for LFO 1.

Unique to LFO 1 is the addition of its own envelope generator, labeled EG to the left of the Rate slider. This enables you to fade in or out the modulation. You can use this to emulate the natural vibrato a musician might employ on a conventional instrument.

5 Drag LFO 1's EG slider up to around 3600 ms towards the delay side.

6 Hold a key on your MIDI controller, listening to the result.

The vibrato fades in gradually after the sound starts.

NOTE ▶ Another unique feature of LFO 1 is that it is polyphonic; each voice played (key press) has its own wave cycle that is independent of the others. This helps to avoid static, phase-locked modulation. In the case of the vibrato example, each note in a chord would have its own unique LFO, no matter when it is played.

7   Turn the mod wheel all the way down on your MIDI keyboard, turning off the vibrato effect.

NOTE ▶ LFO 2, while being monophonic, offers the capability of syncing to Logic's bars and beats to create tempo-based effects. Do this by dragging the Rate slider to the bottom half.

Using the Envelope Generators

The ES2 offers three different envelope generators per voice. Both Envelope 1 and 2 do not do anything unless you assign them as modulation sources. Envelope 3, on the other hand, is hard-wired to the volume of the sound. With it you can define how a sound changes in dynamics when a key is struck, held, and released.

You can use this envelope to change the organ-like dynamics your sound has now to those of a swelling pad or string sound.

1   Drag Envelope 3's Attack slider (A) upwards about halfway (1000 ms).

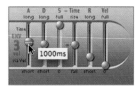

2   Play a key on your MIDI keyboard, listening to the result.

The sound swells, and then dies out quickly once the key is released.

3   Drag Envelope 3's Release slider upwards to about 1800 ms.

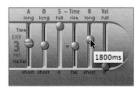

4   Play a key on your MIDI keyboard, listening to the result.

The sound swells, and then dies out slowly once the key is released.

Similar to the intensity slider you looked at earlier within the modulation router, the attack of each envelope can be set to a range that is hard-wired to respond to velocity.

If a range is set, playing softly will increase attack time (towards the top of the range), and playing hard will decrease attack time (towards the bottom of the range).

5 Drag the bottom of Envelope 3's Attack slider downwards to around 280 ms, creating a range.

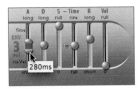

6 Play a key with varying velocity on your MIDI keyboard, listening to the result.

As mentioned earlier, all three envelope generators can be assigned as modulation sources. When you look at the first modulation slot, you can see that it is set to modulate the cutoff frequency of Filter 2 by Envelope 2. Currently, it is bypassed (the b/p button is orange). Let's turn it back on to hear the result.

7 Click the bypass (b/p) button next to the Target parameter in the first slot of the modulation router.

8 Play a key on your MIDI keyboard, listening to the result.

The cutoff frequency of the low-pass filter (Filter 2) changes over time, as dictated by Envelope 2.

TIP ▶ Understanding the differences between LFOs and envelope generators can be confusing at first. LFO modulation can be thought of as regular, or cyclic, change between two states (like a pendulum). Envelope generators can be thought of as change that happens over time and are therefore linear (like a timeline).

Now that you've explored some existing routings, it's time for you to create your first modulation routing. This routing will change the blend between the two parallel filters, using Envelope 1 as the modulation source.

9   In the fourth slot in the modulation router, click the Target menu and choose FltBlend.

10   Click the Source menu and choose Env1.

11   Drag the intensity slider upwards to around 0.77.

NOTE ▶ Intensity can be set to a negative value, which creates a negative offset to the target instead of a positive one.

Now that you've set up the modulation routing, you can set Envelope 1's parameters as you wish.

12   Drag Envelope 1's Attack slider to around 1200 ms.

13   Drag Envelope 1's Decay slider to around 4900 ms.

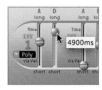

14   Play a key on your MIDI keyboard, listening to the result.

The sound slowly crossfades between Filter 1 and 2, governed by the settings of Envelope 1.

Using the Vector Envelope Generator

The ES2 vector envelope generator is unique among the others in its ability to evoke change represented by specific points along an adjustable timeline that triggers with each key pressed. These points can be looped as well, offering myriad ways to change the sound over time.

In order to keep screen real estate demands to a minimum, the vector envelope controls are hidden behind the modulation router.

1   Click the Vector button, located to the right of the modulation router.

The vector envelope controls are revealed.

The vector envelope controls only two targets: oscillator mix (Triangle), and parameters assigned to the X-Y (Planar) pad in the output section. You assign the targets within the Vector mode menu below.

2   Click the Vector Mode menu and choose Mix.

Take a look at the main area of the vector envelope. There are three numbered points along a timeline, which can store different states of the target control (in this case, the mix Triangle). Essentially, the vector envelope moves from state to state along the timeline, changing the target parameters.

These states are set by first selecting the point and then setting the square within the Triangle.

3   Click the first point, selecting it.

4   In the Triangle, drag the square to approximately the middle (all oscillators).

This will be the beginning state of the sound, almost identical to how it has been sounding previously.

5   Click the second point, selecting it.

NOTE ▶ By default, the second point is designated as the sustain point (represented by the small *s* symbol above it). This is similar to a standard envelope generator, wherein the sustain point is held for as long as the key is pressed. You can change the sustain point by clicking the blue strip above the designated point.

6   In the Triangle, drag the square to the lower-right corner (Oscillator 3).

7   Click the third point, selecting it.

8   In the Triangle, drag the square to the far left (Oscillator 2).

By default, the vector envelope is set to Solo Point, which will only let you hear the state of the selected point in the timeline. In order to hear the sound move from state to state, you need to turn this mode off.

9   In the lower-left corner of the vector envelope area, click the Solo Point button, which deselects it.

10   Hold a key on your MIDI keyboard, listening to the result.

When you press a key, you can hear the oscillator mix changing from all three oscillators sounding equally to just Oscillator 3. When you release the key, the mix changes from Oscillator 3 to Oscillator 2.

The amount of time it takes to move from one point to another can be changed as well. You do this by dragging the numerical time display between the points.

11   Drag the time display between points 1 and 2 downwards to 380 ms.

12   Hold a key on your MIDI keyboard, listening to the result.

The oscillator mix changes between the first two states a bit quicker than before.

NOTE ▶ Additional points can be added by Shift-clicking directly on the vector envelope timeline. To delete a point, Control-click it and choose Delete Selected Point from the shortcut menu.

You can add further sonic movement by looping points within the timeline. These loops can move forward, backward, and alternately forward and backward, depending on the setting.

13   At the bottom of the vector envelope area, click the Loop Mode menu and choose Alternate.

A loop area is defined starting at point 1 and ending at point 2.

14 Hold a key on your MIDI keyboard, listening to the result.

The oscillator mix changes, going back and forth from the states defined in point 1 and 2.

NOTE ▶ Loop start and end points can be defined by clicking below the points on the blue strip below the timeline.

The rate of the loop is usually determined by the timing between the two points. You can, however, adjust the rate proportionally by using the Loop Rate control. The rate can be set to free time (as Hz) or as divisions of the beat (Sync), which locks to tempo.

15 Drag the Loop Rate control to the left, setting the rate to a 1/2-note interval.

16 Hold a key on your MIDI keyboard, listening to the result.

The oscillator mix changes, going back and forth from the states defined in point 1 and 2 at the rate of a 1/2 note (the default tempo of the project is 120 bpm).

TIP ▶ You can always revert back to the original timeline by clicking the As Set button just below the Loop Rate slider.

The X-Y, or Planar, pad is a freely assignable controller allowing you to control two parameters at once. You can assign these as sources within the modulation router, but if you are planning on using the vector envelope, you can conveniently assign them without leaving Vector mode.

In the following steps, you will assign X in the Planar pad to modulate the pitch of Oscillator 2 (which changes the character of the oscillator synchronization), and Y to modulate the pulse width of Oscillator 3.

17 Click the X Target menu at the far right and choose Pitch 2.

18 Double-click the intensity setting under X Target, and enter 1. Press Return.

19 Using the same technique, assign the Y Target to Osc3Wave, with an intensity of 1.

20 Hold a key on your MIDI keyboard while dragging the square within the Planar pad, listening to the result.

Now that you've heard the modulation effect controlled manually, let's assign it to the vector envelope to change the settings on the Planar pad over time.

21 Click the Vector mode menu and choose Mix+XY.

22 Select the vector envelope points one by one as you did earlier, this time changing the Planar pad square location for each point.

23 Hold a key on your MIDI keyboard, listening to the result.

You can now hear the oscillator mix, pitch of Oscillator 2, and pulse width of Oscillator 3 change dynamically over time.

Exploring the Output/Processing Section

Now it's time to add the finishing touches within the output/processing section. Here you can attenuate overall volume level, add an additional sine wave oscillator, or use processing to further shape the sound.

You might have noticed that the levels on the channel strip are getting pretty hot, especially at high velocities. To rectify this, you can turn down the Volume knob.

1 Drag the volume knob downwards, to approximately –8.5 db.

You now have a little dynamic headroom with which to add some further processing.

In addition to distortion, the ES2 offers modulation effects (chorus, flanger, and phaser) to further develop your sound at the output stage. These can only be selected one at a time by clicking the buttons labeled the same (chorus is selected by default) and adjusting the Intensity and Speed knobs below.

2 Drag the Intensity knob upwards, to around 52.

3 Hold a key on your MIDI keyboard, listening to the result.

The chorus effect increases, creating a spacious, swirling stereo sound.

Now that you've spent quite a bit of effort creating your sound with the ES2, it's good idea to save it.

4 From the preset menu, choose Save Setting As.

5 In the file selector dialog, name the preset *Advanced Logic*, and then click Save.

TIP ▶ If you are feeling stuck, or need some inspiration, try using the ES2's Randomize function. Located just below the filter section, it lets you set a target for randomization within the menu on the right and then use the slider to set the intensity of randomization (1 to 100%). When you click the Randomize button on the left, all specified parameters within the target will be randomized by the amount specified. You can also make variations of existing sounds by using low intensity values with limited parameter targets (filters, LFOs, and so on).

Lesson Review

1. Which direction does signal flow in the ES2?

2. Each of the three oscillators in ES2 offers what in addition to analog-style waveforms and modulation options?

3. When in FM mode, Oscillator 1 acts as the carrier, and Oscillator 2 acts as what?

4. When in Ring Modulation mode, Oscillator 2 acts as the carrier, and Oscillator 1 acts as the what?

5. When using oscillator synchronization, which oscillator is the master?

6. How can the ES2 filters be configured?

7. In the ES2, modulation is assigned where?

8. The ES2 vector envelope can be assigned to what two targets?

Answers

1. Signal flow moves from left to right, which helps with understanding the instrument as well as locating controls.

2. Each oscillator offers 100 Digiwaves.

3. Oscillator 1 acts as the carrier, and Oscillator 2 acts as the modulation source.

4. Oscillator 2 acts as the carrier, and Oscillator 1 acts as the modulation source.

5. Oscillator 1 is the master when using oscillator synchronization.

6. The filters can be configured in either series or parallel.

7. Modulation is assigned within slots of the modulation router.

8. The ES2 vector envelope can be assigned to Mix (Triangle) and the X-Y (Planar) pad.

4

Lesson Files   Advanced Logic 9_Files > Lessons > 04_EXS24_Start.logic

Media   Advanced Logic 9_Files > Media > EXS24

Time   This lesson takes approximately 60 minutes to complete.

Goals   Build new sampler instruments from audio regions

Assign pitch mapping and tuning to zones

Create loop points for sustaining sounds

Use groups to assign common parameters to multiple zones

Use filters and modulation to change the character of sampled material

Route output of specific groups for individual processing

Sampling with the EXS24 mkII

A sampler is an extremely versatile tool. Essentially, it allows you to map digital audio files, or *samples*, across pitch ranges for triggering via MIDI. It does this by dynamically changing the playback speed of the samples in real time to match the pitch specified by the MIDI note value.

Individual samples are referenced and mapped within a *sampler instrument*. In this lesson, you will explore the abilities of the EXS24 mkII by creating unique sampler instruments using specific audio regions from the Arrange window.

Creating Sampler Instruments

Traditionally, new sampler instruments are produced by first creating a blank sampler instrument, and then adding and mapping individual samples one by one, building it from the ground up. However, one of the new features in Logic Pro 9 is the ability to use a single command to automatically create a new EXS24 mkII track loaded with a new sampler instrument wrapped around a selected audio region in the Arrange window. This makes it especially easy to extend the creative possibilities of audio files, placing under your fingertips the ability to trigger and process.

1   Choose File > Open.

2   In the file selector dialog, navigate to Music > Advanced Logic 9_Files > Lessons and open **04_EXS24_Start.logic**.

3   Use the Mute tool to unmute the Vox Note region on Track 1.

4   Play the project, listening to the Vox Note audio region.

You will use this recording of a singer holding a single pitch for your first sampler instrument.

5   Stop playback.

6   Go to the beginning of the project.

7   In the Arrange area, select the Vox Note region, if it's not already selected.

8   From the local Audio menu, choose Convert Regions to New Sampler Track.

The Convert Regions to New Sampler Track dialog appears.

Here, you can set how the selected audio region will be initially mapped within the new sampler instrument. Samples are mapped within zones, which contain settings controlling how the sample will be played back, including key ranges.

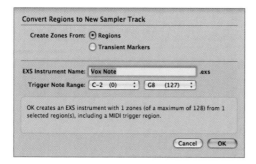

9   Select Create Zones From Regions, if it's not selected already.

This will create a single zone that references the Vox Note audio region (as outlined at the bottom of the dialog).

You can also set the pitch range of the zone that will be created, as specified by the Trigger Note Range menus (low to high). Since only a single audio region was selected (you can also select multiple), it will only utilize the lowest trigger note to map the region.

10 Click the first Trigger Note Range pop-up menu and choose C3 (60).

This will create a new zone at C3, right in the middle of the keyboard.

11 Click OK.

A new EXS24 track (named Vox Note) is created below the original track, along with a new MIDI region. This new region contains a held C3 note that triggers the newly mapped audio file for the same duration as the original audio region. Note that the original region is muted. The new MIDI region in effect replaces the original one in the arrangement.

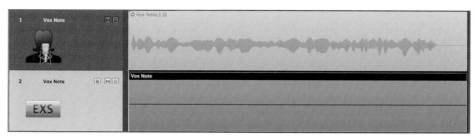

12 Play the project, listening to the new Vox Note MIDI region played through the EXS24.

The playback sounds identical to before.

This new zone will be automatically velocity mapped; the harder you strike the key, the louder the file playback.

13 Press the C3 on your MIDI keyboard at varying velocities, listening to the result.

The Vox Note audio file plays as long as you hold down the key, changing volume (amplitude) along with your keyboard velocity.

Using the EXS24 Instrument Editor

Let's take a look inside the newly created sampler instrument, with the goal of exploring the creative potential offered by the EXS24. Sampler instruments are edited within the EXS24 Instrument Editor, which is accessible from within the EXS24 interface.

1 In the Inspector, double-click the EXS24 in the Arrange channel strip to open the EXS24 interface.

The EXS24 Parameter window opens, with the newly created sampler instrument, Vox Note, displayed. You will be working with the parameters in this window later on in the lesson, but for now, you will use it to quickly access the EXS24 Instrument Editor.

2   Click the Edit button, located at the top right.

The EXS24 Instrument Editor opens.

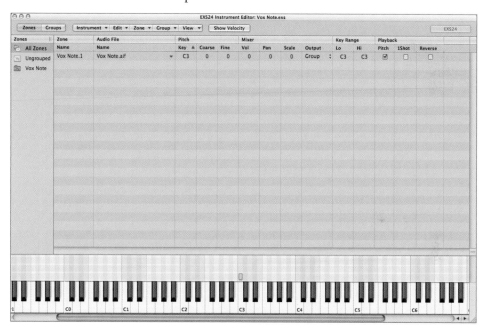

For now, you can close the window to save some screen real estate.

3   Close the EXS24 Parameter window (not the EXS24 Instrument Editor).

The EXS24 Instrument Editor has two views: Zones and Groups. You are currently looking at the Zones view (more on Groups later), as indicated by the selected button at the top left.

The top portion of the EXS24 Instrument Editor is called the Parameters area, and it displays the settings of each sample referenced by the sampler instrument. The bottom portion of the window displays how each sample is mapped to various pitches, represented by the keyboard at the bottom of the window. As you can see, a new zone, named Vox Note.1 was created, mapped to C3 on the keyboard.

When you create a sampler instrument with the Convert Regions to New Sampler Track command, the zone created is without range—that is, only mapped to a single pitch.

You can, of course, extend the zone's range to map the audio file to multiple pitches. This is done either by changing settings within the Key Range columns of the Parameters area, or by dragging directly on the zone in the bottom area.

4   Within the Key Range parameters, double-click the Hi field and enter *c4*. Press Return.

The zone extends in range to the right, from C3 to C4.

5   In the bottom area of the EXS24 Instrument Editor, drag the zone's left border to the left, extending the range to C2.

6   Play the C2 to C4 keys on your MIDI keyboard, listening to the result.

The pitch (and speed) of the sample shifts up and down, mapped in relation to your MIDI keyboard input.

NOTE ▶ You can also create new sampler instruments by choosing New from the EXS24 Instrument Editor's Instrument menu, or by clicking the Edit button on the EXS24 interface when an instrument isn't currently loaded. This creates a blank sampler instrument where you can manually add zones by choosing New Zone or Load Multiple Samples from the Zones menu. You can also create new zones by dragging and dropping audio files from the Logic Bin or Browser, or even the Finder.

If you have perfect pitch, you might have noticed that the sung note is a little flat compared to standard tuning (A440). This wouldn't be a problem if this was the only instrument used in the project, but if other instruments will be played at the same time, it would sound out of tune. Using the zone's Pitch parameters in the Instrument Editor, you can compensate for tuning discrepancies (Coarse equaling semitones, and Fine equaling cents, or 1/100th of a semitone).

The best way to tune a zone by hand is by inserting a Tuner plug-in on the EXS24 channel, monitoring the results as you adjust parameters.

7   Click the top insert slot of the new Vox Note (EXS24) channel, and select Metering > Tuner > Stereo.

The Tuner opens.

8   While watching the Tuner readout, hold down the C3 key on your MIDI keyboard and drag the zone's Fine parameter upwards to about 28 cents (the Tuner's readout should bob around the 12 o'clock position).

The sample plays back in tune in relation to standard tuning.

9   Close the Tuner window.

Creating Loop Points

Looping is a technique that stems from the day when samplers had tiny memory stores (by today's standards) in which to load samples. Many sounds start off with complex attacks but soon settle into a more or less steady waveform. By repeating this "settled" area, a sample can be sustained indefinitely without using valuable memory space. Even with modern software samplers that have access to gigabytes of memory (like the EXS24), looping is a useful technique to create sustaining sounds out of material that is otherwise quite short, like the audio file you are working with in this exercise.

By default, this editor only displays some of the Zone parameters, while hiding others, including the Loop parameters. You can select the parameters that you want to display within the View menu.

1   Click the local View menu and choose View All.

All Zone parameters are displayed, including the Loop parameters.

NOTE ▶ Depending on the size of your EXS24 Instrument Editor window, you might need to scroll to the right to view the Loop parameters.

In order to enable looping, you first need to select the Loop On box.

2   In the Loop parameters, click the Loop On box.

Although you could enter start and end times (by sample number) in the parameters area, this would be arbitrary and counterintuitive. It is much easier to select an area on the waveform itself by using the Sample Editor.

3   In the Audio File parameters for the zone, click the small disclosure triangle to the right of the audio file name and choose Open in Sample Editor.

The Sample Editor opens, displaying the referenced audio file, Vox Note.aif.

NOTE ▸ You most likely will need to expand the Sample Editor window to do the following exercise. If you have limited screen real estate, you can minimize the EXS24 Instrument Editor window, temporarily storing it in your Dock.

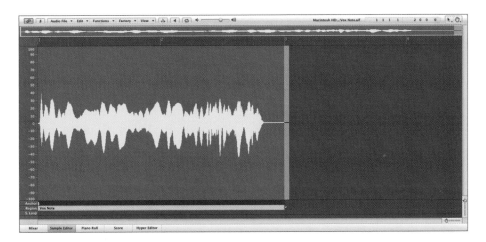

TIP ▸ Double-clicking an audio file within a zone also opens the audio file in the Sample Editor.

By default, the Sample Editor displays bars/beats in its timeline. It is much more helpful to view the timeline when setting loop points in samples (1 sample = 1 ÷ sample rate per second). This will correspond to the numerical display within the EXS24 Instrument Editor.

NOTE ▸ Samples as a measurement of time is not to be confused with the term *samples*, mentioned earlier in the chapter. The latter is another way of saying "digital audio files," while the former refers to the tiny components that make up a digital waveform.

4   From the local View menu, choose Samples.

The timeline is now displayed in samples.

The trick to setting loop points is to find a sustaining portion within the audio file that can be repeated without interruption. In order to make smooth edits, it is necessary to make selections that do not interrupt the waveform above or below the zero axis (thereby creating an audible click). When Snap Edits to Zero Crossings is enabled within the Sample Editor, all new selections will be justified to the nearest point the waveform crosses the zero axis.

5   From the local Edit menu, choose Snap Edits to Zero Crossings.

6   Using the help tags, select an area from approximately 28800 to 91900 samples (refer to the following illustration).

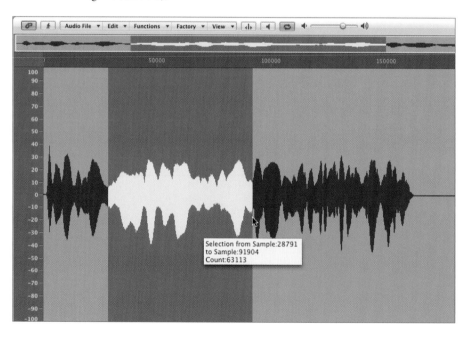

You can audition your selection by selecting the Prelisten and Cycle buttons at the top of the Sample Editor.

7   Click the Prelisten and Cycle buttons to listen to your selection looping.

8   Click the Prelisten button, stopping playback.

> **TIP** ▶ Your loop points may sound a bit rough at first, but with further massaging, you can create a smoother result. This is done by zooming in on the start and end loop points and fine-tuning the selection while auditioning.

Now that you've identified the area you want to be looped, you need to set the start and end loop points to the zone in the EXS24 Instrument Editor.

9   From the Sample Editor's local Edit menu, choose Selection > Sample Loop.

The Sample Loop lane within the Sample Editor displays the selected area in green.

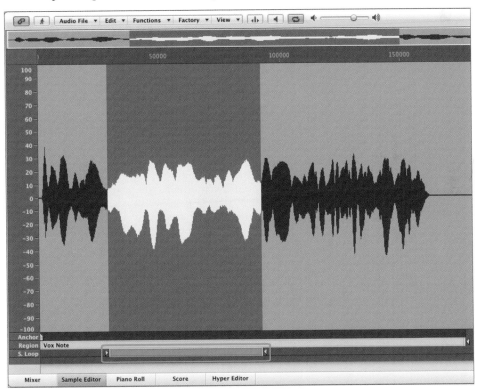

10 Close the Sample Editor.

The results of your selection appear within the Loop parameters of the EXS24 Instrument Editor.

11 Hold down a C3 on your MIDI keyboard, listening to the result.

The sample plays, now looping the selected area for as long as you hold down the key.

To aid you in helping to smooth out the repeating loop's start and end points, you can apply a short crossfade. This is similar to how you smooth region transitions in the Arrange window.

12 In the Loop parameters, double-click the Xfade field and enter *30*. Press Return.

There is also an option to have the crossfade be equal powered, which creates an exponential curve with a 3 db boost in volume in the middle to compensate for the dip in volume that normally occurs within a linear crossfade.

13 In the Loop parameters, click the E. Pwr box to enable it.

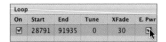

14 Hold down a C3 on your MIDI keyboard, listening to the result.

The sample plays, smoothly looping the selected area for as long as you hold down the key.

Using the Parameter Window

After a sampler instrument is loaded, the triggered sounds are further refined and processed by the global playback parameters located on the interface of the EXS24 mkII itself. These parameters are nearly identical to the sound processing functionality of a synthesizer, allowing you to further shape your sampler instrument sounds.

1 In the EXS24 Instrument Editor window, click the EXS24 button.

The EXS24 Parameter window (interface) opens. This offers a convenient way to access the EXS24 playback parameters without having to go back to the channel strip.

2   Close the EXS24 Instrument Editor.

A Save dialog appears.

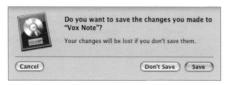

3   Click Save.

Now look at the EXS24's interface. Note that the EXS24 shares many interface characteristics with the ES2 synthesizer covered in Lesson 3. It has filter, output, modulation routing, and modulation source sections in similar places within the interface.

In this exercise, you will use the amplitude envelope to change the character of the Vox Note sampler instrument to that of a swelling choir-like pad that decays slowly. In the EXS24, Envelope 2 is hardwired to amplitude, and it controls the dynamics of how the sound is shaped over time for each key pressed.

4   In the controls for Envelope 2, drag the Attack slider upwards to about midway (about 820 ms).

TIP ▶ You can split the Attack controls of both Envelopes 1 and 2 to create a range. This intensity range is modulated via note velocity, wherein high values trigger the sound more quickly (represented by the lower half of the control), and low values trigger the sound more slowly (represented by the upper half of the control).

5   In the controls for Envelope 2, drag the Release slider upwards to about midway (about 820 ms).

6   Hold down a chord between C2 and C4 on your MIDI keyboard, listening to the result.

You should hear a swelling, sustained choir sound, based off of the original audio file, Vox Note.aif.

7   From the preset menu, choose Save Setting As.

8   In the file selector dialog, name the preset Vox Note and then click Save.

9   Close the EXS24 window

Creating Multiple Zones from Region Transients

In the previous exercises, you created a single zone sampler instrument from an audio file in the Arrange window. Using a similar technique, you can create a sampler instrument with multiple zones based off of detected transients in the audio file. This is especially useful when dealing with rhythmic material such as drum and percussion loops that have clear transients.

In the following exercises, you will create a new sampler instrument from a basic drum loop and explore ways to extend and transform the sound using the EXS24 playback parameters and routing flexibility.

1   Use the Mute tool to mute the new Vox Note region (Track 2).

2   Select the Basic Drums track (Track 3).

3   Use the Mute tool to unmute the Basic Drums regions on Track 3.

4   Play the project, listening to the Basic Drums region to become familiar with the material.

5   From the Arrange window's local Audio menu, choose Convert Regions to New Sampler Track.

The Convert Regions to New Sampler Track dialog appears.

6   Select Create Zones From Transient Markers.

NOTE ▶ When you select to create zones by transient markers, Logic performs a quick transient detection similar to the one performed when you activate Flex view for the first time. The number of detected transients is displayed in the info area at the bottom of the Convert Regions to New Sampler Track dialog.

7   Click OK.

A new EXS24 track (also named Basic Drums) is created, along with a new MIDI region. This new region contains multiple note events that trigger each of the created zones in order, and for the same duration as the original audio region, replacing the original audio region in the arrangement.

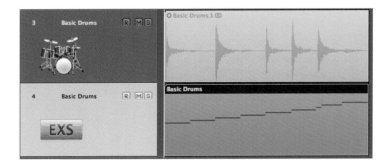

NOTE ▶ This is similar to using the Slicing Flex mode, wherein an audio region is chopped up according to its transients.

8   Play the project, listening to the new Basic Drums MIDI region played through the EXS24.

The playback sounds identical to before.

9   In the Inspector, double-click the EXS24 in the Arrange channel strip to open the EXS24 interface.

10 Click the Edit button, located at the top right.

The EXS24 Instrument Editor opens, displaying the multiple zones created from transients.

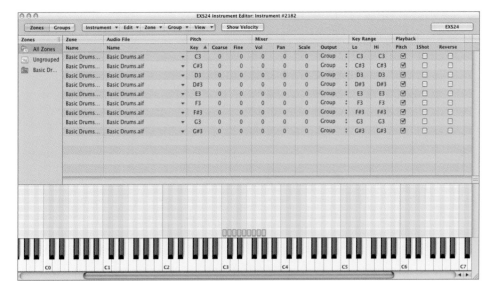

As you can see within the Parameters area, each transient from the original audio file is mapped chromatically to MIDI pitches C3 through G#3.

11 Play the C3 through G#3 keys on your MIDI keyboard, listening to the result.

When playing the associated MIDI pitches on the keyboard, you hear each individual slice. However, the slice only plays for as long as you hold down the key, and it can sound truncated if you let go before the slice plays out in its entirety. In order for the sample to play back its complete length irrespective of the key release, you need to have 1Shot enabled within the Zone parameters.

12 Choose Select All from the EXS24 Instrument Editor's Edit menu.

13 On any of the selected zones, click the 1Shot box to enable it for all.

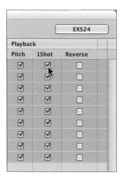

14 Play the C3 through G#3 keys on your MIDI keyboard, listening to the result.

The slices play through in their entirety.

Although this provides an effective way to trigger the drums as a performance instrument, let's explore additional playback parameters within the EXS24 Instrument Editor to further process the sound.

15 Click in the background of the EXS24 Instrument Editor to deselect all zones.

16 In the Parameters area, Command-click the zones mapped to C#3, D#3, and G#3 to select them.

> **TIP** ▶ To use your MIDI controller to select zones, choose Zone > Select Zone of Last Played Key.

17 Click the Reverse box for one of the selected zones to enable it for all selected zones.

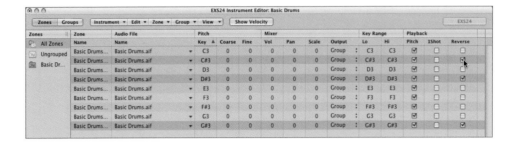

18 Play the C#3, D#3, and G#3 keys on your MIDI keyboard, listening to the result.

The samples play back in reverse.

19 Close the EXS24 Instrument Editor window.

20 Click Save in the Save dialog that appears.

Using Filters and Modulation to Process the Sound

Just like you used the ES2 synthesizer to process the oscillators' signal, you can use EXS24's filter and extensive modulation options to process the sampler instrument you created. In fact, the EXS24's filter and modulation router directly mirror the ones in the ES2, with the exception of only offering a single filter, instead of a pair.

The filter in the EXS24 is a multimode filter, offering high-pass, low-pass, and band-pass modes. In order to take advantage of its sound-shaping properties, you first need to switch it on.

1 Click the filter on/off button located at the right side of the filter section.

NOTE ▶ Having an on/off switch for the filter enables you to quickly audition sounds with and without the filter's influence. It also is worth noting that when the filter is active, it takes up more processor power, so it is a good idea to switch it off when you don't need it.

Now that the filter is switched on, you can apply filter settings to shape the sound.

2   Do the following with the EXS24's filter settings (refer to the illustration below to double-check):

▶   Click the 6 db low-pass (LP) filter mode/slope button to gradually attenuate frequencies above the cutoff frequency.

▶   Drag the Cutoff knob to about 68%.

▶   Drag the Resonance knob to about 45%, accentuating the cutoff frequency by applying a gain boost.

▶   Click the Fat button, enabling you to retain the low frequencies that are naturally diminished by high-resonance settings.

▶   Drag the Drive knob to about 20% distorting the filter and adding harmonics.

Now that you've created your filter settings, it's time to hear the result.

3   Play the C3 through G#3 keys on your MIDI keyboard, listening to the result of the filter settings.

You can further expand on the filter's sound-shaping properties by applying modulation to the cutoff frequency. The goal is to create a surging filter sweep that is timed to the tempo of the song. You can do this by using the EXS24's modulation router, which is nearly identical to the ES2's modulation router, except that it calls the parameter that will be changed dynamically the destination instead of the target.

4   In the third (empty) slot in the modulation router, choose filter cutoff (Flt Cutoff) as the destination (Dest), and LFO1 as the source (Src).

5   Drag the Intensity slider to about +7.7%.

6   Select the top sawtooth setting for LFO1's waveform.

7   Drag LFO1's Rate knob to the left, setting it to 1/8.

This will create a filter sweep for every eighth note, no matter what the tempo of the project is.

NOTE ▸ The EXS24's LFO1 is polyphonic with its own envelope generator, just like the ES2.

Now it's time to test your modulation routing. Because it's tempo-dependent, let's listen to it playing in the Arrange window.

8   In the Transport bar, click the Cycle button.

9   Play the project, listening to the result.

You should hear a sweeping, pulsing, swelling drumbeat that is quite transformed from the original.

10   Stop the project.

While the loop was playing, you might have noticed the EXS24 distorting, and the channel volume pushing well into the red. This is because of the extra gain introduced by boosting the Drive and Resonance controls. You can buy back a little headroom by lowering the EXS24's own Volume control, located at the far right of the interface.

11 Drag the Volume knob downwards to a value of –7 db.

Using Groups

In the EXS24 Instrument Editor, zones can be organized into groups in order to apply common parameters to multiple zones simultaneously. Groups contain many of the same parameters used in zones, but they also offer some unique parameters of their own, such as the ability to offset both the filter settings and the envelopes. This allows you to create, for example, different cutoff and resonance values for different zones.

In the sampler instrument you created, the low-pass filter cuts out the high frequencies of all samples. By using groups, you can, in effect, apply a different cutoff frequency for just the snare hits.

1 On the EXS24 interface, click the Edit button.

The EXS24 Instrument Editor opens.

2 From the local menu, choose Group > New Group.

A new group is created, Group #2, which appears within the Zones column.

NOTE ► In addition to the newly created group, the Zones column displays All Zones, Ungrouped, and Basic Drums groups. The All Zones group contains all zones, regardless of their assignment. The Ungrouped group contains only zones that have no assignment whatsoever. The Basic Drums group, created by default when you imported the samples into the EXS24 Instrument Editor, contains all of the slices created by using the Convert Regions to New Sampler Track setting.

3   In the Zones column, double-click the name of the new Group (Group #2), and enter *Filter*. Press Return.

To display the parameters for the newly created group, you need to switch to Groups view.

4   Click the Groups view button.

The group parameters are displayed.

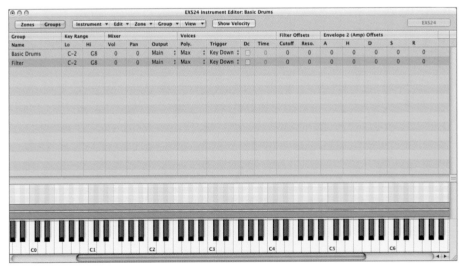

NOTE ▸ By default, the editor only displays some of the group parameters, while hiding others. As you did with zones in an earlier exercise, you can select the parameters you want displayed within the View menu while in Groups view.

5   In the Filter Offsets parameters, double-click the Cutoff field and enter –5. Press Return.

This will lower the filter cutoff frequency for any zone assigned to this group.

Now that you created and modified the group, its time to assign the zones to the new group. This is done back in the Zones view.

6   Click the Zones view button.

You might be asking yourself "where did the zones go?" Not to worry; you are currently viewing the Filter group, which as of yet does not have any zones assigned to it.

7   Click the All Zones group.

All zones are displayed.

Zones can be easily assigned to groups by dragging and dropping onto the groups within the Zones column.

8   Command-click the zones mapped to D3 and G3 to select them.

9   Drag the selected zones to the Filter group.

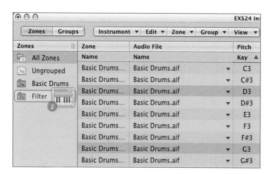

10 In the Zones column, select the Filter Group.

The two zones you added are displayed.

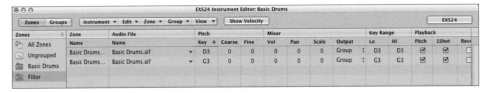

11 Play the project, listening to the result.

The snare samples mapped to D3 and G3 have a slightly different filter cutoff frequency, changing the sound.

Routing Individual Sounds for Processing

As if the options offered by the EXS24's modulation and filter sections weren't enough, Logic allows you to further process the sound emanating from the EXS24 by inserting plug-ins in the signal chain. When you do this, the entire EXS24 signal is processed. Although this normally isn't a problem, there are some instances when you want to apply separate processing to individual zones within a sampler instrument.

To do this, you need to isolate the zone or group on its own mixer channel for individual processing. Fortunately, the EXS24 allows you to route individual sounds through separate virtual "outputs" to accomplish just that. These routings are selected by the Output menu in the Mixer parameters in either the Zone or Group parameters.

1 Click the Groups view button.

2 Click the Output field for the Filter group (it currently displays "Main"), and choose 3-4.

NOTE ▶ The first five selections represent stereo routings, and the last six selections represent mono.

3   In the local Instrument menu, choose Save.

To use this special function, you need to instantiate the EXS24 as a multi-output instrument. So far you've been working with the EXS24 as a stereo instrument and have done quite a bit of work modifying the zones and groups. Luckily, Logic allows you to keep all of the current settings when changing from stereo to multi-output instantiations.

NOTE ▶ For any software instrument, all settings and content contained in a software instrument will be transferred when switching modes (mono, stereo, multi-output, and 5.1).

5   At the bottom of the Arrange window, click the Mixer button to open the Mixer.

6   On the Basic Drums channel strip (Track 4), click-hold the Instrument slot to open the Instrument Plug-in menu and choose EXS24 (Sampler) > Multi Output (5xStereo, 6xMono).

The EXS24 interface opens after reloading the associated samples and current settings.

7   If necessary, move the EXS24 window so you can see the EXS24 Basic Drums channel strip (Track 4).

8   Just under the Solo button, click the small plus button (+) on the EXS24 Basic Drums channel strip (Track 4).

A new Aux 1 channel strip is created immediately to the right of the EXS24 Basic Drums channel strip (Track 4). This will be the receiving channel for our Filter group. By default, Logic creates an aux channel with the default stereo input of 3-4 for the associated multi-output instrument (in this case, the EXS24).

9   Play the project, stopping after you've had a chance to observe the output of the Aux 1 channel.

The zones assigned to the Filter group play through the Aux 1 channel, while the remaining zones play through the EXS24 Basic Drums channel (Track 4).

TIP ▶ This technique works well for drum sampler instruments that need separate compression, EQ, and ambience treatments for individual drums (kick, snare, and so on).

Now that the snare slices are isolated on their own mixer channel, you can insert plug-ins or use send effects for further processing and not affect the other slices in the sampler instrument. In the following steps, you will send the snare slices through a simple Echo plug-in to create rhythmic echoes.

10   Click the Aux 1 channel's top insert slot, and choose Delay > Echo >Stereo.

The Echo plug-in is instantiated, and its interface window opens.

11 Click the Time menu, and choose 1/8T.

This sets the repeat time to eighth-note triplets.

12 Drag the Wet slider down to 23%.

This will lower the volume level of the repeats so as not to overpower the original signal.

13 Play the project, listening to the effect of all of the EXS24 programming you've done in the last few exercises.

The result is a surging, shuffling, processed drum loop, quite abstracted from the original audio file.

14 From the preset menu, choose Save Setting As.

15 In the file selector dialog, name the preset Vox Note and then click Save.

To give perspective on just how much has been changed, let's finish by listening to the original loop.

16 Close both the Echo and EXS24 windows.

17 Close the Mixer.

18 Using the Mute tool, select the Basic Drums.1 region on Track 3, unmuting the original region.

19 In the Transport bar, click the Solo button to enable it.

20 Play the project.

21 While the project is playing, select the original Basic Drums audio track (Track 3) and EXS24 Basic Drums software instrument track (Track 4) alternatively, soloing them.

22 Stop the project.

23 In the Transport bar, click the Solo button to disable it.

Lesson Review

1. Individual samples are referenced and mapped within what?
2. What contains the settings for how a sample will be played back, including key ranges?
3. Which tuning parameter in the EXS24 Instrument Editor would be used to tune by cents, Coarse or Fine?
4. Are loop points set within zones or groups?
5. What parameter in the EXS24 Instrument Editor is used to smooth out transitions between the end points and start points of a loop?
6. How are groups used in the EXS24 Instrument Editor?
7. Are filter and envelope offsets set within zones or groups?
8. What do multi-output instruments do?

Answers

1. Samples are mapped within sampler instruments.
2. Zones contain the settings for how a sample will be played back, including key range.
3. The Fine parameter is used to tune by cents.
4. Loop points are set within zones, as they refer to specific samples.

5. The Xfade parameter allows you to assign a crossfade between the end and start points of a loop, making it smoother.

6. Groups are used to assign common parameters to multiple zones.

7. Filter and envelope offsets are set within groups.

8. Multi-output instruments (such as Ultrabeat and EXS24 mkII) can route individual sounds to separate channel strips for isolation or further processing.

5

Lesson Files	Advanced Logic 9_Files > Lessons > 05_Sculpture_Start.logic
Media	None
Time	This lesson takes approximately 45 minutes to complete.
Goals	Explore different material characteristics on which to base your sound
	Apply different objects to select how the material is played
	Process the sound using the Waveshaper and Body EQ
	Morph between variances of the sound using the Morph Pad
	Record your movements in the Morph Pad to use as a modulation envelope

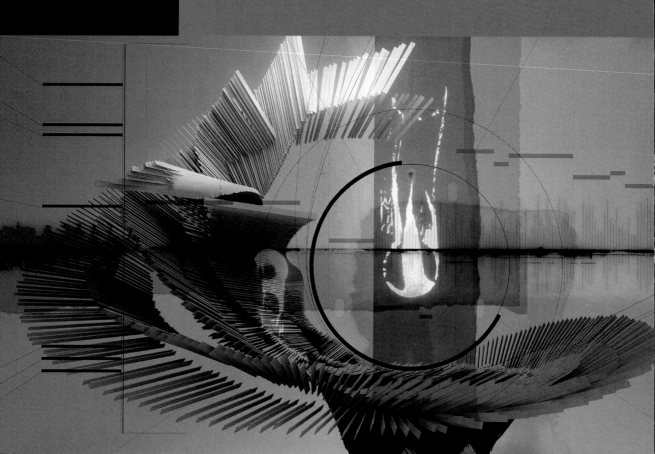

Lesson **5**

Sound Design with Sculpture

Sculpture represents a unique approach to synthesis. It uses sophisticated algorithms to recreate the way sound is generated in the natural world. Specifically, it simulates the characteristics of a vibrating string or bar. This technique is called component or physical modeling, and it closely mirrors the sound generation found in Logic's vintage keyboard instruments (EVP88, EVD6, and EVB3).

One way to wrap your head around Sculpture is to imagine a synthesizer that lets you control how all the components of a real "physical" instrument interact, and what materials they are made from. In effect, you are building a physical instrument from scratch.

Because Sculpture is so innovative, many people have difficulty when they first approach it, unsure of how to begin designing sounds and editing settings. In the next exercise, you will walk through the key components of Sculpture and create a sound from scratch.

Understanding the User Interface

Let's start off our journey in sound design by taking a brief look at the Sculpture interface to identify where essential controls are located.

1 Choose File > Open.

2 In the file selector dialog, navigate to Music > Advanced Logic 9_Files > Lessons and open **05_Sculpture_Start.logic**.

The project opens, displaying the Sculpture interface.

Although there are many unique controls available here, the Sculpture interface also aligns itself closely with the instruments discussed in previous lessons. There are sections dedicated for sound generation, filtering, processing, and modulation.

Sound generation section

Output/processing section

Filter section

Modulation section

Signal flow also generally follows a path similar to the previously discussed instruments, going from left to right.

Understanding the String

In Sculpture, the central synthesis element is called the *string*. This is a bit of a misnomer, since the basic physical material it represents can be any material that would generate sound as the result of a physical action—such as striking, picking, blowing, and so on—upon it.

1   Play your MIDI controller.

The string animates, depicting its vibration. This animation is an effective tool when you're programming sounds with Sculpture, as it provides visual feedback reflecting how your choices are affecting the string.

TIP ▶ You can turn the string animation off by Control-clicking the string and selecting Disable Screen Animation. This can conserve the CPU resources used to generate the animation."

Using the Material Pad in the center of the interface, you can construct the string by blending the properties of four basic materials: steel, nylon, wood, and glass.

2   Drag the ball in the Material Pad around the square while playing your MIDI controller.

The sound changes as you move the ball, modifying the Inner Loss (damping) and Stiffness (rigidity) of the string material.

3   Position the ball about halfway between nylon and steel at the far left edge of the Material Pad.

The outside ring of the Material Pad contains additional parameters that determine the sound-making properties of the selected material.

4   Try dragging the Media Loss slider, listening to the sound by playing your MIDI controller, eventually settling on a value of about 0.25.

Media Loss controls the damping of the string caused by its environment. Imagine a string vibrating in air, water, or pea soup to visualize what this parameter does.

5   Drag the Resolution slider, listening to the sound by playing your MIDI controller, eventually settling on a value of about 55.

The material's resolution has to do with the number of harmonics it generates. The higher the value, the richer and more complex the sound as more overtones are produced. Be aware that higher resolution values carry a higher CPU load.

6   Drag the Tension Mod(ulation) slider, listening to the sound by playing your MIDI controller, eventually settling on a value of about 0.25.

The Tension Mod control adds pitch displacement of the string to higher note velocities. This is similar to the slight initial pitch change that occurs when you strongly pluck a stringed instrument.

Using Objects in Sculpture

Sculpture has three objects that determine how the string is excited or disturbed (how it is played). Remember physical instruments need an action applied to the sound-producing material to make a sound: a guitar string needs to be plucked or picked, a violin string needs to be bowed, a marimba bar needs to be struck with a mallet, and so on.

1   Click the 1 button next to the Object 1 controls (at the far left of the interface).

The button turns from blue to gray, indicating that the object is off.

2   Play your MIDI controller.

You shouldn't hear any sound.

Why is no sound produced? This illustrates the dependent physical interaction between objects and strings. Without an object exciting the string, nothing happens, just as in the real world.

3   Turn on Object 1 again by clicking the 1 button.

4   Click the Type button located to the right of Object 1's Strength knob.

The menu that appears lists various exciter types for exciting the string.

5   Try choosing each exciter type one at a time, testing each sound by playing your MIDI controller and observing the effect on the string animation.

6   Conclude by choosing the Pick exciter type for Object 1.

Object 1 is now set to simulate the action and sound of a guitar pick acting on a string. The parameters are controlled by the object's Strength knob and surrounding sliders: Variation, Timbre, and, for Objects 1 and 2, VeloSens (velocity sensitivity). The parameters are context sensitive, meaning that the exciter type determines what the controls do. For example, the Timbre slider sets hammer mass when the exciter type is Strike, and bow pressure when the type is Bow.

MORE INFO ▶ See the "Sculpture Excite Table (Objects 1 and 2)" section in the Logic Pro 9 Instruments manual for a chart describing the parameters for each exciter type.

7   Drag the Strength knob and try different values, listening to the result while playing your MIDI controller.

In the case of Pick, the Strength parameter determines pick force and speed.

8   Option-click the Strength knob to return the value to the default.

TIP ▶ You can Option-click most controls in Logic to return them to their default settings.

9   Drag the Variation slider, listening to the sound by playing your MIDI controller, eventually settling on a value of about 0.61.

The Variation slider determines plectrum stiffness when the exciter type is set to Pick.

10   Click the 2 button next to Object 2 to turn it on.

11   Click the Type button to open the menu, and then choose Disturb.

Note that this menu is considerably longer than the Object 1 menu. Object 2 offers all of the same exciter types as Object 1 but also contains a variety of others, which are referred to as *disturbers*. The nature of a disturber type is not to *start* the string material vibrating (as the exciter types do), but to disturb the vibration in some way through a physical interaction. Therefore, disturbers work in conjunction with exciters to produce a complex result.

12 Play your MIDI controller to hear the result of the applied disturber.

With Disturb chosen, you are introducing a physical object at a fixed distance from the string that keeps it from freely vibrating. Think of an object positioned close to the strings of a guitar so that it is nearly touching. When the guitar strings are plucked, the strings hit the object, creating a buzzing sound.

13 Adjust the Strength of Object 2 to about 0.43, listening to the results by playing your MIDI controller.

Just as they do with the exciter types, the Strength, Variation, and Timbre controls modify aspects of the chosen disturber. In the case of Disturb, Strength sets the hardness of the object positioned near the string.

MORE INFO ▶ See the "Sculpture Disturb and Damp Table (Objects 2 and 3)" section in the Logic Pro 9 Instruments manual for a chart describing the parameters for each disturber type.

14 In the Gate settings for Object 2, select the Always button, and then play your MIDI controller to hear the result.

The Gate settings determine when the object interacts with the string in relation to the MIDI controller keystroke: on depressing the key (and not when the key is let go), on letting go of the key (and not when the key is pressed), or always.

15 Click the 3 button, and then choose Bouncing from the Type menu if necessary.

Notice that Object 3's Type choices are limited to disturbers (no exciters). Bouncing simulates a loose object lying on the vibrating string. Imagine a piece of paper or small wood block lying directly on a guitar's strings to get an idea of what this produces.

16 Set Strength to about 0.11, playing your MIDI controller to hear the results as you adjust the value.

Strength controls the effect of gravity on the bouncing object.

17 Adjust the Timbre slider to approximately –0.22, listening to the results as you do so.

In the case of a bouncing object, the Timbre parameter controls the stiffness of the object.

Now that you have determined the basic sound generation by choosing object types, you can further work with the sound by determining where each object interacts on the length of the string. This is similar to picking a guitar string at the bridge, at the neck, or in the middle.

You can position objects by moving sliders representing each object in the Pickup display.

18 Drag the Object 1 slider in the Pickup display to the right, positioning it in the middle of the string.

19 In the Pickup display, drag the Object 2 slider to the left, positioning it slightly to the right of the left end (a value of 0.03).

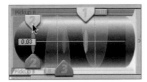

20 In the Pickup display, drag the Object 3 slider to the left, positioning it between the Object 1 and Object 2 sliders.

21 Listen to the sound by playing your MIDI controller.

Adjusting the Pickups

To sense vibrations from the string, Sculpture uses pickups that function identically to an electric guitar's electromagnetic pickups. As on an electric guitar, the pickup's location is of importance; different positions along the length of the string create different timbres.

TIP ▶ To hear these subtle differences, play your MIDI controller while you do the following adjustments.

1 Drag the Pickup A slider to the left, roughly between Objects 2 and 3.

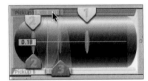

2 Drag the Pickup B slider over Object 1.

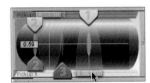

The resulting sound emphasizes the Pick exciter, similar to the way the neck pickup works on an electric guitar.

Processing the Sound

The extensive processing options in Sculpture allow you to further shape the sound using a variety of means (multimode filter, Waveshaper, stereo delay, and Body EQ). Examine some of the choices, working with the sound you have constructed so far.

1 Turn on the Waveshaper by clicking the Waveshaper button above the Material Pad.

The Waveshaper provides interesting distortion effects, including tube simulation, for harmonically rich results.

2   Drag the Input Scale knob to a value of 0.39.

3   Drag the Variation knob to a value of –0.69.

4   Play your MIDI controller to audition the sound.

You have just applied soft, tube-like saturation to the sound.

The Body EQ section uses a unique approach to equalization, providing some great sound-shaping possibilities. A standard EQ changes individual frequency bands, but Body EQ also offers spectral models that emulate the resonating properties of specific instruments. These models can be shaped by adjusting formant-related parameters.

5   If Body EQ is not already turned on, click the Body EQ button to the right of the Material Pad.

By default, Body EQ is set to the Lo Mid Hi model, emulating a standard three-band EQ.

6   Click the Model button to open the Model pop-up-menu.

As you can see, the choices range from various string instruments (guitars, violin, cello, double bass, and so on) to kalimba and types of flutes (alto and bass).

7   Choose Dobro Guitar.

The controls change to reflect the formant parameters of the resonating body (Dobro Guitar), and the graphic display to the right now depicts a detailed spectrum.

8   Try playing your MIDI controller to hear the Dobro Guitar spectral model applied to your sound.

In effect, you are coupling the sound generator you constructed (through the interaction between string and objects) with the resonating body of a Dobro guitar (a metal-body guitar with an acoustic speaker cone).

9   Try changing the three formant-related controls, which adjust how much the harmonics are emphasized (Intensity), how closely they are spaced (Stretch), and how far their frequency moves up or down (Shift).

Using Modulation in Sculpture

The modulation section in Sculpture is extensive, offering everything from low-frequency oscillators (including two jitter generators that produce random variations) to Note On Random modulators and user-created envelopes.

Of special interest is the Morph Pad, which enables you to morph between parameter settings for the entire instrument. The Morph Pad can be controlled manually by MIDI controllers or by its own time-based envelope.

1   If the Morph Pad is not already turned on, click the Pad button in the morph envelope display.

The Morph Pad has five morph points, represented by center and corner points (A, B, C, D). Each point can be thought of as a memory location that stores the parameter settings of everything from string material to object and pickup placement.

Instead of setting each state manually, let's randomly generate deviants of the original state in each point.

2   Select the 4 Points button, located to the left of the Morph Pad.

By selecting this, you are targeting only the four outermost points (A, B, C, D) for randomization, leaving the original (center point) sound alone.

3   Drag the Intensity (Int) slider to the right of the Morph Pad to a value of 25%.

4   Click the Randomize (Rnd) button above the Intensity slider.

To see what just happened, look at how the controls for the various states (points) were affected.

5   Click each point in the Morph Pad (click the letters), one at a time, looking at how the Material and Object controls change.

NOTE ▶ The small red dot appearing in the controls' graphic readout represents the original state (at the center point within the Morph Pad). Each state, then, is a variation of these original settings, depending on how much randomization (Intensity) was applied.

6   Hold down a note on your MIDI controller, and on the Morph Pad, move the morph (red) ball to various points, listening to the sound.

The controls (and the sound) change smoothly to reflect the various states.

Sculpture even allows you to record your movements within the Morph Pad, creating a unique envelope that animates the sound whenever a key is depressed.

In order to record your movements, you must first "arm" the morph envelope record function by clicking the Record Enable button to the left of the morph envelope display.

7   Click the Record Enable button.

The Record Enable button flashes, waiting to record.

To guarantee an accurate start time, Sculpture is set by default to trigger recording only when a MIDI note is detected *and* the morph ball is moved within the Morph

Pad. This ensures that you will be recording only your movements within the Morph Pad, and not the time it takes to prepare your mouse and keyboard.

NOTE ▶ Sculpture can also be set to trigger a Morph Pad recording to just a simple MIDI note-on message, or note plus sustain pedal. These trigger modes are set within the Record Trigger menu, next to the Record Enable button.

8   Hold a key on your MIDI controller while moving the morph ball around the Morph Pad. Release the key when you are done.

NOTE ▶ Your morph ball movements will still be recorded for the length of the sound's decay phase, after the key is released.

When the note completes its decay phase, the recording stops. The envelope information is now displayed in both the Morph Pad itself as well as in the morph envelope display, located directly below.

9   Hold a key on your MIDI controller again, watching the envelope move along the path, recreating your movements.

Saving and Trying Presets

As you can see, Sculpture is a truly exceptional instrument. Let's end this section by saving the sound you just made as a preset.

1   Click the Settings button to open the menu, and then choose Save Setting As.

2   In the Save As field, enter a name that suits the sound you just made.

3   Click Save.

Let's conclude by taking a brief look at some of the expertly programmed settings in Sculpture, which show off the diverse capabilities of the instrument. With each of these, try playing your MIDI controller while holding chords and single notes to hear the sound evolve over time. Also try playing with the Morph Pad (if active) and modulation wheel of the MIDI controller, as these are frequently deployed to control sound changes.

Some Presets to Try

Preset Location	Description
07 Blown Instruments > Saturated Air	Highly expressive modeled flute sounds
02 Modeled Pads > Ambient Light	Evolving harmonic pad
10 Motion Sequences > Reverse Rhythms	Rhythmic groove using extensive modulation
13 Warped Sculptures > Marble on a Journey	Randomly bouncing and rolling marble using Morph Pad

Lesson Review

1. What is the basis for sound generation in Sculpture?
2. What controls the basic material of the string?
3. What does an object do?
4. What is used to control where each object interacts with the string?
5. What is used to sense vibrations along the string?
6. Besides the sound-generation and modulation sections in Sculpture, what other components are used to further process the sound?
7. Which modulation control enables you to program smooth transitions between various parameter states?

Answers

1. Sculpture utilizes a string acted upon by objects as the basis for sound generation.

2. The Material Pad controls the damping and stiffness of the string.

3. The objects determine how the string is excited or disturbed (how it is played).

4. The object sliders can be positioned anywhere along the length of string by adjusting within the Pickup display.

5. The pickups are used to sense vibrations along the string, similar to an electric guitar.

6. Components such as the Waveshaper, Body EQ, and Delay allow you to further process the instrument in interesting ways.

7. The Morph Pad enables you to smoothly move from various states of control settings.

6

Building Drum Sounds with Ultrabeat

Ultrabeat's inspiration stems from the drum machines of the 1980s, as well as the currently popular sample-based hardware groove boxes. Ultrabeat is similar to them in functionality, offering both sound generation and integrated step sequencing.

What sets Ultrabeat apart, however, is its multiple sound sources, built-in signal processing, sophisticated step sequencing, and highly flexible sound architecture.

In this lesson, you will explore the many synthesis features implemented within Ultrabeat, as well as the unique traits it offers for modifying sound.

Selecting Sounds in the Assignment Section

When you look at Ultrabeat for the first time, you can tell that its interface is based on classic synthesizer design, offering sound generation, filter, modulation, and output sections. It also reflects a similar signal flow path to the other Logic software instruments we looked at in previous lessons, moving from left to right.

1   Choose File > Open.

2   In the file selector dialog, navigate to Music > Advanced Logic 9_Files > Lessons and open **06_Ultrabeat_Start.logic**.

The project opens, displaying the Ultrabeat interface.

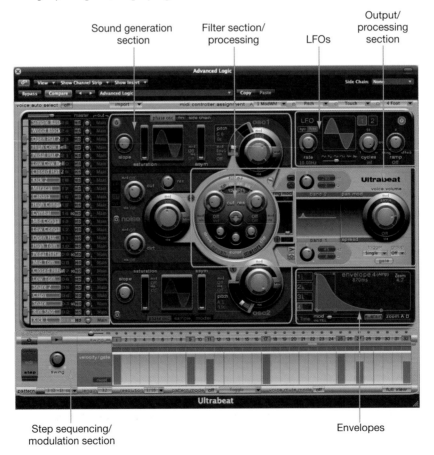

Although Ultrabeat's interface is unique in its incorporation of a step sequencer at the bottom, it has sound generation, filter, and output/processing sections in roughly the same places as the software instruments discussed in earlier lessons.

At the left side of the interface resides the Assignment section, which contains 25 drum sounds and a mixer. Each drum sound, or voice, has independent parameters that can be adjusted for volume, soloing, muting, pan position, and audio output.

3   Select a few of the drum voices by clicking the names (kick, snare, and so on).

The main section of the interface changes with each selected voice. This is because each drum voice has its own independent sound-generation, filter, modulation, processing, and volume settings, which are viewed by clicking its name.

NOTE ▸ In addition to two octaves (C1 to B2) of individually mapped percussion sounds, each kit reserves the C3 slot for a sound that is automatically pitch-mapped over three octaves.

4   At the upper left of the interface, click the Voice Auto Select On/Off button so that voice auto select is turned on.

5   Play a few notes in the C1 to B2 range.

The interface changes with each new note played. When voice auto select is on, the most recent note triggered is displayed.

TIP ▸ If you do not have a MIDI controller, try clicking the onscreen musical keyboard to the left of the drum name to audition the sound in the Ultrabeat window. You can also use Logic's Caps Lock Keyboard as you program the sounds in this lesson.

Exploring the Sound Generators

Ultrabeat represents an amalgamation of the synthesis features looked at specifically in the last three lessons: analog waveforms (including noise), frequency modulation (FM), ring modulation, sample playback, and physical modeling.

Creating your own drum sounds from scratch can be a little daunting for the novice programmer. In order to aid in speedy construction, Ultrabeat offers a few handy voice presets that can be called up as starting points.

Creating Kick Drum Sounds

1   Control-click the kick drum voice (C1) and choose Init > Kick from the shortcut menu.

The parameters in the main area change.

2   In the main part of the interface, look at the top oscillator (Osc1).

It is the only oscillator currently active (the power button at the left is lit), so it is responsible for generating the raw sound that makes up the kick drum.

The oscillator is set to Phase Osc, which uses the Slope, Saturation, and Asymmetry (asym) controls to shape the waveform into almost any basic analog synthesizer waveform. The best way to get a handle on how each control shapes the sound is to try them and listen to the sound each produces.

3   Repeatedly press the C1 key on your MIDI controller while you drag the Slope, Saturation, and Asymmetry controls, listening to the result.

The sound changes timbre as you shape the waveform.

The pitch and volume of the signal generated by Oscillator 1 is governed by the controls located immediately to the right of the Phase Osc controls.

Modulation routing in Ultrabeat is done not via a dedicated modulation router, as with the ES2 and EXS24, but instead by small menus situated around the targeted control. You can see these routings showing up in blue (source) and green (via) around the pitch and volume controls for Oscillator 1.

Ultrabeat has four assignable envelopes that can be used for sources of modulation. One of the tricks used in creating analog kick drum sounds is to use an envelope to quickly drive the oscillator pitch downwards, creating the immediately familiar, deep vintage kick sound. The initialized kick preset has this routing in place for you by default, as evidenced by the Env3 mod setting within the pitch parameters.

To investigate the shape and timing of envelope 3, you need to first select the corresponding button in the lower-right area of the interface.

4   Click button 3 to select envelope 3.

TIP ▸ When you click any of the four envelope buttons, all modulation assignments using it as a source will highlight on the interface. This also works for the two LFO buttons at the top right of the Ultrabeat interface. You can use this to easily trace modulation routings in complicated setups.

Ultrabeat's envelopes can be adjusted graphically by dragging attack and decay time handles, and the envelopes can be further shaped by Bezier curves.

5   Drag the decay time handle to the right, leaving it at a setting of around 740 ms.

6   Play C1 on your MIDI controller, listening to the result.

The pitch change of Oscillator 1 now decays at a slower rate.

Although this is an exaggerated example, it illustrates the ingenuity of using envelopes to quickly modulate pitch, creating a unique bass drum sound.

7   Drag the decay time handle to the left, leaving it at its original setting of around 50 ms.

Now that you've dialed in your kick drum sound, let's name it.

8   In the Assignment section, double-click the kick voice (currently Init:Kick), and then enter *Kick*. Press Return.

Creating Snare Drum Sounds

Snare drums are traditionally built with noise generators, which supply the nonpitched, irregular vibrations that define the snare drum character. Ultrabeat has a dedicated noise generator, placed between the two oscillators in the sound generation section.

1   Control-click the snare drum voice (D1) and choose Init > Snare from the shortcut menu.

The parameters change, turning on the noise generator.

2   Audition the snare by clicking the musical keyboard to the left of the Assignment section or playing your MIDI controller (D1).

TIP ▶ The sound you are hearing is made up primarily from the noise generator, with some bottom-end resonance supplied from Oscillator 1's Phase Osc setting. This layered technique is highly recommended for approaching your own drum sound construction.

The noise generator has its own multi-mode filter in addition to the main filter section, offering low-pass (LP), high-pass (HP), and band-pass (BP) modes. By default, high-pass is enabled, allowing you to attenuate unwanted low frequencies produced by the noise generator.

3   Repeatedly press the D1 key on your MIDI controller while you drag the Cutoff knob to a setting of about 0.75, listening to the result.

The snare becomes brighter.

In order to make the sound more responsive to player input, it is common to modulate the cutoff frequency with an envelope whose intensity is governed by velocity. Let's duplicate this routing for the snare drum.

4   Click the blue mod menu above the Cutoff knob and choose Env3.

Look closely and you will see that an indented blue control has appeared on the outer edge of the Cutoff knob. This controls the depth of the assigned modulation source.

5   Click the green via menu below the Cutoff knob and choose Vel (velocity).

A green control "handle" appears on the outer edge of the Cutoff knob. This controls the intensity of the modulation, in this case governed by velocity.

6   Drag the blue modulation control to a value of 0.66 (–0.09).

7   Drag the green via control to a value of 0.9 (+0.15).

NOTE ▶ The values displayed within the parentheses reflect the offset to the current state.

The controls should look like this:

8   Play the D1 key on your MIDI controller at varying velocities, listening to how the cutoff opens up a bit at higher values and closes at lower ones.

NOTE ▶ The snare init setting utilizes Ultrabeat's two bands of EQ to shape the sound further after the filter section.

9   In the Assignment section, double-click the snare voice (currently Init:Snare), and then enter *Snare*. Press Return.

Creating Hi-Hat Sounds

As you explored in the ES2 lesson, frequency modulation (FM) and ring modulation are used to create metallic timbres with lots of harmonics. You can use these effects within Ultrabeat to create interesting hi-hat sounds.

1   Control-click the closed hi-hat voice (F#1) and choose Init > Hat1 from the shortcut menu.

The parameters change.

This setting contains the routing necessary to create FM, with Oscillator 1 being the carrier and Oscillator 2 being the modulator. The FM depth is controlled by the FM Amount knob located to the left of the waveform display in Oscillator 1.

2   Repeatedly press the F#1 key on your MIDI controller while you drag the FM Amount knob to a value of about 0.86, listening to the result.

A metallic ringing sound is produced, as harmonics are increased.

3   In the Assignment section, double-click the hi-hat voice (currently Init:Hat1), and then enter *Closed Hat*. Press Return.

Oscillator 2 is set to Phase Osc by default within the Init:Hat1 setting, but you can also use the other sound generation modes to modulate the carrier, including physical modeling. This will result in an entirely different, but related, timbre that can be assigned to another drum voice.

4   Control-click the Closed Hat voice (F#1) and choose Copy (Voice & Seq) from the shortcut menu.

5   Control-click the Pedal Hat voice (G#1) and choose Paste Voice from the shortcut menu.

Your original hi-hat sound has been copied to the new voice, ready for variation.

6   In the Assignment section, double-click the newly copied hi-hat voice (currently Closed Hat), and enter *Pedal Hat*. Press Return.

7   In Oscillator 2, click the Model button, switching the synthesis mode to physical modeling.

Similar to Sculpture, Ultrabeat's model utilizes a string that is excited by objects. Ultrabeat's component model sound generation is greatly simplified compared to what you saw in Sculpture, only offering two types of exciters, a material pad, and resolution controls. Even so, interesting sounds can be generated, including those created by using it as a modulation source.

8   Repeatedly press the G#1 key on your MIDI controller while you click the two exciter buttons, comparing the results. Select type 2 after you've had a chance to listen to both.

▶ **Processing Audio Input with Ultrabeat**

In addition to offering Phase Osc and FM choices, Oscillator 1 has a side chain setting that provides the ability to route external audio signals into the signal flow, triggered by incoming MIDI notes or the step sequencer. To set this up, do the following:

1.   Select the channel that will send the signal from the Side Chain menu at the top right of Ultrabeat's interface.

2.   Mute the channel sending the side chain signal so it doesn't reach the outputs (if you want to hear the original track in addition to Ultrabeat's processing, keep this unmuted).

3.   Play the project.

Whenever MIDI messages are sent to Ultrabeat (MIDI keyboard, recorded regions, triggered patterns, and so on.), the side chain signal should be heard, layered with the other sound generators, and processed by the filters and modulation of Ultrabeat.

For more information on side chaining, see "Using Side Chain Effects" in Lesson 10.

Loading Samples

As stated earlier, Ultrabeat also offers sample playback through Oscillator 2, similar to the EXS24 (discussed in Lesson 4).

1   Control-click the Cymbal voice (C#2) and choose Init > Sample from the shortcut menu.

The oscillator switches to sample mode, displaying No Sample Loaded.

If you were to hit the C#2 key now, you wouldn't hear anything because you haven't yet loaded a sample. You add one by dragging and dropping your own audio files from the Finder, or by loading one of Ultrabeat's large library of samples via a menu.

2   Click the disclosure triangle next to No Sample Loaded and choose Load Sample from the pop-up menu.

A file selector dialog appears, displaying the contents of the Ultrabeat Samples folder.

NOTE ▸ The Load Sample command automatically brings you to the location where Logic Pro installed the default Ultrabeat samples (Library/Application Support/Logic/Ultrabeat Samples). This makes it easy to browse samples specially designed for use in Ultrabeat. You can also drag and drop audio files from the Finder.

3   Open the Crash Cymbals folder and select **Special Crash.ubs**.

NOTE ▸ The .ubs extension signifies a proprietary sample format that has multiple velocity layers built into the file. Although no user-accessible way exists to create files in the .ubs format, you can convert velocity-mapped EXS instruments into .ubs files by clicking the Import button at the top of the Ultrabeat window.

4   Click the Open button.

5 Play the C#2 key on your MIDI controller, or click the musical keyboard to the left of the Assignment section to audition the crash.

The sample is triggered.

As with the EXS24, you can change the pitch of the sample by using coarse and fine adjustments. These are located to the right, and can be quickly adjusted by dragging the Pitch slider next to the oscillator's volume controls.

6 Repeatedly press the C#2 key on your MIDI controller while you drag the Pitch slider to E4 (659.3 Hz).

The sample plays back higher (and shorter).

Let's finish by creating a fast tremolo (amplitude modulation) using one of Ultrabeat's two LFOs to modulate volume. You do this by first assigning the routing around the oscillator's Volume knob.

7 Click the blue mod menu (currently set to Env1) above Oscillator 2's Volume knob. Choose Lfo1 from the menu.

8 Drag the blue modulation control to –14 dB (–8 dB).

9   Play the C#2 key on your MIDI controller, listening to the result (a pulsing cymbal sound).

Ultrabeat's two LFOs are located at the top right. These contain rate, wave shape, and envelope controls similar in function to what you encountered in previous lessons. What makes Ultrabeat's LFOs unique, however, is the ability to limit the amount of cycles that the LFO generates from one to infinity. This enables you to evoke change in limited doses, only enacting modulation at the beginning of the sound.

10   Drag the Cycles knob to a setting of 4.

11   Play the C#2 key on your MIDI controller, listening to the result.

The pulsing enacted by the LFO is limited to only four cycles.

> **TIP** ▶ You can easily create your own sample-based kits by dragging and dropping audio files to Oscillator 2. There is a special Ultrabeat preset that saves you the hassle of configuring each drum voice's Oscillator 2 setting for samples. You can find this preset under 01 Drum Kits > Drag & Drop Samples.

Processing with the Filter and Bitcrusher

Right smack in the middle of the interface is a circular area that contains Ultrabeat's filter and distortion circuit. In order to send a signal from the sound generators to the filter and distortion circuit, you need to have the Signal Flow buttons selected. These are located next to the oscillator's Volume knob.

1   Click the Signal Flow button (above and to the left of Oscillator 2's Volume knob).

Now that signal can flow from the oscillator to the filter, let's use it to process the cymbal sound.

Similar to the ES2 and the EXS24, Ultrabeat has a multimode filter that can be set for low-pass (LP), high-pass (HP), band-pass (BP), or band reject (BR) with adjustable slope and resonance.

2   Click the HP button, selecting high-pass mode.

3   Drag the Cutoff knob to 0.60.

4   Drag the Resonance knob to 0.75.

5   Play the C#2 key on your MIDI controller, listening to the result.

The timbre changes slightly, attenuating some of the lower frequencies.

Ultrabeat's distortion circuit can be used to add grit and harmonics to the sound, and also has the added bonus of a bitcrushing mode for lo-fi sounds.

6   At the bottom of the circle, click the Crush button to select it.

7 Drag the Drive knob to 5.0 dB.

8 Drag the Color knob to 6x.

9 Play the C#2 key on your MIDI controller, listening to the result.

The cymbal sound's sample rate is reduced, adding grit to the sound.

NOTE ▸ You can determine whether the distortion circuit is inserted before or after the filter by clicking the arrow button located at the center of the circular area.

10 In the Assignment section, double-click the cymbal voice (currently Init:Sample), and enter *Cymbal FX*. Press Return.

Now that you've constructed a basic kit, let's test it out by playing one of Ultrabeat's step sequences.

NOTE ▸ The integrated 32-step sequencer located at the bottom of Ultrabeat's interface greatly aids in the production of drum loops and beat patterns. These patterns, including any user-created patterns, are saved within each of the Ultrabeat settings. To learn more about how to do this, please refer to David Nahmani's Level 1 Apple Pro Training Series book, *Logic Pro 9 and Logic Express 9.*

11 Turn on the sequencer by clicking the power button at the upper left of the sequencer.

12 Click the Play/Stop button located immediately to the right of the power button.

The sequencer starts, and Ultrabeat plays a sequenced pattern.

13 Click the Play/Stop button, stopping the sequence after you've had a chance to listen to the drums you programmed.

> **TIP ▶** Each pattern in Ultrabeat can be triggered via an incoming or recorded MIDI note; this allows the starting and stopping of patterns on the fly (especially advantageous for live performances). Each pattern has a number designating the slot, as well as a MIDI note number (in parentheses) next to it. The MIDI note number indicates which incoming MIDI note will trigger which pattern.

Automating Parameters in Step Mode

Ultrabeat not only lets you program sound triggers via step sequencing, it also lets you do the same for each sound's parameters. This mode, called Step mode, provides step-by-step automation of any sound-shaping control within the synthesizer.

For this exercise, you will be using Step mode to offset the pitch of the snare voice's Oscillator 1.

1 Select the snare drum voice in the Assignment section (or play D1 on your MIDI controller).

2 On the bottom part of the Edit Mode switch (located in the lower left of the interface), click Step.

The sound-editing area darkens, and yellow frames appear around all of the parameters that are available for automation. In addition, the step grid changes to display parameter offset instead of velocity/gate.

When in Step mode, the step grid is used to effect changes to the yellow highlighted parameters by offsetting the current sound settings.

NOTE ▶ When you move a control, you define the target parameter for Step mode.

3 Click within the step select row for step 1, right below the trigger row.

4 Drag the Pitch slider for Oscillator 1 to G2.

Notice that the Offset menu now reads Osc1 Pitch, and the step grid displays your adjustment as a positive offset (above center line) to the original pitch (F2). This offset is expressed as a percentage.

TIP ▶ You can also drag the value bars up and down within the step grid to create offsets of the selected parameter's value.

If desired, you can have Ultrabeat create randomized offsets for each trigger.

5 Control-click the step grid area and choose Alter from the Offset shortcut menu.

Small offsets are created for each trigger.

NOTE ▶ The Alter and Randomize selections in the Offset shortcut menu differ from each other in how they randomize the offset values within the step grid. Alter randomizes all current parameters by a few percent of the current setting, in essence varying input that is already present. Randomize, on the other hand, creates brand-new, random values from scratch, no matter what offset values were already present.

6 Play the sequence, and stop when you've heard the results.

The pitch of the snare voice changes for the altered steps.

7 Click the Mute button located at the lower left of the step grid.

This control enables you to mute the currently displayed parameter offsets, returning the part back to its unaltered state.

TIP ▶ When creating offsets in Step mode, you may decide that you want to make a quick change in the original drum sound. To quickly do this without losing your momentum, press Option-Command to temporarily toggle Ultrabeat back into Voice mode.

8 On the Edit Mode switch, click Voice.

9 Click the preset menu and choose Save Setting As.

10 In the file selector dialog, name the preset *My Kit* and click Save.

TIP ▶ Ultrabeat can address multiple channel outputs (eight stereo and eight mono), just like the EXS24. These routings are selected in the Assignment section, under the "out" column.

Lesson Review

1. Oscillator 1 offers what modes of sound generation?
2. Oscillator 2 offers what modes of sound generation?
3. Source modulation routings appear in what color on the interface?
4. Via modulation routings appear in what color on the interface?
5. Routing to the filter and distortion circuit is done by enabling what?
6. In order to define the target parameter for Step mode, you need to do what?

Answers

1. Oscillator 1 offers phase oscillator and frequency modulation synthesis (as well as side chain input).
2. Oscillator 2 offers phase oscillator, sample playback, and physical modeling.
3. Source modulation routings appear in blue.
4. Via modulation routings appear in green.
5. You can route to the filter and distortion circuit by enabling the Signal Flow buttons, located around each oscillator's Volume knob.
6. You need to click a control first in order to define it as the target parameter for Step mode.

7

Lesson Files   Advanced Logic 9_Files > Lessons > 07_Anatomy of a Human Bomb_Start.logic

Media   Advanced Logic 9_Files > Media > Anatomy of a Human Bomb

Time   This lesson takes approximately 90 minutes to complete.

Goals   Use specialized playback commands for editing tasks

Create and edit markers using a variety of techniques

Understand playback and transport hierarchy

Perform global edits to add and subtract song sections

Navigate via markers using a variety of techniques

Rearrange song sections using folders

Use locators to skip over entire sections in the project

Learn zoom techniques to visualize and edit material

Working with the Arrangement

A computer-based system offers distinct advantages over other methods of developing and arranging musical material. First and foremost is the ability to work with visual representations of sound, whether as audio waveforms or as graphical data (such as MIDI or notation). You can create detailed edits and work with arrangements by moving sections around as you would text in a word processor. A nonlinear approach to editing lets you jump around in a composition, manipulating multiple aspects of a piece of music and playing back sections for instant feedback.

Many of Logic's features are geared toward manipulating and developing musical material. This lesson focuses on techniques that enable you to efficiently view, organize, and move large chunks of data within a project.

Navigating the Arrangement

Before you can begin arranging, you must be familiar with the various pieces that make up the overall project. Quickly creating a connection between what you see in Logic's Arrange area and what you hear during playback is the first critical step before arranging a project.

In this set of exercises, you'll gain an understanding of Logic 9's new play position prioritization and Cycle mode features while familiarizing yourself with the song used in this and the following two lessons. Emphasis will be placed on using key commands so that you can keep one hand on your computer keyboard and the other on your mouse for peak efficiency.

There are a multitude of ways to position Logic's playhead and initiate playback. The Arrange area's Bar ruler, Cycle mode, and Marquee tool are particularly helpful for positioning the playhead, especially when compared to the use of the Transport area's transport controls.

Playing the Arrangement

First you'll need to get familiar with how the project sounds and begin to understand the visual layout of the song. Rather than use traditional transport controls such as fast forward and rewind, you'll use the specialized playback functions that come with Logic's nonlinear capability.

1   Choose File > Open.

2   In the file selector dialog, go to Music > Advanced Logic 9_Files > Lessons and open **07_Anatomy of a Human Bomb_Start.logic**.

> **NOTE** ▶ This project opens zoomed out so you can see all regions in the song. The Inspector and Media and Lists areas are closed—they are not needed for the purpose of arranging. As discussed in Lesson 1, this view is locked into a screenset so that you can quickly return to this overall view by pressing the number 1.

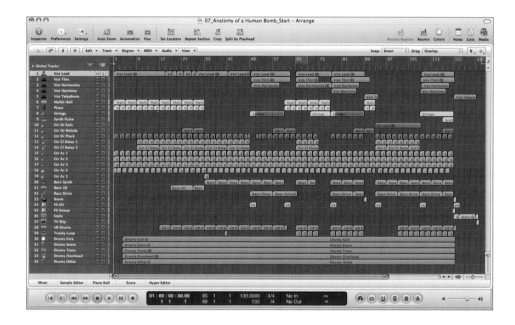

3   Start playback by double-clicking the lower half of the Bar ruler near bar 1.

As the song plays, take note of where it transitions from verse to chorus.

In order to quickly familiarize yourself with the arrangement, it's useful to be able to move the playhead without having to constantly start and stop playback.

4   While playback continues, click in the lower half of the Bar ruler to move the playhead.

The playhead jumps to your selected position and continues playing.

5   Continue to click at various positions in the Bar ruler.

Be sure to listen to the song at bar 49 and 65 to become acquainted with both a chorus and verse.

6   Double-click the lower part of the ruler near the beginning of the song.

Playback stops, and the playhead sits at the position you double-clicked.

Although the Marquee tool is primarily thought of as an editing tool, it's actually one of Logic's primary transport mechanisms, letting you position the playhead by clicking directly in the Arrange area. In this project the Marquee tool has already been configured as the Alternate (Command) tool.

7   Hold the Command key to bring up the Marquee tool, and then click just before the first region on the UB Drum track at bar 20.

It won't look like much has happened, but a very thin and barely visible marquee selection has been made at the position you clicked.

8   Click Play.

The playhead jumps to the marquee selection and begins playback.

NOTE ▶ If playback happens only for an instant and then stops, it's most likely because you slightly dragged the pointer when clicking with the Marquee tool, creating a very small marquee selection. If the marquee selection is more than 1 pixel wide, playback will stop at the end of the selection. Use the Deselect All command (Shift-Command-A) to clear your selection and try again.

9   While the song is playing back, use the Marquee tool to click another position in the arrangement.

Unlike when you clicked in the lower half of the ruler, the playhead does not immediately jump to the new position. In order to move the playhead, you must first stop
and then start playback.

10 Press the Spacebar once to stop and then again to start.

The second time you pressed the Spacebar the playhead moved to the new marquee
position and began playback.

11 Press Spacebar to stop.

12 Press Shift-Command-A to clear your marquee selection.

Prioritizing Playback

In this exercise you'll learn how Logic chooses where the playhead moves each time you
click Play. Understanding this will help you take full advantage of Logic 9's new transport
prioritization options.

1 With the Pointer tool, select the Gtr Solo region and click Play.

Notice that playback does not jump to the selected region. In many instances it makes
sense to play from the beginning of selected regions so you'll now modify how Logic
prioritizes playback position.

2 Click Stop.

3 Hold down the mouse on the Play button in the Transport area.

The top four items in this menu show how Logic prioritizes play position. If none of
the items in this list were checked, Logic would start playback at the current playhead
position. Notice that the first option, Play Marquee is checked. This explains why the
marquee selection affected where the playhead moved earlier in this lesson. As you

can see, Play From Selected Region is an option, but it is unchecked, meaning selected regions are not being considered. This is why the playhead did not move to the Gtr Solo region for the first step in this exercise.

NOTE ▶ If two or more checked conditions are met, Logic moves the playhead based on the condition that's highest on the list. In this example, marquee selection overrides a cycle area.

4   Select Play From Selected Region and release the mouse.

5   Hold the Play button and verify that there is a checkmark next to Play From Selected Region.

6   Release the mouse and press Spacebar to play.

Now playback occurs from any selected region.

7   Stop playback and then drag the pointer around the vocal regions at bar 49 and click Play.

Playback occurs exactly where the Vox regions begin. It's often helpful to hear the selected material without all the other parts playing. Soloing parts helps you to better connect the regions you see with the parts you hear.

8   Engage Solo mode by pressing S.

The Solo button in the transport turns yellow, as does the ruler and the highlighted border around the Vox regions.

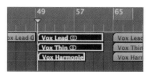

9   Press the Spacebar once to stop and again to start playback from the beginning of the soloed regions.

10   Take a moment to familiarize yourself with other regions in the project by selecting them and then playing them back both with and without Solo mode engaged.

> **NOTE ▶** When toggling Solo mode, it's normal to have a brief pause before hearing the transition between soloed and unsoloed regions.

11   Hold the Play button and deselect the Play From Selected Region option.

12   Make sure Solo mode is off.

> **NOTE ▶** The default setting for playback hierarchy is to have Play Marquee Selection and Play Cycle enabled. The settings you choose are project settings that will not be retained when you open other projects. If you wish to use settings other than the default on a regular basis, consider adding them to a session template as explained in Lesson 1.

Using Specialized Playback Commands

In some instances it makes the most sense to initiate playback from the beginning of the area you're looking at, regardless of any selections. In this exercise you'll configure a specialized play command to start playback from the left window edge.

1   Select the three Vox regions at bar 65.

2   Press Z to zoom on the Vox regions.

Now that you deselected Play From Selected Region in the playback hierarchy, clicking Play will no longer start the playhead from the start of the selected region. It's practical to want to play what you see without having to make additional selections, so you'll customize a key command to do just that.

3 Press Option-K to open the Key Commands window.

4 In the search field, enter *play window*.

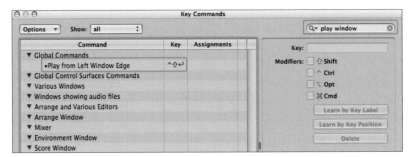

5 Click Play From Left Window Edge.

The Key column shows that keys have already been mapped to this command, but the default setting requires using the Enter button on a numeric keypad, which makes it difficult to press with one hand.

Click the Learn by Key Label button and press Control-Spacebar.

6   Close the Key Commands window.

Now it's time to try it out.

7   Press Control-Spacebar

Playback starts at the left window edge.

A useful thing to note about this command is that it works with your window's horizontal scroll bar.

8   Move the horizontal scroll bar to the left and press Control-Spacebar.

Playback immediately starts from the left side of the visible area. Now you are using what you see as the reference point for playback.

> **TIP** ▶ This technique also works brilliantly with any hardware that can control a window's horizontal scrolling, such as the Apple MacBook trackpads, Mighty Mouse, or Magic Mouse.

Isolating Material with Cycle Mode

Play From Left Window Edge is a useful feature, but you still must press the command each time you want to hear the section you're looking at. Oftentimes you need to hear sections over and over for critical listening. Cycle mode provides an easy way to temporarily repeat a section of a song for critical listening. In this exercise you'll work with Cycle mode and learn several ways to set the locators that define the boundaries of a cycle area.

> **NOTE** ▶ This exercise uses a key command that was assigned in Lesson 1. If you jumped straight to this chapter, open the Key Commands window and configure the Set Locators and Play command to Shift-Spacebar using the same steps you used to assign the Play From Left Window Edge command earlier in this lesson.

1   Press Z to zoom out.

2   Press C to turn on Cycle mode.

The Cycle button in the Transport area turns green, and a cycle area appears in the upper part of the ruler at bar 65.

3   Click Play.

Because Play Cycle is a checked item in the playback hierarchy, the playhead jumps to the beginning of the cycle area and plays repeatedly over the four-bar section.

4   Without stopping playback, select the Gtr Solo region at bar 93 and press Shift-Spacebar.

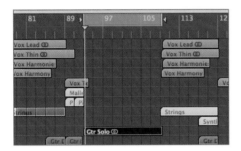

The cycle area immediately adapts to the same length as the Gtr solo region and after a brief pause play begins at the guitar solo.

5   Without stopping, click the lower part of the bar ruler just before the Gtr Solo region.

The playhead jumps just before the cycle area, letting you hear how the song transitions into the guitar solo. This also demonstrates how moving the playhead by clicking in the lower part of the ruler always takes priority over anything checked in the playback hierarchy. Once the playhead reaches the end of the guitar solo, it will loop back to the beginning of the cycle region.

6   Press Z to zoom on the guitar solo.

7   Hold Control-Option and press the Left Arrow key several times to zoom out until you can see a few measures before the guitar solo.

NOTE ▶ While zooming, the displayed area of the window is justified either to the current playhead position or to a selected region. When you want to zoom in to a given playhead position, you must make sure that nothing is selected before you zoom. If you want to zoom in to an individual region, you need to select it first.

8   Press Control-Spacebar (Play From Left Window Edge) to now hear playback begin just before the guitar solo.

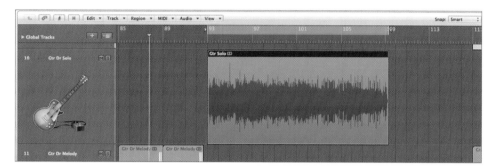

This also shows that specialized play commands take priority over anything in the playback hierarchy.

Now take a closer listen to the guitar solo.

9   Press S to solo the region, and then press Spacebar to start playback.

There's a subtle click sound around bar 95. Listen to that section a few times to identify the problem. You can further isolate an area within the Gtr Solo region by using the Marquee tool.

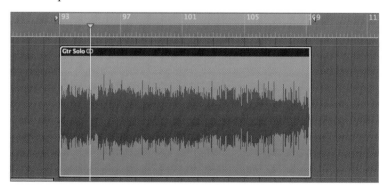

10   Using your Alternate tool (Command), drag a marquee selection from approximately bar 94 to 96.

11 Press Shift-Spacebar.

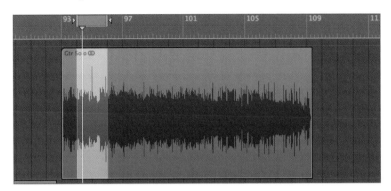

NOTE ▸ As you can see, marquee selections work with the Set Locators and Play command, but the problem is that the Gtr Solo region is no longer soloed. Solo mode works only for regions selected in their entirety with the Pointer tool. Unfortunately, dragging the marquee selection deselects the region as a whole so you cannot audibly isolate the part you wish hear unless you go back and select the region again.

12 With the pointer, click anywhere on the Gtr Solo and click Play.

Now you can hear the soloed area within the region and easily hear the click. Don't worry about the click. Now that you know it's there, you'll fix it in the next lesson.

TIP ▸ Logic 9 features an Auto-Set Locator feature that is useful if you want to quickly audition material using the cycle features. Hold the Cycle button in the transport and choose Auto Set Locators. With this feature enabled, anything you select will automatically function as if you had used the Set Locators and Play (Shift-Spacebar) command you've been using in this lesson.

13 Press S to turn off Solo mode, and then press C to turn off Cycle.

14 Press Z to zoom back out to view the entire arrangement, and then press Return to bring the playhead to the beginning of the song.

> **TIP** ▶ Notice how all of those commands are close together on your computer keyboard, as were all the other commands used in this lesson. Keep them under one hand with your mouse on the other and you'll greatly improve your efficiency with Logic.

Using Markers

Markers serve multiple purposes in a project. They visually identify the sections of a composition, and they also provide navigation points along the Bar ruler. In this way, markers serve as a map that allows you to quickly locate a project's sections for playback, editing, and arranging.

In this section, you will learn several techniques to efficiently create and edit markers that align with each of the project's major sections. Once the markers are in place, you'll name and color them in order to easily identify each part of the song so that you can quickly move to the major song sections using specialized transport commands.

Creating Markers

Markers are positioned and edited on the Marker global track. In this exercise you'll use multiple techniques for creating markers via manual placement, or on the fly as you listen to the song.

1 Click the Global Tracks disclosure triangle.

Currently the only global track configured is the Signature track you'll use later in this lesson.

2 Control-click the Global Tracks header and choose Marker from the shortcut menu.

The Marker track is added in the Global Tracks area.

TIP ▶ Global tracks can be reordered by dragging the marker name to a different position or resized by dragging the lower-left corner.

3   Click the Marker track disclosure triangle.

Additional controls for creating and managing markers appear.

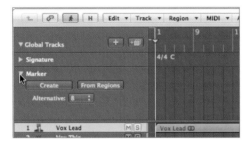

In this project, the first verse starts immediately at bar 1 so you can use the Create button to create a marker at the current playhead position.

4   In the Marker track header, click the Create button.

A marker region named Marker 1 is created in the Marker track and continues through the end of the project. As you add more markers in the song, the first marker will automatically end at the next marker position. The marker is black because it is currently selected.

You're now going to create more markers at various song sections by positioning the playhead using a variety of techniques. See the figure after step 10 as a reference for what you're about to create.

The Period and Comma keys are used to move the playhead forward or rewind one bar.

5 Use the forward command by pressing the Period key (on main part of the keyboard) until the playhead reaches bar 17, and then click the Create button.

Holding Shift while pressing the Period or Comma key makes the playhead fast forward or fast rewind in eight-bar increments.

6 Press Shift-Period twice to move the playhead to bar 33, and then click Create.

7 Press the Go To Position Command (forward slash[/]).

The Go To Position dialog appears, letting you enter the specific measure number to which you want to locate.

8 In the Go To Position dialog's Position field, enter *49* and press Return.

This time you'll use a key command to create the marker.

9 Press Shift-Command-Apostrophe using the modifier keys on the right side of the Spacebar.

TIP ▶ This command uses several keys to do a simple job. If pressing this key combination feels awkward, remember that you can later assign the Create Marker command to a single key.

Oftentimes it's faster and more intuitive to listen to the project and create markers on the fly at the moment you hear the beginning of each song section. You're going to set the next markers as the song plays. Once playback starts, either click the Create button or use the Shift-Command-Apostrophe key command to create markers at the beginning of the major song sections at bars 65, 77, 109, and 121. Do not include a marker for the guitar solo—you'll be doing that later in the exercise. Begin playback just before bar 65 and watch the Bar ruler and the counter in the Transport area carefully. As long as you create the marker close to the desired location, Logic will round the marker to the nearest bar. If you make a mistake, you can simply press Command-Z to undo, and then try again.

So you don't have to wait long between each marker, you can click the lower part of the Bar ruler to jump forward to just before the next marker position.

10 Start playback before bar 65 and create markers at bars 65, 77, 109, and 121, and then click Stop.

TIP ▶ When working with material that doesn't align to the barlines, it is necessary to set markers to locations that are not rounded to bars. In this case you can choose Options > Marker > Create Without Rounding (Command-Apostrophe).

Another method of adding markers is to input them directly into the Marker track with the Pencil tool. For example, you might want to further divide the Chorus section into multiple parts for easier navigation.

11 Press Escape, and then select the Pencil tool.

12 Hold down the mouse in the middle of marker 2 and move until the help tag shows bar 25, and then release.

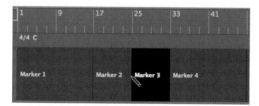

Notice that a new marker was added and all the following markers automatically renumbered themselves.

13 Press the Escape key twice to change back to the Pointer tool.

Oftentimes regions within your arrangement already denote song sections. You can use those regions to quickly create markers by dragging regions from the Arrange area into the Marker track.

It can be difficult to move the region into the Marker track without moving it horizontally in the timeline. Just after you hold the mouse on the desired region, hold Shift so that the region can only be dragged in one direction.

14 Drag the Gtr Solo region into the Marker track but don't release the mouse until you see a thin white highlight around the Marker track, which shows that it's selected.

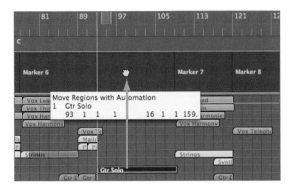

Not only is a new marker created for the guitar solo, but the marker has taken the region's name and color as well. You'll be naming and coloring the other markers you've created later in the lesson.

TIP ▶ Markers can also be created from selected regions by clicking the From Regions button in the Marker track.

15 Press Shift-Command-A to deselect all regions including the markers on the Marker track.

Now you can clearly see where the project's various sections begin and end.

Editing Marker Positions

Invariably, markers that have been created will need to be moved, edited, or deleted altogether. Editing markers works similar to editing regions in the Arrange window but with a few special considerations.

To edit these markers, you'll need to zoom in. Note, however, that Control-Option will not produce the Zoom tool if the pointer is over the global tracks, so you need to start by dragging in the Arrange window.

1 Move the pointer over the Vox Lead track and Control-Option drag from approximately bar 16 to bar 34.

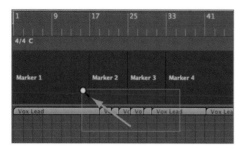

2 Hover the pointer over the upper part of the Marker track where the markers transition at bar 25.

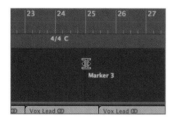

The pointer turns into a Junction tool, letting you change where the transition between the markers occurs.

3 Using the Junction tool, move the transition point from bar 25 to 29.

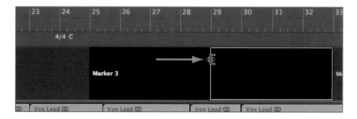

Now Marker 3 identifies where there's a short four-bar interlude before the chorus at Marker 4.

4   Press Z to zoom back out and view the entire arrangement.

For the sake of this exercise, you're going to keep the project broken into simple song sections, so you won't need to identify the interlude at bar 29.

5   With the Pointer tool, click various markers to see how they become selected.

6   Go back and select Marker 3 and press Delete.

Marker 2 stretches back to its original length.

Naming and Coloring Markers

As you saw with the guitar solo, markers are more easily identified when they are named and colored. You will now customize the other markers you created so you can more easily identify sections of the project's arrangement.

1   Double-click Marker 1.

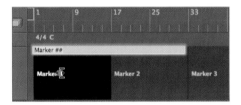

A field to enter the marker's name appears.

2   Enter *Verse 1* and press Return.

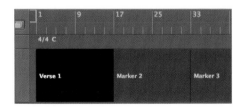

3   With Verse 1 still selected, choose View > Colors or press Option-C.

Logic's color selection window appears.

4   Click a shade of blue for Verse 1 and leave the Color window open.

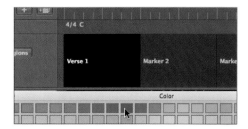

You may not see much change because the marker region is still selected and therefore black. Once you select other markers, the difference will be obvious.

5   Using the same technique, label and color each marker as follows:

Marker 2 – Chorus 1 (green)

Marker 3 – Verse 2 (blue)

Marker 4 – Chorus 2 (green)

Marker 5 – Verse 3 (blue)

Marker 6 – Chorus 3 (green)

Marker 8 – Chorus 4 (green)

Marker 9 – Outro (red)

Use bright colors to distinguish the marker regions from regions in the Arrange area. Reference the figure in the next step to see what you want to achieve.

TIP ▶ Hold Shift to select multiple markers. Once they're selected you can assign a single color to multiple markers at one time.

6   Go back and select the Gtr Solo marker and make it a brighter shade of purple.

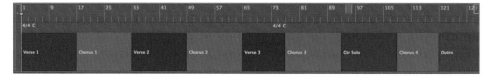

7   Close the Color window.

8   Close the global track header.

Notice that the marker names and colors are superimposed over the lower part of the Bar ruler, making it very easy to see what part of the song occurs at which position in the timeline.

> **TIP ▶** With the global tracks closed, you can still rename markers by Option-double-clicking them in the lower part of the Bar ruler.

Locating with Markers

Now that you have a great visual reference for the primary sections of the song, you can use those markers to navigate the arrangement.

1 Option-click the Chorus 2 marker.

The playhead jumps to the beginning of the second chorus at bar 49.

The Set Locators by Next or Previous Marker and Enable Cycle commands let you quickly isolate a marker for continuous playback.

2 Use the Set Locators by Next Marker and Enable Cycle command by holding Option-Command and use the Left and Right Arrow keys to create a cycle region around Verse 3.

As you can see, this command sets the locators around the next marker while automatically turning on Cycle mode.

3 Click Play.

The Go to Next or Previous Marker command works in a similar way but will move the playhead to the new position without having to first stop.

4 While playback continues, hold Control-Command while pressing the Left and Right Arrow keys.

5 Stop playback and press C to turn off the Cycle mode.

Using Marker Lists

Viewing a vertical list of markers provides a quick visual reference that can be used to navigate to any section of a project when the entire timeline is not visible in the Arrange area's Bar ruler. Logic's Lists area offers a Marker List just for this reason.

1   In the toolbar, click the Lists button, and then click the Marker tab.

Here you see the same markers you created earlier laid out vertically. The exact position of each marker is displayed next to its name.

NOTE ► The right column displays the length of each marker. Markers entered using the Create command show a length of just one tick. That is to indicate that they will extend to the next marker when viewed in the Marker global track.

2   Click the various markers in the list.

Clicking with the pointer does not move the playhead but does allow you to view the marker name and color in a text field at the bottom of the Marker List area.

TIP ► You can edit the text field to include extensive information such as production notes or lyrics. To make changes, double-click the text field. Notes made here will also be visible inside the corresponding regions on the Marker track.

The Marker List makes an excellent transport mechanism because you can quickly click the section of project you want to move to. For this reason it is sometimes helpful to have the Marker List displayed as a separate window.

3   In the main menu bar, choose Options > Marker > Open Marker List.

The Marker List opens as a separate floating window that will always stay on top of Logic's interface, but having it as separate window is extremely handy if you have a second screen. Clicking with the Pointer tool doesn't cause the playhead to locate to a new position, but clicking with the Finger tool will.

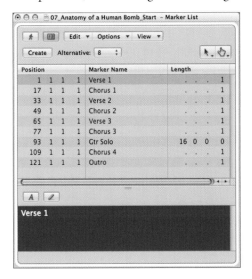

4   In the Tool menu, make the primary tool the Finger tool.

Now you can simply click a marker in the list and the playhead immediately jumps to that position.

5   Close the Marker List window.

Using Global Edits

The ability to rearrange the structure of a composition is an essential part of composing and arranging. However, the seemingly simple task of cutting and repeating sections can become overly complicated, and achieving the desired results often entails multiple steps (dividing regions, selecting areas, cutting, pasting, and so on). Fortunately, Logic offers several features that help with editing multiple regions over numerous tracks by combining multiple steps into single commands.

It is important to understand that the commands used in this lesson can impact all tracks, including global tracks if the global tracks are open. This is a good thing—information in the global tracks such as markers, tempo, and time signature changes should generally be kept intact with the corresponding song sections.

To create these edits, you'll rely heavily on the use of locators. Until now you've primarily used locators for defining Cycle regions. Now you will use locators to define edit points that impact the entire project.

Creating an Intro

You may have noticed that the song jumps right in on Verse 1. You're going to create a short intro section using other parts already in the song. Verse 1 will serve as the basis for the intro.

You want the markers you created in the last section to reflect the changes you're about to make in the arrangement. In order for this to happen, the global tracks need to be displayed.

1   Open the global tracks by clicking the Global Tracks disclosure triangle.

2   Use the Go to Previous or Next Marker commands (hold Control-Command and use the Left/Right Arrow keys) to move the locators around Verse 1.

The locators move around Verse 1, as indicated by the gray shaded area in the upper part of the Bar ruler. Because the edits you're about to make only reference the locator positions, it's OK that the Cycle mode is not turned on. You can confirm the locators cover the area from bar 1 to the beginning of bar 17 in the Transport area.

Left locator

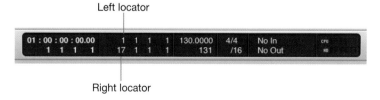

Right locator

3   In the toolbar, click the Repeat Section button.

TIP ▶ The buttons in the toolbar can be different depending on the user's preferences. If the Repeat Section command is not in the toolbar, choose Edit > Cut/Insert Time > Repeat Section Between Locators.

Everything within the locators is repeated, including the marker for Verse 1.

4   Using what you learned in the last exercise, rename the marker at bar 1 *Intro* and change its color to red.

Now you need to remove some of the regions to simplify the sound of the intro.

5   Select everything in the Intro section except for the Mallet-Bell, Piano, and all the Gtr Ac regions.

6   Press Delete.

7   Play the song from the beginning.

Although the intro is in place, it is too long.

8   This time use the Set Locators by Previous/Next Marker and Enable Cycle commands (hold Option-Command with the Left/Right Arrow keys) to create a cycle region around the intro.

The reason for using this command is that it turns on the cycle area, which in turn can be used to adjust the locators. In this case your interest in the cycle area is not to play the intro but to define a section you want to eliminate from your arrangement.

9   Move the cycle area's right locator to bar 13.

Notice that the help tag will display a length of 12 complete bars.

10 In the Arrange area's local menu, choose Edit > Cut Insert Time > Snip: Cut Section Between Locators.

The Intro is shortened to four bars in length, and all regions following the snipped selection have moved to the left to fill in where the measures were removed.

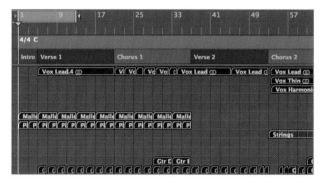

NOTE ▶ All the commands in the Edit > Cut Insert Time menu rely on the use of locators, and their operation will impact all tracks, including global tracks.

All regions and information in the global tracks have been removed from the area between the locators, and all subsequent material has been moved left in the timeline to fill in the gap. You can see this by the new position of the Verse 1 marker, which is now at bar 5. Now the intro is a nice length. Make it a bit more interesting by grabbing a region from later in the song.

11 Option-drag the Vox Telephone region at bar 93 to bar 1. Hold Shift after selecting the region to prevent it from moving to a different track.

12 Turn off Cycle mode and play from the beginning

13 Click Stop.

Inserting Space

The song's form alternates between verse and chorus sections. Adding an unexpected rest in the arrangement can add interest to the composition by catching listeners off guard. Play from bar 49 and pay particular attention to where the song transitions from Verse 2 to Chorus 2 and then stop.

You're going to add two beats of space between these sections; as before you'll need the help of locators to achieve this. This time you'll manually enter the locators using the locator display in the Transport area.

1   In the Transport area, double-click the left locator. Enter *53* in the displayed field and press Return.

2   In the Transport area, double-click the right locator. Enter *53.3* and press Return.

NOTE ▶ When entering positional values, you can use periods, spaces, or most any nonnumeric character to separate bar, beat, division, and tick values.

This number indicates that the right locator is positioned at bar 53, beat 3, or two beats after the left locator. The locators might be hard to see at this zoom level.

3   Zoom to show the area from approximately bar 50 to bar 60.

4   In the Arrange area's local menu, choose Edit > Cut/Insert Time > Insert Silence Between Locators.

A dialog asking if you want to add a time signature change appears. This is because Logic recognizes that adding two beats of space into the arrangement would cause the musical downbeats of the song to fall away from the bar lines. Changing bar 53 to a measure of 6/4 will correct this problem.

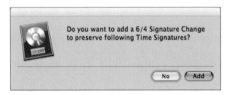

5   Click Add.

You can see the change reflected in the Signature global track.

Although it works, many musicians would consider that having a bar of 6/4 time overlapping the transition between a verse and chorus to be awkward. So let's fix that.

6   Press Escape and select the Scissors tool. Click the second beat in bar 53, which is also where the right locator can be seen.

This corrects the time signature issue by creating a bar of 2/4 during the space you inserted.

7   Press Escape twice to return to the Pointer tool.

8   Play the song beginning near bar 49 and listen to the transition with the space you added.

9   Click Stop, and then click the Global Tracks disclosure triangle.

Working with Folders

Consider that when people think of arranging, they visualize it in terms of blocks representing the different sections of their songs. Organizing a song should be as simple as placing these blocks in a desired order. While the methods of executing bulk edits in the previous exercise work well, the large-scale shifting of potentially hundreds of regions is far from the simplicity that many would prefer. Logic features a system not of blocks, but of folders that can function in nearly the same way.

Packing Folders

The first step is to pack the entire song into a folder region that will reside on a special folder track.

1   Press 1 to recall screenset 1.

2   Click the Vox Lead track header, and then press Command-A to select all regions.

3   Choose Region > Folder > Pack Folder.

The entire project has been placed into a folder on a newly created folder track. You still see the empty tracks where the regions of this song once resided. The folder region assumes the name and color of one of the selected regions. Don't worry about that; you'll be renaming things soon enough.

4   Play the project.

Notice that the meters on the unused tracks move. That's because the channel strips that produce the sounds from those tracks are still being used in the project. The empty tracks can be a bit distracting, and they aren't required to still hear your song.

TIP ▸ You can delete the unused tracks by choosing Track > Delete Unused. However, when you unpack a folder, the track order may change from your original arrangement. Leaving the unused tracks insures that when you unpack a folder the track order remains the same, as you will see at the end of this lesson.

5   Stop the song.

6   Make sure the folder region is selected, and then press Z to zoom.

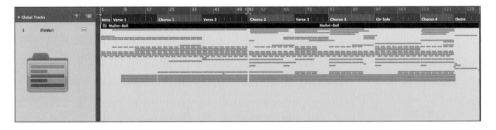

Notice that the folder region shows an overview of the regions that it contains.

Subdividing Folders for Rearranging the Project

To rearrange this project, you need to subdivide the large folder region into smaller sections. You've already defined those sections with markers, so you'll use those as a guide.

1   Hold Control-Command and use the Left/Right Arrow keys to move the playhead to the beginning of verse 1.

2   Choose Regions > Split > Split Regions by Playhead or use the backslash (\) key command.

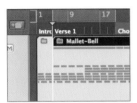

3   Using this technique, divide the folder region at the beginning of each song section.

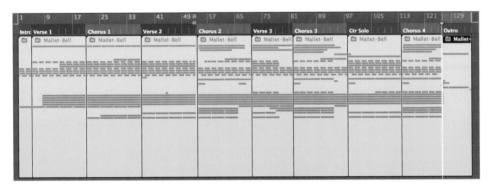

To more easily see the song structure, you'll now name and color the folder regions as you did with the marker regions.

4   Select the Text tool.

5   Using the marker as a guide, hold Shift and select each of the verses.

This may look a little strange, as you get a text field when you click each verse, but that's OK here.

6   In the text field for the last verse region you select, enter *Verse 1* and press Return.

It doesn't matter which one you name Verse 1 since Logic sequentially numbers the regions from left to right.

With the verse regions still selected, choose View > Colors and select a similar color to the one you used for the verse markers.

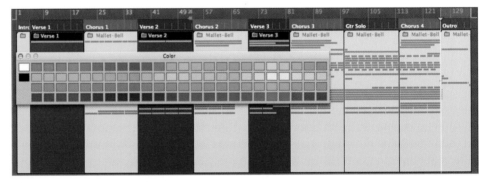

7   Continue to name and color the folder regions to match the marker regions.

8   When finished naming and coloring the folder regions, close the Color window and compare your work to the following figure.

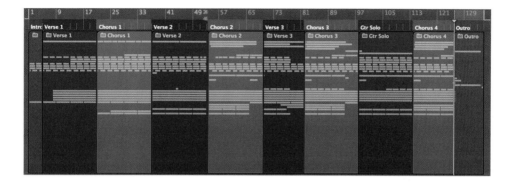

9   Press Escape twice to return to the Pointer tool.

Creating Alternate Arrangements

Now that your folders are prepped, you're ready to start rearranging the song. You'll create a second folder track so you can experiment with another arrangement by dragging and rearranging regions without losing the current one.

1   Double-click the (Folder) track header, enter *Version 1*, and press Return.

2   On the Version 1 track, click the Mute button.

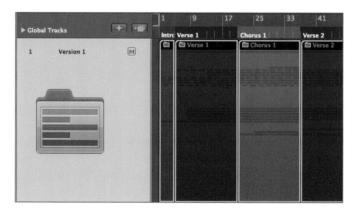

You are about to create another folder track for an alternate arrangement. Muting this track prevents multiple arrangements from being active at the same time.

3   At the top of the track list, click the Duplicate Track button.

4   Double-click the new track header, enter *Version 2*, and press Return.

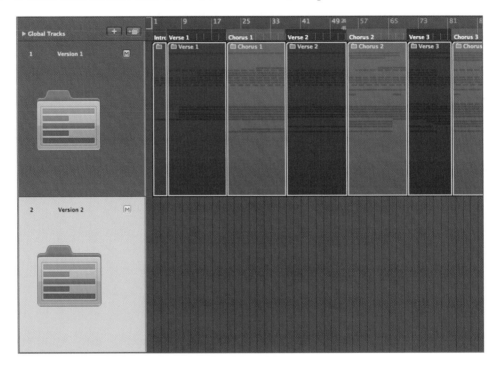

Consider the Version 1 track as your source track and the Version 2 track as your destination.

You'll now start your new arrangement by copying the original arrangement through Chorus 2 to the Version 2 track.

5   On the Version 1 track, select all regions from the beginning through Chorus 2.

6   Copy the regions from the Version 1 track by holding Option and dragging the regions to the Version 2 track directly below.

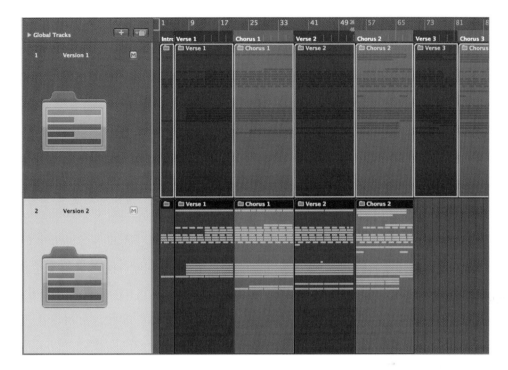

The choruses sometimes feel like they lose energy due to the long turnaround before the next verse. To keep the energy going, you're going to remove the turnaround from Chorus 2. To do this you first need to separate the beginning of Chorus 2 from the turnaround by dividing the Chorus 2 region at bar 66.

7 Move the playhead to bar 66.

8 Make sure the Chorus 2 region on the Version 2 track is selected, and then use the Divide at Playhead command (\).

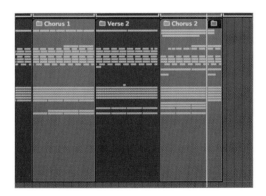

9   Press Delete.

The Chorus 2 region is shortened.

TIP ▶ It's not a good idea to shorten folder regions by trimming them with the Pointer tool. Although they will sound fine, they can cause unexpected results if you later unpack the folder. It's safer to divide a folder region and delete the undesired section.

As you start to build the arrangement on the Version 2 track, use the playback techniques found earlier in this lesson to hear how the transitions are working.

10   Option-drag the Verse 3 region from the Version 1 folder track to the Version 2 folder track at bar 66.

NOTE ▶ This transition sounds awkward because the vocal phrase at the end of Chorus 2 gets chopped off. You'll fix this in the final exercise.

Now you'll try something quite different from the original arrangement by placing the guitar solo after Verse 3.

11   Option-drag Version 1's Gtr Solo to Version 2 at bar 78.

The guitar solo now comes after Verse 3, whereas before it came after Chorus 3.

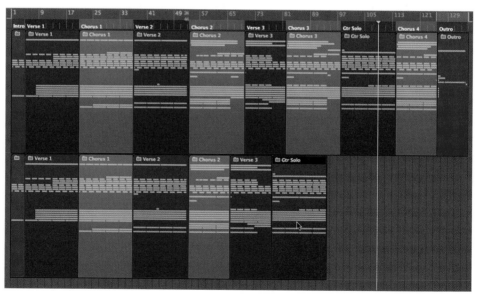

Editing Folder Regions

Although it sounds good to have the guitar solo play coming out of Verse 3, the guitar solo as a whole feels a bit long. You'll now use some of the commands learned at the beginning of this lesson to identify and remove a section of the solo guitar. The goal is to make the guitar solo section half as long. Because the transitions between the solo and the song sections on either side sound good, you'll work to remove the middle eight bars of the solo.

1   Select the Gtr Solo on the Version 2 track and press Z.

2   Using the Marquee tool, drag a marquee selection from bar 82 to 90.

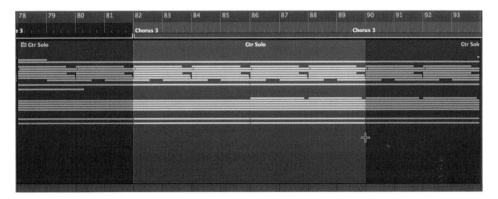

3   Press Shift-Spacebar to audition the area you selected.

4   Press C to turn on Cycle mode.

You're turning on Cycle mode in order to use a feature for auditioning edits called Skip Cycle. Skip cycles can be created by dragging from right to left in the upper part of the Bar ruler, which results in the left locator having a higher bar number than the right locator. This lets Logic know that you temporarily don't want to play that section of the song. In this case since the section of the song you want to leave out is already in a standard cycle area, you can flip-flop the locators to create a skip cycle with a key command.

5   Use the Swap Left and Right Locator command (J) to create a skip cycle.

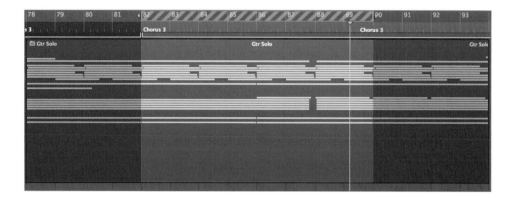

6   Press Control-Spacebar to play from the left window edge in order to audition the potential edit, and then stop when you've heard the result.

Skipping the middle eight bars sounds perfect, so now it's time to make this permanent.

7   With the Pointer tool, click in the marquee selection to divide the region, and then press Delete.

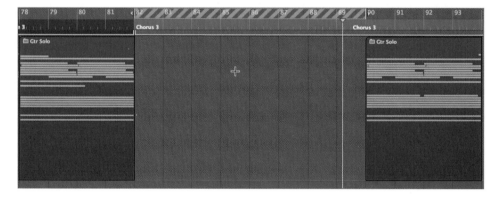

As you can see, edit tools and workflows generally work the same on folder regions as they would on standard audio or MIDI regions.

8   Move the second part of the solo to the end of the first at bar 82.

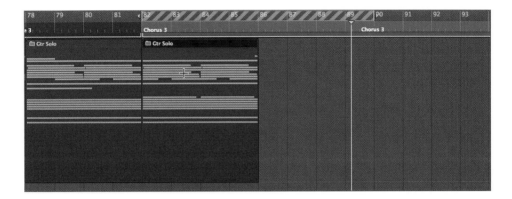

In order to keep the guitar solo intact as a single region, you need to merge the two Gtr Solo regions.

9 Select both Gtr Solo regions and choose Region > Merge > Regions (Control-=).

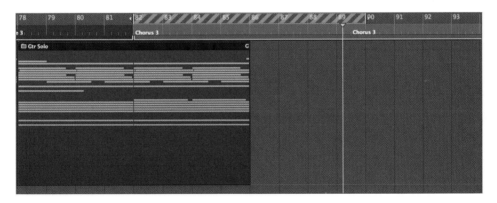

10 Press C to turn off Cycle mode, and then zoom out to see the entire arrangement.

Working Inside Folders

When rearranging at the folder level, the transitions don't always sound smooth. This is because it's very common for musical phrases to overlap song sections. When the regions representing these phrases are organized differently than the way they were originally recorded, unnatural transitions often occur. In this exercise you'll rearrange the final chorus and then work inside a folder to fix any transitional problems.

1 Option-drag the Chorus 4 region from the Version 1 track to the Version 2 track at bar 94.

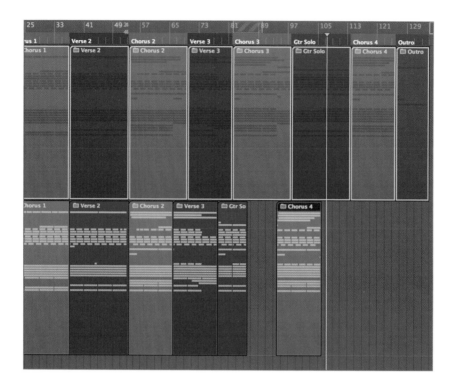

The gap between the solo and Chorus 4 is intentional. You'll fill in the blank space by copying a section from the end of the region you just moved in order to make the main hook in the chorus play a total of four times before the turnaround.

2   Position the playhead at bar 102 and divide at the playhead.

3   On the Version 2 track, Option-drag the first part of Chorus 4 (at bar 94) to bar 86, copying it.

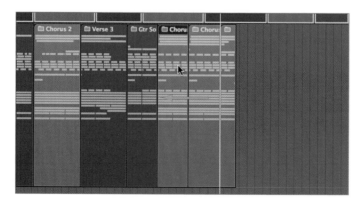

4   Select all three Chorus 4 regions and merge them by pressing Control-=.

This will be the last chorus in the version of the arrangement, creating a shorter song with only three chorus sections.

5   Use the Text tool to rename the newly merged region to *Chorus 3*.

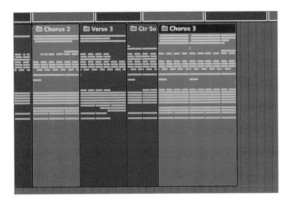

6   Play back the Chorus 3 region on the Version 2 track from about bar 90.

The transition where the choruses repeat at bar 94 sounds odd, because the vocal tracks were cut off prematurely. You'll need to go inside the folder to fix the problem.

7   With the Pointer tool, double-click the Chorus 3 region on the Version 2 track.

Now you're looking inside Chorus 3.

8   Press Command-A, and then press Z to zoom out.

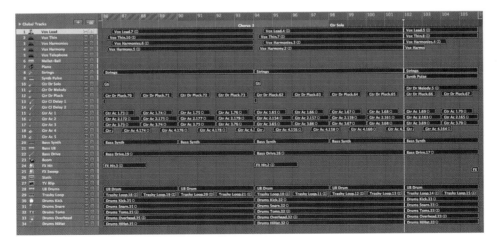

NOTE ▸ When viewing the contents of a folder region, the Bar ruler only shows measures within the boundaries of the region.

The Vox group of Vox regions ends prematurely at bar 94. You'll need to extend their length to hear the natural cutoff of their vocal phrases. Because you're going to be dragging the ends of these regions over the top of the next group of Vox regions, you need to make sure that you don't overlap the regions. Overlapped audio regions can create unexpected results where the region on top may not be the one you hear.

9 Set Logic's drag mode to No Overlap.

10 Select only the four Vox regions that end at bar 93.

11 Drag the end of any one of the Vox regions to meet the beginning of the next vocal phrase at the third beat of bar 94.

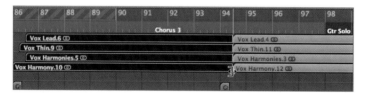

Because they were all selected, all the regions have their lengths extended.

12 Double-click in the lower part of the bar ruler at bar 92 to audition the transition, and then stop when you've heard the result.

Now that the transition is fixed, you need to get back to see things at folder level, as you had before.

13 Click the Hierarchy button, and then zoom to see the entire arrangement.

14 Option-drag the outro to the end of the Version 2 arrangement at bar 106.

Your new arrangement is complete. Take a moment to listen to the new version.

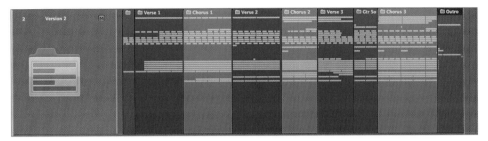

Managing Multiple Arrangements

You just completed a second version of the song's arrangement, but the markers don't reflect your changes. In this exercise you'll create a new alternate Marker track to reflect these changes, and see how you can switch between multiple arrangements of the project within the same project file.

Switching between arrangements is as simple as muting one folder track and unmuting the next. This can occur while playback is happening, but it may take a few seconds to transition between versions.

1 Click Play and experiment with switching between the versions by muting and unmuting the version track headers.

2 After you've had a chance to listen to your results, mute the Version 1 track header and unmute the Version 2 track header before clicking Stop.

You may have noticed that the current markers do not match the Version 2 arrangement. The Marker track has an alternative Marker option that lets you quickly conform the markers to your new arrangement without losing the original set of markers.

3 Click the Global Tracks disclosure triangle.

4 Click the Marker track's disclosure triangle.

5   In the Marker track's Alternative pop-up menu, choose 2.

The markers disappear. Don't worry; they're still stored in the Alternative 1.

6   Click the Version 2 track header to select all regions on that track.

7   In the Marker track, click the From Regions button.

Markers are automatically created from the folder regions you created.

8   Deselect all regions.

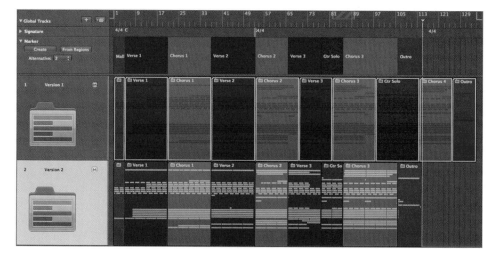

Now the Marker track reflects your new arrangement.

In the next exercise you're going to learn how to unpack your arrangement so you'll now delete the Version 1.

9 Make sure the Version 1 track header is selected and press Delete to delete the regions on the Version 1 track.

10 Press Delete again to delete the Version 1 track from the track list.

Unpacking Folders

Sometimes it's helpful to see your arrangement without it being compartmentalized into song sections. Achieving this is as simple as unpacking your folders.

1 Make sure all the regions on the Version 2 track are selected and choose Region > Folder > Unpack Folder (Use Existing Tracks).

A dialog asking what to do with overlapping regions is displayed. Creating separate tracks anytime there is an overlapping region can result in many duplicate tracks in the Arrange window.

2 Click No.

Instantly your entire song is laid out as if you had done all the edits region by region. The folder track is just an empty shell.

3 Select the folder track header and press Delete.

4 Zoom out to see the entire project.

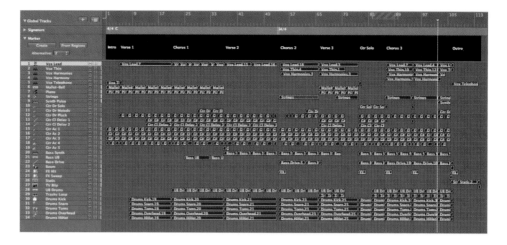

Now you can easily fix the bad transition between Chorus 2 and Verse 3.

5   Zoom in and select only the Vox Lead and Vox Thin regions that end at bar 65.

6   Drag the lower-right corner of either Vox region to end just before you see the wave-
    form begin on the Lead Vox region at bar 66 beat 3.

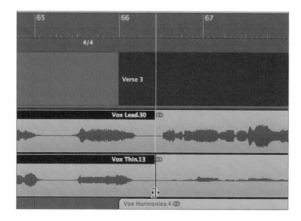

7   Play from the beginning to hear the new arrangement.

Lesson Review

1. How do markers aid in a production?

2. How is changing the text and color of markers useful in a production?

3. Where are markers accessed?

4. How can you initiate playback from the bar number displayed on the far left side of Arrange area?

5. How are locators set?

6. Where do you configure playback hierarchy?

7. How can you insert or delete measures across all tracks of a project (including global tracks) at once?

8. How can you compartmentalize large groups of regions for quick, simple rearranging of projects?

Answers

1. Markers can designate section material or serve as navigation points.

2. Changing the appearance of markers (including production notes) helps you easily identify and navigate to sections within the arrangement.

3. Markers can be accessed in the Bar ruler, Marker track, or Marker List.

4. Use the Play From Left Window Edge key command.

5. Locators can quickly be set by dragging within the Bar ruler or by creating cycle areas for any region, event, or marker.

6. Hold the Play button in the Transport area.

7. Set locators around the measure to be added or deleted and then choose Cut/Insert Time commands from the Edit menu.

8. Pack all regions of a song into a folder. The folder can then be divided into song sections and rearranged.

8

Lesson Files
Advanced Logic 9_Files > Lessons > 08_Anatomy of a Human Bomb_Start.logic

Media
Advanced Logic 9_Files > Media > Anatomy of a Human Bomb

Time
This lesson takes approximately 75 minutes to complete.

Goals
Apply crossfades to multiple regions simultaneously

Draw out clicks in audio files

Create a composite take using take folders

Edit multiple tracks simultaneously with groups

Use phase-locked editing to edit and quantize drums

Replace bad drum hits with good ones using transient detection techniques

Use drum replacement/doubling to replace recorded drum sounds with samples

Use Soundtrack Pro as an external audio editor

Lesson 8
Advanced Audio Editing

The flexibility of editing digital audio is one of the distinct advantages of working with nonlinear hard-disk recording systems. The user can precisely fix mistakes, adjust timing, rearrange section material, and combine elements in every conceivable way. What was once incredibly difficult or impossible to do with analog tape is now almost routine if you have the right set of tools and skills.

Modern production is both blessed with and plagued by this flexibility. On the one hand, it allows sophisticated edits to be performed with great accuracy. On the other, falling into obsessiveness is all too easy, and you can worry a track to a lifeless lump of 1s and 0s.

That said, good editing techniques can take your material to another level, turning a raw performance into a polished piece of music.

In this lesson you'll pick up where you left off in Lesson 7 by further refining the audio recordings used in this song. Using Logic's wide variety of powerful features, you'll not only learn how to fix problems out of necessity but how to edit creatively to bring new energy to the song.

Smoothing Transitions with Crossfades

Unwanted clicks and pops are an unfortunate byproduct of working with digital audio. These anomalies can occur when the audio waveform unnaturally jumps from the end of one region to the beginning of another. Clicks and pops can also occur in an otherwise great recording due to inappropriate buffer or clock settings on the audio interface at the time of recording. In this section you'll learn techniques to fix these issues with minimal fuss so you can focus on more creative endeavors.

Working with Crossfades

Crossfades are the easiest way to smooth over unnatural transitions between newly adjoined regions. Because the last lesson created so many new transitions, this exercise will show you how to apply crossfades *en masse*. First you'll get rid of the click between the two halves of the guitar solo to better understand Logic's crossfade features, and then you'll apply crossfades across all the drum regions to make their edits sound more natural.

1   Go to Advanced Logic 9 > Lessons and open **08_Anatomy of a Human Bomb_Start.logic**.

The project opens zoomed around the Gtr Solo regions. A cycle area is already enabled, and the Gtr Dr Solo track is soloed.

This guitar solo contains several audible clicks that have occurred for different reasons. The click at bar 82 is caused when the waveform abruptly moves in an irregular way where the regions transition.

2   Play the guitar solo and listen for the click at bar 82.

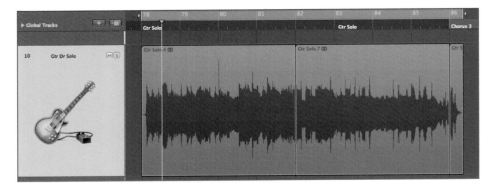

You can smooth this transition and eliminate the click at bar 82 by adding a crossfade.

As you add the crossfade, it's important to see what's happening in the selected region's Parameter box.

3 Select the first Gtr Solo region, and then open the Region Parameter box by clicking its disclosure triangle.

The Region Parameter box displays parameters for the Gtr Solo.4 region. Notice that the Fade parameter displays Out. This indicates that the region selected is set to have a fade-out applied to it, but since there is no numerical value to the right of the setting, there is no audible effect.

4 With the Pointer tool, hold Control-Shift and drag a selection area that overlaps the two regions by about a beat.

Upon releasing the mouse, white shaded areas appear, illustrating the applied crossfade.

Notice in the Region Parameter box that the Fade type has been set to EqP (Equal Power) with a numerical value next to it. Equal Power uses logarithmic curved fades to keep the volume level from dipping during the transition. The value to the right represents the length of the fade in milliseconds.

TIP ▶ With the Pointer tool, holding Control-Shift serves the same purpose as the Crossfade tool found in the tool selection menu. As with the Crossfade tool, holding Control-Shift lets you change the shape of the curve by dragging the middle of the shaded area.

5 Play the same section to hear that the click is now gone.

Unless you're zoomed in closely, dragging a crossfade between regions often creates a crossfade area that is much bigger than is needed to remove clicks created by transitions. Crossfades that are too long can sometimes sound awkward because both regions can be heard at the same time, so keeping crossfades just short enough to eliminate the click is ideal. You can create small crossfades by using numerical values in the Region Parameter box.

6 Double-click the fade time, enter *50*, and press Return.

The shaded area representing the crossfade resizes to reflect the change.

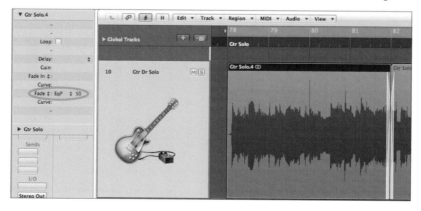

7   Play the transition.

With only a 50-millisecond crossfade, the click is still inaudible.

Applying Crossfades to Multiple Regions

In the last lesson you rearranged many audio regions that in their new order can create clicks or other noticeable glitches at transition points. To help smooth out abrupt edited transitions, it's a good idea to apply a short crossfade to all edited regions as a group.

1   Turn off solo for the Gtr Solo track and zoom out to see the entire arrangement.

2   Solo the drum tracks by dragging down the Solo buttons across all their track headers.

3   Turn off Cycle mode, and then play the song and listen to the transition between Chorus 2 and Verse 3.

Although there's no click or pop, the transition sounds a little abrupt. Similar unnatural transitions can be heard throughout the drum tracks, so you'll apply crossfades across all the drum regions at once.

4   Select all the drum regions except for the small regions at the very end of the song.

> **NOTE** ▶ Crossfade settings only need to be applied to the region preceding a transition, which is why it's not necessary to select the last regions on each track.

5   In the Region Parameter box, change the Fade type to Equal Power Crossfade and set the time to *50*.

TIP ▸ The Fade In parameter just above the Fade parameters is only used to create a volume fade-in at the beginning of a region if there is no preceding region with a cross-fade value. In the event that there is a region with a crossfade value before a region with a Fade In value, the crossfade will take priority and the Fade In value will be ignored.

6   Zoom on the drum regions at the end of the song to see that the crossfades have been applied.

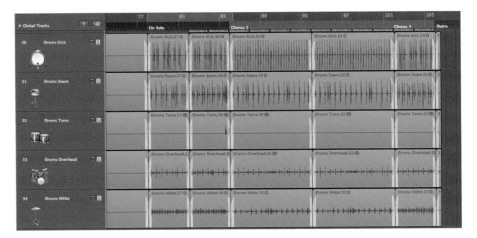

7   Listen to the transition between Chorus 2 and Verse 3.

The transition still feels abrupt, even with the 50-millisecond crossfade. A longer fade time for this specific section can help to smooth the transition.

8   Select the drum regions during Chorus 2.

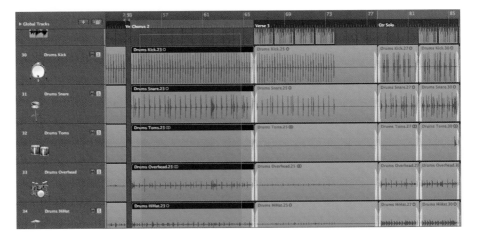

9 Set the fade value to *5000* and play the same transition again.

A setting of 5000 means it takes a full 5 seconds to crossfade between the two sets of regions. This allows for the cymbal crash in the Drums Overhead track that was originally played coming out of Chorus 2 to be heard over the beginning of Verse 3, which sounds much more natural then when it was chopped off.

TIP ▶ The Curve parameter just below the Fade parameters can be adjusted to control the shape of the crossfade curves providing more options for shaping the sound of transitions between sections.

10 Deselect Solo on all of the Drums tracks by Option-clicking the Solo button on any of the Drums track headers.

Fixing Clicks in the Sample Editor

Sometimes clicks and pops appear within the body of an audio region such as the case at bar 80 in the guitar solo. This can be a result of clipping that occurred during their recording, sample rate clocking errors, or even the result of edited audio files being bounced together without proper crossfades. Regardless of the cause, this exercise shows how to find them visually and audibly and then literally draw them out of the picture.

1 Double-click the first region of the original guitar solo at bar 78.

The Sample Editor opens displaying the Gtr Solo region.

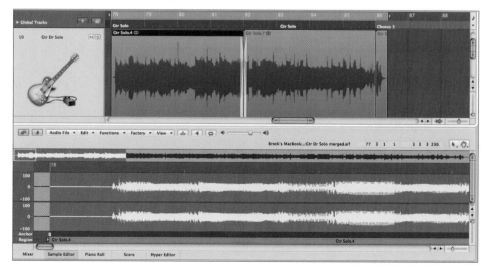

Clicks that may be almost unnoticeable without added effects can become obvious when reverb and delays are added to the sound. In order to hear the click in context with all the channel strip effects, you need to make sure that the Sample Editor is set to Auto-select Channel Strip.

2 Control-click the Prelisten button and choose Auto-select Channel Strip from the shortcut menu.

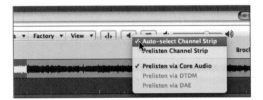

3 Click the Prelisten button to audition the region's audio file and click the Prelisten button again when you've identified the click.

4 Scroll to bar 80 and look for the spike in the waveform that represents the click.

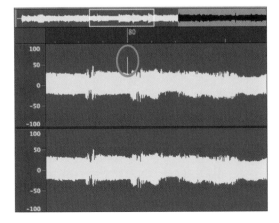

It's clear that the click only exists in the left channel of the stereo recording.

You can also use scrubbing to quickly move back and forth at varying speeds. This technique is especially useful to zero in on a click's location when it might not be visible in the waveform.

5   Hold the mouse in the upper part of the Bar ruler and drag left or right to scrub the audio around the click.

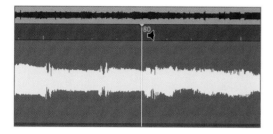

TIP ▶ Double-clicking the Bar ruler starts and stops playback just as it does in the Arrange area.

6   Hold Control-Option and zoom until the click is clearly visible.

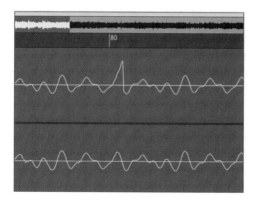

7   Change the alternate tool to the Pencil tool.

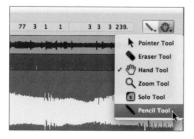

8   Using the Pencil tool, draw out the click.

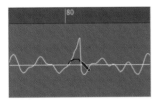

TIP ▶ The process of drawing out clicks can be hit or miss. If after you draw out the click you still see a spike in the waveform, try to draw out the remaining spike. Sometimes you may inadvertently overwrite a good part of the waveform. In that event, press Command-Z to undo your change and try again.

Once the waveform looks good, make sure it sounds good. Use the scrub method you just learned to see if the click is truly gone. Sometimes completely eliminating the click is impossible, but the drawing you do may minimize the problem and be sufficient in the context of the mix.

NOTE ▶ Because you're updating the actual audio file, the click will be removed from all regions that reference this audio file.

9   Close the Sample Editor at the bottom of the Arrange area, and then listen to the guitar solo with the rest of the tracks.

Creating New Parts from Existing Ones

One of the advantages offered by digital editing is the ease with which new parts are created from existing material through copying and pasting. In order to achieve a convincing result, however, it is of equal importance to use judicious edits to assemble the new part as well as create seamless transitions between the constituent building blocks.

In the previous lesson you cut the guitar solo in half by removing the middle 8 bars of the solo. Although the result sounds good, you might discover that combining various sections of the original 16-bar solo yields a better variation. In the following exercises, you'll learn how to divide the original guitar solo into smaller pieces so that it can be packed into a take folder for use with Quick Swipe Comping. You'll also exploit Logic 9's new ability to use conventional editing within the take folder to realign the timing of parts for perfect placement.

Packing a Take Folder

You're going to create a new 8-bar-long guitar solo using portions of the original 16-bar performance. To achieve this you'll begin by splitting the guitar solo in half, creating an A and B section. You'll then position the A and B sections on different tracks so that they start at the same time. Since you don't really want both parts to play simultaneously, you'll pack the A and B sections into a take folder, which you'll use in the next exercise to choose which parts of each section you want to hear.

1   Double-click the Gtr Dr Solo track header and rename the track *Gtr Solo (v1)*.

This track will be kept muted so that you can revert to the original edit if you end up liking it better than the comp you're about to make.

2   Mute the Gtr Solo (v1) track.

3   At the top of the track list, click the Duplicate Track button to create a new track, and then rename it *Gtr Solo (v2)*.

This track will hold the new comp of the guitar solo you're going to create in the next exercise.

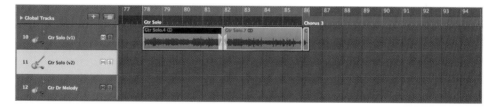

Now you need to bring the original guitar solo down to the new track.

4   Hold Option and drag the first Gtr Solo region at bar 78 to the same measure on the Gtr Solo (v2) track.

Because the region is only referencing the beginning section of the original 16-bar guitar solo, you now need to expose the rest of the solo on the track.

5   Drag the lower-right corner of the region as far right as it will go.

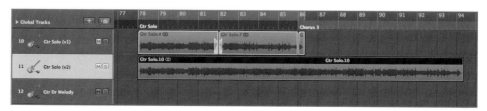

In order to do intermix parts from the entire 16-bar solo, you need to make both halves start at the same point in time.

6   Press Escape, and then press 5 to select the Scissors tool. Click the region at bar 86 to divide it in half.

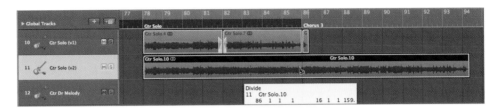

7   Press Escape twice to go back to the Pointer tool, and then drag the region to the Gtr Dr Melody track at bar 78.

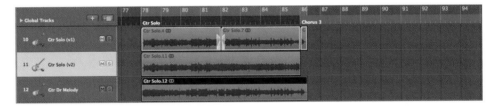

It's OK that you put the solo on the melody track because it's only going to be there for a moment.

Naming the regions will help to identify which part you're hearing when you start to edit.

8   Use the Text tool to rename Gtr Solo.11 to *Gtr Solo A* and Gtr Solo.12 to *Gtr Solo B*.

To make it even easier to see which parts are playing, set each region to a different color.

9   Press Option-C to open the Color window.

10   With the Pointer tool, select the Gtr Solo A region and choose a color from the Color window, and then apply a slightly different color to Gtr Solo B.

11 Close the Color window.

Now you're ready to pack the two regions into a single take folder.

12 Select the Gtr Solo A and Gtr Solo B regions. Control-click one of the selected regions and choose Folder > Pack Take Folder from the shortcut menu.

Gtr Solo B region is moved into a new take folder region named Gtr Solo (v2): Comp 1, which also contains the Gtr Solo A region.

Creating a Comp

Now that you have both halves of the guitar solo packed into a take folder, you'll use Quick Swipe Comping to quickly create a preliminary edit that transitions between the Gtr Solo A and B performances. Although Quick Swipe Comping is very good at transitioning between two or more regions in a take folder, it doesn't permit moving the parts in time. This can be problematic as it's often necessary to move phrases forward or backward in time in order for them to sit into the overall arrangement. To overcome this you'll learn how it is now possible to bypass Quick Swipe Comping so that you can freely reposition regions within a take folder using Logic's conventional editing tools.

1 Double-click the Gtr Solo (v2) take folder, and then press Z to zoom.

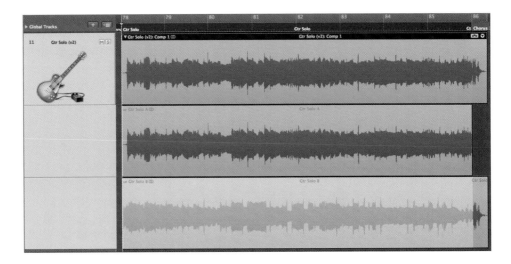

The take folder shows the current composite on the track with two take lanes below. Take lanes are used to display the content of different regions that can be used to create your comp. Only one take lane can be heard at one time. Colored sections of a take lane indicate which parts of a region will be heard; dimmed areas are not heard. In this case Gtr Solo A is played in its entirety, but only the tail end of Gtr Solo B will be played. This transition is displayed in the comp above the take lanes where the region changes colors at bar 86.

2   On the Gtr Solo (v2) track header, click the Solo button to solo the track. Press Shift-Spacebar to begin playback, and then press C to turn on the Cycle mode. Gtr Solo A plays with the last part of Gtr Solo B played at the end.

3   In the Take Folder menu, choose Guitar Solo B and play it to become familiar with that part.

Now you're going to use Quick Swipe Comping to create transitions between the two takes.

4   Be sure the Guitar Solo B take is selected in its entirety

5   In Guitar Solo A, drag from just before bar 80 to bar 82, and then play to hear the
transition.

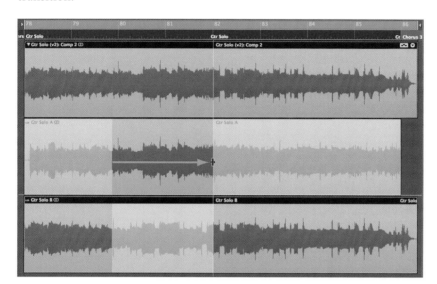

You're going to leave the notes that begin Guitar Solo B, but transition to the descending line that starts Guitar Solo A. To do this you must move the beginning part
of Guitar Solo A in time. Moving parts in time is not possible with Quick Swipe
Comping engaged, so you must first turn off Quick Swipe Comping mode.

6   In the upper part of the take folder, click the Quick Swipe Comping mode button.

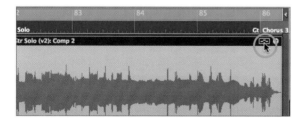

When Quick Swipe Comping mode is off, you're free to use all of Logic's existing editing features to manipulate the regions within the take folder. Most importantly this
includes the ability to create new regions and move them in time.

7 Hold Command and marquee select Gtr Solo A from 78 3 1 1 to halfway between it and 79 2 2 1. Watch the help tag to confirm your exact positions.

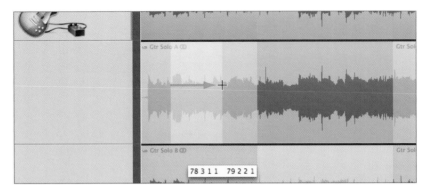

8 Click the marquee selection to divide the region at the selection borders, and then drag the new region to start at bar 79.

9 Turn Quick Swipe Comping back on, and then select the newly moved region so that it is added to the comp.

10 Turn off Solo in the track header, and then play the new version of the guitar solo with the rest of the tracks.

NOTE ▸ When you edit the timing of regions within a take, all comps that reference the take will be affected by the change. This can create unwanted changes to alternate comps.

11 Take a moment to experiment with creating other versions of the solo with and without using Quick Swipe Comping.

12 Close the take folder by clicking the disclosure triangle in its upper-left corner and turn off Cycle mode.

TIP ▸ The Take Folder menu offers various tools for converting the content of a take folder back to conventional audio regions. Flatten will convert the current comp into discrete audio regions on the current track while deleting the takes used to create the comp. Unpack works in a similar way but retains the original takes by placing them on muted duplicate tracks.

Editing with Mixer Groups

Drums, background vocals, and layered guitar performances are each comprised of multiple tracks, but we often look at them as a single entity when it comes to making adjustments such as volume and in this case, making edits.

In this section you'll use Logic's Mixer groups to organize the drum tracks into a group for editing. You'll also learn how to temporarily disable group editing when you want to edit to individual regions within the drum group.

You'll also use Logic Pro 9's new ability to maintain phase-lock while performing edits on grouped tracks. Phase-locked editing insures that all the tracks within the group maintain their timing relationships down to the sample level.

Configuring an Edit Group

Logic's Mixer groups can be used to apply a variety of operations such as volume, panning, and automation to multiple channels at the same time. In addition you can also use Mixer groups to permit simultaneous editing of tracks. In this exercise you will use Logic's Mixer group feature to place the drum tracks into an edit group in order to quickly make changes to the regions across all the drum tracks.

1   At the bottom of the Arrange area, click the Mixer tab.

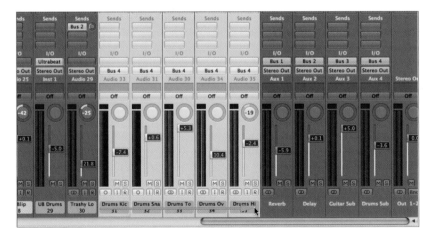

2   Drag across the names of the Drum tracks to select their channel strips.

3   Click the Group slot on any of the selected channel strips, and then in the Group selection menu choose Group 1.

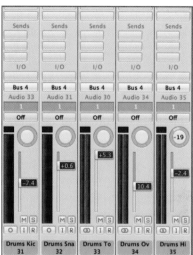

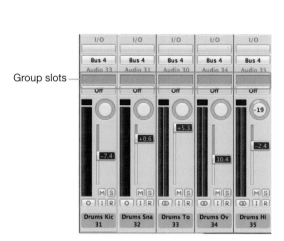

Group slots

The drum channels are assigned to Group 1.

Creating a group name is especially helpful to quickly identify groups in the project. These names will be displayed in the Group slot in the Mixer.

4 Click any of the group selection boxes and choose Open Group Settings.

5 In the Group Settings window, double-click the Group 1 Name field, enter Drums, and press Return.

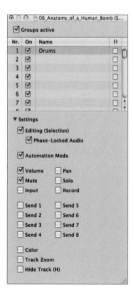

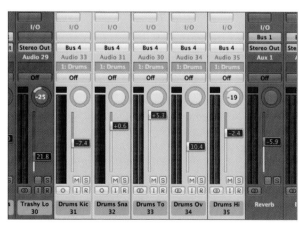

By default, channels within groups have their volume and mute controls linked. In order to be able to perform edits as a group, you need to activate the Editing setting.

6   Click the Editing (Selection) checkbox.

NOTE ▶ The Phase-Locked Audio checkbox also becomes active. You'll learn about phase-locked audio later in this section.

Activating and Deactivating Groups Using Group Clutch

Now that your group is defined, an edit you make to any of the drum regions will be reflected on all the other drum tracks as a whole. To get a feel for this process, you'll first make a simple edit to mute the sound of unnecessary open mics at the beginning of the drum tracks. You'll see how to use the Group Clutch feature to temporarily disable groups when you need to make an adjustment to an individual track. The Group Clutch works like an automobile's clutch, temporarily taking the group "out of gear" while letting you perform the necessary adjustments.

1   Close the Mixer, and then create a marquee selection from the beginning of the Drums HiHat region just before the transients in bar 12. Mute the selection by pressing M.

All the drum regions automatically reflect the same marquee selection so they were all muted at the same time.

Sometimes it's necessary to temporarily bypass groups in order to make an individual change to a track within the group. In this case you'll mute the snare drum in Verse 3 in order to back off the energy in that section of the song. In order to minimize the side-stick part that's being played in Verse 3, use group clutch to mute the snare region in that section.

2   Toggle the group clutch by pressing Command-G.

All groups are bypassed, and the group numbers and names in the channel strips become dimmed.

3   Click the Snare region during Verse 3 at bar 66, and press M to mute the region.

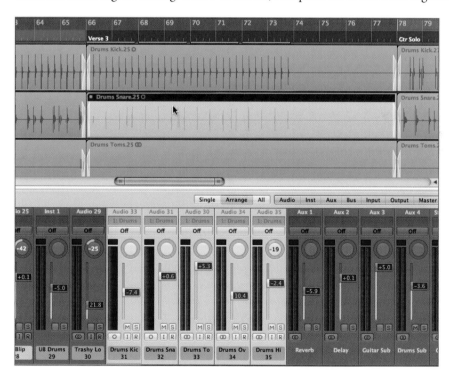

4   Use the Toggle Group Clutch command (Command-G) to turn groups back on.

Understanding Phase-Locked Editing

Phase-locked editing is a new feature in Logic 9 that works in cooperation with the flex editing techniques you learned in Lesson 2. When this group edit option is selected, it means that the timing relationship between all members of the group stay intact regardless of how any one track is moved, stretched, or quantized. This is especially important where there is some spill into all channels (especially the overheads). Without phase-locked editing, moving the snare on the snare track without also moving the corresponding section of the overhead track can produce unwanted doubling effects and a sonic degradation called *phase cancellation* that can smear the overall image. To best understand how phase-locked editing works, you'll compare how flex edits are affected with and without phase-locked editing engaged.

1   Zoom on the Drums tracks at bar 102 and deselect the Phase-Locked Audio checkbox in the Group Settings window. Then turn on Flex View and choose a Flex mode for the Drums tracks. Because they are in a Mixer Group, you only need to change the Flex mode for one of the Drums tracks.

2   Turn on Flex View and change the Flex Mode on the Drums tracks to Slicing.

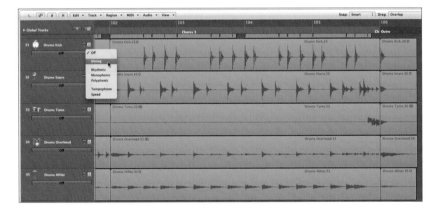

3   Click any one of the drum regions at bar 102, and in the lower half of the Drums Snare region drag the snare hit at bar 103 beat 2 to the left of bar 102.

Notice how the different colors indicate the uneven way in which the time compression is being applied to the different drum tracks. This is because each track is independently snapping to transient markers that are unique to each track.

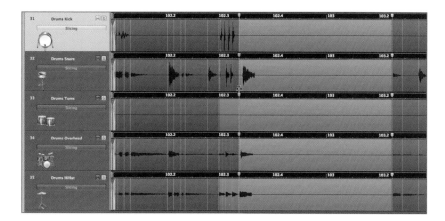

If you had an extreme amount of time compression in one of your regions, you may be prompted with a message asking if you really want to create a high-speed section.

4   Press Command-Z, or click Cancel in the dialog, to undo your last edit.

5   Click the Phase-Locked Audio checkbox in the Group Settings window, and then drag the same snare to the left again.

Notice how the flex mode time compression is being applied in the same amount across all the drum tracks.

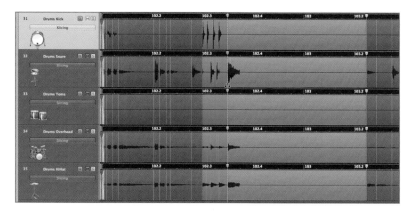

6   Press Command-Z.

To create an unexpected sense of urgency in the drum part just before the outro, you'll now move the snare hit at 103 2 1 1.

7   In the lower half of the region, drag the snare from 103 2 1 1 to 103 1 3 1 to move it an eighth note earlier.

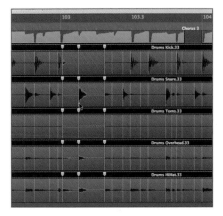

TIP ▸ Since no help tag is displayed when moving the flex marker, watch the playhead position in the Transport bar for reference.

8   Repeat the last step for the snares in the same relative positions at bars 104 and 105.

9   Listen to the result both soloed and with the rest of the tracks.

While soloed, the result may sound unnatural, but when blended with the rest of the tracks, the result provides a surprising change to the rhythmic form just before the end of the song.

TIP ▸ Try other flex modes to achieve different sonic results. Remember, though, that flex modes are applied at the track level, so making a change could impact other flex edits in the track.

Quantizing Drums with Phase-Locked Editing

Because phase-locked editing maintains the relative time of all tracks within the group, this feature is ideal for quantizing audio across groups of tracks such as a drum kit. You may have noticed that when you chose phase-locked editing in the Group Settings window, a button with the letter Q was displayed in the track header of all the drum tracks. Tracks with the letter Q lend their transients as reference points when using the quantize parameters found in the Region Parameter box. For this song, it's important that the kick drum is as rhythmically rigid as possible, so you'll use it as the quantization reference track.

1   Deselect Q on the all the drum track headers except for the Drums Kick. Now only the kick will be referenced when quantizing.

NOTE ▶ It is normal for there to be a brief pause between clicking the Q button and seeing the Q button's status toggle.

2   Click any of the drum track headers. Because the drum tracks are grouped, the regions on all the drum tracks are selected.

3   Zoom in on Chorus 2 so that you can clearly see the transient markers.

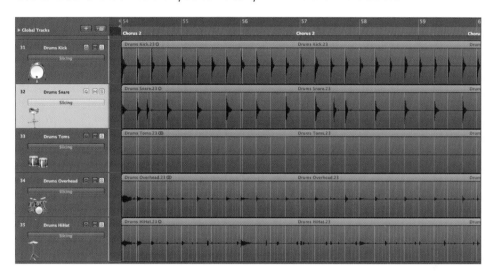

4   Select any of the drum regions, and then in the Region Parameter box set the Quantize value to 1/4-Note.

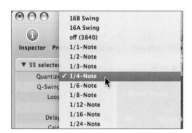

The drum regions display orange and green highlighted waveforms indicating where timing shifts have occurred. Notice that the colors for any particular beat are the same across all the drum tracks, indicating they have all been moved forward or backward in time together in order to maintain their relative time relationship.

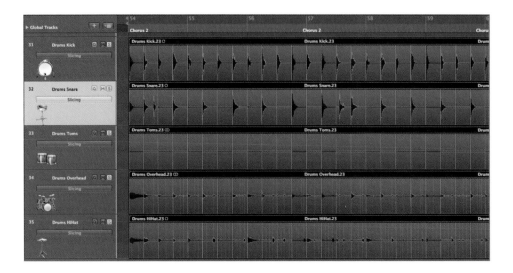

5   Turn off Flex view by clicking the Flex View button in the toolbar or pressing Command-F. Turn off the Drums edit group by pressing Command-G.

Repairing Drums with Marquee Transient

The snare drum hits that fall on the backbeat should be loud and powerful compared to the ghost notes the drummer also played, but some of the backbeat snares are noticeably quieter than the others. In this lesson you'll replace the bad snare hits by using a better snare hit from elsewhere in the same track. To speed up this workflow you'll use Marquee selection techniques that use transients in the audio waveforms as a guide to quickly isolate selections for copying and pasting.

1   With the Pointer tool, select the Drum Snare region at bar 54 and zoom in around the first few measures of that region.

    The snares at bar 56 beat 2 and bar 58 beat 2 sound like they weren't hit as hard as the others in the track.

2   Deselect Solo on all drum tracks except for the Drums Snare track header, and then play the song and listen for consistency in the snare hits.

    You'll now select a good snare hit to serve as a replacement for the bad ones. You'll use Logic's ability to snap transients to make exacting selections faster and easier than making manual selections.

3   Draw a marquee selection around the last snare in bar 54. Leave a generous area on each side of the waveform.

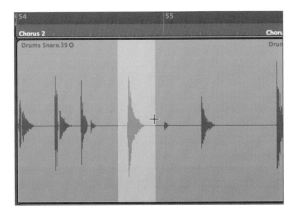

It's important to leave ample space after the snare decay so that when it gets copied to the bad snare positions it completely covers the bad hit. However it's important to tighten the left side of the marquee selection to the first transient of the snare hit. Holding Shift and pressing the Left/Right Arrow keys will move the left side of a marquee selection to the previous or next transient. In this case the left side of the marquee selection now snaps perfectly to the first transient of the snare.

4   Hold Shift and press the Right Arrow key.

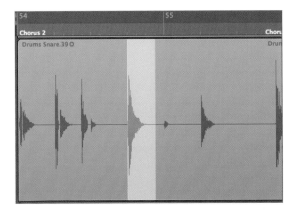

TIP ▶ If the marquee selection does not snap to the transients you would like to reference, you can define the transient markers for a region by using the Sample Editor, as discussed in Lesson 2.

5 Copy the snare to the clipboard by pressing Command-C.

6 Hold Shift and continue to press the Right Arrow key until the marquee line is at the first bad snare hit in bar 56.

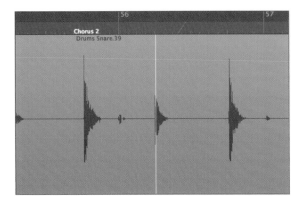

TIP ▸ If you press the Right Arrow key too many times, let go of Shift and use the Set Marquee End to Previous Transient command (Left Arrow key) to move the marquee selection to the previous transient.

7 Press Command-V.

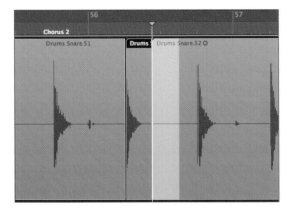

The good snare hit has replaced the bad one. Now you can quickly move to the next snare that needs to be replaced.

8 Hold Shift and move the marquee to the next bad snare at bar 58. Press Command-V to replace it.

9   Listen to the repaired snare drums.

10 Stop playback.

> **TIP** ▶ You can use the marquee selection techniques shown in this lesson with MIDI regions as well. The beginning or end of a MIDI note is used as the transient point that the marquee selection references.

> **NOTE** ▶ Holding Shift-Command with the Left/Right Arrow keys normally defaults to moving both a marquee selection's beginning and its end to the next or previous transient position, but you changed the Shift-Command arrow keys to move locators to different marker positions in Lesson 7. You can accomplish the same result by pressing the Left Arrow key to move the marquee selection to the left or hold Shift and press the Right Arrow key to move it to the right as you did in this lesson.

Editing Drums in Soundtrack Pro

You're going to be making some creative edits to the snare regions that play during the guitar solo using features found not in Logic, but in Soundtrack Pro 3.

Soundtrack Pro 3 is a completely separate application that is included in Logic Studio, and it should be considered as part of your audio editing workflow when using Logic. Soundtrack Pro can function as a full-fledged digital audio workstation, but its main attraction to Logic users is as a file-based audio editor with powerful features not found in Logic's own Sample Editor.

In this set of exercises, you learn how to move an audio file from Logic into Soundtrack Pro, manipulate it using features unique to Soundtrack Pro, and return the results to Logic.

Preparing Files for Use in Soundtrack Pro

Because the file editing capabilities in Soundtrack Pro need to see a single audio file, you'll first merge the two snare regions during the guitar solo into a new audio file that will then be sent to Soundtrack Pro.

1   Scroll to the Gtr Solo section of the song and select the Drums Snare.27 and Drums Snare.30 regions.

2 Press Shift-Spacebar to familiarize yourself with the snare performance, and then click Stop.

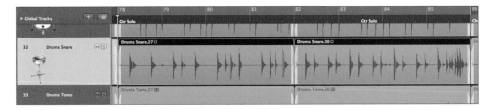

3 Control-click either of the selected Drums Snare regions and choose Bounce and Merge > Merge from the shortcut menu.

A dialog appears, asking if you want to create a new audio file.

Because you will ultimately be modifying the original audio file stored on your hard drive, it's always best to create a new copy of the region you're going to edit in Soundtrack Pro. In this case, merging serves this purpose.

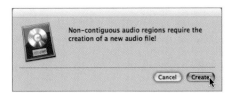

4 Click Create.

A new audio file called Drums Snare merged is created in place of the previous Drums Snare regions.

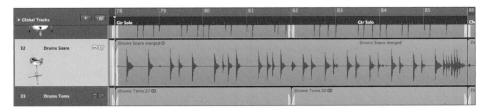

TIP To create a new audio file from a single region, Control-click the region and choose Convert > Convert to New Audio File(s) from the shortcut menu.

5   Select the Drums Snare merged region, and then in the main menu bar choose
    Options > Audio > Open in Soundtrack Pro.

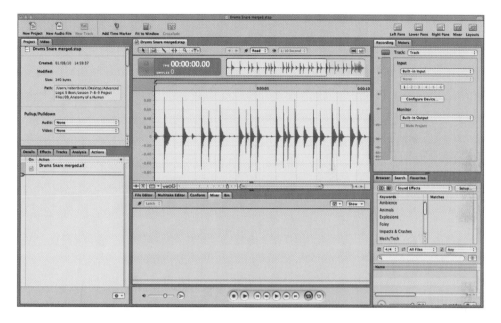

Soundtrack Pro automatically opens, and it creates a new Soundtrack Pro audio file
project that displays the Drums Snare merged waveform.

NOTE ▶ Multitrack projects (.stmp files) are similar to Logic projects (minus the
MIDI capabilities), whereas audio projects (.stap files) allow you to edit and manipulate individual audio files similar to Logic's Sample Editor.

Understanding the Soundtrack Pro Interface

At first it might seem a little daunting to dive into an entirely new application, but there
are only a few things you need to understand in order to enjoy the power of this application in your Logic workflow.

Soundtrack Pro uses panes to display information in tabbed windows for quick viewing.
The panes that are visible depend on which ones were open when the program was last
closed. Only the left pane is necessary for most audio editing workflows.

1   In the toolbar, click each of the three pane buttons, or hold Control and press the A,
    S, or D keys until only the left pane is open.

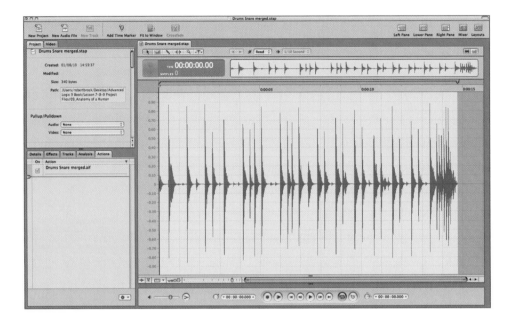

Because you're now working in a different program, volume levels may be different than what you were accustomed to in Logic. To be safe it's best to start with a low playback level.

2   Lower the playback volume using the Monitor Volume slider.

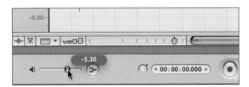

3   Press the Spacebar to toggle playback, and adjust the Monitor Volume slider to your liking.

4   Press Return to move the playhead to the beginning.

> **NOTE** ▸ If you don't hear sound, it's most likely because Soundtrack Pro is assigned to a different audio interface than Logic. To fix this, go to Soundtrack Pro > Preferences. In the Recording tab, select the desired audio interface from the Monitor pop-up menu.

TIP ▶ Soundtrack Pro uses the J, K, and L keys to scrub audio back and forth.

5 Press Return to bring the playhead to the beginning.

The upper-left corner of the Waveform Editor displays a list of tools similar to those found in Logic.

6 Click the Zoom tool (Z).

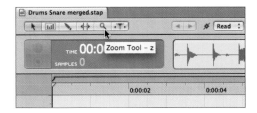

Zooming with the Zoom tool works differently in Soundtrack Pro than in Logic.

7 With the Zoom tool, either click or drag around a section of the waveform to zoom in.

8 Hold Option and click the waveform to zoom out.

You can also drag the Zoom slider at the bottom of the waveform area as an alternate way to zoom.

9 Zoom to display the first five seconds of the waveform.

Editing in Soundtrack Pro

In this exercise you'll use Soundtrack Pro's ability to apply effects on selected parts of a file. You'll use this to create a long reverb tail on a single snare hit.

1 Click the Selection tool (A), and then select the snare drum that occurs about two seconds in.

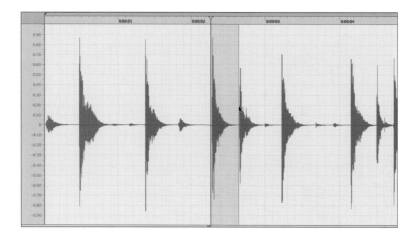

2   Press the Spacebar to hear your selection looped over and over.

3   Press Spacebar again to stop.

4   In the main menu bar, choose Process > Effects > Reverb > Space Designer.

This is the same Space Designer found in Logic. Most of Logic's effects plug-ins are available in Soundtrack Pro; however, in Logic's channel strips, plug-ins work in real-time whereas effects you choose via Soundtrack Pro's Process menu are applied to the file.

5   Double-click the Decay Time value and enter 5. Press Return.

6   Move the Rev slider to the top to increase the volume of the reverb.

7   Click Apply.

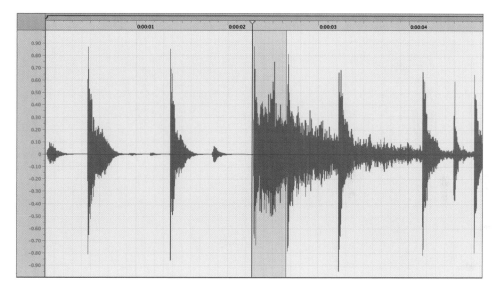

You'll notice that the waveform rebuilt itself, and you can clearly see that the reverb affects the waveform beyond the original selection area. In this case only the snare was used to create the reverb, but the 5-second-long reverb tail is mixed back with the original dry snare sounds.

8   Click toward the beginning of the waveform to clear your selection, move the play-head, and then play the file.

Using Frequency Spectrum View
Although you can clearly see the result of the effect of the reverb in the waveform, you'll now use a unique way to look at your sound that is not available in Logic.

1   In the upper-right corner, click the Frequency Spectrum view button.

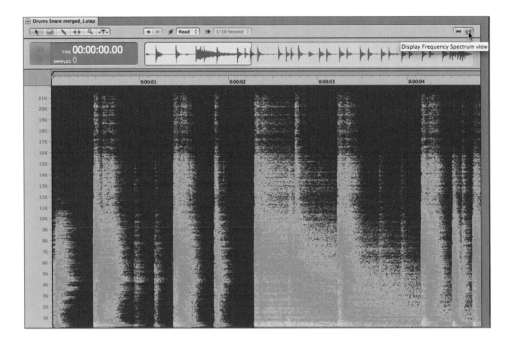

This view shows amplitude with color. Yellows and reds are louder, greens are soft, and blue represents no sound at all. To the left there is a scale that shows the frequency of sound that relates to the colors. The default scale that Soundtrack Pro uses is not very musical, with most of the information that we recognize as pitch being represented in the bottom few percent of the scale.

2 Control-click the Frequency scale on the left and choose Logarithmic from the shortcut menu.

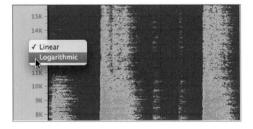

Now you can begin to see the red colors at around 200 Hz representing the snare drums' loudest frequencies.

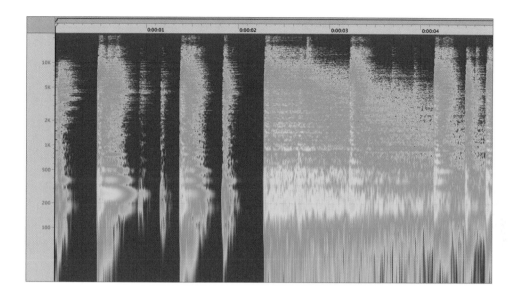

3 Scroll to the right and select the snare hit that occurs a little more than halfway between the 9-and 10-second mark.

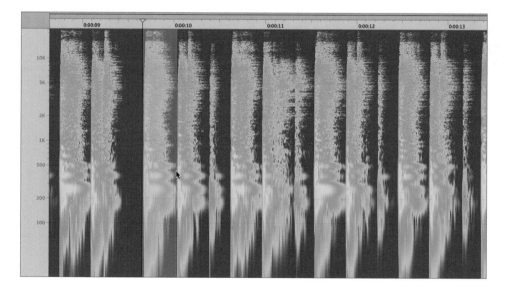

4 As before, choose Process > Effects > Reverb > Space Designer, and then set a 5-second decay and maximum reverb level. Click Apply.

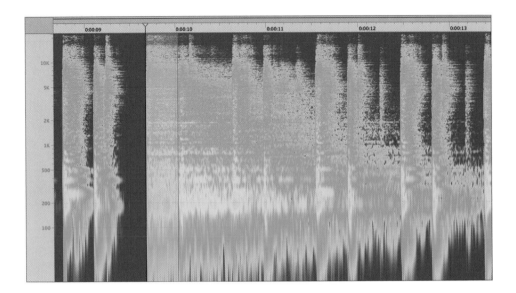

The visual result of the reverb is obvious.

5 Listen to playback.

> **TIP** Not only can you see specific frequencies, but you can select specific frequencies with the Frequency Selection tool, found to the right of the Selection tool. Although you can't apply signal processors to specific frequencies, you can delete, copy, and paste selected frequencies. It is an excellent tool for removing clicks and pops with minimal impact to the rest of the audio signal.

In Soundtrack Pro's lower-left corner, the Actions tab shows every change made to the file in the order in which they were done. At any time you can bypass an edit by clicking the checkbox next to the action. Regardless of when you made the edit, Soundtrack Pro will immediately render the waveform as if you had never performed that action. You'll now remove the last reverb you applied.

6 Click the checkbox on the second Space Designer button in the Actions list.

The reverb on the snare is removed.

7   Return to a waveform display by clicking the Waveform view button.

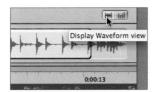

You are returned to a waveform display in the editor.

Working with Multiple Audio Files

Soundtrack Pro can easily manage working with multiple audio files. Tabs at the top of the Waveform display allow you to quickly switch between audio file projects. Soundtrack Pro even lets you quickly copy and paste information between audio file projects. Using this capability you'll create a reverse reverb effect that builds energy towards the end of the file.

1   Make sure the snare is still selected, and in the main menu bar choose File > New > File From Selection.

Soundtrack Pro creates a completely new audio file project, indicated by the Untitled tab above the Waveform Editor.

Your Drums Gtr Solo project is still active on the tab to the left, and you'll jump back to it after you edit the individual snare hit. By default, you're zoomed so far out that you can hardly tell there is audio in the Waveform Editor, so you'll need to take a closer look.

2   Choose View > Fit to Window or press Shift-Z.

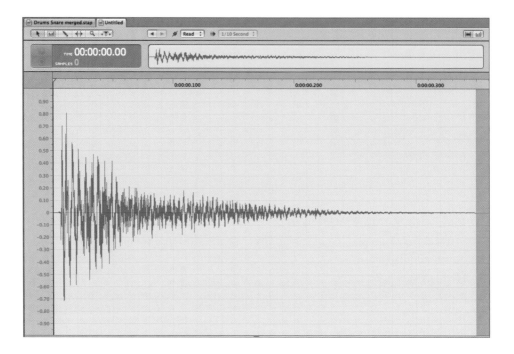

3   Press Command-A to select the entire snare hit.

4   Choose Process > Space Designer.

You'll use the same settings as before, except this time you'll remove all the dry signal so that only the reverb remains.

5   Change the decay time to 5 seconds, turn the reverb level all the way up, and completely turn down the dry level. Click Apply.

Now you're going to reverse the reverb tail.

6 Press Shift-Z to zoom to fit the waveform in the editor, and press Command-A to select all.

7 In the main menu bar, choose Process > Reverse.

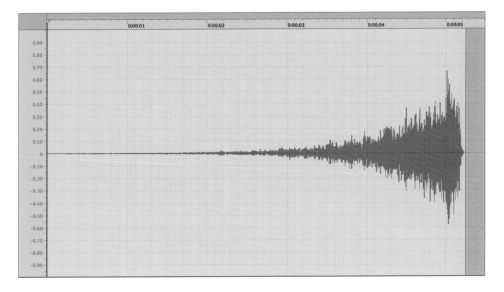

8 Play the file.

You're now going to copy the reverse reverb back into the Drums Snare merged.stap file.

9 Press Command-A to select all, and then press Command-C to copy the reverse reverb into the clipboard.

10 Click the Drums Snare merged.stap tab.

The original Drums Snare merged file appears in the editor, and the snare hit just before 10 seconds is still selected. In order to mix the clipboard contents into this file, you must select the entire area that should include the reversed snare.

11 Press Shift-Z to zoom out on the entire file, and then drag a selection from the currently selected snare hit through the end of the file.

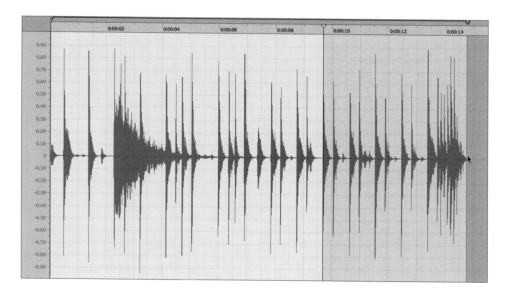

12 In the main menu bar, choose Edit > Paste Special > Paste Mix.

A dialog opens that lets you mix the audio copied into the clipboard with the audio in the file.

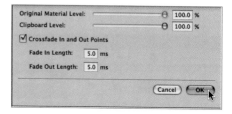

In this case you want the original material and the reverse snare reverb to be mixed together equally, so accept the defaults.

13 Click OK.

You can see the waveform change to reflect where the reverse reverb sound reaches its apex at the end of the file.

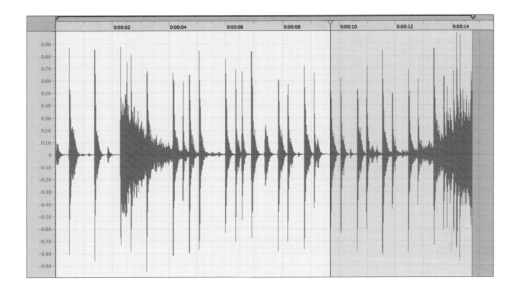

14 Press Shift-Command-A to deselect the entire waveform.

15 Press Return to move the playhead to the beginning, and then play the Drums Snare merged file.

You can hear the reversed reverb effect build towards the end of the file.

Seeing Soundtrack Pro Edits in Logic

The edits that have been made in Soundtrack Pro have yet to be rendered to the Drums Snare merged file that Logic is referencing. You only need to save your changes in Soundtrack Pro in order to update the file before returning to Logic.

1 Choose File > Save or press Command-S.

2 Press Command-Tab to go back to Logic.

Logic immediately updates the Drums Snare merged waveform.

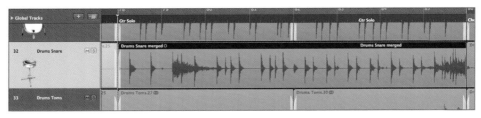

3 Play the song at the Gtr Solo section with the Drums Snare track soloed and unsoloed to hear how your Soundtrack Pro edits sound in Logic.

4 Click Stop.

You've now completed a roundtrip of the Logic Pro/Soundtrack Pro editing process by modifying the snare part with a series of edits that would have been much more difficult using Logic Pro alone.

Replacing Drums

The kick drum track in this song is, for the most part, a static four on the floor pattern very popular in electronic music, but the acoustic sound of the drum doesn't lend itself to that style. You'll remedy this by turning each kick hit into a MIDI note message using Logic 9's new Drum Replacement/Doubling feature. Once converted, the resulting MIDI events will trigger an electronic kick drum sample to give the pulse of this song an even stronger foundation.

1 Solo the Drums Kick track header, and then audition a short section in Chorus 1.

Drum replacement/doubling works at the track level and not just the regions, so you need to be sure the desired track header is selected.

2 Click the Drums Kick track header.

3 In the Arrange area's local menu, choose Track > Drum Replacement/Doubling.

A number of things happened all at once. The Drum Replacement/Doubling dialog appeared. The Library opened in order to let you quickly choose the type of drum sound you want to hear. The Drums Kick track automatically zoomed in vertically in order to let you more easily identify the transient positions that are used to generate MIDI notes. Lastly, an entirely new software instrument track (using an EXS24 software instrument) called Drums Kick + was created with a new region that contains MIDI notes for each drum hit that was detected.

NOTE ▸ The Drum Replacement/Doubling dialog is a floating window that will remain on top of the Arrange window. You can still make adjustments such as zoom settings in the Arrange window while the Drum Replacement/Doubling dialog is open. For the following lesson steps, you may need to move the Drum Replacement/Doubling dialog depending on your screen layout.

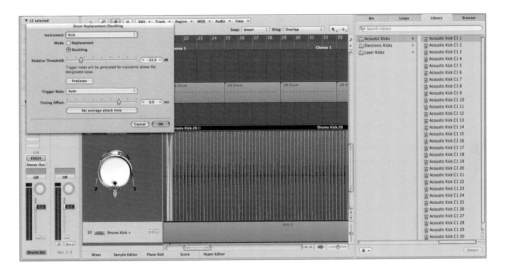

With all these options, you may feel like you don't know where to start. Begin by helping Logic determine where to create MIDI notes that represent the original kick drums.

In the Drums Replacement/Doubling dialog, the Instrument parameter is used as a preset to automatically choose a Relative Threshold, MIDI note number assignment, and EXS24 library presets for the sound that will be used. In this case the default Kick setting is appropriate.

Relative Threshold sets the minimum amount of amplitude needed to trigger a note. There is a preset value, but you'll likely need to adjust the Relative Threshold control to tailor the selection based on the volume of transients on the recording. Yellow lines represent positions where notes have been created. As you adjust this setting, the yellow lines will appear or disappear on the Drums Kick track.

4   Slide the Relative Threshold control all the way to the left and then back to the right.

As you moved left, you lowered the threshold for transient detection, creating yellow lines that represent where MIDI notes will be placed to trigger a drum sample.

Ideally you want one yellow line for each kick you see in the waveform, but you're zoomed too far out to visually confirm that the threshold setting is at an appropriate value.

5   With the Drum Replacement/Doubling dialog open, zoom on a drum region near bar 54 so that you can clearly see each kick transient.

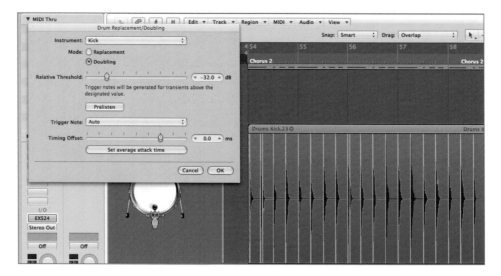

Now that you can more clearly see the transients of each kick drum, gradually lower the threshold until you see a yellow line at each kick transient. Because the Relative Threshold setting impacts the entire track, you may need to scroll the Arrange area window left and right to see if the setting is low enough to pick up all the kick hits.

6   Slide the Relative Threshold parameter to −32.

A problem with setting the threshold low enough to pick up all the kick hits is that it can sometimes detect unwanted material and create doubled notes on single instrument hits.

There is clearly an unwanted double detection on the first two kicks of bar 54 as well as elsewhere in the track. It's better to set the threshold low and generate extra notes, because editing out unwanted notes is much easier than creating missing notes.

Now you can select the kick sound you want to trigger from the Library.

7   In the Library, click the Electronic Kicks folder and select Electronic Kick C1 55.

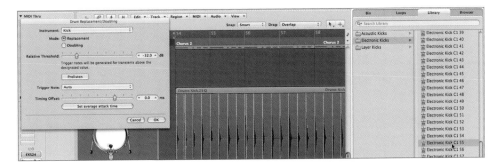

Now you need to hear the kick sound you selected in context. Although the Prelisten button in the dialog will accomplish this, it will begin playback based on the playback prioritization discussed in Lesson 7. In this instance the playhead would move to the beginning of the song where there are no kick drums. Instead, you can double-click the lower part of the Bar ruler to start and stop prelisten anywhere in the song. While listening, you can also click the Solo buttons on the original Drums Kick and Drums Kick + track headers to hear how the triggered kick sounds by itself, with the original kick, or in context with the entire song. You can also use the Arrange channel strip to blend the two kicks together.

8   With the Drum Replacement/Doubling dialog open, double-click the Bar ruler to stop and start playback. Try soloing the Drums Kick and Drums Kick + track headers.

NOTE ▸ The Timing Offset parameter should be placed at 0.0 unless there is a noticeable delay between the original and sampled drum.

9 Now that you've heard the results, you need to decide if you want to double or replace the original kick region. The only difference is that selecting replace will mute the original kick region. Since you're going for an electronic feel, you'll replace the kick.

NOTE ▶ The Trigger Note assignment determines the MIDI note number that will be used. If this parameter is set to auto, the value in the drum type selected in the Instrument parameter will be used to automatically generate an appropriate note number that corresponds with the General MIDI drum map.

10 Select the Replacement option and click OK.

A new region is created on the Drums Kick + track just below the original audio region, and the regions on the Kick Drums regions are muted.

11 Zoom the new region near bar 21 to see how the MIDI notes shown in the region align to the transients of the kick drum.

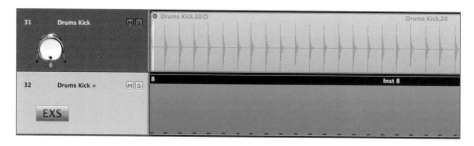

To avoid confusion, name the new region to be the same as the Drums Kick + track header.

12 With the new region selected, choose Region > Name Regions by Tracks / Channel Strips.

Now you need to correct the problem of the doubled kicks. Logic's Event List editor is an ideal place to address this.

13 In the toolbar, click the Lists button. Click the Event tab if it's not already selected.

14 Scroll down the list until you see bar 54.

The note event at 54 1 1 102 and 54 2 1 126 represent just two of the notes that were incorrectly assigned to the kick drum, producing a doubled kick sound that shouldn't be there.

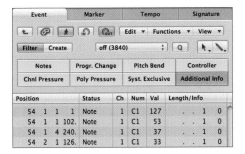

Logic has a specific command for removing doubled notes, but in order for it to work, both notes must occur at the exact same location. To get the doubled notes to completely overlap the correct note, you'll quantize the entire region.

15 Press Command-A to select all events, and then set the quantization menu to 1/8-Note.

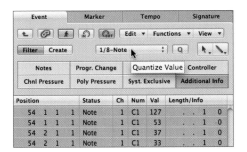

Now you see two note events at 54 1 1 1 as well as 54 2 1 1. Leaving two notes to play at the same moment can lead to subtle phase cancellation problems, so you'll delete one note anytime there are two notes at the same position.

16 In the Event List's local menu, choose Functions > Delete MIDI Events > Duplicates.

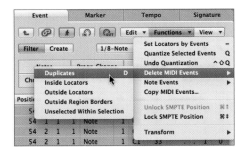

All doubled kicks are removed, but in some cases the kick with the lower velocity value was left. The number in the Val column represents the velocity of the first note, and as you can see the velocities vary from note to note. To create an electronically programmed feel for the kick drum, you're going to change all the velocities to the same value with a key command that is only available in the Event List.

17   Scroll to the top of the Event List and press Shift-Command-A to deselect all notes.

18   Press Shift-Command-A to deselect all notes. Double-click the 127 value for the first event, enter *120*, and press Return.

You changed the velocity of the first event, and because the other events in the list were also selected, you also changed them on a relative scale. You need to set all the other note events to the same value as the first note you just changed.

19   Press Shift-V to use the Copy Value to All Following Events command.

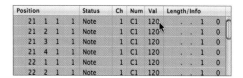

Now all the electronic kicks have consistent velocity throughout the project, helping to solidify the pulse of the project.

TIP ▶ The Copy Value to All Following Events command also works when changing other values in the Event List such as note number or length.

Lesson Review

1.   How can you smooth transitions between edited regions?

2.   How can you eliminate clicks and pops within an audio file?

3.   How can you create new parts from existing material?

4.   How can you edit multiple tracks of a drum recording?

5.   How can you quantize an acoustically recorded drum kit?

6.   How can you quickly replace bad sections of audio with good sections?

7.   What features exist within Soundtrack Pro that are not found in Logic?

8.   How do you move audio edited in Soundtrack Pro back to Logic?

9.   How can you replace the sound of a drum instrument?

Answers

1. Smooth transitions with crossfades. To accomplish this for large numbers of regions, set crossfade parameters in the Region Parameter box.

2. In the Sample Editor, zoom in on the waveform and draw out the click with the Pencil tool.

3. Pack a take folder of selected regions and then use Quick Swipe Comping to edit the parts together.

4. Using Mixer groups, create an Edit group with phase-locked editing enabled.

5. Assign drum tracks to a phase-locked edit group and then enable quantization parameters in the Region Parameter box.

6. Cut and paste material using marquee selections that are precisely tuned using the Snap to Transient commands.

7. Actions, Paste Mix, and Frequency Spectrum view.

8. Save over the exported audio file, making sure the file type and bit depth match the original.

9. Apply the Drum Replacement/Doubling command to convert audio tracks into a MIDI track that will trigger sampled instruments.

9

Lesson Files
Media
Time
Goals

Advanced Logic 9_Files > Lessons > 09_Anatomy of a Human Bomb_Start

Advanced Logic 9_Files > Media > Anatomy of a Human Bomb

This lesson takes approximately 60 minutes to complete.

Utilize aliases to repeat performances in other parts of the project

Edit regions by applying playback parameters

Use quantization techniques to change the rhythmic feel

Use specialized selection techniques to edit MIDI events

Modify MIDI data using the Transform window

Split multipart MIDI regions into individual parts for editing

Advanced MIDI Editing

At its heart, MIDI is a command protocol consisting of status messages that indicate when and how events are performed. While digital and analog audio represent actual sound, MIDI data numerically represents the actions that create or control sound generation. As a result, MIDI editing can be somewhat counterintuitive.

Logic provides similar editing tools and parameters for both MIDI and digital audio recordings, especially at the region level (for example, for copying and dividing). However, editing the two differs significantly at the finer, note level.

Even considering Logic's powerful digital audio tools, MIDI still has a distinct advantage when it comes to editing, offering extreme flexibility through real-time and nondestructive processing of all data.

In this lesson, you will use several methods of creating expressive musical parts out of existing material, and you will learn selection and editing techniques that enable you to work efficiently at the note level.

Using Aliases

An alias in Logic functions much as it does in the Finder; it is a reference to another region. It does not contain any actual data but refers to the content of the original item from which it was created. Like the repeated segments of a looped region, aliases update themselves when the original region is modified, but aliases have the added flexibility to be freely moved anywhere in the timeline or even to other tracks independent of the original region. In this exercise you'll convert looped regions into aliases and copy those aliases to another track in order to layer the strings with another sound.

1   Go to Advanced Logic 9 > Lessons and open **09_Anatomy of a Human Bomb_Start.logic**.

The project opens with a cycle region around Chorus 3. The Strings region at bar 86 is selected and its contents are shown in the Piano Roll Editor. Notice that the looped region repeats the 2-bar Strings region until the end of Chorus 3.

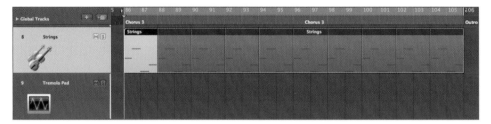

2   Play the song in Chorus 3 and toggle Solo on the Strings track header to listen to the Strings region by itself and with the rest of the tracks.

In order to have more flexibility with the Strings region, you'll now convert the loops into aliases.

3   In the arrange area's local menu, choose Region > Loops > Convert to Aliases.

The name and information displayed in the alias is italicized. The information listed after the arrow in the alias refers to the region name and track number from which it was derived.

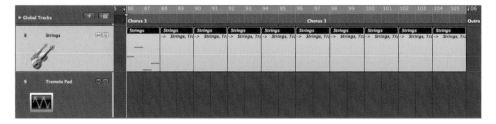

You can easily double the string part with another instrument by copying one of the aliases.

NOTE ▶ In this version of the Anatomy of a Human Bomb project, the Tremolo Pad track has already been added for you.

4   Press Shift-Command-A to clear the current selection, and then hold Option while dragging any of the aliased regions to bar 86 of the Tremolo Pad track.

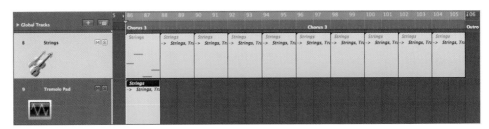

5   Choose Region > Repeat Regions, and in the Number of Copies field enter 9. Click OK.

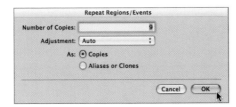

NOTE ▶ Because the region being repeated is already an alias, it doesn't matter in the dialog window if you select Copies or "Aliases or Clones."

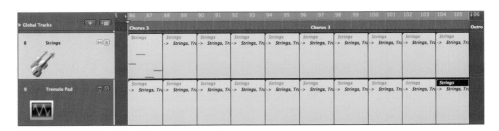

6   Use the Solo buttons on the Strings and Tremolo Pad track headers to listen to the tracks as well as in context with the rest of the mix.

The string line consists of four notes that ascend in pitch; however, the pitch of the last two notes of the phrase stand out a little too much in the mix. You can quickly resolve this issue by editing those notes using the Piano Roll Editor.

Although your intent is to edit the original Strings region, in large projects that region may be difficult to find. Double-clicking any aliased region will provide the option of either editing the original region the alias references or converting the alias to copy.

7   Double-click any of the aliased regions, and then click the Original button in the resulting dialog.

The Piano Roll Editor opens in the bottom of the Arrange window.

8   In the piano roll, select all four notes in bar 55 and then drag them down one octave (−12 notes).

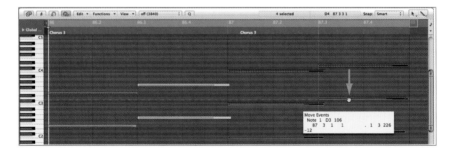

9   Close the Piano Roll Editor, and then play the song.

All the aliased Strings regions on both the Strings and Tremolo Pad track play the last half of the phrase in a lower octave.

10 Turn off Solo on the String and Tremolo Pad tracks and listen to the new part with the rest of the song before clicking Stop.

As you can see, aliases are extremely effective when you want to repeat a theme throughout a project but retain the ability to make changes to that theme later in production.

Working with Region Parameters

MIDI regions are data containers that hold various types of MIDI events. The events in a MIDI region can be altered individually using one of Logic's MIDI editors (Piano Roll Editor, Event List, Hyper Editor, Transform window, and so on) or altered all at once using the Region Parameter box.

The Region Parameter box gives you access to a variety of parameters that affect the data in MIDI regions. These functions invite experimentation, as they are entirely nondestructive, and the MIDI data can be returned to an unaltered state at any time. Think of these parameters as filters that can be applied to single or multiple MIDI regions in varying degrees of intensity, without permanently altering the data.

In this series of exercises, you'll be making changes to region parameters on the fly so you can instantly hear the result of your work. Start and stop playback and solo tracks as you feel the need.

Transposing Regions

Note events in any MIDI region can be transposed all at once by changing the Transpose parameter in the Region Parameter box.

You'll help add a bit of energy leading up to the outro by transposing the aliased String and Tremolo Pad regions you created in the last exercise up one octave.

> **NOTE ▸** With exception to quantization settings, region parameters on alias regions can be set independently from the region they reference.

1   Select the regions on the Strings and Tremolo Pad tracks starting at bar 102 through the end of the song.

Four regions on two tracks are selected.

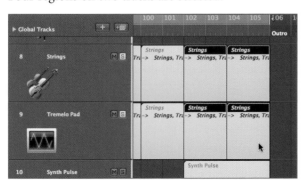

Region parameters can be applied to single regions and also to multiple regions simultaneously. When doing so, the Region Parameter box displays the number of selected regions that will be affected by the parameter adjustments. In this case, instead of displaying the name of the individual selected region, the box displays "4 selected."

2   In the Region Parameter box, hold the mouse just to the right of the Transposition parameter and drag the mouse up until the value reaches +12, or click the double-arrows to the right and choose the same value from the octave menu.

3   Play the song just before the selected regions and listen for the transposed strings.

> **TIP** ▸ The settings in the Region Parameter box can also be applied to incoming MIDI signals. This is done by changing settings when no region is selected (the box reads "MIDI Thru" instead of a region name). Once the recording is complete, the resulting region inherits the same parameter settings as MIDI Thru.

Modifying Velocities in a MIDI Region

In Lesson 8, you converted an audio recording in the Drums Kick track to MIDI. This created varying velocity values for each drum hit that resulted in more dynamic change than in the original performance. Rather than setting all the kick velocities to the same value (as you did in the last lesson), in this lesson you'll limit the range of velocity values for the kick drum notes in order to control the dynamics while still providing a degree of expression that reflects how the drummer played the part.

The Velocity and Dynamics parameters provide a fast way to alter all note velocity values in a region. The Velocity parameter simply offsets note velocities. The Dynamics parameter also acts on MIDI note velocities, but—instead of adding or subtracting a fixed value—it scales the difference between the highest and lowest velocity values. In this way, it functions similarly to the way a compressor or expander acts on the dynamics of an audio signal, increasing or decreasing the dynamic range for the selected MIDI region.

When applying a value larger than 100 percent, the differences between "soft" and "loud" notes are increased (as they would be by an expander), and they are decreased with values of less than 100 percent (as they would be by a compressor).

1   Scroll down to display the Drums Kick + track, and then Option-click the Solo button on the Drums Kick + Track, turning off all other solos.

2   Play from the beginning of Chorus 3.

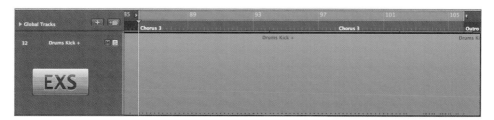

3   Click the Drums Kick + region to select it. In the Region Parameter box, choose Fixed from the Dynamics menu.

Fixed sets the notes to a velocity of 64, producing a consistent timbre and volume.

4   Change the Dynamics setting to 50%.

Now the difference between the highest and lowest velocities is half what it was before, creating a kick part that maintains the accents and nuances of the original performance but keeps the volume and tone more consistent.

Although the kick part is more consistent, it is also a bit quieter. As with the makeup gain in a compressor, you can correct this by raising the velocity values with the Velocity parameter.

5   Drag the Velocity parameter up to +20.

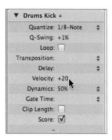

6   Listen to the Drums Kick region in context with the rest of the song and adjust the
    Dynamics and Velocity parameter to your liking.

    NOTE ▸ Settings made in the Region Parameter box, with the exception of Loop and
    Quantize, aren't reflected in the editors. The changes take effect during playback.
    These changes can also be written permanently to the region: In the Arrange area's
    local menu bar, choose MIDI > Region Parameters > Normalize Region Parameters.

Using Delay to Adjust the Feel

The Delay parameter is used to move a region forward or backward in time. By choosing
a positive value, you can delay the playback of a region, achieving a laid-back or dragging
feel. Negative values push the region earlier, creating a rushing or driving feel in relation
to the beat.

The current project's musical material warrants a driving rhythm, especially in the drums.
You can use the Delay setting on the Drums Kick + region in order to further push the
energy of the song.

1   Play the project, listening to how the Drums Kick + works with the rhythm section.

    Delay settings can be displayed in ticks (the smallest possible bar subdivision or
    system quantization), note values, or milliseconds. Most people who have worked
    with digital delay devices are used to thinking in terms of milliseconds, so switch the
    default setting of ticks to milliseconds before changing the Delay setting.

2   In the Arrange area's local menu bar, choose View > Delay in ms.

3   In the Region Parameter box, click the arrows to the right of the Delay parameter to
    open the Delay pop-up menu and choose 1/192 = 9.6.

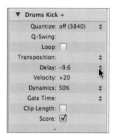

TIP Logic automatically converts musical time increments like you just saw in the Delay pop-up menu into milliseconds based on the tempo of your project. Therefore projects with different tempos will show different millisecond values. To further refine the delay setting, you can adjust in half-millisecond intervals by dragging up or down in the blank space to the right of the Delay parameter.

By selecting this value, you are advancing the playback of the Drums Kick + region by a 1/192 note, or 9.6 milliseconds.

4   Play the project from Chorus 3, and disable Solo in the Drums Kick + track header to hear how the kick drum plays in the arrangement so you can continue to adjust the delay parameter to your liking.

TIP The Delay parameter always displays in musical values in addition to ms or ticks, ranging from 1 bar of delay to a 1/4 note of advance. This is especially useful for creating echo effects between regions of similar content on separate tracks.

Using Gate Time to Alter Articulation

The Gate Time parameter directly affects the length of MIDI events, but not in the way that you might expect. Instead of uniformly decreasing or increasing the length of all MIDI events in a region, the Gate Time parameter changes notes by a percentage of their lengths, thereby allowing you to adjust the articulation of a performance from, say, staccato to legato.

The first region on the Bass Synth track needs a little tightening up, as the longer notes sustain a bit too long, bleeding into the shorter ones. By adjusting their lengths with the Gate Time parameter, you can modify the length of notes to change the articulation of the performance.

1   Select the first region in the Bass Synth track, displaying it in the Region Parameter box.

2   Press Shift-Spacebar to set the cycle region around the Bass Synth region, and then
    press S to engage Solo mode.

    To clearly hear the effect of the Gate Time parameter, you can test an extreme setting
    and observe the results.

3   In the Region Parameter box, click to open the Gate Time pop-up menu and choose
    Fixed.

    Each note is played with the shortest possible duration, creating an extremely staccato
    performance.

4   Click to open the Gate Time pop-up menu and choose 50%.

    All events are adjusted to 50 percent of their length, creating an articulate
    performance.

    Now you'll create a legato feel.

5   Click the Gate Time pop-up menu and choose Legato.

    Each note's duration extends to the beginning of the next note, creating a fluid bass
    line that sounds appropriate for this part of the song.

6   Press S to disengage Solo mode, and then stop playback.

Correct and Modify Rhythm with Quantize

Just as musical rhythm is expressed in relation to the grid formed by beat and meter, so
sequencers map MIDI event timings to a grid determined by a base resolution provided
by the software application. To ensure that the placement of an event in time is as accurate
as possible, Logic offers a resolution of a 1/3840 note (one tick).

This division allows for a vast range of rhythmical placement, but there will be occasions when you need to adjust the accuracy of events in relation to more musical divisions (eighth notes, sixteenth notes, triplets, and so on). This can be done with *quantization*, which compares events to a chosen resolution and then corrects their time placement by moving them to the nearest position on a beat/time grid.

Logic offers multiple ways of quantizing events, including adjusting the data in the Region Parameter box. In this exercise, you'll check out the aural and visual effects on note events when quantizing by correcting the timing of the Mallet-Bell region that plays in the intro.

1 Double-click the Mallet-Bell region at bar 1.

The Piano Roll opens.

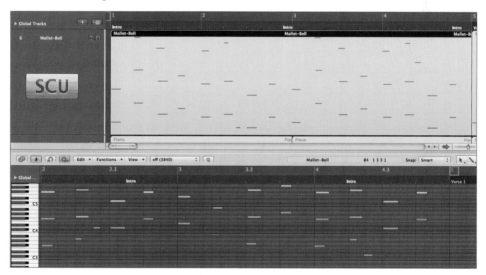

Adjustments to Quantization parameters are visually reflected in the editors, so keep your eye on the Piano Roll Editor to see how the changes you're about to make affect the note positions.

2 Engage Solo mode by pressing S. Press Shift-Spacebar to set the cycle area around the Mallet-Bell and start playback.

You can hear the rhythmic unevenness in the Mallet-Bell part.

To more easily see the changes you're going to make, you'll need zoom in a little closer.

3   In the Piano Roll Editor, zoom in on the notes that play in the first two measures.

Notice that most of the notes are played late and clearly not aligned to the grid lines that represent quarter-note divisions.

Although the Mallet-Bell line is primarily playing a quarter-note pattern, a few eighth-note pickups are played, so you will need to choose an eighth-note quantization value in order to avoid having those pickups rounded to quarter-note positions.

There are many variations of eighth-note quantization settings, of which all but one are intended for the purpose of swinging the eighth-note feel.

4   While keeping your eye on the Mallet-Bell part in the Piano Roll Editor, click to open the Quantize menu and choose 8F Swing.

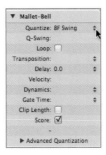

You can hear and see that the pickup notes in bars 2 and bar 4 have been shifted later in time to create a swing feel.

TIP ▸ Swing settings for both eighth and sixteenth note feels are available with letters from A to F that respectively increase the swing feel. Another way to get finer control over the intensity of the swing feel is to choose a Quantize parameter without swing and adjust the Q-Swing parameter. Values above 50% move every alignment gridline more to the right, and values below 50% move them more to the left.

In this case the part needs to be played with a straight feel.

5   Change the Quantize parameter to 1/8-Note.

The Mallet-Bell part is now played perfectly in time.

In some instances you may want to tighten the rhythm of a part, but you'll want to preserve some of the human feel. You can do this by correcting only the notes that are the most out of time. This is easily accomplished by using the Q-Strength parameter. This is an Advanced Quantization parameter, so you must first click the Advanced Quantization Parameter disclosure triangle to reveal this setting.

6   Click the Advanced Quantization disclosure triangle to display the Advanced Quantization parameters.

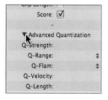

Q-Strength lets you choose just how much the Quantize setting pulls the start of each note to the timing grid. A value of 0% means quantizing has no effect; changing to higher percentages creates tighter timing. If no value is displayed next to the Q-Strength parameter, it is considered to be at 100%, and thus the notes are perfectly aligned to the timing grid.

7   Double-click the blank space to the right of the Q-Strength parameter and set the value to 50%.

The notes move to a position that is half the distance between the eighth-note grid lines and the notes' original position, tightening up the rhythm but still maintaining a human feel.

Using the Q-Range parameter it is also possible to include or exclude notes from quantization based on how close a note is to the quantization grid. This can be helpful when you only want to quantize the notes that were played the farthest out of time.

It's easiest to understand how Q-Range works by first looking at the region without the effects of quantization.

8 Turn the Q-Strength value down to 0%.

The notes revert to their originally played position.

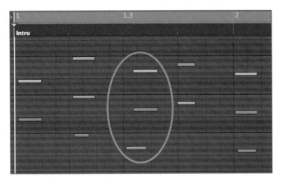

A three-note chord plays at bar 1 beat 3. The lowest note in the chord is fairly close to the beat grid line, but the top two notes are played considerably later.

9 Click the Q-Range pop-up menu and choose $-1/32 = -120$

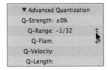

You won't see any change just yet because the Q-Strength is still set to 0%.

10 Drag the Q-Strength parameter back to 75%.

Only the top two notes in the chord move closer to the beat grid line. The lowest note is not affected.

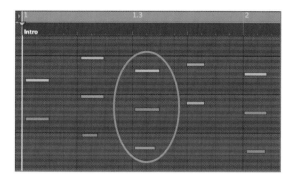

Because your setting has a negative value, only notes that were more than 1/32nd note away from the quantization grid line will be selected for quantization. If you had set the Q-Range settings using a positive value, only the notes that are less than 1/32nd note of the quantization grid line would be selected for quantizing.

TIP ▶ You can adjust Q-Range values in single tick increments by dragging up or down in the space next the to the Q-Range parameter.

Now that you understand how the Quantize, Q-Strength, and Q-Range parameters work and relate to each other, you can adjust these settings to create the feel you want for the Mallet-Bell region.

11 Adjust the Quantize, Q-Strength, and Q-Range settings for the Mallet-Bell region to your preference, and then click Stop.

Arpeggiating Chords with Q-Flam

The term *flam* is typically associated with hitting a drum with one stick just a moment before hitting it with the other to create a fatter sound. In Logic, the Q-Flam region parameter can be used to create a similar effect when multiple notes are positioned at the same exact point in time. Small values can be used to create subtle timing offsets between notes of a chord, while larger values can create arpeggio effects.

The Piano region at the beginning of the song plays blocks of chords. Because the notes were step recorded, you'll use Q-Flam to break the chords apart.

1 Select the first two Piano regions at the beginning of the song, and then press Shift-Spacebar to set the locators and play the regions.

You can clearly see in the Piano Roll that all the notes in each chord are played at the same time.

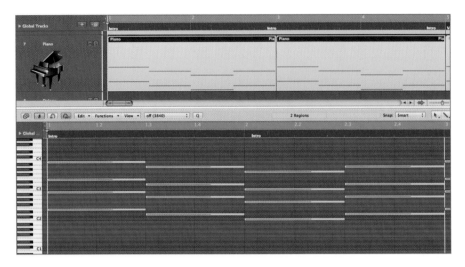

In order for Q-Flam to function, a quantize value must be selected in the Quantize parameter even when notes are already aligned.

2   In the Region Parameter box, set the Quantize parameter to 1/4-Note. Click to open the Q-Flam menu and choose 1/64.

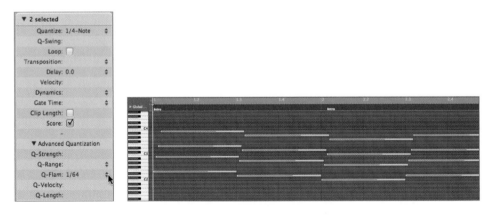

The chords sound more "rolled," and as you can see, each note in the chord plays 1/64th note after the previous one. Positive Q-Flam values create an ascending arpeggio (low notes play first) of the notes; negative values create a descending arpeggio.

Create more of a musical pattern by using larger values.

3   Change the Q-Flam value to –1/8, and then press S to turn off Solo mode to listen to the new part with the rest of the mix.

Now the piano part plays a descending eighth-note pattern that works nicely in the intro.

Using Template Parameters

In Lesson 2 you learned how to create groove templates from audio regions. In fact, all of Logic's Quantization settings are based upon similar premade templates that include timing as well as note velocity and length information that can be applied to the content of regions. You can tailor these templates to better match the region content by adjusting the Q-Velocity and Q-Length parameters.

The Q-Velocity and Q-Length parameters let you choose how closely you want those values in the selected region to match those of the groove template. These values are expressed as percentages, where 100 means that the velocity or length matches the template exactly.

In this exercise you'll adjust the settings of an eighth-note Synth line that was step recorded resulting in a lifeless feel. Using the Q-Velocity and Q-Length parameters, you'll modify the line to include rhythmic and dynamic accents.

1   Select the Synth Pulse region at bar 102, and then press Shift-Spacebar to set the locators and play the song in Solo mode.

Even though the notes are already aligned to the grid, you must first choose a Quantize parameter setting to serve as the map to which velocity and note lengths conform.

2   In the Region Parameter box, set the Quantize parameter to 1/8-Note and raise the Q-Velocity parameter to 100%.

As you raise the value, you can see in the Piano Roll how the original note velocities gradually change to the velocities provided by the 1/8-Note template. It's clear that the 1/8-Note template accents notes that fall directly on each beat.

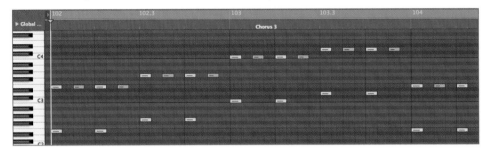

3   Raise the Q-Length parameter to 100%.

Notice how the 1/8-Note quantize template contains longer notes on the quarter-note positions as compared with the eighth-note positions.

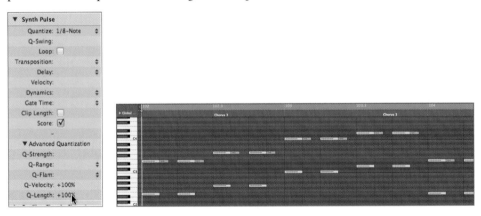

4   Stop playback.

TIP It is sometimes helpful to render the effect of region parameters to the MIDI events as if they had been recorded that way. This is especially useful to see the result of parameters that are not reflected in the editors such as Velocity and Delay settings. The Quantize settings can also be rendered into the region by choosing MIDI > Region Parameters > Apply Quantization Settings Destructively.

Selecting MIDI Events for Editing

Let's continue developing the Synth Pulse line by editing at a finer level: individual MIDI events. You can do this in any of Logic's MIDI editors, but the Piano Roll Editor works particularly well for quickly selecting and viewing region contents.

You'll be using a variety of specialized commands found in Logic's menus that work particularly well for music production workflows because of their ability to quickly select and edit information based on musical context.

The Synth Pulse part is an eighth-note pattern that alternates between an octave interval and single note. Your goal is to create a part that consists entirely of individual notes that toggle between an upper and lower pitch. You'll achieve this by using specialized commands to select and delete the top notes in each octave interval.

1   In the Piano Roll Editor's local menu, choose Functions > Note Events > Select Lowest Notes, or press Shift-Down Arrow.

   The lowest note of each octave interval is selected, as are the single notes played between the intervals.

   The notes you want to delete are in fact the notes that aren't currently selected, so you can simply invert your selection.

2   Choose Edit > Invert Selection, or press Shift-I, and then press Delete.

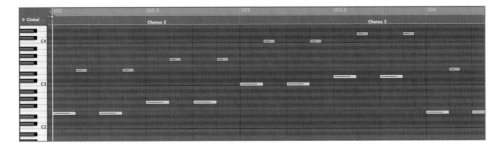

   The Synth Pulse now sounds more like an arpeggio.

   Now you'll make the phrasing sound more interesting by lengthening some of the upper notes.

3   Hold Shift and select the second and fourth green notes in bar 102.

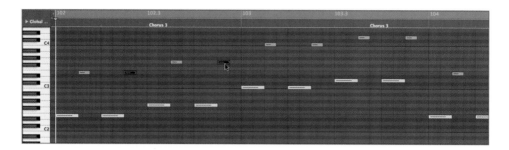

The goal is to select the remaining notes that happen in the same relative position, but this can be tedious to do manually. The Select Equal Subpositions command is a powerful tool that will select any other notes in the region that occur at the same position relative to the barline.

4   In the Piano Roll Editor's local menu, choose Edit > Select Equal Subpositions, or press Shift-P.

5   Choose Functions > Note Events > Note Force Legato (selected/any).

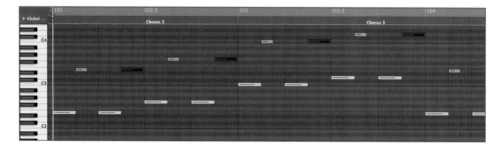

Each of the selected notes extends its length so that it ends when the next note begins.

6   Listen to the edit in the context of the mix.

Using Transform Functions

Transform functions are powerful selection and processing tools that allow you to manipulate all types of MIDI information in almost all conceivable ways. Each function employs a set of conditions and operations to specify exactly what data is selected and how it will be manipulated.

The functions can range from the simple to the complex. In this section, you will learn how to use one of the many preset transform functions, and you'll also create a custom transform set to use in your projects.

Working with Transform Sets

Transform sets are essentially transform function presets that can be accessed through the Transform window or through the local menus in any of the editors that can manipulate MIDI information. You'll familiarize yourself with how transform functions work by first working with a transform set.

Earlier in the lesson, you used the Q-Flam parameter to arpeggiate chords played by the piano in the intro. You'll now return to those regions to modify them to have a more human feel.

1   Select and audition the two Piano regions in the intro.

2   In the Piano Roll Editor, choose Functions > Transform > Humanize.

The Transform window opens.

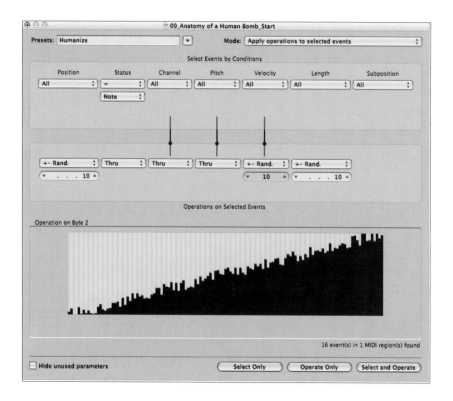

The Humanize function applies a slight randomization to events, creating a looser and more natural-sounding performance.

The Transform window is divided into three main sections: Select Events by Conditions, Operations on Selected Events, and Operation on Byte 2. Although these headings might sound a little confusing, they can be explained in a straightforward manner.

Basically, to use the transform functions on MIDI data, you must indicate exactly what you want to affect in the Select Events by Conditions section. Here, you specify the criteria of the desired target, whether you want a simple selection based on event type (or status) or a complex selection having multiple conditions (for example, events that have a specific length, position, and value).

The Operations sections indicate how you want to modify the selected MIDI events. This can be almost any kind of MIDI transformation you can dream up, even converting one type of event to another for further processing. With the Humanize transformation, for example, selected notes are randomized in position, velocity value, and length. Each transformation has a specific extent assigned to it, which can be anything from a single number or note to a range of operations. Here, the position, velocity, and length of the selected note events are randomized within a positive or negative range of 10 ticks.

The Operation on Byte 2 section is a graphical representation of the transformation itself and directly depicts the values for byte 2 of the MIDI event chosen in the Status column. (A MIDI channel voice message consists of a status byte followed by one or two data bytes.) In the case of note events, byte 2 is velocity; for controllers it is the value for the assigned controller.

All of this translates to a function that slightly varies note events, imparting a looser, more human feel.

3 At the bottom of the Transform window, click the "Select and Operate" button.

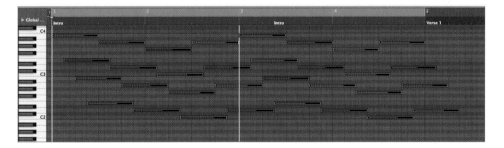

The note events displayed in the Piano Roll Editor change slightly in position, length, and velocity.

You can repeatedly click the "Select and Operate" button to further increase the amount of humanization that is applied. It's best to listen as you add more humanization, so this time you'll play back the part while making the changes.

NOTE ▶ If you feel like you've applied too much humanization, you can press Command-Z to undo the last operation.

4 Play the project and continue to click the "Select and Operate" button while listening to the effect. Continue clicking until you see blue colored notes in the Piano Roll Editor.

5 Play the project, listening to the "humanized" part.

Creating New Transform Functions

You probably noticed when navigating through the Transform menu that Logic offers numerous preset transform functions. These functions are capable of accomplishing many common MIDI editing tasks in an efficient manner. However, there will most likely be a time that you will need to create your own transform set to address a specific need, whether it be the quick selection of specific MIDI data for editing, or selecting and performing an operation on the MIDI data via a single step.

For this exercise, you will create a transform function designed to humanize only notes that are above the root note of the piano chords that begin at bar 5. With the lowest note of the chord anchored directly on the beat, this helps to preserve the tightness of the track even though the upper notes will be humanized and slightly out of time. In the last exercise you may have also noticed that after humanizing the piano, notes that had high velocities tended to stick out too much, and lower velocities may not have been loud enough. To address this you'll configure your transform set to only randomize velocities between a defined upper and lower range.

1   In the Arrange area, select the Piano region at bar 5 and audition it while cycling in Solo mode.

   Creating a new transform set is done in any open Transform window, whether opened in a MIDI editor or from the main Window menu.

2   In the main menu bar, choose Window > Transform.

   The Transform window opens, displaying the last selected preset (in this case, Humanize).

3   Click the disclosure triangle next to the Presets menu and choose **Create Initialized User Set**.

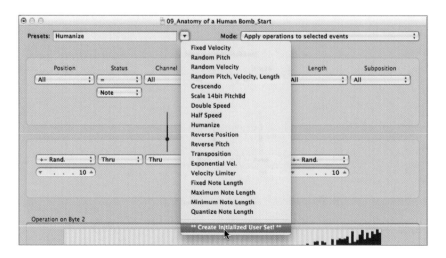

A dialog appears, asking if you'd like to create a new transform set or rename the current one.

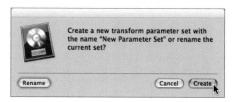

4   Click Create.

A new, blank transform set is created.

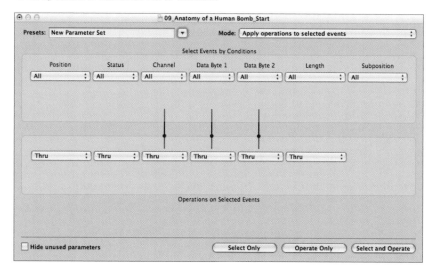

Notice that many more parameters are accessible (via pop-up menus) than there were when you opened the Humanize preset. This is because preset transform functions open with unused parameters hidden from view, presenting only the relevant parameters for selection or operation.

> **TIP** ▶ Preset transform functions will display all parameters if you deselect the "Hide unused parameters" checkbox in the lower-left corner of the Transform window. Having all parameters displayed allows you to further extend the capabilities of the preset by adding more selection and operation data.

5   Select the text in the Preset menu ("New Parameter Set") and enter *Custom Humanization*. Press Return.

A dialog appears, asking if you'd like to rename the current, empty set or create a new one.

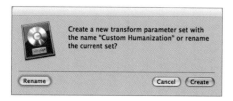

6 Click Rename.

When you create a new transform set, it is advisable to start off by defining just what you want to transform. In the Select Events by Conditions area, "All" is displayed by default for every parameter, signifying that no discrimination will be made when selecting MIDI data (all event types, positions, and channels will be selected). In order to narrow the focus of the selection, you need to specify the relevant parameters instead of leaving them in their default state.

It is best to start defining selection criteria by choosing the MIDI event type, which is done from the Status menu.

7 Click the Status pop-up menu and choose = (equal sign).

A new menu is created just below the option you chose, allowing you to specify the event type.

8 Click the new pop-up menu and choose Note.

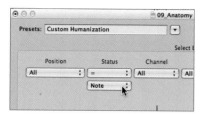

By specifying Note as the Status parameter, you are excluding all events but MIDI notes in the selection. This is still far too general a selection. The goal of the transform function is to select only the MIDI notes that have a pitch equal or higher than F2. In order to do this, you need to define further criteria in the selection parameters.

9 Click the Pitch pop-up menu and choose >= (greater than or equal to).

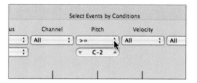

A value field appears below the menu. Entering a number in this value field defines a selection greater than or equal to the inputted number.

10 Double-click the number in the value field and enter *F2*. Press Return.

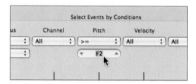

Now that your selection criteria are defined, you can specify what will happen to the selected data when the operation runs. This is done by choosing operations from the parameter menus in the Operations on Selected Events area.

11 In the Velocity column in the Operations on Selected Events area, click the pop-up menu to view the list of operations that can be performed (do not choose anything as of yet).

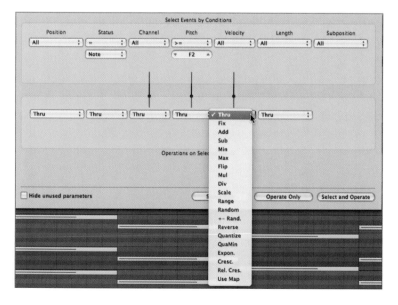

As you can see, there are many possibilities that can transform MIDI data in simple to complex ways.

MORE INFO ▶ Definitions of the available operations are provided in the Logic Pro 9 User Manual.

12 Choose Random from the Velocity pop-up menu.

Two value fields appear below the Random menu. Rather than randomize within a certain range from a note's current velocity value (as with the +- Rand setting used in the Humanize transform set), a randomly selected value between these two numbers will be applied irrespective of a note's original value. In this case you want a low number that will still produce a piano note that is loud enough, and a high number that won't trigger the fortissimo samples that stand out too much.

13 Double-click the Random value fields and enter *70* in the top (lower value) field and *115* in the bottom (higher value) field.

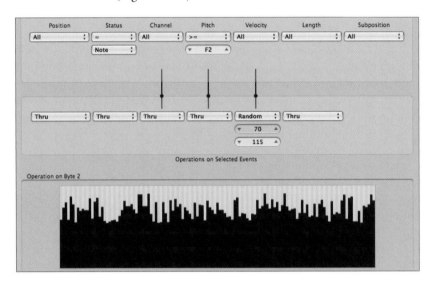

14 In both the Position and Length column in the Operations on Selected Events area, choose the +- Rand setting.

15 Change the value fields for both parameters to 20 ticks.

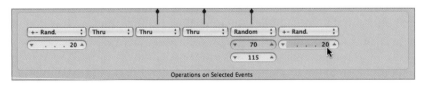

You have now created a new transform set that, when activated, will humanize the start and length of each note within 20 ticks of the current value, and randomly assign velocity values between 70 and 115 on any notes at or above F2.

16 Click the "Select and Operate" button.

All MIDI notes at F2 or higher have been humanized without risking the velocities being too low or too high.

17 Play the project, listening to the newly transformed MIDI data.

> **NOTE** ▶ If you want to select only specific MIDI data without processing, click the Select Only button. Likewise, you can also choose to process only previously selected MIDI data by clicking the Operate Only button, bypassing the selection criteria altogether.

Applying New Transform Sets

All newly created transform sets are immediately available in any MIDI editor's Functions > Transform menu. This puts your transform set creations within easy reach whenever you are editing MIDI data.

1 Close the Transform window, turn off Cycle mode, and in the Arrange area, select all the Piano regions from bar 7 through the end of the song.

2 Zoom out in the Piano Roll Editor so you can see all the Piano notes from the separate regions from bar 7 through the end of the song.

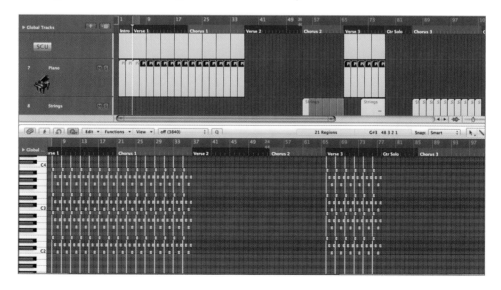

> **TIP** ▶ You can view more than one region's note data in the same Piano Roll Editor. The Piano Roll Editor (and other editors as well) will automatically display all selected regions. This can get a bit confusing when you're working with lots of events, so it helps to display each region's events with separate colors. To do this, first make sure that each region is colored differently in the Arrange area. Then, in the Piano Roll Editor's local menu bar, choose View > Region Colors.

3   From the Arrange area's local menu bar, choose MIDI > Transform > Custom Humanize.

The Transform window opens, displaying the transform set you created earlier.

4   Click the "Select and Operate" button.

All MIDI notes with velocity at or above F2 are humanized.

5   Close the Transform window.

6   Play the project from the beginning, listening to the newly transformed material in the context of the project.

> **TIP** ▶ Newly created transform functions are saved in the project file itself. In order to be able to use your newly created transform functions in other projects, you need to import them first. You can do this by choosing File > Project Settings > Import Settings and making sure that the Transform Sets checkbox is selected. Then select the project file where the new transform set resides and click the Open button.

Separating MIDI Events

It is not unusual to record MIDI drum parts by triggering multiple sounds in a single pass, creating a single region containing both the kick drum and snare parts. This technique can help create a track that locks into a groove. Having the kick drum and hi-hat on the same track, on the other hand, can make it more difficult to edit the parts using techniques learned in this lesson, and there's less flexibility when mixing.

Because a MIDI file transmits a stream of commands with discrete events, it allows for some fancy editing functions. One such function is Separate by MIDI Events, which enables you to break out a MIDI region into components based on specific criteria to separate regions on separate tracks. You can try this on the bass drum and hi-hat part, splitting them into separate tracks for independent editing.

1   Turn off Cycle mode and click the UB Drums track header to select all the regions on that track.

The Piano Roll Editor shows the upper hi-hat line with kick drum hits at the beginning and end of each region.

To separate the kick drum from the hi-hat, you must first combine the UB Drum regions into a single region, otherwise a new pair of tracks will be created for each of the current UB Drum regions.

2   Click the UB Drum track header, and in the Arrange area's local menu choose Region > Merge > Regions, or press Control-=.

When using the Separate By Note Pitch function, a new track and a new region are created for every note number found. In addition, the newly created tracks are automatically assigned to the same instruments as the original MIDI region.

3   In the Arrange area's local menu, choose MIDI > Separate MIDI Event > By Note Pitch.

A new track is created for each of the notes contained in the UB Drums region, and the UB Drums track is now empty and no longer necessary.

4   Select the empty UB Drums track header that is now empty and press Delete.

For easier identification, name the new tracks and regions with their corresponding instruments.

5   Double-click the Track header that contains the newly created regions and rename the first *UB Kick* and the second *UB Hi-Hat*.

6   Select both of the newly created regions and choose Region > Name Regions by Tracks/Channel Strips.

Lesson Review

1.   How are aliases used?

2.   What does the Region Parameter box do?

3.   How can you quickly modify the timing a MIDI region?

4.   What are the Q-Velocity and Q-Length parameters used for?

5.   What does the Invert Selection command do in a MIDI editor?

6.   What does the Select Equal Subpositions command do in a MIDI editor?

7.   Where can you access the transform functions?

8.   How are the transform functions useful?

9.   What does Separate by MIDI Events do?

Answers

1.   Aliases are used for duplicating material that needs to automatically update when the original is edited.

2.   The Region Parameter box allows real-time control over various playback parameters, enabling you to transpose and adjust the feel of events in a MIDI region.

3.   Select a Quantize setting to determine the timing grid that notes will be aligned to. Use the Q-Swing and Q-Strength to further refine how the notes are placed in relationship to the grid.

4.   Q-Velocity and Q-Length can be used to conform MIDI notes to the length and velocity values defined in a quantization template that is selected using the Quantize parameter.

5. The Invert Selection command selects all regions (in the Arrange area) or events (in a MIDI editor) that are not currently selected and deselects any regions or events that are selected.

6. The Select Equal Subpositions command selects all regions or events with a similar bar or beat relationship to the selection.

7. The transform functions can be accessed via the main Window menu, or via the Functions > Transform menu in all MIDI editors.

8. The transform functions contain many helpful operations for processing MIDI data, such as humanizing performances.

9. Separate by MIDI Events separates combined parts recorded in a single MIDI region into individual regions for further editing.

10

Managing the Mix

Logic provides dedicated channels for MIDI, audio, and software instruments. These channels are accessed via Logic's integrated Mixer, which shows them in an organized display.

Each channel offers a set of controls for working with the signal throughput (volume, pan, sends, and so on). These controls can be linked together so that groups of channels respond with the manipulation of a single control.

In this lesson you will use the Mixer to efficiently view and access the Mixer channels, as well as navigating plug-ins in the insert chain. In addition, you will utilize groups to link controls of multiple channels, helping you to streamline the mix process.

Importing Channel Strips and Data

New to Logic 9 is the ability to import both track content, channel strip configuration (including plug-ins and routings), and automation data from one project into another. This makes it easy to transfer mix and region data from sessions recorded at a separate place and time.

In this first exercise, you will open the project file you'll use throughout the lesson, and import additional data from another project file, adding it to the mix.

1   Choose File > Open.

2   In the file selector dialog, go to Music > Advanced Logic 9_Files > Lessons and open **10_I Was Raised_Start.logic**. The project file opens.

3   Play the project to familiarize yourself with the material, clicking the Stop button when you are finished.

A double-tracked guitar riff was recorded within a separate project in another studio. You can use Logic's import features to add these tracks into the open project, including the channel strips and automation.

4   Choose File > Import.

5   In the file selector dialog, go to Music > Advanced Logic 9_Files > Lessons and select **10_I Was Raised_Guitar.logic**.

NOTE ▸ The Open File menu at the bottom of the file Import window needs to be set to All Logic document types or Logic songs in order to select the project file.

6   Click Import. The Media area opens, displaying all the channels that are available for import from the selected project file.

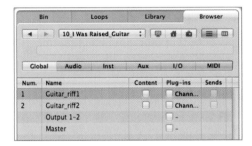

In the Browser tab, you can select what data you want to bring in from the imported tracks. This includes Content (region data and placement), Plug-ins, Sends, I/O, and Auto (automation data).

7   In both the Guitar_riff1 and Guitar_riff2 rows, select the Content, Plug-ins, I/O, and Auto checkboxes.

NOTE ▸ The Sends checkbox is dimmed because the imported channel strips from this project do not have an active send setting. If sends are imported, Logic will also create an aux that reflects the bussing of the original track, complete with inserts.

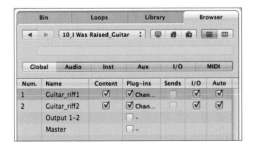

8   Click Add.

The two Guitar_riff tracks and channel strips are added to the project and are displayed in the Arrange window.

9   Close the Media area.

10   Select the Guitar_riff1 and Guitar_riff2 tracks in the Arrange track list, looking at their channel strips in the Inspector. Each channel strip is imported with both insert effects and volume information intact.

Working with the Mixer

The Mixer has three display modes that access the channels of a mix: Single view, Arrange view, and All view. Understanding how the three differ will help you navigate through your mix efficiently.

Using Arrange View

The Mixer's Arrange view is often referred to as an adaptive mixer. In this display mode, Logic creates a Mixer setup adapted from the Arrange area's track list, reflecting aspects such as track order, track names, and assigned colors. The Mixer's Arrange view will reflect the Arrange area's track list, even when new tracks are created and reordered.

The Mixer's default setting, Arrange view, will probably be the view you use most often when mixing, as it allows you to focus on those elements that are directly involved with the project's musical arrangement.

With the project open, you can observe firsthand the relationship between the Arrange area and the Mixer's Arrange view by rearranging the track order for a more ergonomic mixing setup.

1   Open Screenset 2.

This screenset contains an open Mixer with a small Arrange area (based on the template you created in Lesson 1).

2   In the Arrange area, use the vertical scroll arrows at the far right or the Up and Down
     Arrow keys on your keyboard to examine the tracks in the arrangement.

     NOTE ▶ If you are using a smaller screen resolution than 1140 x 900, it is possible
     that the vertical scroll arrows will be hidden from view. If this is the case, use the Up
     and Down Arrow keys to scroll through the track list instead.

     There are 29 tracks displayed vertically in the track list.

3   In the Mixer, use the scroller to examine the channels used for the project.

     This is a fairly large session, with 37 channel strips displayed side by side. Notice that
     the first 29 channel strips correspond to the tracks listed in the Arrange area's track
     list, in both order and number.

     NOTE ▶ The aux, output, and master channel strips are included because they are
     a part of the signal chain used by the Arrange area's tracks (including sends and
     returns, and master bus). You can hide them by deselecting Add Signal Flow Channel
     Strips in the Mixer's View menu.

4   In the Mixer, try selecting different channels by clicking the name at the bottom of
     each channel strip.

When a channel is selected, it is highlighted with a light green border. Note that the corresponding track is highlighted in the Arrange area, which automatically scrolls to display the track selected in the Mixer.

5   In the track list of the Arrange area, try selecting a few of the tracks.

When a track is selected in the Arrange area's track list, the Mixer automatically scrolls to display the corresponding channel.

6   In the Mixer, select channel 25, the drum overheads channel (Drum_overhds).

Note that this channel is located between the Snare and Toms_rack channels. It would be more conveniently located in the Mixer next to the other stereo drum tracks (Drum_intro and Loop).

You can move the track in the Arrange area while observing the changes in the Mixer.

7   In the Arrange area's track list, drag the track downward (the pointer switches to a hand), dropping it after the Toms_floor track.

The track order changes in the Arrange area and the Mixer, and the Drum_overhds track is inserted between the Toms_floor and Loop tracks.

Arrange area track list

Mixer

Using the Channel Strip Filters

The channel strip filter buttons, located at the upper-right side of the Mixer, define the types of channels displayed in the Mixer. They can be selected singly or in combination. When the filter buttons are used in Arrange view, the display will show only the tracks in the Arrange area that are of the selected types defined by the filter buttons. Limiting the displayed channels can be helpful when concentrating on a specific aspect of the mix, or when screen real estate is in high demand. By default, all the filter buttons are selected, thereby displaying every type of channel available in a given view.

1   Click the Audio channel strip filter button (it is currently active), deselecting it.

All audio channels in the arrangement are hidden, leaving a single instrument channel, plus the aux, output, and master channels used by the Arrange area tracks.

2   Click the Audio button again.

All channel types are now active, and the complete arrangement is visible.

Using All View

The Mixer's All view displays all the channels available in the project, grouped by type (audio, software instrument, Aux, and so on) and organized in ascending order (Audio 1, Audio 2, Audio 3, and so on).

Since the channels displayed in All view correspond to type and not to tracks in the Arrange area, you can use this view mode to look at channels—such as output and master channels—that are not otherwise contained in your arrangement. As in Arrange view, channels in All view are displayed via the channel strip filter buttons. The channel strip filter selections made for the Arrange and All views are independent, and they remain intact even when you toggle between the display modes.

Rather than use All view to display multiple (or all) types of channels, it is most useful to dedicate All view to a single type of channel, such as output channels. All view then becomes an "alternative" Mixer that provides quick access to a frequently used channel type in a mix.

In this exercise, you will set up All view as a dedicated output mixer.

1   In the Mixer menu bar, click the All button.

By default, all filter buttons are turned on, displaying all channel types available in the project's Environment. To view only channels of a specific type, you need to disable all channel strip filter buttons for channels you do not wish to view. This can be time-consuming, but Logic supplies a single-action shortcut.

2   In the menu bar, Option-click the Output button.

All channels disappear and are replaced by the output channels (four stereo channels) available to the project.

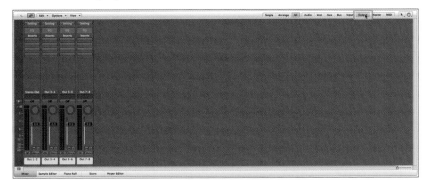

NOTE ▶ You need to have an audio interface with at least eight outputs for the output channels to appear active (having a fader, pan control, inserts, and so on). Otherwise, the output channels will appear labeled but blank.

Option-clicking a channel strip filter button displays only the selected channel type. You can add other channel types to the view by clicking (without Option) additional filter buttons.

3   Click the Master button to turn it on. The master channel is added to the Mixer.

4   Click the Arrange and All buttons to toggle between the view of the output and master channels (All view) and the tracks used in the arrangement (Arrange view).

Notice that the display modes remember the channel filter settings you last assigned, even when switching between Arrange view and All view.

TIP ▶ The channel strip filter settings are saved in the screenset, so you can make this a part of the permanent Mix setup.

This setup enables you to conveniently access individual outputs on your audio interface as you adjust volume levels, apply signal processing, or perform bounces.

Using Single View

Single view essentially limits the Mixer display to a single selected channel and all channel strips that are a part of its signal path. This offers an effective way to trace the signal flow from track to output, including all send destinations (aux channels). You can leave Single view enabled as you select source channels via the Arrange area's track list, but toggling it on and off while you're mixing in the other view modes makes more sense. Doing so allows you to quickly focus in on, and make adjustments to, a single channel's signal flow and then return to working on the total mix.

1   In the menu bar, click the Arrange button if it's not already selected.

2   Click the Violin1 channel strip (track 11).

3   Click the Single button.

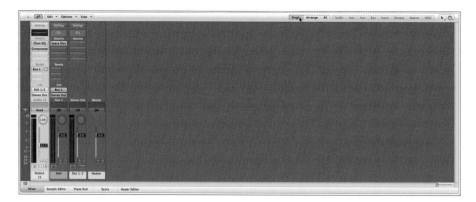

The complete signal flow stemming from the Violin1 channel is displayed, including the send destination (Aux 1) and the output and master channels.

4   Click the Arrange button to return to the overall mix.

Creating Production Notes

Also new to Logic 9 is the ability to quickly create production notes, allowing you to comment on takes, indicate mix settings, and save session information along with the project file. Notes can be created both in a dedicated Notes area adjunct to the Arrange window, as well as in the Mixer window itself.

1   At the upper-right corner of the Arrange window, click the Toolbar button, revealing the toolbar.

2   Click the Notes button. The Notes area opens.

As you can see, project information has already been entered in the Notes area under the Project tab. The Notes area also has a Track tab that allows you to enter notes associated with a selected track.

3   Click the Track tab.

4   In the Mixer, scroll to the right and select the Kick track (track 22). The Notes area displays the track number and name (22 Kick).

5   In the Notes area, click the Track Text Edit button.

6   In the Track pane, enter *Kick needs more low end*.

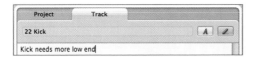

NOTE ▸ You can change the font, size, and style of the note text by selecting it and then clicking the Font button.

7 Close the Notes area by clicking the Notes button.

As mentioned earlier, you can create and view track notes in the Mixer window.

8 In the Mixer, click the Notes button.

The Mixer expands vertically, revealing the Notes area beneath the channel strips. You can see the note you created earlier for the kick track displayed underneath the channel strip.

Panning Stereo Tracks

Logic's Mixer channels offer true stereo functionality without requiring the user to dedicate two tracks (a left and a right channel) for playback. This provides playback of interleaved stereo files, stereo software instruments, and stereo busses through a single mixer channel, providing ease of use when working with stereo sources.

On stereo channels in the Mixer, the Balance control balances the relative levels of the left and right signals that make up the stereo signal. Adjusting the balance of a stereo track reduces one side in favor of the other.

For example, imagine a stereo drum overheads track that has the hi-hat on the left side of the stereo field and the ride cymbal on the right. If the Balance control for the track is turned to the left, the right side of the signal diminishes, losing the ride. If the knob is turned to the right, the opposite happens, reducing the hi-hat signal in favor of the ride.

While this stereo balance function provides considerable ease of use, it also represents a limitation when it comes to the placement of a sound in a mix's stereo field. It is often necessary to reposition the center of a recorded stereo signal within the mix while changing the spread (stereo width). Fortunately, Logic offers a handy plug-in, the Direction Mixer, that does this on any stereo track. This plug-in allows for a more focused sound, as you are truly panning a stereo signal instead of adjusting the signal level of the left and right sides.

1 On the Piano channel strip (track 14), click the second Insert slot and choose Imaging > Direction Mixer > Stereo from the pop-up menu. The Direction Mixer plug-in window opens.

You can also click a plug-in name in the pop-up menu to insert it, rather than choosing the format (mono, stereo, or 5.1) within the subsequent menu. When doing so, Logic automatically selects the format that best matches the channel.

The Direction Mixer plug-in offers the panning functionality just described by means of the Direction parameter. Graphically, the Direction knob is quite different from the Pan control used on mono tracks. Values within the range of –90 to +90 degrees represent the full stereo field; greater and lesser values (from +90 to +180 or from –90 to –180 degrees) bring the middle of the signal back toward the center, but with the left and right sides reversed. At +180 (or –180) degrees, the signal is dead center, but with the left and right sides inverted.

2 Drag the Direction knob up to set a value of +51.

This places the center of the Piano signal slightly to the right side of the mix.

In addition to positioning the middle of the stereo signal across the stereo field, you can use the Direction Mixer plug-in to widen or tighten the spread of the stereo base by adjusting the Spread parameter. A setting of 1.0 maintains the width of the original signal. Lower settings bring the sides toward the center, decreasing the spread.

3 Drag one of the Spread sliders to set a value of 0.8.

This will tighten up the stereo signal so that it doesn't take up quite as much width in the stereo mix.

4   Click the Solo button for the Piano channel.

5   Press Shift-Enter (or click the Play from Selection button on the transport) to play the project from the beginning of the Piano part.

6   While the project is playing, click the Bypass button on and off to hear the Piano track with and without the Direction Mixer.

   Notice that with the Direction Mixer active, it feels as though the piano is sitting to the right of the vocalist, but the stereo image is not compromised. If you had used the main Balance control to do the same thing, you might have lost the sound of the low notes on the piano, because they are normally heard in the left side of the stereo image.

7   With the Direction Mixer plug-in active (bypass is off), stop playback and close the Direction Mixer window.

8   On the Piano channel, click the Solo button to unsolo the channel.

9   Play the project again, this time listening to how the Piano track fits within the stereo mix.

   NOTE ▶ The Direction Mixer plug-in also decodes MS (middle-side) encoded stereo recordings. Once the MS mode is engaged (by clicking the MS button), you can alter the stereo signal with the Spread and Direction controls as you would with standard left-right stereo signals.

Switching the Contents of the Plug-in Window

Accessing the multitude of active plug-ins in a project can be a clumsy process requiring the opening and closing of each plug-in window. Menus in a plug-in window provide a simpler way to navigate around active plug-ins, allowing you to view any plug-in in the same window regardless of its channel or its order in the signal chain.

This navigation technique also helps when you're copying presets from one location to another and identical processing is required. The two violin tracks are a good example of this, since they could both benefit from similar EQ and dynamics processing. In this exercise you navigate from the Violin1 channel to the Violin2 channel using the plug-in window menus, copying and pasting settings from one plug-in to another.

1   In the Mixer, look at the two adjacent Violin tracks (tracks 11 and 12).

Notice that they have identical plug-ins at the same Insert slots in the channels. However, the Violin1 plug-ins have customized settings, which you will copy to Violin2.

To use this plug-in settings technique, you need to have a plug-in window open.

2   In the Violin1 channel (track 11), double-click the Channel EQ plug-in to open the plug-in window.

The EQ curve indicates a subtle dip at around 395 Hz and a smaller boost at around 3450 Hz.

3   Click the Copy button.

Now that you have copied the EQ plug-in settings from Violin1, you can paste them into the Channel EQ in the Violin2 channel. You will use the two "Show" pop-up menus located at the top of the plug-in window to view the Channel EQ setting for Violin2 in the same plug-in window.

The Show Channel Strip menu accesses the same numbered Insert slot on any channel that has an active plug-in.

4   Click the Show Channel Strip pop-up menu and choose Audio 12 - Violin2.

The Violin2 Channel EQ settings (default) are now displayed in the open plug-in window.

5   Click the Paste button.

The plug-in settings from Violin1 are pasted into the Channel EQ of Violin2.

6   Click the Show Channel Strip menu and choose Audio 11 - Violin1.

This returns you to the Violin1 Channel EQ. Let's move on to display the Compressor plug-in, located in the second Insert slot for the channel. Each Insert slot for a single channel can be accessed by the Show Insert pop-up menu.

7   Click the Show Insert menu and choose Comp.

The Compressor interface now appears in the plug-in window.

8   Click the Copy button.

9   Click the Show Channel Strip menu and choose Audio 12 - Violin2.

The Compressor inserted in the second Insert slot on the Violin2 channel is displayed in the plug-in window.

10   Click the Paste button.

The plug-in setting from Violin1 is pasted onto the Compressor of Violin2.

11   Close the plug-in window.

Changing Plug-in Locations

Where you place an effect in the signal flow is as important as what effect is chosen. Inserting effects at different places in the signal chain can lead to different results depending on the processing involved.

Changing effect placement is easily done in Logic's Mixer by dragging with the Hand tool. You can try this by changing the order of the lead vocal signal chain (track 1), placing the EQ after the Compressor.

1   Solo the Vox_Lead channel by clicking the Solo button.

2   Click the Cycle button to turn on Cycle mode.

3 Use the Set Locators by Previous/Next Marker and Enable commands (Option-Command-Left Arrow and Option-Command-Right Arrow) to create a cycle region around the Verse 1 section.

4 Select the Hand tool. This tool allows you to grab and move plug-ins in this window.

TIP ▶ By default, you switch from the Pointer tool to the Hand tool in the Mixer by pressing Command as you click.

5 Drag the Channel EQ in the first Insert slot on track 1 (the Vox_Lead channel), placing it between Insert slots 3 and 4 (a yellow line will appear between Insert slots 3 and 4).

The signal chain reflects the new order, inserting the Channel EQ (including the settings) after the Compressor.

NOTE ▶ When dragging plug-in locations with the Hand tool, pay special attention to the area where you release the mouse button, as this affects placement in the signal chain (top to bottom). To aid in this, a light yellow rectangle or line is displayed indicating where the plug-in will be placed. With careful placement, you can put plug-ins above or below the others (indicated by a yellow line) in the signal chain, and even swap locations (an empty target slot will be indicated by a yellow rectangle).

6 Play the project and listen to the lead vocal channel with the new plug-in order.

7 While it's playing, drag the Channel EQ plug-in back to the first Insert slot. The plug-in changes position, even when the project is playing.

8 Stop the playback.

> **TIP ▶** This technique also works for dragging Insert plug-ins from one channel to another. If you do this, make sure to keep format (mono, stereo, or 5.1) compatibility between the two channels in mind. You can even copy plug-ins from location to location by pressing the Option key while dragging.

Using a Plug-in's Extended Parameters

Many of Logic's plug-ins (both instruments and effects) offer extended parameters that are hidden from the standard interface by default. These settings are worth exploring and are easily accessed by clicking the disclosure triangle at the lower left of the plug-in interface.

The Compressor parameters on the Vox_Lead channel sound great but could benefit from a little coloration to make the result sound more like the pleasing harmonic distortion associated with tube-based audio hardware. You can add this coloration using the Output Distortion parameter located in the Compressor's extended parameters.

1 In the Vox_Lead channel (track 1), double-click the Compressor plug-in to open the plug-in window.

2 At the lower left of the Compressor's interface, click the disclosure triangle. The extended parameters appear at the bottom of the plug-in window.

3 From the Output Distortion menu, choose Soft. While subtle, the Soft setting introduces gentle audio clipping at the output, which is quite pleasing to the ear.

4 Click the Solo button to unsolo the Vox_Lead channel, and then listen to the effects processing applied to the track within the context of the mix.

5 Close the Compressor window and stop the playback.

Using Mixer Groups

A *group* is used to link similar controls (panning, volume, and so on) in different channels. This creates a direct relationship among all the channels in the group assignment.
As a result, when you adjust the parameters on one channel, the same parameters are
adjusted in all the group's channels.

Assigning Channels to Groups

In this exercise, you will assign similar backing vocals to a group using the same process
you learned in Lesson 8 ("Editing with Mixer Groups"). This time, instead of using this
function for editing, you will be linking together specific properties to control in the Mixer.

1   On the Harm1 channel (track 2), click the Group slot and choose Open Group
    Settings from the pop-up menu.

    The Group Settings window opens.

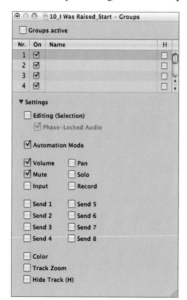

In this window, you can set the channel properties to be linked.

NOTE ▸ In addition to sharing channel strip parameters, groups can share attributes such as viewing and editing settings in the Arrange area, the channel strip color, and the automation mode.

2   Select the Solo and Send 1 checkboxes.

This links the Solo button and topmost Send knob for the group.

3   Double-click in the Name column in the Nr. 1 row, enter *HrmVox*, and press Return.

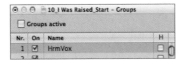

4   Close the Group Settings window.

5   On the Harm1 channel (track 2), click the Group slot and choose Group 1: HrmVox from the pop-up menu.

1: HrmVox now appears in the Group slot on the track. This signifies that the channel is assigned to Group 1.

6   On the Harm2 channel (track 3), click the Group slot and choose Group 1: HarmVox from the pop-up menu.

The Harm1 and Harm2 channels both display *1: HrmVox* in the Group slot.

TIP ▶ You can assign the most recently selected group to any channel by Option-clicking its Group slot.

Now that you have assigned the two channels to a group, you can adjust both tracks simultaneously, including the solo and send controls you specified in the Group Settings window.

In this mix, the harmony vocals (Harm1 and Harm2) need additional reverb processing to create a more reflective sound. Both tracks have sends set for Aux 3 (a long, more reflective reverb).

Since the two channels are similar in character and material, it is desirable to have the same send level for both sent to this longer reverb. Because Send 1 was selected in the HrmVox Group Settings window, changing either channel's Send 1 value will also cause the other to change.

7   Use Control-Command-Right Arrow and Control-Command-Left Arrow to set the locators around the Chorus 2 section.

8   Click the Solo buttons for the Harm1 (track 2) channel. The Solo button becomes engaged for both channels.

9   Play the project. While listening to the playback, drag up the Send knob on either of the channels, applying additional reverb to your liking. Both Send knobs move as you adjust one or the other.

10 When you are finished setting the reverb level for the channels, stop the playback.

Temporarily Disabling a Group

It is often necessary to adjust individual channels of an assigned group without affecting the entire group. At these times, you can temporarily disable the group by using the group clutch, similar to how you used it in Lesson 8 ("Activating and Deactivating Groups Using Group Clutch"). In the current project, the Harm2 channel is a little too loud to blend with the part sung on the Harm1 channel. To change the fader without affecting the other channel, you need to engage the group clutch, make an adjustment, and then reengage the group by turning off the group clutch.

The group clutch can be activated via a menu selection in the Mixer's local menu bar (Options > Group Clutch) or a key command (Command-G). You will probably be performing this most often during playback, so the keyboard shortcut makes for a more ergonomic mix process.

1   Play the project, listening closely to the HrmVox group.

2   Press Command-G, the group clutch key command.

    The Group display turns from yellow (active) to gray (inactive), indicating that the group clutch is engaged.

3   Drag the Harm2 fader down to –13.0 (dB).

4   Press Command-G again.

    The group display turns from gray (inactive) to yellow (active), indicating that the group clutch is disengaged.

5   With the song still playing, turn off soloing on the Harm1 and Harm2 tracks by click-ing either channel's Solo button. The entire arrangement can now be heard.

6   In one of the HrmVox group channels, drag up the fader to adjust the level of the group in relation to the mix (to about –6.7 dB and –9.0 dB, respectively).

    Both faders move in tandem, maintaining the relative gain between them.

7   Stop the project when you are happy with the volume level of the harmony vocals in relation to the overall mix.

Lesson Review

1. What track data can you import from one project to another?

2. Explain the difference between the Mixer's Arrange, All, and Single view modes.

3. Notes can be created for both the project and what?

4. Which insert plug-in aids in accurate stereo placement within a mix?

5. A plug-in's Show Channel Strip and Show Insert menus allow what?

6. Which tool allows you to change the insert order, thereby affecting signal flow?

7. How do you link the controls of multiple channels while mixing?

8. How do you temporarily disengage a group?

Answers

1. You can import track content, channel strip configuration (including plug-ins and routings), and automation data from one project into another.

2. The Mixer's Arrange view adapts to the Arrange area's track list, and vice versa. The All view mode displays all the channels existing in a project's Environment, and it can be used to create an alternative mixer with commonly accessed channels. The Single view displays the entire signal flow from a selected channel, including send channels and output.

3. Notes can be created for both the project and tracks.

4. Stereo tracks can be accurately balanced and their images adjusted by means of the Direction Mixer plug-in.

5. A plug-in's Show Channel Strip and Show Insert menus allow navigation from plug-in to plug-in within the same window, making it easier to copy and paste settings between plug-ins.

6. The Hand tool allows you to change the insert order by dragging and dropping plug-ins within a single channel, or from channel to channel.

7. Use groups to link the controls of multiple channels while mixing.

8. Engage the group clutch (press Command-G or, in the Mixer's menu bar, choose Options > Group Clutch).

11

Lesson Files Advanced Logic 9_Files > Lessons > 11_I Was Raised_Start.logic

Media Advanced Logic 9_Files > Media > I Was Raised

Time This lesson takes approximately 60 minutes to complete.

Goals Create submixes for processing multiple channels

Create a headphone mix

Use plug-in side chains

Use parallel compression while maintaining stereo placement

Incorporate external effects processors into Logic's Mixer

Bounce both regions and tracks in place

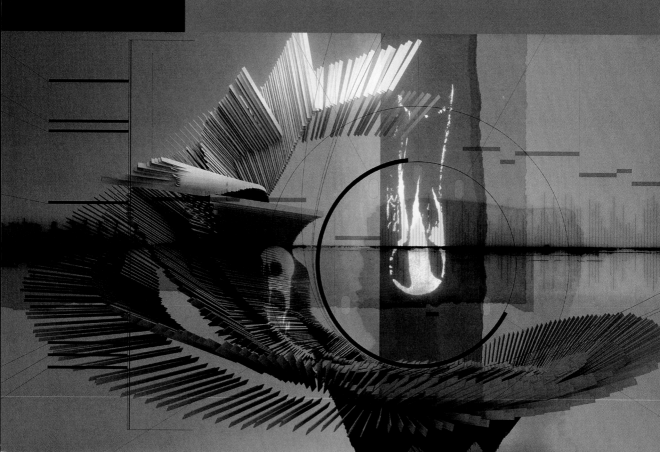

Controlling Signal Flow

In the software world of Logic, a signal is routed from one channel to another via the sends and input/output fields of each channel. Signals are often sent to multiple destinations simultaneously and can even interface with external devices by leaving the audio interface and coming into it again.

In this lesson, you will configure the Mixer to route audio signals to accomplish specific mixing tasks such as submixing and side chaining. You will also create bounces of individual regions and tracks that take into account the signal flow of their respective channels. In addition, you will learn how to integrate external effects processors into your signal flow, interfacing the physical world with the virtual one.

Using Aux Channels as Submixes

In addition to acting as effects returns, aux channels can act as submix channels that receive signals from multiple audio channels. Using an aux channel for a submix allows you to work with multiple routed channels as a single set while retaining the relative differences of individual channels.

Using aux channels as submixes is similar to assigning channels to groups, as you did in Lesson 10. Both techniques enable you to simultaneously adjust the output of multiple channels while maintaining the relative levels of the individual tracks.

However, the two techniques differ profoundly in function: aux channel submixes directly control the signal flow, whereas groups link the channel controls, keeping the respective signal paths separate.

A common use for a submix is to provide processing for multiple tracks (such as those for backing vocals or drums) by using a single effects-processing chain. This form of processing is referred to as *serial processing*, because the entire output of one or more channels is fed in a series directly into another channel. Using submixes eliminates the need to assign the same effects chains to several tracks separately; it also saves valuable CPU power.

In this exercise, you will assign backing vocals (tracks 2–10) to a shared aux channel, creating a submix that applies the same EQ processing to all the tracks at once.

1   Choose File > Open.

2   In the Open window's file selector dialog, go to Music > Advanced Logic 9_Files > Lessons and open **11_I Was Raised_Start.logic**. The project opens to the Mixer/Arrange area screenset you used in the previous lesson.

3   Drag over the track names of the backing vocal tracks (tracks 2–10) in the Mixer. The channel strips are selected as you drag over them.

4   Click any selected track's Output slot and choose Bus > Bus 6. All the Output slots for the selected channel strips change to Bus 6.

Logic automatically creates a new aux channel when you select an unused bus as an output.

NOTE ▸ When multiple channel strips are selected, a "temporary group" is created that also works for assigning send destinations on multiple tracks, as well as adjusting channel controls.

5   On any of the selected channels, double-click the Output slot (Bus 6).

The Mixer automatically locates to a newly created aux channel (Aux 6).

To differentiate between the submix channel and the other aux channels, it's a good idea to give the submix channel a more descriptive name and assign it a new color. Doing so also makes the submix channel easier to locate in the Mixer layout and in the menus that access aux channels (such as the Send and Output menus).

6   Double-click the name of the newly created aux channel strip (Aux 6) and enter *BkVox Sub* to rename the Aux 6 channel. Press Return

7   Choose View > Colors from the Mixer menu bar. The Colors window appears.

8   Choose a color by clicking any color square in the palette. After you've chosen it, close the Colors window.

By setting the selected tracks to output directly to an aux channel, you can process the full signal of the combined channels using the aux channel's Insert slots (applying EQ, de-essing, compression, and so on). Let's try this by instantiating a channel EQ onto the newly created submix.

9   On the BkVox Sub channel, click the top Insert slot and choose EQ > Channel EQ > Stereo from the pop-up menu. A Channel EQ is instantiated and ready for use.

10   In the Settings menu, choose 05 Voice > Backing Vocals.

At this point, you could easily continue to apply additional processing to the backing vocals (such as de-essing and compression) by adding more inserts, which would affect all the signals at once.

11 Close the Channel EQ window.

12 On the BkVox Sub channel, click the Solo button.

> **NOTE ▸** When an aux channel is soloed, Logic uses automatic mute suppression on the tracks that feed the aux. This allows you to hear the contributing signals without having to find the separate channels and solo each of them.

13 Press Control-Command-Right Arrow/Left Arrow (the Go to Next/Previous Marker command) to locate the playhead to the Refrain section.

14 In the Transport bar, click the Cycle button.

15 Play the project, listening to the backing vocals as sent through the EQ on the aux channel.

16 While the project is playing, drag the BkVox Sub channel's volume fader up and down. All backing vocal tracks change their volume, adjusted by a single fader.

17 Return the volume to 0.0 (dB) by Option-clicking the fader.

18 Stop the project playback.

Setting up the aux channel as a submix allows you to control the volume of all participating tracks while maintaining the relative volume levels set by each track's fader.

Applying Send Effects to Submixes

The submix channel you just created also works well for assigning a group of channels to a common send effect, such as reverb. Conveniently, aux channels also contain sends, which allow you to assign the submix containing the backing vocals to any send effect configured on the other aux channels.

1 On the BkVox Sub channel, click the top Send slot and choose Bus > Bus 5 (Vox verb) from the pop-up menu.

2 Play the project.

3 On the BkVox Sub channel, drag up the Send knob, listening to the backing vocals as you adjust the amount of signal sent to the vocal reverb to taste.

4 Stop the project playback.

NOTE ▶ This routing is frequently referred to as *parallel routing,* wherein the signal is split (via the send) and fed to separate channels.

5 On the BkVox Sub channel, click the Solo button to take it out of Solo mode.

6 Play the project, dragging the fader on the BkVox Sub channel to adjust the volume level of the backing vocals.

7 Stop the project playback when you are happy with the volume level of the backing vocals in relation to the overall mix.

TIP ▶ The methods of signal routing described in these exercises invite experimentation! Try combining both methods to create interesting signal processing chains.

Using Side Chain Effects

Side chaining processors is a valuable mixing technique wherein the signal from one channel is used to control an effect on another channel. When side chaining with Logic, the plug-ins involved and how they are routed can take many forms, depending on the desired result.

In this exercise, you will explore a side chain technique employed by mix engineers to add low-end to a kick drum by using a gated sine wave oscillator that is triggered by the kick drum signal itself.

1 Use the Set Locators by Previous/Next Marker and Enable commands (Option-Command-Left Arrow and Option-Command-Right Arrow) to create a cycle region around the Intro section.

2 In the Mixer, select the Kick track (track 22), click the Solo button for the Kick channel, and play the project, listening to the Kick track.

The kick has a lot of beater sound but could use a bit more low-end body.

3 In the Arrange window's submenus, choose Track > New.

4 Use the New Tracks dialog to create one new mono audio track with an output setting of Output 1-2.

A new channel is created (Audio 29) that appears next to the original Kick track.

5 Double-click the name area of the new track, and enter *Kick Osc* to rename it. Press Return.

6 On the new Kick Osc channel strip, click the top Insert slot and choose Utility > Test Oscillator > Mono from the pop-up menu.

The Test Oscillator plug-in window opens.

The Test Oscillator generates raw waveforms at a set frequency. You will use this to generate the sine wave that will supply the low-end for the kick sound you are trying to create.

By default, when you bring up a Test Oscillator on an audio track, it will start producing a constant signal. Since the Kick track is still soloed, the Kick Osc channel is muted. You'll be hearing the signal shortly, but for now let's use this advantage to finish setting up the signal chain without the Test Oscillator's incessant sound.

7   In the new Kick Osc channel strip, click the second Insert slot, and choose Dynamics >
Noise Gate > Mono from the pop-up menu. The Noise Gate plug-in window opens.

The Noise Gate only allows a signal to pass through when it is above a set threshold,
opening the "gate." When the signal is below the threshold, it reduces the gain by a
specified amount, closing the "gate."

Since it is placed after the Test Oscillator in the signal chain, the Noise Gate plug-in
receives the generated sine wave signal in series. By using a side chain for input, you
can have the Noise Gate "listen" to another channel's signal level instead of the Test
Oscillator's to open and close the gate, allowing the sine wave to pass through only when
the side chain signal is above the set threshold. Using this technique, you can use the
original Kick channel (Audio 21) to open and close the gate in time to the kick drum.

8   In the Side Chain menu at the top right of the Noise Gate plug-in window, choose
Audio 21 - Kick.

NOTE ▶ The list displayed in the Side Chain pop-up menu corresponds to the channel type and number, not to the channel order in the Mixer. Channel type and number are displayed in the Mixer in the middle of each channel strip.

9 Click the Solo button for the Kick channel (track 22), unsoloing it.

10 Click the Solo button for the Kick Osc channel (track 23).

11 Play the project.

The kick drum track plays, with its output routed to the side chain of the Noise Gate. Whenever the signal rises above the threshold level, the Activity indicator lights and the gate "opens," allowing the Test Oscillator to be heard. The result is a sine wave playing in time to the kick drum.

The frequency of the sine wave is much too high to supply the needed low end that is the goal of the exercise. You can change the frequency of the Test Oscillator's generated sine wave by using the Frequency knob.

12 While playing the project, drag the Test Oscillator's Frequency knob down to about 50 Hz.

You can monitor the side chain signal coming into the Noise Gate by selecting the Monitor option in the Side Chain section. This is an excellent way to troubleshoot the signal flow if you are experiencing any problems.

13 Select the Monitor checkbox, enabling it.

The original Kick track sounds through the Kick Osc channel, routed in through the side chain.

TIP ▶ The Noise Gate's Side Chain section also contains controls to limit the side chain input to a specific frequency, enabling you to key into a specific frequency range for the trigger.

14 Deselect the Monitor checkbox, disabling it.

You might have noticed that the original kick part plays a different rhythm than the generated sine wave signal. You can clearly hear this when you play the two together.

15 Click the Solo button for the Kick channel (track 22).

The Kick Osc channel is not as articulate as the original kick part. This is because the threshold level needs to be set to close the gate at a higher gain setting, when the original kick signal level falls after the initial transient.

16 Raise the Threshold slider to about –32 dB.

The sine wave now triggers in time with the original kick track.

TIP ▶ You can further shape the generated sine wave by using the Noise Gate's Attack, Hold, and Release knobs, extending or shortening the envelope characteristics of the sound for different effects.

17 Close the Noise Gate and Test Oscillator plug-in windows.

Now that you've created your routing, it's time to balance the two signals, blending them to create a single kick sound.

18 While playing the project, reduce the Kick Osc channel's volume so that it is barely noticeable (around -17 db or lower), supplying a bit more low end to the original kick drum sound.

19 Click the Solo buttons for both the Kick and Kick Osc channels, unsoloing them.

20 Click the Cycle button, disabling it.

21 Listen to the newly layered kick drum sound in context of the mix. Stop playback.

▶ **Side Chain Techniques**

Side chaining is used for many tasks. Try using some of the following techniques for both mixing and sound-generation purposes:

▶ Use a Noise Gate on a bass track set to receive side chain input from the Kick drum, opening the gate only when the kick sounds. This tightens the timing of the two parts, locking them together.

▶ Use a Compressor on a rhythm instrument or entire mix set to receive side chain input from a vocal track, "ducking" the sound when the vocal signal is present.

▶ Use the side chain input on the EVOC 20 PS Vocoder Synth to route a vocal (or other) track in as the analyzed signal.

▶ Use the side chain input on the ES1, ES2, or Ultrabeat to route audio signals into the synthesizers. Use the filters, envelopes, and modulation sections to shape the sound.

Positioning Sends Pre or Post Channel Strip Controls

In Logic's channels, signal flows from the inserts to the volume fader, followed by the pan control. The send controls can be configured to route signals at various points in the channel strip's signal chain. When you first bring up a send on a channel, it routes the signal post-volume, and pre-pan. This means that the signal routed to the busses will change along with the volume fader movements, but not be affected by the pan control. This is the default, and it reflects the standard setup for mixing when sending signals to reverbs and delays that are inserted on aux channels.

However, there are situations where more flexibility is required, providing the ability to send a signal either pre-fader or post-pan. In this exercise, you will use post-pan sends for parallel compression on the drum channels, as well as set up a headphone mix using pre-fader sends.

Creating Parallel Compression Using Post-Pan Sends

Parallel compression is a mixing technique that applies compression to a channel's signal via a bus instead of using a channel insert. This setup is often utilized to layer a heavily compressed signal with the original one, providing the sonic coloration of aggressive compression while maintaining the dynamic characteristic of the original channel's signal.

When you use this technique with a group of channels, it is important to maintain the pan relationship of the original channels when you send to the aux channel for processing. By sending post-pan, the panning of the individual tracks is retained, and it is reflected in the stereo bus.

In this exercise, you will use parallel compression on the drum channels using post-pan sends to maintain the stereo image.

1   In the Mixer, drag over the track names of the drum channels (channels 22–29).

2   On any of the selected *stereo* drum channels (Drum_overhds or Loop), click the next available Send slot and choose Bus > Bus 7.

NOTE ▶ When creating new aux channels in this manner, Logic assigns the format (mono, stereo, surround) of the new aux channel based on the channel from which you assigned the send. In this instance, you need to create a stereo bus, so therefore you need to assign the send from one of the stereo channels.

All selected channels now have a send assigned to Bus 7, and a new aux channel is created with its input set to Bus 7.

3   Click-hold any of the newly created Bus 7 sends and choose Post Pan.

When sending a signal post-pan, you are also sending post-fader. This means that both the panning and the volume levels for each channel are maintained when sending to the bus. For this reason, you should set all send levels to the same setting (unity gain, or 0 dB, is best) when doing parallel compression, as the amount hitting the compressor should reflect the volume levels set in the faders.

4   On any of the selected channels, Option-click the Send level knob, setting them all to unity gain.

NOTE ▸ The Send knobs are displayed in blue when configured post-pan (as opposed to green for the default post-fader setting).

5   On any of the selected channels, double-click the Send slot (Bus 7) you just created.

The Mixer automatically locates to a newly created aux channel (Aux 7). This channel will be used to apply parallel compression to the signal sent from the drum channels.

6   Using the technique you learned earlier in this lesson, color the Aux 7 channel and name it *Drm Comp*. Press Return.

7   On the Drm Comp channel, click the top Insert slot and choose Dynamics > Compressor > Stereo from the pop-up menu.

A compressor is instantiated and ready for use. As stated earlier, the bus compressor in parallel compression is usually set to a fairly aggressive setting, creating a heavily compressed signal to mix in with the original one.

8   In the Settings menu, choose 05 Compressor Tools > VCA Smashed.

Now it's time to test the parallel compression routing.

9   On the Drm Comp channel, click the Solo button, enabling it.

10   Play the project. You should hear the drum channels signal, heavily compressed. Stop the project.

Because the signal is being sent to the bus post-fader (in addition to post-pan), any change in volume level of the source channels will change the level of the compressed signal. This can be a handicap when trying to blend the signals during a mix, as one is dependent upon the other. By using a submix as you did earlier in the lesson, you can change the volume level of the unaffected signal independently of the affected.

11 Drag over the track names of the drum channels (channels 22–29), selecting them.

12 Click any selected track's Output slot and choose Bus > Bus 8. All the Output slots for the selected channel strips change to Bus 8.

13 On any of the selected channels, double-click the Output slot (Bus 8) you just created.

The Mixer automatically locates to a newly created aux channel (Aux 8). This channel will be your submix fader for the unaffected drum signal.

14 Color the Aux 8 channel and name it *Drm Sub*. Press Return.

Now it's time to test out your signal routing and fine-tune the relationship between the heavily compressed bus (Drm Comp) and the original channels (Drm Sub).

15 Click the solo button on the Drm Sub channel (Aux 8), enabling it.

16 Play the project.

You should now hear the signals from the original drum channels layered with the heavily compressed Drm Comp channel.

17 Listening to the mix, blend the Drm Sub channel signal with the heavily compressed Drm Comp channel by adjusting their volume faders.

18 Option-click any of the active Solo buttons (disabling solo for all channels) and listen to the parallel compressed drums in relation to the entire mix.

19 Stop playback, close the compressor window.

Creating a Headphone Mix Using Pre-Fader Sends

If you have an audio interface that has more than two outputs, you can create an independent headphone mix for tracking sessions. This allows you to give recording artists their own custom mixes for tracking. You can do this by using sends on each channel to pass signal to an aux channel set to output on a different pair of audio outputs than your main mix.

In order for the control room's mix to be independent of the headphone mix, however, you need to configure the sends pre-fader, which will send the signal before it reaches the volume fader in the channel strip. This creates a setup where you can adjust the control room mix normally (by adjusting the faders) and adjust the headphone mix via the send levels.

1 In the Mixer's local menus, choose Edit > Select All (Command-A). All channel strips are selected.

2 On any of the selected *stereo* channels, click the next available Send slot and choose Bus > Bus 9. All channels (including the reverb returns and submixes) now have a send assigned to Bus 9.

3 Click-hold any of the newly created Bus 9 sends and choose Pre Fader. The Bus 8 sends turn green, indicating that they are now configured pre-fader.

4 On any selected channel double-click the Send slot (Bus 9) you just created. The Mixer automatically locates to a newly created aux channel (Aux 9).

5 Using the technique you learned earlier in the lesson, color the channel and name it *Phones*. Press Return.

As of now, the Phones aux channel is set to output to the main stereo outs. In order to create an independent headphone mix, you need to assign the output of the bus to a spare pair of outputs on your audio interface (connected to a headphone amplifier box and headphones).

TIP ▶ Some audio interfaces have built-in headphone amplifiers that can be assigned separately from the other inputs and outputs. Using these eliminates the need for an external headphone amplifier box.

6   On the Phones aux channel, click the output field and select an available pair of outputs on your audio interface.

NOTE ▶ If your system configuration does not include at least four outputs, you can still follow along with the exercise by using output 1-2 for the Phones channel, and assigning all other channels to No Output.

Each channel's send level dictates how much signal will be sent to the bus (irrespective of the channel faders), allowing you to create an entirely independent mix for headphones by using the send controls on each channel.

7   Play the project.

8   While listening to your headphones, adjust the send amount to Bus 9 on all channels, one at a time, creating a headphone mix.

9 Stop the project.

> **TIP** ▶ You can create as many headphone mixes as you have free pairs of audio interface outputs. For each headphone mix, you will need to create a pre-fader send. This allows independent mixes to be created for each artist tracking.

Incorporating External Effects Processors

Although software effects processors can offer distinct advantages over external processors, having high-quality hardware processors in the signal chain can uniquely improve the sound. External effects processors are easily incorporated into Logic's software Mixer with a "helper" plug-in that manages the flow to the processor from the audio interface's inputs and outputs.

With the I/O plug-in, you can treat the external processor almost as if it were itself a plug-in, inserting it into a channel or applying it as a send effect in Logic's Mixer. To illustrate this technique, you will insert an imaginary hardware reverb unit as a send effect.

To enable the integration in this exercise, you need to physically send a signal from your audio interface to your hardware processor and back again. This is done by connecting an open pair of outputs from your audio interface to the stereo inputs of the hardware reverb, and connecting the stereo outputs of the hardware reverb back to an open pair of stereo inputs on the audio interface.

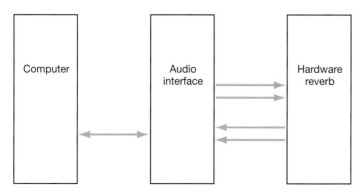

If you have a hardware reverb processor, try this by connecting the equipment according to the preceding diagram, using inputs 5–6 and outputs 5–6 of your audio interface. If not, follow along with an "imaginary" external processor connected.

> **NOTE** ▶ Ideally, your system configuration should include at least six inputs and outputs to create the following routing without de-coupling the headphone mix created in the previous exercise. However, if your system configuration includes only four inputs and outputs, you can still follow along with the exercise by assigning all track channels to Stereo Output, and the Phones channel to No Output, freeing up a pair to use for the following exercise.

Once this physical cabling has been completed, you need to create a new aux channel to feed the external hardware.

1   Choose Options > Create New Auxiliary Channel Strips. The New Auxiliary Channel Strips dialog appears.

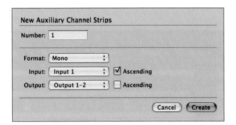

In this dialog, you can specify the number, format, and I/O configuration of the aux channels you've created.

> **TIP** ▶ New auxiliary channels are easily created by clicking the Add (+) button at the far left of the Mixer.

2   From the Format menu, choose Stereo.

3   From the Input menu, choose Bus > Bus 10.

4   Click Create. A new aux channel, Aux 10, is created in the Mixer.

5   Double-click the track name for Aux 10 and rename it *Ext verb*.

NOTE ▶ Clearly naming aux channels that feed external hardware is useful to differentiate them from Logic's internal send effects.

If this channel is to function as a send effect, you'll need to route to the external effects processor. This is done via the I/O plug-in.

6   In Aux 10, click the top Insert slot, and choose Utility > I/O > Stereo. The I/O plug-in window opens.

The next step is to assign the appropriate inputs and outputs of the audio interface to access the hardware processor. This is done via the Input and Output menus.

7   Click the Output menu and choose 5–6.

8   Click the Input menu and choose 5–6.

You can now send signals to the hardware reverb inserted on Aux 10 using the same means you would use for any send effect: the channel Send menu.

9   In the Guitar_riff1 channel (track 19), click the top Send slot and choose Bus > Bus 10 from the pop-up menu.

NOTE ▶ As when reverb plug-ins are inserted as bus effects, the wet-dry ratio on the external hardware reverb should be set to 100% wet.

10 Solo the Guitar_riff1 channel by clicking its Solo button.

11 Press Control-Command-Left Arrow to locate to the Intro section.

12 Enable Cycle mode in the Transport. The cycle area now encompasses the Intro section.

13 Play the project. While the project is playing, on the Guitar_riff1 channel, drag up the Send knob to adjust the amount of signal sent to the hardware reverb on Bus 10.

14 Raise the return level by dragging the Aux 10 channel fader up until you can hear the effect.

> **NOTE ▶** All external hardware processors are different. You might need to adjust the send and return levels in Logic to achieve optimum gain staging. You can also apply additional signal gain going to and from the external effects processor by dragging the Output Volume and Input Volume sliders on the I/O plug-in. When using this setup, do not change Logic's master channel strip fader or master fader in the Transport bar, as this changes the volume level of all output channels and, therefore, your send levels to the external hardware.

15 Stop the project playback.

16 Turn off Cycle mode in the Transport.

> **TIP ▶** The I/O plug-in can also be used as an insert effect, sending signals to and from external effects processors such as hardware compressors, EQs, stomp boxes, and so on.

Bouncing in Place

New to Logic Pro 9 is the ability to bounce both regions and tracks "in place," or in their original position on the timeline. This is extremely useful for "rendering," or creating a version of the data with all channel strip processing applied, saving CPU resources. Logic's Bounce in Place features provide a great deal of flexibility when producing the new file, enabling you to bounce the channel's audio signal with or without plug-ins, effect tail, and volume and pan automation.

NOTE ▶ It is not possible to perform an in place bounce of a region routed to a MIDI channel strip.

1   Open Screenset 1.

2   In the track list, select the Drums_intro track (track 30). The region at the beginning of the project becomes selected.

3   Use the Zoom tool to zoom in on the selected Drums_intro region.

4   In the track header, on the Drums_intro track, click the Solo button, enabling it.

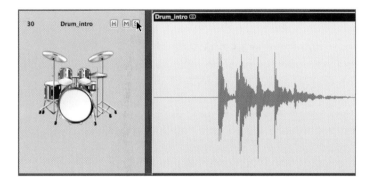

5   Play the project from the beginning, stopping after you've had a chance to listen to the selected Drums_intro region.

6   Take a look at the track's channel strip in the Inspector.

As you can see (and hear), the channel has plug-ins inserted, applying EQ, compression, and reverb to the selected region. In this exercise, you will use the Bounce in Place feature to create a new version of the Drums_intro region, with signal processing applied, exactly at the same point in the timeline.

7   In the Arrange window's submenus, choose Region > Bounce Regions in Place.

NOTE ▶ This command can also be activated by a toolbar shortcut, as well as a key command.

The Bounce Regions in Place window appears.

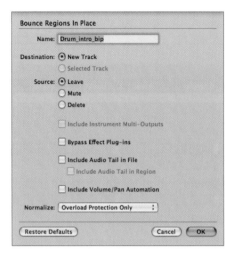

There are a few things to consider before performing the bounce. One such consideration is whether or not to create a new track (and channel strip) for the bounced region, and what will be done with the original region once the bounce is performed.

8   In the Destination section, select New Track, if it's not already selected.

9   In the Source section, select Mute, if it's not already selected.

Having these settings enabled will create a bounced region on a new track, muting the original region automatically.

Another thing to consider when bouncing is whether or not to apply the channel's active inserts, printing the effect to the new file. To do this, you need to have the Bypass Effect Plug-ins option deselected.

10   Deselect the Bypass Effects Plug-ins checkbox, if it's not already deselected.

If you were to click OK at this point, you would create a new file without the full decay, or "tail" of the reverb plug-in that is inserted on the channel, as it lasts longer than the length of the original region.

Logic's Bounce in Place feature can compensate for the added time incurred by the tail, creating a new recording that allows the tail to die out naturally without clipping it short.

11 Select the Include Audio Tail in File checkbox and the Include Audio Tail in Region checkbox.

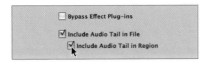

NOTE ▶ If the Include Audio Tail in Region checkbox is deselected when bouncing, a new audio file is created as before, including the added time incurred by the tail. This time, however, the region length is preserved, and does not adapt to include the added time. In effect, Logic will not play the tail, but you can still make it available by dragging the region borders.

12 Click OK.

A new track and region (Drums_intro_bip) are created underneath the Drums_intro track (now muted). Note that the newly created channel does not have any plug-ins instantiated, but it does have the same volume setting as the original channel.

13 Play the project from the beginning, listening to the newly created region and channel. It should sound exactly the same as the original.

NOTE ▶ Once the original region and channel is deemed no longer necessary, you can delete the channel and region, conserving valuable CPU power.

Rendering Software Instrument Tracks as Audio

Bouncing in place also works great for rendering software instruments into audio tracks for additional editing, processing, or even export to another software application.

1 Press 1 to bring up Screenset 1 again.

2 Select the Piano track (track 14) in the track list.

3 On the Piano track, Option-click the track Solo button, enabling it and disabling solo for the Drums_intro and Drums_intro_bip tracks.

4 In the Arrange window's submenus, choose View > Track Automation. Track automation is revealed for all tracks.

5 Note the automation and channel strip plug-ins for the Piano track.

The goal here is to replace the original software instrument track with an audio track that also has the same signal chain, including the inserted plug-ins, and volume automation. This will enable you to work with the piano as audio, while still retaining the ability to do any additional mixing tweaks that are deemed necessary.

6 Choose Track > Bounce Track in Place.

The Bounce Track in Place window appears.

NOTE ▶ This window is virtually identical to the Bounce Regions in Place window, but it leaves out the Source and Include Audio Tail options.

7 In the Destination section, select Replace Track.

> **NOTE** ▶ When bouncing software instruments that have multi-output capabilities (EXS24 and Ultrabeat), you can choose to include the signals from all outputs into the bounce. To do this, select the Include Instrument Multi-Outputs option. You can also have each separate output bounced as individual tracks by selecting the As Additional Tracks option.

8 Select the Bypass Effects Plug-ins checkbox, if it's not already selected.

9 Deselect the Include Volume/Pan Automation checkbox, if needed.

> **NOTE** ▶ In addition to providing standard normalization when bouncing the new file, the Normalize menu also offers downward normalization via the Overload Protection Only item. This acts as a safety net, keeping levels that rise above 0 dB from clipping.

10 Click OK. A new track and channel, Piano-bip, are created with the signal flow and automation intact, replacing the original.

Lesson Review

1. What is the most efficient way to apply effects processing to multiple channels at once?
2. Side chaining plug-ins allows you to do what?
3. Sends can be configured in what three ways?
4. How do you insert an external effects processor into the signal chain?
5. When bouncing regions or tracks in place, a channel's audio signal can be rendered to a new audio file with and without what?

Answers

1. Use aux channels as submixes to apply effects processing to multiple channels.
2. Side chaining plug-ins allows you to control an effect on one channel by the signal from another channel.
3. Sends can be configured post-fader, pre-fader, and post-pan (and fader).
4. Insert external effects processors into the signal chain using the I/O plug-in.
5. When bouncing regions or tracks in place, a channel's audio signal can be rendered to a new audio file with or without plug-ins, effect tail, and volume and pan automation.

12

Lesson Files	Advanced Logic 9_Files > Lessons > 12_I Was Raised_Start.logic
Media	Advanced Logic 9_Files > Media > I Was Raised
Time	This lesson takes approximately 60 minutes to complete.
Goals	Automate an aux channel
	Copy automation data between tracks
	Scale automation
	Apply automation to multiple tracks at once
	Map your MIDI controller to Logic's controls

Controlling the Mix

A good mix is a performance of sorts. Like an instrument in an ensemble, each element of a mix speaks its part clearly and expressively, complementing the other elements. This is a dynamic process, frequently involving the continuous adjustment of individual signals as a project progresses.

To create a dynamic-sounding mix, you have to be able to control audio signals over time. Adjusting volume, panning, or even plug-in parameters through the course of a project is an important part of breathing life into a mix.

Logic's comprehensive track-based automation system allows you to change over time the settings of virtually all channel-related software controls. These movements can be recorded offline or made in real-time by using a mouse, dedicated hardware MIDI control surface, or MIDI controller. Whichever entry method you use, the automation data can be easily edited and manipulated after the initial input, giving you control over all the sonic elements in a composition.

In this lesson, you will learn various methods for efficiently tackling specific automation editing tasks, focusing on techniques that get the most from the data you have already entered. In addition, you will learn how to assign MIDI knobs and faders to Logic's plug-in parameters and volume and pan controls, transforming your MIDI controller into a powerful control surface.

Automating an Aux Channel

Offline automation can be easily created by clicking in the automation lane of any visible track in the Arrange window. Although this is a simple process, it is not immediately apparent how to create automation for an aux channel. This channel, used primarily as an effect send or submix, exists only in the Mixer as part of the signal flow. It is not represented in the Arrange area, where offline automation is performed. In order to perform the offline automation of a channel control or plug-in inserted on an aux channel, you must add it to the Arrange area's track list.

In this exercise, you will automate the bypass of a reverb plug-in inserted on an aux channel by first adding it to the Arrange area.

> **NOTE ▶** This lesson assumes that you are familiar with the basics of creating and editing automation in Logic. If you need a refresher, please take a look at "Automating the Mix and Using Control Surfaces" from David Nahmani's Level 1 Apple Pro Training Series book, *Logic Pro 9 and Logic Express 9.*

1   Choose File > Open.

2   In the Open window's file selector dialog, go to Music > Advanced Logic 9_Files > Lessons and open **12_I Was Raised_Start.logic**.

3   Drag-select the Track Solo buttons for both the Crunch_Gtr1 and Crunch_Gtr2 tracks (tracks 17 and 18, respectively), soloing them.

4   Create a Cycle region from measure 7 to measure 9.

5   Play the project, listening carefully to the two tracks for the length of the cycle. Click Stop.

You can distinctly hear the reverb tail continue from the last strummed chord of the Intro into Verse 1. Although this makes perfect sense from an engineering perspective, it does not fit the aesthetic of the project. All instruments stop precisely at the end of the Intro section, leaving the voice and piano exposed. By using automation, you can bypass the reverb at this point, eliminating the hanging tail that overlaps the verse.

Adding Channels to the Track List for Automation

To automate the reverb bypass, you must first add the aux channel where the reverb effect resides to the Arrange track list. This is done in the Mixer.

1 Press 2 to open Screenset 2.

2 Double-click the Send slot on either of the Crunch_Gtr channels.

The Mixer locates to the Aux 4 channel, selecting it.

3 In the Mixer's local menu bar, choose Options > Create Arrange Tracks for Selected Channel Strips.

4 Press 1 to open Screenset 1.

A new track, Aux 4, is created in the Arrange area and positioned below the Piano track.

5 In the track header, drag the Aux 4 track down, positioning it below the Crunch_Gtr2 track.

This is where you will automate the reverb bypass that will apply to both Crunch_Gtr tracks.

6 Using the Zoom tool, draw a selection rectangle around the two Crunch guitar regions in the Intro section as well as in the track below (Aux 4).

The magnification level expands, allowing you to view the selected area for both the Crunch_Gtr tracks and the Aux 4 track.

7 In the Arrange area's local menu bar, choose View > Track Automation.

The header of the selected track displays the automation menus.

8   In the Aux 4 track, click the Automation Parameter menu and choose Main > Insert #1 Bypass.

Insert #1 Bypass corresponds to the SilverVerb plug-in in the first Insert slot in the Aux 4 channel.

9   In the Aux 4 track, click the top of the automation track close to measure 8.

Two new nodes are created, both displaying *Bypassed*.

10 Drag the node at the beginning of the project down to to the bottom of the automation track.

11 If necessary, use the guideline to drag the new node so that it occurs just after the last bit of the waveform in the Crunch_Gtr tracks (around 8 1 1 41).

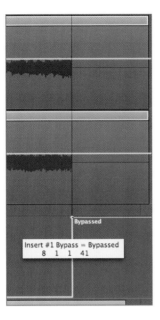

12 Play the project to hear the automated bypass silence the reverb. Stop the project.

Snapping Automation Data to the Timeline

The transition from the Bridge to Verse 4 is nearly identical to the transition between the
Intro and Verse 1, and could benefit from the same automation effect. You can easily do
this by Option-dragging the previously created automation nodes, copying it to the new
location. To make it easier to place the copied automation at the same relative location on
the timeline, you can enable Snap Automation. When Snap Automation is turned on, all
created nodes and edits are snapped to the grid.

1 Use the Zoom Horizontal Out key command (Control-Option-Left Arrow) to zoom
   out far enough to see the Bridge and Verse 4 sections.

2 Holding down the Shift key, draw a selection rectangle around the two bypass nodes
   you created in the previous exercise.

   NOTE ▶ Make sure you draw the selection rectangle within the automation area, as
   you could inadvertently select a region along with the automation nodes.

   The two nodes are selected, along with the area between them.

3 At the top of the Arrange area, click the Snap menu and choose Snap Automation.

4   Option-drag the selected area, using the guideline to position the copied set of nodes to the beginning of the Verse 4 section (the help tag will display 47 2 4 196).

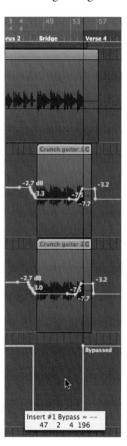

The automation nodes you created for the transition from the Intro to Verse 1 are copied to the transition between the Bridge and Verse 4.

> **TIP** ▶ Snap Automation is especially useful for creative automation that repeats on specific beats or at other intervals.

5   Turn Cycle mode off.

6   On the Crunch_Gtr tracks, click the Track Solo buttons, disabling them.

7   Play the project around the two locations where you created the bypass automation, listening to your work and observing the SilverVerb plug-in in the Arrange channel strip.

8   Stop the playback.

> **NOTE** ▶ Although Logic's automation is sample-accurate, its timing can still be affected by plug-in delays and hardware latencies. You can compensate for these delays by adjusting the Snap Offset parameter in Preferences > Automation. This will offset the automation on all tracks by a selected tick value (negative or positive).

Copying Automation Data Between Tracks

Doubled tracks are commonplace in musical productions, and they create a thicker, more complex sound when mixed with each other. These doubled channels most often need similar, if not identical automation, which can be laborious to recreate. Instead, try copying the automation data from one track to another, making any further adjustments starting with the newly copied data.

The doubled kick you created in Lesson 11 with a gated sine wave oscillator is a prime example of an instance when copying automation data is useful. In this exercise, you will copy the automation from the Kick track to the Kick Osc track, scaling it to an appropriate level.

1   Scroll downward to view the Kick and Kick Osc track (tracks 23 and 24) in the Arrange window.

At the end of Verse 4, all drum tracks (including the Kick track) contain automation that dips their volume level, followed by a brief build in intensity when entering the refrain. The side chain signal you sent to the Kick Osc track is sent pre-fader of the original channel. This signal is used solely to open and close the gate, and therefore does not adjust the gain of the Test Oscillator as it dips in volume. In order for the

Kick Osc track to exactly follow the dynamic shape of the Kick track, you need to copy and paste the automation.

2 Hold down Shift and drag to select all the nodes in the Kick track (track 23).

NOTE ▸ It is important to include the node located at the beginning of the project for this technique to work.

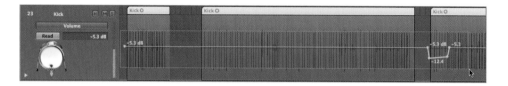

3 Press Command-C to copy the automation.

4 Select the Kick Osc track.

5 Press Command-V to paste the automation.

The automation you previously created now appears on the Kick Osc track. Since you did not enter these nodes manually, Read mode was not automatically enabled for this track. You need to make sure to enable Read mode to ensure that the copied track automation will be performed.

6 For the Kick Osc track, click the Automation Mode menu and choose Read.

TIP ▸ Automation data can also be copied from one parameter to another in a single track. You can do this by holding down the Command key while selecting parameters in the Automation Parameter menu. When doing so, Logic will prompt you to either convert or copy and convert the data, allowing you to either transfer the automation of one parameter onto another, or copy the data keeping the original automation intact.

Scaling Automated Values

Often you'll want to boost or reduce levels for an entire track proportionally while maintaining the automation shape and node relationships. The automation data you copied to the Kick Osc track has the correct dynamic shape but puts the track at a much higher volume level than before (it was originally −17 dB).

Instead of selecting each automation node and dragging the nodes to adjust the levels, you can scale the existing values up and down using the value fader with the Command key. In this exercise, you can try your hand at scaling the relative values of the volume automation data.

1   In the Kick Osc track header, Command-drag the value fader up and down, observing the changes to the automation.

Notice how the difference in levels between the nodes becomes greater as you scale up, and how the node levels move closer together when scaling down. When you adjust the levels for the entire automation track at once, all the values are changed proportionately by a percentage.

2   In the Kick Osc track, Command-drag the value fader until the first node of the track reads −17.0 dB.

3   Play the project from the end of Verse 4 (around measure 58), listening to the Kick Osc track and observing the volume fader in the Arrange channel strip.

4   Stop the playback.

TIP ▶ Automation data can also be scaled, copied, and pasted in the Automation Event List. This list cannot be accessed via the standard Event List in the Lists area, but only by using a key command. The default command is Control-Command-E.

Applying Automation to Multiple Tracks at Once

Channels that have been grouped in the Mixer not only can share automation modes, but they will also mirror any automation written to any of the tracks when the group is active (that is, group clutch is off). Any edits made to individual automation tracks in a group will be reflected by the other tracks as well. This enables you to quickly create offline automation, as well as edit real-time automation for groups while working on a single track.

In this exercise, you will add and alter automation data to an entire group of tracks at once.

1   Press 2 to open Screenset 2.

2   In the Mixer, scroll to the far right to view the drum tracks.

3   Drag-select the drum tracks (tracks 23 to 31).

4   In any of the selected tracks, click the Group slot and choose Open Group Settings from the pop-up menu. The Group Settings window opens.

5   Double-click the Nr. 2 row in the Name column, enter *Drums*, and press Return.

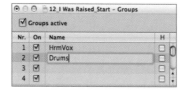

NOTE ▶ The automation mode setting of the channels in the group can be linked or unlinked by having the Automation Mode checkbox enabled in the Group Settings window. This is on by default.

6   Close the Group Settings window.

7   In any of the selected tracks, click the Group slot and choose Group 2: Drums from the pop-up menu.

All selected tracks are assigned to the Drums group.

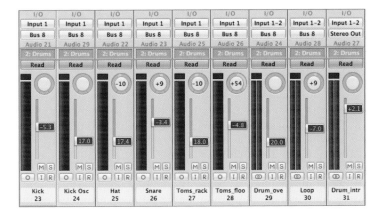

8 Press 1 to open Screenset 1.

9 In the Arrange window's track list, Shift-select tracks 23 through 31 (Kick through Drum_intro).

10 Use the Toggle Zoom to Fit Selection or All Contents key command (Z) to zoom the selected tracks.

11 Choose View > Track Automation. All drum track automation is displayed.

12 In any of the selected drum tracks, click in the track automation area around measure 89. New automation nodes are created in each track.

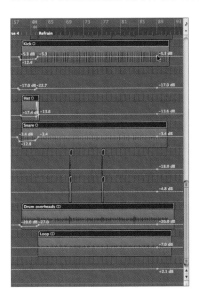

13 In the Kick track, drag the newly created automation nodes upwards to –0.3 dB (5 dB higher than the previous node).

> **TIP** ▶ You can alter Volume and Send automation nodes in 0.1 dB increments by holding the Control key while you change the value.

Notice that each track's automation node also increases in value, but not by the same value of 5 dB. This is because automation edits that are made on a track belonging to a group make relative, rather than absolute, changes to the automation on other tracks in the group.

> **NOTE** ▶ This relative relationship is also maintained when writing real-time automation to grouped tracks.

14 Choose Edit > Undo (or press Command-Z) twice, returning to the state before you entered the new automation nodes.

15 Save the project as *12_I Was Raised_Done*, saving it to Advanced Logic 9_Files > Media > Completed.

Using Control Surfaces

Although the mouse is suitable for setting controls, you will quickly discover that it is not the ideal tool for performing common mixing moves (such as dragging sliders and faders). The inability to click more than one thing at a time is a major hurdle you must overcome to effectively refine your mix.

To truly benefit from using real-time automation, you need to control the channel with something other than the mouse. A hardware control surface that is designed to integrate with Logic's Mixer will provide the best control for real-time automation, but any MIDI controller will do. In addition to standard MIDI controllers like mod and pitch bend wheels, most modern MIDI keyboards have integrated faders, knobs, and buttons that send out MIDI messages that can be assigned to Logic.

In this set of exercises, you will assign the buttons, knobs, and faders on a MIDI controller to transport controls, plug-in parameters, and channel controls in Logic's Mixer, giving you hands-on control over your mixes.

> **NOTE** ▶ Logic supports many leading hardware control surfaces with little or no setup. See the Logic Pro 9 Control Surfaces Support manual for details on supported devices and individual configuration directions.

Assigning Transport Controls

Most modern MIDI controllers have integrated transport buttons that send out MIDI messages. When assigned to Logic's transport controls, these buttons provide remote control of the project from wherever you are playing.

The easiest way to assign MIDI controllers to Logic's transport is through the Key Commands window.

> **NOTE** ▶ This exercise requires that you have a MIDI controller connected, preferably with integrated transport controls. However, you can still try the outlined steps with any MIDI button, pad, or key, as long as they are set to send an on/off MIDI command. Refer to your MIDI controller manufacturer's manual for further information as to what would send an on/off message on your keyboard.

1   Press 1 to reopen Screenset 1, making all tracks visible.

2   Choose Logic Pro > Preferences > Key Commands.

The Key Commands window opens. Note that below the standard Learn by Key Label and Learn by Key Position buttons (which we looked at back in Lesson 1), there is an Assignments window. This area displays MIDI messages that have been assigned to the selection in the command column.

You can assign MIDI messages to selected commands by clicking the Learn New Assignment button, located below the Assignments window.

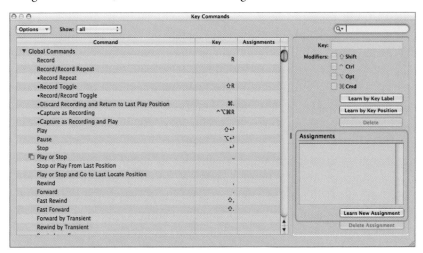

3   If necessary, clear out any text in the search field by clicking the cancel button.

4   Scroll to the top of the key commands list. Click the Global Commands disclosure tri-angle to display its commands, if they're not already displayed.

You should see all the basic transport controls listed in the Command column (record, play, stop, rewind, and forward).

5   In the Command column, select Play.

6   Click the Learn New Assignment button.

At this point, Logic is "listening" for MIDI messages coming in (as evidenced by the selected Learn New Assignments button) and will assign the next message coming in to the play command.

7   Press the play button on your MIDI controller.

The incoming MIDI message is displayed in the Assignments window followed by "Learned," and the Learn New Assignments button is turned off.

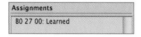

NOTE ► Avoid sending double commands by making sure that you press only a single button on your MIDI controller, and that you press it one time only. Also make sure to wait for the Learn New Assignment button to turn off before playing your MIDI controller.

Most likely you noticed that the project started playback when you assigned the MIDI command. This illustrates that the command assignment worked.

8   Stop the project.

Let's continue to assign transport buttons in the same manner.

9   In the Command column, select Stop.

10   Click the Learn New Assignment button.

11   Press the stop button on your MIDI controller and wait for the Learn New Assignment button to turn off.

The button is now assigned to the Stop command.

12 Using the same technique, assign buttons on your MIDI controller to the Forward, Rewind, Cycle Mode, and Record commands.

> **NOTE** ▶ When you first assign the Record command, it will put Logic into record mode, possibly prompting you for a save location and even initiating recording onto the currently selected track. After assigning the command, make sure to click Stop and delete any recordings that have inadvertently been made.

13 Close the Key Commands window.

14 Try out your new key commands by locating around the project, playing selected material.

Controlling Plug-in Parameters

Using a control surface to manipulate a control on a plug-in is a much more gratifying experience than using the mouse. This provides gestural control over a parameter, as well as the tactile connection lost to computer-based modern electronic music making.

In this exercise, you will assign your MIDI controller's mod wheel to the filter cutoff of the EXS24, letting you tweak the sound with your fingers.

> **NOTE** ▶ Automation Quick Access also allows you to assign any knob, fader, or wheel on your MIDI controller to the currently visible automation parameter on a track. While similar to the mapping of controller assignments done in this lesson, it is limited to automating only one parameter at a time. The Automation Quick Access controller assignment is done in the preferences, under the Automation tab.

1 Press 2 to open Screenset 2.

2 Select the Piano track (track 14).

3 In the channel's Input field, double-click the EXS24 to open the EXS24 interface.

In order to tell Logic which parameter you want to assign, you need to click it first.

4 Click the EXS24's filter cutoff knob without adjusting the control.

5 Choose Logic Pro > Preferences > Control Surfaces > Learn Assignment for "Filter Cutoff."

> **NOTE** ▶ The last selected parameter or channel control is always displayed in this menu, representing the assignment target.

The Controller Assignments window opens.

6   Click the Easy View button at the top of the Controller Assignments window, if it's
     not already selected.

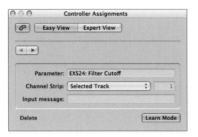

Note that "EXS24: Filter Cutoff" is displayed in the Parameter field, and that the
Learn Mode button is activated. Logic is now "listening" for MIDI input and will
assign it to the EXS24 filter cutoff.

7   Move your MIDI controller's mod wheel up and down all the way.

     NOTE ▸ When sending a continuous controller, it is important that you move it from
     smallest value to largest, so that the entire range is learned.

8   Click the Learn Mode button, deactivating it.

     The assignment is learned, and the mod wheel (Controller 1) is displayed in the Input
     message field.

     TIP ▸ You can also use the Learn New Controller Assignment key command
     (Command-L) to put Logic into Learn mode when the Controller Assignments window
     is not open. When doing this, you need to keep holding the Command key while you
     are moving the physical control on your MIDI controller, then release it when you're
     done. Essentially, Logic is listening for MIDI input as long as the Command key is held.

     You can now try out your new assignment.

9   Move your mod wheel, watching the EXS24's filter cutoff knob move in accordance.

     NOTE ▸ In this exercise you are using the mod wheel, but any knob or fader that
     sends a MIDI controller message works as well.

In the Controller Assignments window, you may have noticed that the Channel Strip menu is set to Selected Track. In effect, this dictates that the assignment applies to any selected track with an EXS24 instantiated, allowing you to control the filter cutoff with your mod wheel.

10 Close the EXS24 window.

TIP ▶ By repeating this technique, you can assign the same continuous controller on your MIDI controller to the filter cutoff controls of every synthesizer at Logic's disposal. This provides you with a single control that always manipulates the filter cutoff on the selected track, regardless of the software instrument.

Using Expert View

So far you've been working in the Controller Assignments window's Easy view. In order to visualize the assignment mappings you are creating, as well as perform more complicated assignments, you need to use Expert view.

1 In the Controller Assignments window, click the Expert View button. The window expands to display the Expert View parameters.

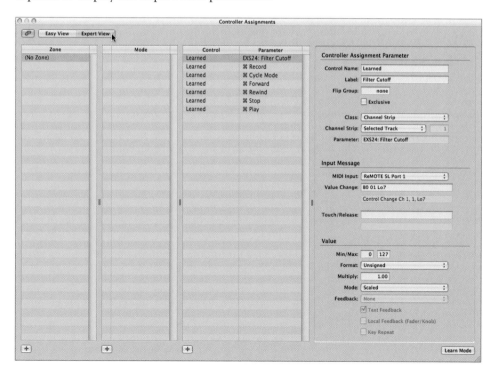

In the Control/Parameter list in the middle of the window, you can see all the assignments you have created so far, including the transport assignments made in the Key Commands window.

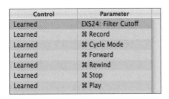

The right side of the window contains specific information for the selected assignment (currently EXS24: Filter Cutoff), including the assigned parameter, MIDI input message, and any value settings.

2   Select a few assignments in the Control/Parameter list and observe their settings in the Controller Assignment Parameter, Input Message, and Value areas.

In the following set of exercises, you will be using Expert view instead of Easy view to make and organize your assignments, as Expert view provides more control over the mappings you create.

Assigning Channel Controls

The knobs and faders that come on most modern MIDI controllers are commonly found in sets of eight or more, perfect for pairing each with a specific channel control in Logic's Mixer (volume, pan, sends, and so on). When assigning a set of MIDI controls to a set of channel controls, it is best to think of them as a consecutive series (fader 1, 2, 3, and so on), or bank, instead of isolated controls. These controls should be linked with a one-to-one relationship; for example, fader 1 on the control surface only controls the volume fader for channel 1 in Logic, fader 2 should only control channel 2's volume fader, and so on. This is a different linking strategy than the one used in the last exercise, where the mod wheel controls any EXS24 filter cutoff on any selected track.

While you can always reassign these links by selecting in the Channel Strip menu, Logic creates these relationships automatically, depending on whether the parameter you want to control is on a selected channel. In order for Logic to create a one-to-one assignment, as just described, you need to make sure that the currently selected channel is different from the one that contains the parameter you want to control.

In this exercise, you will assign a series of eight knobs or faders on your MIDI controller to the volume faders on channels 1–8 in Logic's Mixer.

NOTE ▶ The following exercises are designed for MIDI controllers with at least eight knobs or faders. However, you can still complete the lesson by creating a similar setup using a smaller set of knobs or faders at your disposal.

1   Deactivate groups by using the Group Clutch key command (Command-G).

NOTE ▶ Temporarily deactivating groups helps when assigning channel parameters, so each control will be independent from another. You can always activate them again for group control.

2   In the Mixer, make sure that channels 1–8 are not selected (the Piano channel should still be selected from the previous exercise).

3   In the Controller Assignments window, click the Learn Mode button, activating it. Logic is now waiting for MIDI input.

4   Click channel 1's volume fader. This defines the targeted parameter you want to control, which is displayed in the Control/Parameter list.

5   Move the first fader or knob of the series of eight on your MIDI controller up and down all the way.

The assignment is learned, and the MIDI message source and value is displayed in the Input Message area.

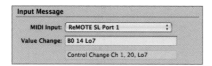

6   With Learn mode still activated, click channel 2's volume fader.

7   Move the second fader or knob of the series of eight on your MIDI controller up and down all the way.

The assignment is learned.

8   Repeat the process, clicking the volume fader on channels 3–8 and moving the appropriate knob or fader on your MIDI controller one at a time (while Learn mode is still activated).

9   When done, click the Learn Mode button, deactivating it.

You should now have a series of assignments that appear in the Control/Parameter list.

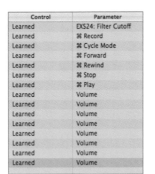

> **NOTE** ▸ If you make a mistake when assigning a parameter, you can delete the assignment by selecting it in the Control/Parameter list and pressing the Delete key.

10 Close the Controller Assignments window.

11 Move the knobs or faders you assigned, watching Logic's channel volume faders move in accordance.

If you look at the Channel Strip settings for the selected assignments, you will see that they are set for Fader Bank instead of Selected (as they were in the Filter Cutoff assignment). This indicates that each channel will be part of a consecutive series of faders, as specified in the number field to the right.

> **NOTE** ▸ A MIDI controller only sends 128 different values. In order to achieve smooth control over parameters that inherently have much finer resolution, Logic scales the MIDI value to match. This is the default when you make a channel control assignment, and it can be seen in the Mode menu in the Value area. Also in the Value area, the Min/Max fields let you set a range for the scaled controller, and the Multiply field lets you apply simple math to the input message, thereby changing the speed in which the parameter reacts to the controller's movement

Mapping the Same Controls to Multiple Parameters

Even if you only have a single set of eight knobs or faders on your MIDI controller, you aren't limited to controlling a single set of channel controls. By creating zones and modes in the Controller Assignments window's Expert view, you can use the same set of physical controllers for volume, pan, sends, and so on, toggling between these mappings via a button from your MIDI controller.

In this exercise, you will create two mapping modes for volume and pan, allowing you to assign the same set of knobs or faders to achieve independent control over both.

1   Choose Logic Pro > Preferences > Control Surfaces > Controller Assignments (or use the key command, Command-K).

The Controller Assignments window opens in Expert view.

You're going to assign the same set of knobs or faders to the pan controls on channels 1–8. You could assign them one at a time as before, but it is much easier to assign these series of controls using Logic's "fill up" feature. This requires you to assign only the first and last of the series; Logic will automatically fill in the missing controller assignment information.

NOTE ▶ In order to use the "fill up" feature, your MIDI controls must be sending consecutive continuous controller (CC) numbers (for example, CC 8–16) or MIDI channel numbers (for example, CC 7, Channels 1–8) for Logic to extrapolate the missing assignments. You can check what messages are being sent from the MIDI controller by observing Logic's MIDI Activity display while you move controls. If your MIDI controller isn't sending consecutive messages, you can use your MIDI controller's editing software to create these mappings before you try using Logic's "fill up" feature. If all else fails, you can assign the controllers one at a time using the technique you learned earlier.

2   Click the Learn button.

3   Click the pan knob for channel 1.

4   Move the first fader or knob of the series of eight on your MIDI controller up and down all the way.

The assignment is learned.

5   With Learn mode still activated, click channel 8's pan knob.

A dialog window appears, asking if you'd like to reassign the duplicate controls.

6   Click "Keep both." This is important, because you want to keep the correct MIDI message assigned to the parameters you specified. Don't worry about doubling the assignment for now.

7   With Learn mode still activated, move the last fader or knob for the series of eight on your MIDI controller up and down all the way.

8   Click the Learn mode button, deactivating it.

Another dialog window appears, similar to before, asking if you'd like to reassign the duplicate controls.

9   Click "Keep both."

Another dialog window appears, asking you whether you'd like Logic to automatically fill up in between the two assignments you made.

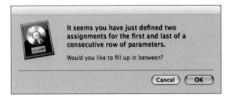

10 Click OK.

Logic creates eight consecutive assignments, mapping the first eight channels' pan controls to the eight consecutive knobs or faders on your MIDI controller.

Creating Zones and Modes

If you were to move one of the assigned knobs or faders on your MIDI controller, both the volume fader and the pan knob would respond (try this to see). The goal is to have separate modes that can be toggled, allowing you to control volume faders and pan knobs separately. To do this, you first need to create a zone, which represents your MIDI controller. Once created, you can make as many modes as you'd like in the zone.

Currently, the mappings have no zone assignment, indicated by "(No Zone)" in the Zone list.

NOTE ▶ (No Zone) is used to contain assignments that will work irrespective of any active user-created zone.

1   In the Controller Assignments window, click the Add (+) button beneath the Zone list.

A new zone is created in the Zone list, ready to be named.

2   Name the new zone after your MIDI controller. Press Return.

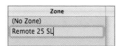

Notice that there aren't any assignments displayed in the Control/Parameter list when this new zone is selected. That is because they still reside in the (No Zone) area. Once you create the modes, you can add the assignments you created in the (No Zone) area into their associated modes.

3   Click the Add (+) button beneath the Mode list.

A new mode is created in the Mode column.

NOTE ▶ There is a bug in Logic Pro 9 that highlights "(No Mode)" when the first mode is created. This can make things a little confusing when you want to name a new mode, as this mode cannot be renamed.

4   In the Mode list, double-click New Mode, and then type *Volume*. Press Return.

5   Use the same technique to create another mode named *Pan*.

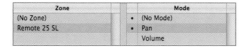

NOTE ▶ Similar to (No Zone), the default mode, (No Mode), contains assignments that will work irrespective of any active user-created mode.

Now that you have created the modes, you can fill them each by cutting and pasting the volume and pan assignments you made previously in the (No Zone) area.

6　In the Zone list, click (No Zone).

7　Command-select each pan assignment in the Control/Parameter list, and then press Command-X to cut.

8　In the Zone list, click the zone you created (and named after your MIDI controller).

9　In the Mode list, click the Pan mode, and then press Command-V to paste the assignments. The assignments are added to the Pan mode.

Zone	Mode	Control	Parameter
(No Zone)	• (No Mode)	Learned	Pan
Novation	• Pan	Learned	Pan
	Volume	Learned	Pan
		Learned	Pan
		Learned	Pan
		Learned	Pan
		Learned	Pan
		Learned	Pan

10　Using the same technique, cut and paste the volume assignments from the (No Zone) area to the Volume mode in your new zone.

Now that you've separated the pan and volume assignments into different groups, they will not interfere with each other. The active mode has a small black dot next to it in the Mode list. Because you selected the Volume mode last, it will be active.

11　Move one of the assigned knobs or faders on your MIDI controller.

The channel volume faders move, linked to the movement of the physical controller.

12　In the Mode list, select the Pan mode.

A black dot appears next to it, indicating that it is the active mode.

13　Move one of the assigned knobs or faders on your MIDI controller.

The channel pan knobs move, linked to the movement of the physical controller.

Assigning a Button to Switch Modes

You can select modes with the mouse, but it defeats the purpose of liberating yourself from having to use the mouse to mix. Instead, you can assign a button on your MIDI controller to change mode, acting as a toggle between the two modes you created.

Because you want this control to work regardless of the active mode, you need to create this in the (No mode) area.

> **NOTE ▶** You need a button that sends a simple on/off MIDI message to make the following exercise work. This can be a dedicated button, pad, or even a key on the MIDI controller, as long as it sends either a note on/note off or a toggled (on/off) continuous controller message. To find out what message the physical control sends, try hitting it while observing Logic's MIDI Activity display.

1   Select (No mode) in the Mode list.

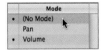

2   Click the Learn Mode button, activating it.

3   Press a button on your MIDI controller.

4   Click the Learn Mode button, deactivating it.

You probably noticed that Pan is listed in the Parameter field in the Controller Assignment Parameter area. That's because a pan knob was the last selected channel control. In order to create a mode switch, you need to assign the MIDI button to a different class in the Class menu.

5   In the Controller Assignment Parameter area, click the Class menu and choose Mode Change.

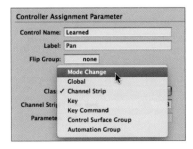

In order for the MIDI button to step through the modes, you need to make one more change in the Value area.

6   In the Value area, click the Mode menu and choose Rotate.

Now it's time to test out your assignment.

7   Press the button on your MIDI controller you assigned to switch modes. The Volume and Pan modes become active in turn with every button press.

8   Try toggling back and forth between the Volume and Pan modes while moving the knobs or faders you assigned previously.

You can now use the same set of knobs or faders to control both volume and pan in Logic's Mixer, changing their function with a button press.

Changing Fader Banks

The assignments you have done so far work great, but only for the first eight channels of the Mixer. You can use the same set of knobs or faders to control all channels of the mix by assigning two bank buttons that shift their targets to the next or previous group of eight. Like the mode change switch you created in the preceding exercise, you need to place this control in the (No mode) area so that it remains functional regardless of the active mode.

1   Click the Learn Mode button, activating it.

2   Press the button on your MIDI controller you want to assign to move to the next bank of faders.

3   Click the Learn Mode button, deactivating it. A new assignment is created.

Considering you will be assigning two buttons with nearly identical functions (next and previous bank), it's a good idea to name them.

4   In the Controller Assignment Parameter area, click in the Control Name field and enter *Bank +*. Press Return.

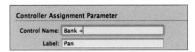

5   Click the Class menu and choose Control Surface Group.

6   Click the Parameter menu and choose Fader Bank for Current View.

By choosing Fader Bank for Current View, you are specifying that the bank control will work regardless of the view mode in Logic's Mixer.

7   Click the Bank Type menu and choose By Bank.

This will create the banking in groups of eight channels, which reflects the number of assigned channels you made earlier.

8   In the Value area, click the Mode menu and choose Relative.

This setting is used for buttons that increment/decrement by the amount set in the Multiply field just above it (currently set to 1.00).

This completes the setup for the next bank button. The previous bank button assignment is almost identical, except for two small things.

9   Using the same technique, assign another button on your MIDI controller to the same Class, Parameter, and Bank Type settings

10 In the Control Name field, type *Bank –*.

11 In the Value area, change the Multiply field to –1.00.

This step specifies that the button will move by bank decrementally.

Now that you've assigned your bank buttons, it's time to test them out.

12 Close the Controller Assignments window.

13 Press the button you assigned to Bank + and Bank –, and move one of the previously assigned knobs or faders, observing the channels in the Mixer.

You can now move in the Mixer in banks of eight channels, accessing the volume and pan controls via your MIDI controller.

14 Try your hand at using your new assignments to mix the project live, moving around the project, dynamically setting volume and pan levels, and writing automation.

NOTE ▶ All the assignments you created in the last set of exercises are saved in the com.apple.Logic.pro.cs preference file located in ~/Library/Preferences. All mappings done in the Controller Assignments window are global and apply to all project files. This file is updated whenever you quit Logic.

Lesson Review

1. How can you automate an aux channel?
2. Snap automation is enabled where?
3. How is automation data scaled?
4. What must be done in order to apply automation to multiple tracks at once?
5. Where do you assign MIDI controls to Logic's transport?
6. How do you assign MIDI controllers to plug-in parameters and channel controls?

Answers

1. Aux channels are automated by first adding them to the Arrange window with the Create Arrange Tracks for Selected Channel Strips command.

2. Snap automation is enabled in the Arrange area's Snap menu.

3. You can scale automation data by Command-dragging the value fader for the automation parameter.

4. In order to apply automation to multiple tracks at once, the channels must be grouped.

5. MIDI controls are assigned to Logic's transport in the Key Commands window.

6. MIDI controllers are assigned to plug-in parameters and channel controls in the Controller Assignments window.

13

Lesson Files   Advanced Logic 9_Files > Lessons > 13_A Blues for Trane_Start.logic

Media   Advanced Logic 9_Files > Media > A Blues for Trane

Time   This lesson takes approximately 60 minutes to complete.

Goals   Configure Logic for surround sound mixing

Position signals in the surround field

Apply multi-channel effects

Check your mix with multi-channel analysis tools

Encode your surround mix for DVD-Audio and DVD-Video

Working with Surround

The demand for surround sound production has rapidly increased in recent years, due mostly to the proliferation of home theater systems. Not only is surround sound the de facto standard for video (film, DVD-Video, Blu-ray, and so on), but it also has growing influence on interactive media (video games, web-based) and music (soundtracks, DVD-Audio titles).

As surround sound becomes more and more prevalent in the audio world, it becomes increasingly important to acquire at least a working knowledge of surround mixing. Logic provides sophisticated tools to produce a professional surround sound mix, whether you are creating content for video or interactive media, or producing music-only projects in surround sound.

In this lesson, you will explore the entire workflow of a surround music project, from setup to mixing to encoding.

> **NOTE** ▸ To complete this lesson, you will need an audio interface with at least six outputs wired to a six-channel surround sound playback system. If you do not have such a setup, you can still follow the exercises, but you will hear the results in stereo only.

Configuring Logic for Surround

Working in surround can encompass multiple surround formats, depending on the target playback system (home theater, movie theater, and so on). Logic can accommodate all popular surround configurations from quadraphonic to 7.1, but you will most likely work in the 5.1 (ITU 775) format for your surround productions. This format consists of three speakers across the front (left, center, right) and two speakers in the rear (left surround, right surround). The *.1* in the name represents a sixth channel for low-frequency effects (LFE) sent to a subwoofer.

> **MORE INFO** ▶ The Logic Pro 9 User Manual provides excellent explanations and diagrams of the various surround formats. See the "Working with Surround" section for details.

In this lesson, you will mix a jazz quintet session in 5.1 surround format and place the listener in the middle of the performers. Let's start by opening the project file used in this lesson.

1   Choose File > Open.

2   In the Open window's file selector dialog, go to Music > Advanced Logic 9_Files > Lessons and open **13_A Blues for Trane_Start.logic**.

3   Play the project to familiarize yourself with the material you will be mixing.

Assigning Audio Interface Outputs

To enable Logic to play a project through each speaker in your surround sound setup, the amplifier for each speaker must be connected to a separate output in your audio interface. Before you can begin mixing, you need to configure Logic to specify which output is connected to which speaker. This is done in Logic's preferences.

1   Choose Logic Pro > Preferences > Audio. The Audio preferences are displayed.

2   Click the I/O Assignments tab.

    The I/O Assignments tab contains options for configuring your surround setup.

3   Click the Output tab, if it's not already selected.

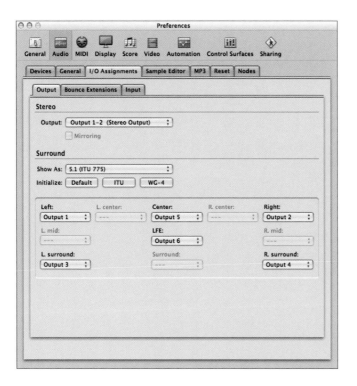

In the Output tab, you can specify which surround channel connects to which output of your audio interface (and, ultimately, to your speakers). Although you can match all conceivable setups, the default configuration is highly recommended, and it represents the established 5.1 (ITU 775) standard.

Notice that several channel assignments are dimmed and cannot be set in the Output Assignment area (L. center, R. center, L. mid, R. mid, Surround). These channels are filtered by the Show As menu, which is set to 5.1 (ITU 775) by default. The surround format chosen in the Show As menu makes available only the appropriate output channels.

4   Click the Show As pop-up menu to see the available configurations. When you're done, make sure to leave the setting at its default, 5.1 (ITU 775).

5   Look at each of the channel assignments in the Output Assignments area to verify that your system corresponds to this routing.

6   Close the Preferences window.

Setting the Project Surround Format

The Surround preferences are global (and remain the same from project to project), but each project can be independently configured to any surround format. The surround format is set in the Audio project settings.

1 Choose File > Project Settings > Audio. The Audio settings for the project are displayed.

By default, a project's surround format is set to 5.1 (ITU 775), as shown in the Surround Format menu. Alternative formats can be selected in that menu.

2 Click the Surround Format pop-up menu to see the available configurations, making sure to leave the setting at its default, 5.1 (ITU 775).

3 Close the Project Settings window.

Mixing in Surround

In the Mixer, look at the output assignments of the channels. The mix includes mono and stereo channels set to output through a single stereo output channel (Output 1-2). Some channels are also routed via buses to various submixes (Aux 2, 3, and 4), which, in turn, are also set to output through the single stereo output channel. In short, everything is configured to create a stereo mix.

To create a surround mix, you need to change the channel outputs from stereo to surround. You can do this by changing the assignment from stereo output to surround in the Output slot.

NOTE ▶ In this session, the trumpet, bass, and drum parts are made up of multiple tracks using different mic placements, which are then submixed. It is important not to change the output settings for the channels being routed to submixes, as that would change the signal flow. Instead, change the output settings for their respective submix channels (Aux 2 through 4) from stereo to surround.

1   Shift-click the Sax M130, Piano LR, Tpt Sub, Bass Sub, and Drums Sub channels to
    select them.

2   On any of the selected channel strips, click the Output slot and choose Output >
    Surround in the pop-up menu.

The Pan or Balance control on each selected channel changes to a Surround Panner.
To the right of the Mixer, you'll notice that the Stereo Output channel has been eliminated and that the Master channel now has a multisegment level meter.

3   Click the Mixer background to deselect all channels.

Using the Surround Panner

The Surround Panner is used to position signals in the surround field. Each speaker in the output array (except for the LFE) is represented by a small blue dot on the circumference of the circle, and the white dot represents the signal position. You can change a channel's position in the surround field by dragging the white dot in the Surround Panner.

1   On the Sax M130 channel, click the Solo button.

2   Press Control-Command-Right Arrow and Control-Command-Left Arrow (the Go to Next/Previous Marker key commands) to locate to the head marker.

3   Turn on Cycle mode.

4   Start playback, listening to the saxophone.

5   In the Surround Panner, drag the white dot to about the 10 o'clock position, slightly in from the edge.

The saxophone emanates from the front left side of the surround field.

As you most definitely discovered, it is difficult to precisely position a sound using the tiny Surround Panner in the channel. Fortunately, you can open the Surround Panner in a magnified window.

6   Unsolo the Sax M130 channel and solo the Tpt Sub channel.

7   On the Tpt Sub channel, double-click the Surround Panner.

The Surround Panner window opens.

8   Drag the blue dot to the 2 o'clock position, just in from the edge.

9   Stop playback.

In this enlarged view, it is much easier to accurately position a signal in the surround field. In addition, the Surround Panner window also provides precise visual feedback as to the angle (±180°) and diversity (distance from the surround field's center) of the positioning. These values are represented both graphically and numerically.

TIP ▶ The signal sent to the speakers can be muted by clicking the speaker icons in the Surround Panner.

Adjusting Center and LFE Levels

The Surround Panner window includes sliders to independently adjust the amount of signal sent to the center and LFE channels. By default, the Center Level slider is set to unity (feeding signal to the center channel), while the LFE is muted.

In this exercise, you will adjust the center and LFE levels of various channels. To most easily do this, start off by improving the Mixer's ergonomics.

1   Drag the Surround Panner window to the Mixer, just to the right of the last mixer channel.

2   At the top left of the Surround Panner window, click the Link button.

When the Link button is on, you can use a single window to display the Surround Panner of any channel strip, without the clutter of multiple windows.

3 Play the project.

4 In the Surround Panner window, drag the Center Level slider all the way to the left, muting the output.

As the amount of signal sent to the center channel is eliminated, the placement of the trumpet should become more focused on the front right side of the surround field.

5 Unsolo the Tpt Sub channel and solo the Bass Sub channel.

6 On the Bass Sub channel, double-click the Surround Panner.

The Surround Panner window displays the settings for the Bass Sub channel (because linking is turned on).

7 While watching the visual readouts, position the blue dot at an Angle of about 150 (degrees) and a Diversity of about 0.40.

TIP▶ Double-clicking the numeric displays at the top of the Surround Panner window and entering a number will precisely set angle and diversity.

8 Drag the Center Level slider all the way to the left, muting the output.

9 Drag the LFE Level to the right, to a value of –15.5 dB.

As the amount of signal sent to the LFE channel is increased, the bass frequencies should become more pronounced, reinforced by the subwoofer.

10 After you've had a chance to hear the results of your actions, stop playback.

11 Unsolo the Bass Sub channel.

Balancing Stereo to Surround Signals

Depending on the type of input signal (mono, stereo, or surround), Logic uses slightly different types of Surround Panners. So far you've been working with mono source signals. In this exercise, you will use the Surround Panner to accurately position stereo signals in the surround field.

> **NOTE** ▶ A signal's channel input format is indicated by the number of level meters and by the symbol on the button below them. See the section "Setting the Input Format of Channel Strips" in the Logic Pro 9 User Manual for detailed descriptions and illustrations of each input format.

1   Solo the Sax M130, Piano LR, Tpt Sub, and Bass Sub channels.

In this exercise, you will adjust the surround placement of the stereo piano channel in the context of other instruments that are already positioned.

2   On the Piano LR channel, double-click the Surround Panner.

The Surround Panner window displays the Piano LR channel, which is a stereo source.

When using a stereo source, the Surround Panner window contains an additional parameter, Spread, which indicates the width of the stereo signal in the surround field. This is represented graphically by the L and R dots (representing the left and right side of the stereo image), and numerically at the top of the window.

3 Play the project, listening to the piano's position in the surround field.

As you can hear, the piano sounds a bit wide, crowding the saxophone and trumpet on either side of it.

The spread of the signal can be adjusted by dragging the L and R dots in the Surround Panner window.

4 Try dragging the L dot to the left and right, increasing and decreasing the spread while listening to the results.

You have to be careful when dragging the L or R dots, as you can inadvertently change the angle and diversity. To avoid doing this, Command-drag the L or R dot. This will lock down the diversity and angle, allowing you to adjust only the spread.

5 Position the blue dot to an Angle of 0.0 and Diversity of 0.12.

6 Command-drag the L dot toward the center blue dot until the Spread value is +34.

In effect, you narrowed the stereo signal slightly, causing less overlap with the saxophone and trumpet in the surround field.

7 Stop playback.

8   Option-click an active Solo button on any of the soloed channels.

All the Solo buttons are turned off at once.

Let's now do the same thing with another stereo source, placing the drums submix in the surround field while listening to the entire mix.

9   In the Drums Sub channel, double-click the Surround Panner to display its settings in the Surround Panner window.

10   Play the project.

11   By moving the dots or changing the numeric values, position the stereo source in the surround field at an Angle of –157.0, Diversity of 0.27, and Spread of +91.

12   Remove any signal fed to the center channel by muting the center level.

This places the drums behind and to the left side in their own space in the surround mix.

13   Stop playback.

14   Close the Surround Panner window.

Using Surround Effects

To preserve imaging, surround mixing often requires the use of specialized surround processors. These are, in essence, effects that independently process the individual channels of the given surround format. There are two types of surround processors available in Logic: multi-channel and multi-mono. With multi-channel effects, the surround channels are tightly integrated, or coupled, processing the entire surround source at once. Multi-mono effects, on the other hand, are essentially multiple mono plug-ins that are individually applied to each surround channel in the signal path.

In this exercise, you will assign both types of surround format plug-ins to channels, creating surround send and insert effects to aid in producing a professional-sounding mix.

> **NOTE** ▶ Logic's surround plug-ins work in all surround formats available to the application (Quadraphonic, LCRS, 5.1, 6.1, 7.1, and so on). The surround format chosen for the project determines the surround format of the plug-ins.

Using Multi-channel Effects

Immersing the listener in an artificially created ambience is the primary goal of surround production. To aid in this task, multi-channel reverb is used to simulate acoustic environments in the surround field. What differentiates the surround reverb processor from its mono and stereo cousins is its ability to simultaneously receive input from and send output to more than two channels.

For this exercise, you will use a multi-channel version of Logic's convolution reverb, Space Designer, as a send effect. This plug-in not only sends and receives over multiple channels; it also utilizes specialized surround recordings of real acoustic spaces for impulse responses.

1   Solo the Sax M130 channel.

2   On the Sax M130 channel, click the first Send slot and choose Bus > Bus 1.

    A new aux channel is created, receiving input from Bus 1.

3   Below the meters on the Aux 1 channel, click the channel Format button and choose Surround from the pop-up menu.

The channel switches from mono to surround, and the level meters now display six segments instead of one or two (mono or stereo, respectively). These represent each of the six channels used in a 5.1 configuration.

4   On the Aux 1 channel, click the first Insert slot and choose Reverb > Space Designer > 5.1. The Space Designer interface opens.

5   Click the Settings menu and choose 05 Surround Spaces > 01 Surround Rooms > 02.9 Hansa Studio +.

Space Designer loads the surround impulse response recording and any control configurations saved to the preset.

NOTE ▶ The surround impulse responses included with Logic Pro have been recorded with a variety of surround recording techniques, such as circle B-format, omni B-format, and discrete omni. You will even find different format recordings of the same acoustic space.

At first glance, the Space Designer interface looks identical to the stereo version. However, closer inspection reveals that the wet/dry controls are replaced by four sliders. Using these you can adjust the amount of wet and dry signal, and you can control the balance between the front and rear speakers. An additional slider is provided to adjust the amount of signal sent to the center channel.

6   Drag the center channel output slider (labeled C) down to a value of –4.0 dB.

This reduces the amount of reverb signal sent to the center channel, creating a more or less equal dispersion of reverb across the surround field.

7   Close the Space Designer window.

As it is now, the Sax M130 channel is set to send to the surround reverb post fader, but pre Surround Panner. In order to have the surround reverb preserve positional information when generating reflections, you need to assign the send post pan.

8   On the Sax M130 channel, click-hold the Send slot and choose Post Pan.

9   Play the project.

10   On the Sax M130 channel, increase the send amount to Bus 1 (Aux 1) to –14.0 dB.

You should not only hear the saxophone localized off to the left front of the surround field but also hear the processed signal in all five speakers. This creates a convincing ambient effect of the saxophone in a three-dimensional space.

NOTE ▸ The color of the Send level knob ring denotes pre- or post-pan routing. A green ring denotes pre-pan, a blue ring post-pan routing.

11 Unsolo the Sax M130 channel.

12 Assign the sends on the Piano LR, Tpt Sub, Bass Sub, and Drums Sub channels to Bus 1 (Aux 1), and set each to Post Pan.

13 Adjust the send amount of each of the channels in step 12 to the surround reverb, listening to how they sit in the ambient surround field.

14 Stop playback.

Using Multi-mono Insert Effects

When used as an insert on a surround channel, any effect not specifically configured for multi-channel audio is offered in the multi-mono format (this includes third-party plug-ins). These are applied specifically to surround input signals and can be thought of as multiple instantiations of the same effect, one for each surround channel. What makes these multi-mono effects especially powerful is the ability to independently process the LFE channel, which is often called for when you're creating a surround mix.

The surround professional generally can't predict how a carefully crafted mix will translate to consumer setups because the subwoofer is often the most inaccurately configured component in a typical home theater system. In addition, the bass-management systems used in consumer receivers vary widely from manufacturer to manufacturer. For this reason, it is recommended that you apply a low-pass filter to the output of the LFE channel while mixing and mastering to catch any stray high frequencies that might otherwise get through. You can accomplish this by inserting a multi-mono version of the Channel EQ on the Master channel, processing only the LFE channel while leaving the others untouched.

1 On the Master channel, click the first Insert slot and choose EQ > Channel EQ > Multi Mono.

The Channel EQ interface appears.

Multi-mono versions of plug-ins display an additional set of buttons in the plug-in header compared with their mono or stereo versions. These buttons provide access to surround routing and configuration options.

2   At the top of the interface, click the Configuration tab.

The plug-in interface changes to display the configuration of the multiple channels.

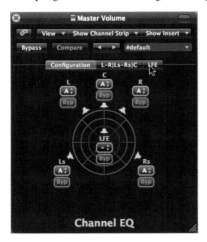

In the Configuration tab, you can bypass the effect on a channel-by-channel basis. The small pop-up menu located under each channel represents a form of grouping, not unlike the channel groups you created in Lesson 9. Assigning multiple channels to a group (A, B, C, or none) in this window allows you to simultaneously bypass all the channels in the same group.

3   Click the Bypass button on any channel except the LFE channel.

All the channels assigned to group A (L, C, R, Ls, Rs) are bypassed, leaving the LFE channel active.

4   At the top of the interface, click the LFE tab.

The plug-in interface changes to display the EQ settings for the LFE channel.

5   Click the Low-Pass Filter button (at the far right), enabling the filter band.

6   Double-click the Frequency setting for the Low-Pass Filter band and enter *120*.

7   Drag the Gain/Slope setting for the Low-Pass Filter band up to 48 dB/Oct.

By using a low-pass filter on the LFE channel, you will remove all frequencies that might cause undue muddiness in the subwoofer channel.

NOTE ▶ There is no hard and fast rule for selecting the frequency for the low-pass filter used on the LFE channel. Usually it is set between 80 Hz and 120 Hz, and it can be different for each monitoring system. To make matters more confusing, some consumer surround systems utilize their own low-pass filters for removing unwanted high frequencies sent to the subwoofer.

8   Close the Channel EQ window.

Checking the Surround Mix

Logic also offers specialized surround plug-ins that enable you to check your mix. These help identify problem spots by isolating individual channels as well as visually displaying the content in the surround field.

1   On the Master channel, click the second Insert slot and choose Utility > Multichannel Gain > 5.1. The Multichannel Gain plug-in appears.

The Multichannel Gain plug-in allows you control the gain and polarity inversion of each channel of a surround track or bus independently. You can also use the plug-in to individually mute each of the surround channels, allowing you to isolate the speaker output.

2   Play the project.

3   Try muting channels individually or in combination to isolate speaker output.

NOTE ► The order of channels as displayed in the channel level meters is determined by the Channel Order setting in the Display preferences (Logic Pro > Preferences > Display, and then click the Mixer tab). Logic's default Internal setting (L, R, Ls, Rs, C, LFE) can be somewhat confusing if you're using the Multichannel Gain plug-in because the two interfaces display the channels in a different order. However, this can be remedied by choosing the Centered setting (Ls, L, C, R, Rs, LFE) in Logic's preferences, which reflects the Multichannel Gain order.

4   After you have a chance to experiment, stop the playback.

5   Make sure that all channels are unmuted in the Multichannel Gain plug-in.

6   On the Master channel, click the third Insert slot and choose Metering > MultiMeter > 5.1. The surround MultiMeter plug-in appears.

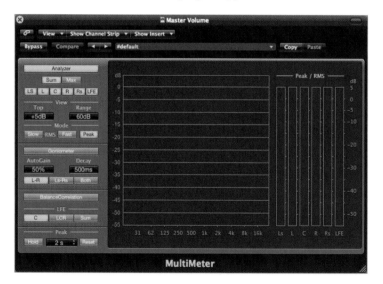

7   Play the project, observing the MultiMeter's frequency analyzer and level meters.

The surround version of the MultiMeter plug-in provides a suite of helpful analysis tools for examining the channels of your surround mix. In addition to a multichannel frequency spectrum analyzer, level meters, and goniometer, the MultiMeter includes an excellent surround balance analyzer.

8   At the lower left of the plug-in interface, click the Balance/Correlation button.

The main window displays sound position in the surround field, which responds dynamically to the signal. You can use this to check the balance of the mix between the Ls, L, C, R, and Rs channels.

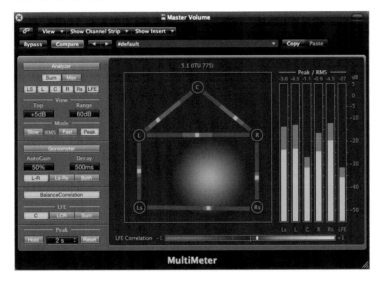

9   Turn off Cycle mode.

10   As the project is playing, listen to your surround mix while watching the balance display.

Now that you've checked sound placement for your surround mix, you can check the LFE Correlation meter to see if the LFE is causing any phase cancellation. This meter can be displayed in a variety of ways, comparing the phase of the LFE channel to the center, the front (left, center, and right), or the sum of all channels.

11   In the LFE section just below the Balance/Correlation button, click the Sum button.

12   If necessary, rewind to the beginning of the project and start playback, watching the LFE Correlation meter at the bottom of the MultiMeter interface.

The LFE Correlation meter moves to the left of the middle point toward −1, indicating that the LFE channel is out of phase with the other channels. This can be remedied in the Multichannel Gain plug-in by reversing the phase of the LFE channel.

13 In the Multichannel Gain plug-in window, click the Phase Invert button for the LFE channel.

The MultiMeter's LFE Correlation meter now moves to the right of the middle, toward +1, indicating that the LFE channel is in phase with the rest of the surround channels.

14 Stop the playback after you've checked your mix.

15 Close the MultiMeter and Multichannel Gain plug-in windows.

Down Mixing

The act of reducing a surround mix to a four-channel (quadraphonic, LCRS) or two-channel (stereo) version is called *down mixing*. To aid in down mixing, Logic Pro includes a specialized Down Mixer plug-in that can be applied to the Master channel, automatically folding down the surround mix to a specified format. As most consumer DVD-Video players incorporate a built-in down mixing process, this enables you to check your mix's compatibility with these down mixing systems, as well as quickly create new format mixes for delivery.

1 On the Master channel, click the fourth Insert slot and choose Utility > Down Mixer > 5.1->Stereo.

The Master channel changes to display stereo level meters, and the Down Mixer plug-in appears in the linked window.

2 Play the project, listening to the stereo down mix, which should now be emanating only from the left and right speakers.

> **NOTE** ▸ If necessary, you can adjust the levels of the input surround channels using the level sliders.

3   Stop the playback.

4   In the Master channel, click the Down Mixer plug-in and choose No Plug-in from the pop-up menu, thereby removing the Down Mixer plug-in from the channel strip.

> **NOTE** ▸ In addition to its suite of surround effect plug-ins, Logic Pro 9 includes surround versions of the EXS24 mkII, ES2 and Sculpture software instruments.

Encoding Surround Projects

Depending upon the delivery format, different techniques exist for encoding a surround project for distribution. In this exercise, you will create a DVD-Audio disc, as well as encode a surround mix in the Dolby Digital (AC3) format, ready for inclusion in a DVD-Video disc.

Creating DVD-Audio Discs

Logic has the ability to create DVD-Audio discs without the need for an external encoding application. This is accomplished in the Bounce window.

1   At the bottom of the Master channel, click the Bnce (Bounce) button.

The Bounce window opens.

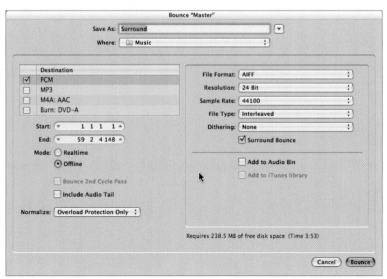

2   In the Destination area on the left, deselect any active checkboxes (PCM, MP3,
    M4A: AAC).

3   Select the Burn: DVD-A checkbox.

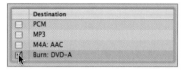

The DVD-A options appear to the right of the Destination box.

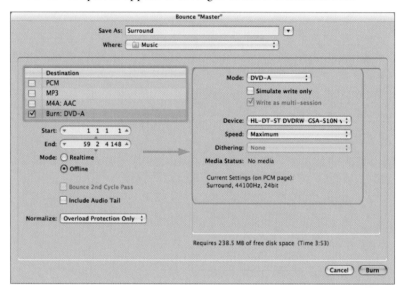

NOTE ▶ If you've never burned a DVD-A before, you might see Burn: CDDA (CD
audio) in the menu instead of Burn: DVD-A. If this is the case, choose DVD-A from
the Mode menu to burn a DVD-A instead of a regular CD.

4   In the Save As field, enter *Working with Surround.*

5   Insert a blank DVD into your DVD burner.

6   Click the Burn button.

After the burn process is completed, you will have a DVD-Audio disc that can be played in the majority of commercial DVD players (make sure your DVD player supports the DVD-Audio format before playing your disc).

NOTE ▶ You cannot use the Bounce command to create compressed surround files (AAC, ALAC, MP3).

Encoding Dolby Digital Files (AC3) Using Compressor

Compressor is a high-quality encoding application that comes with Logic Studio. Among the many audio and video formats it offers for content delivery, Compressor provides Dolby Digital (AC3) encoding, the industry standard format used for DVD-Video surround soundtracks.

Encoding surround sound for DVD-Video entails a two-step process:

▶   Creating a master multi-channel file

▶   Encoding a composite surround format file from the master multi-channel file using compression/encoding software or hardware.

A master multi-channel file is also created in the Bounce window.

1   At the bottom of the Master channel, click the Bnce button. The Bounce window opens.

2   Deselect the Burn: DVD-A checkbox.

3   Select the PCM checkbox.

4   In the options to the right of the Destination box, select the Surround Bounce checkbox.

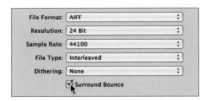

5   At the lower right of the window, click the Bounce button.

> **NOTE ▸** Logic automatically sets the file path for bounces to a Bounces folder created in the project folder.

A bounce is performed, creating an interleaved multi-channel file named Working with Surround.aif.

Now that the master multi-channel file has been created, you can import it into an application such as Compressor for encoding as a Dolby Digital (AC3) file.

> **NOTE ▸** In order to create encoded Dolby Digital (AC3) surround files, some encoder applications need to import multiple "stems," or submix files, corresponding to each surround output channel instead of a single interleaved multi-channel file. You can create these stems when bouncing by choosing Split from the File Type menu in the Bounce window. The resulting files will have extensions added to their names, corresponding to their derived channels (L, R, C, Ls, Rs, LFE).

6   Open the Compressor application.

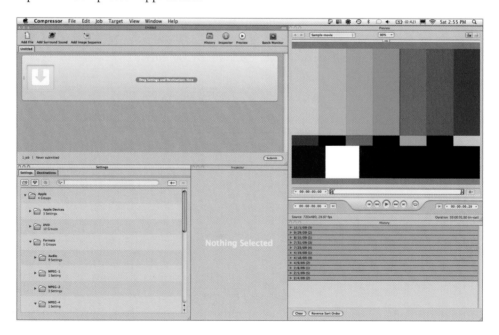

NOTE ► Due to the configurability of Compressor, your window arrangement might appear differently than the one shown here.

7   Click the Add File button.

8   In the file browser, go to Advanced Logic 9_Files > Media > A Blues for Trane > Bounces and select Working with Surround.aif.

9   Click the Open button.

The Working with Surround.aif file is added to the Batch.

10 In the Settings window, choose Apple > Formats > Audio > Dolby Digital Professional 5.1.

NOTE ► The actual data settings are displayed for each of the presets in the Inspector window to the right of the Settings window.

11 Drag the Dolby Digital Professional 5.1 setting and drop it on the Working with Surround.aif icon in the Batch window.

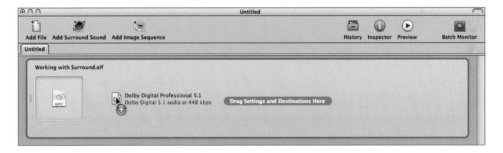

12 At the lower-right corner of the Batch window, click the Submit button.

The submit dialog appears, prompting you to name the submitted batch.

13 Click Submit.

Compressor encodes the interleaved multi-channel file as a Dolby Digital AC3 file, ready for inclusion into a DVD-Video project. The new file will be located in the same folder location as the Working with Surround.aif file (Music > Advanced Logic 9_Files > Media > A Blues for Trane > Bounces).

MORE INFO ▸ For additional information on Compressor, see Brian Gary's *Apple Pro Training Series: Compressor 3.5* from Peachpit Press.

Lesson Review

1.   Where do you assign the outputs of your audio interface to corresponding surround channels?

2.   Where do you set the surround format for an individual project?

3.   How does the stereo input Surround Panner differ from that of other input formats (mono and surround)?

4.   How does the surround version of the Space Designer plug-in differ from the mono and stereo versions when used as a send effect?

5.   How do multi-channel insert plug-ins differ from the mono and stereo versions?

6.   How can you quickly create a four- or two-channel version of your surround mix?

7.   What two steps are involved in creating a Dolby Digital (AC3) file ready for DVD-Video?

Answers

1.   Assigning the outputs of your audio interface to corresponding surround channels is done by choosing Preferences > Audio > I/O Assignments and clicking the Output tab.

2.   The surround format for a project is set in the Audio tab of the Project Settings window.

3.   The stereo input to the Surround Panner offers an additional Spread control.

4.   The surround version of the Space Designer plug-in loads surround format impulse responses, and it has additional controls to adjust the center level as well as the balance between the front and rear speakers.

5.   Multi-channel insert plug-ins have additional configuration settings allowing you to bypass any surround channel. In addition, the LFE channel can be processed independently from the rest of the surround channels.

6. You can quickly create a four- or two-channel version of your surround mix by applying the Down Mixer plug-in to the Master channel.

7. To create a Dolby Digital (AC3) file ready for DVD-Video, you must bounce an interleaved multi-channel surround file from within Logic, and then encode the file using a compression/encoder application such as Compressor.

14

Lesson File   Advanced Logic 9_Files > Lessons > 14_MIDI Processing.logic

Media   Advanced Logic 9_Files > Media > Environment

Time   This lesson takes approximately 90 minutes to complete.

Goals   Use and create layers in the Environment

Understand MIDI signal flow within the Environment

Create objects for processing MIDI data

Create serial and parallel routing for complex real-time processing

Trigger MIDI regions with touch tracks objects

MIDI Processing in the Environment

From the very beginning, the Environment has set Logic apart from other sequencers. The Environment is often thought of as a virtual studio, containing objects that represent your audio channels and MIDI devices. However, the Environment is much, much more, enabling you to process data from MIDI and software instruments in real time by creating complex signal routings and transformations to augment your music.

In this lesson, you will explore useful MIDI processors in the Environment, creating signal routings to affect MIDI input in a variety of ways.

NOTE ▸ You will need to set the "Display Middle C as" preference to C3 (Yamaha) to accurately follow the directions in this exercise (and others throughout the book). This preference can be found in the Preferences > Display > General tab.

Navigating Within the Environment

The Environment is tucked neatly away within its own window, which can be accessed like any other, via the main Window menu. Like other windows, the Environment window can be part of a screenset, which helps to keep things organized.

1　Choose File > Open.

2　In the file selector dialog, go to Music > Advanced Logic 9_Files > Lessons and open **14_MIDI Processing.logic**.

The project opens, displaying Screenset 1, which consists of an Arrange window (with the Library displayed) placed above an Environment window.

The Environment is divided into layers, displaying objects of like type or function to help keep things organized. You are currently looking at the All Objects layer, which provides an easy way to look at all objects currently within the project's Environment. Here, you can see the three software instruments (Marimba, 8bit Kit, and Analog

Lead) assigned to the Arrange track list, as well as other objects being used "behind the scenes" for MIDI input.

NOTE ▶ The top two tracks in the track list are placeholders currently assigned to a special No Output destination. Tracks assigned to No Output will not send any data.

3   In the Arrange track list, click the Marimba, 8bit Kit, and Analog Lead tracks (tracks 3 through 5) one at a time, playing your MIDI keyboard to familiarize yourself with the sound of the software instruments.

When you select a track in the track list, MIDI input from your controller is routed to the track's assigned channel. Notice that when you select tracks in the track list, the corresponding Environment object is also selected.

4   Click the Marimba track (track 3) in the track list, selecting it for MIDI input.

Navigating layers is done by clicking the arrow button next to the Layer menu, located in the upper-left corner of the Environment window.

5   Choose Click & Ports from the Layer menu.

The layer switches, displaying the contents of the Click & Ports layer.

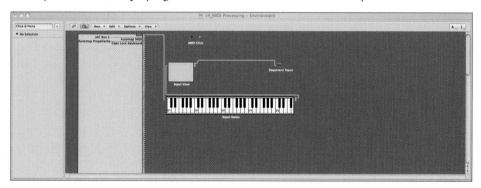

The Click & Ports layer contains objects specific to the routing of MIDI signals from their initial input until they reach Logic's sequencer. The Physical Input object at the far left represents your MIDI interface or MIDI controller (with direct MIDI-to-USB or FireWire connection). All available ports from your MIDI input devices will be listed in the Physical Input object (including the Caps Lock Keyboard and virtual ones like the IAC Bus and Network MIDI). Their corresponding cable outputs are depicted by the small triangles running along the right side.

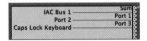

NOTE ▶ The SUM output at the top carries a combination of all MIDI input ports displayed in the Physical Input object that are not currently cabled. When a cable is connected from one of the remaining MIDI ports, its signal will not be passed through the SUM output.

MIDI signals are passed from object to object in the Environment by cabling them together. The left side of an object represents the input; the right side represents the output. As you can see in this layer, the Physical Input is cabled to a keyboard object, labeled Input Notes.

6   Play a few notes on your MIDI controller, observing the keyboard object.

NOTE ▶ If you don't have a MIDI controller handy, the Caps Lock Keyboard will work equally well for the exercises in this lesson.

As you play the keys on your MIDI controller, the software instrument you selected in the track list (Marimba) is triggered, while the corresponding pitches are displayed in the keyboard object.

7   Click some of the keys on the keyboard object.

The Marimba is triggered each time you click the keyboard object.

You have probably noticed that when you play a note on your MIDI controller or click the keyboard object, MIDI events are displayed in the Input View object cabled to the output of the keyboard object. This is a monitor object, which displays all MIDI data passing through it in list form.

The signal chain finally ends with a Sequencer Input object. This represents the connection to Logic's sequencer and routes to the selected track in the Arrange track list.

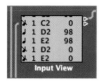

By having the Physical Input cabled to the Sequencer Input (passing through the keyboard and monitor objects), the MIDI signal flows from the MIDI interface or controller providing input, ultimately arriving at the selected Arrange track via the Sequencer Input object.

TIP ▶ If the connection between the Physical Input and the Sequencer Input is severed, MIDI input signals will not be recorded in the Arrange tracks. This connection is a good place to check when you do not see any signal in the Input View object, or are having problems receiving MIDI input in the Arrange window.

Creating Environment Objects

Now that you've had a chance to observe signal flow within the Click & Ports layer, you can try creating Environment objects to process incoming MIDI signals. Although new objects can be inserted in any layer, in this case it makes sense to create an Environment layer to house the new objects you will be exploring in this exercise.

1   Choose Create Layer from the Layer menu.

An empty layer is created.

2   Select "(unnamed)" in the Layer menu text field, and enter *MIDI Process*. Press Return.

You now have a new layer to house your MIDI processing experiments, ready for new objects to be added.

Using Monitor Objects

As you noticed previously in the Click & Ports layer, monitor objects are used to display MIDI signals passing through them. New ones can be created by choosing them from the Environment window's New menu.

1   In the Environment's local menu bar, choose New > Monitor.

A new monitor object appears.

By itself, a monitor object does nothing. In this exercise, you will be using it to both monitor MIDI signals passing through it and to connect to the Marimba software instrument channel selected in the Arrange area. In order to pass the signal, you need to cable the output of the monitor object to the Marimba software instrument channel, which is housed in a different layer (the Mixer layer). Even though these objects exist in different layers, you can still cable them together by first holding down the Option key, and then clicking the cable output of the monitor object.

2   While holding down the Option key, click the cable output (the small triangle in the upper-right corner) of the monitor object.

A menu appears, allowing you to set the destination for the cable.

3   Choose Mixer > Software Instrument > Marimba.

A cable appears, connecting the objects between the layers of the Environment.

NOTE ▶ Once an output from an object is used (cabled to another object), another output triangle automatically appears.

In order to keep things straight, it's a good idea to label objects as you create them.

4   Using the Text tool, click the monitor object to rename it.

5   Enter *To Marimba*. Press Return.

6   Switch back to the Pointer tool and drag the monitor object to the right side of the Environment window, to make room for other objects.

TIP ▶ When creating, moving, and naming objects in the Environment, it helps to alternate between the Pointer tool and the Text tool. These are the default (left-click) and alternate (Command-click) tools in the Environment by default, so you can toggle between them by pressing the Command key.

Using Arpeggiator Objects

Arpeggiator objects receive MIDI note input, outputting each note individually in a variety of selectable patterns, speeds, and lengths. Logic's arpeggiator objects are extremely flexible and can be configured to create complex rhythmic patterns out of static chords.

1   From the Environment's local menu bar, choose New > Arpeggiator.

A new arpeggiator object appears.

In this exercise you will not only be creating new Environment objects but also be cabling them in a variety of ways to process MIDI data. To aid in visualizing the signal routing from one object to the next, you can color the objects and their respective cables.

2   Choose View > Colored Cables.

3   Choose View > Colors.

The color palette appears, allowing you to assign colors to selected objects.

4   With the arpeggiator object still selected, click a shade of green in the color palette.

The arpeggiator object becomes green.

5   Click and hold down the cable output of the arpeggiator object, dragging the new cable to the monitor object.

You now have a connection between the arpeggiator and the Marimba software instrument channel (passing through the monitor).

In order for the arpeggiator to receive input from your MIDI keyboard, you need to bring it up on a track in the Arrange area. Rather than go back to the Arrange area to do this (via Reassign Track or Library), you can use the MIDI Thru tool in the Environment. Any object you click in the Environment using this tool will be configured for the currently selected Arrange track.

6   In the Arrange area, select the top No Output track (track 1) in the track list.

7   Using the MIDI Thru tool, click the arpeggiator object.

The selected Arrange track (track 1) changes to the arpeggiator object.

You can test to see if the arpeggiator is receiving input by playing your MIDI controller.

8   Play a few notes on your MIDI controller, observing the monitor within the Environment window.

You should hear the Marimba software instrument as well as see MIDI data displayed in the monitor object.

The arpeggiator object works with tempo-related material, so in order to have it process the incoming MIDI, the project has to be playing.

9   Play the project.

10 While the project is playing, hold down a chord (any combination of notes) on your MIDI controller.

You should now hear the chord arpeggiated as well as see the resultant MIDI data displayed in the monitor object.

11 Try adding or subtracting notes to your held chord, observing how they change the arpeggio.

NOTE ▶ It is important for the project to remain playing in order for many of the Environment objects to process incoming MIDI notes. Throughout the lesson, if you reach the end of the project, return to the beginning and start playback again.

In the Object Parameter box, you will find many useful settings for the arpeggiator object. Here, you can select from various patterns as well as adjust the velocity, speed, length, and octave of the arpeggiated notes.

NOTE ▶ If it is difficult to both reach your MIDI controller with one hand and adjust the Object Parameter box with the other hand, you can replay the chords after you make the adjustment so you can hear the result.

12 In the Environment area's Object Parameter box, click the Direction pop-up menu and choose Up/Down.

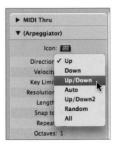

The pattern direction changes, arpeggiating up and then down the notes of the chord.

13 In the Object Parameter box, click the Direction menu again, this time choosing Random.

The pattern changes, randomly arpeggiating selected notes from the chord.

The Velocity parameter allows you to adjust the velocities of the arpeggiated notes of the original chord. You can set a positive or negative offset, or even randomize the velocities.

14 In the Object Parameter box, drag the Velocity parameter (it currently displays "Original") down to choose Random.

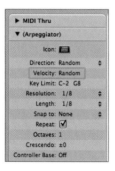

The velocities of the arpeggiated notes are randomized.

The speed of the arpeggio is governed by the Resolution parameter, which is defined by note divisions (half note, quarter note, and so on).

15 Click the Resolution menu and choose 1/16.

The arpeggiated notes change to a sixteenth-note resolution, playing twice as fast as before.

To enable synchronization with other MIDI data, the arpeggiator can be set to wait for a specific note division before starting. This is done with the "Snap to" parameter.

16 Click the "Snap to" menu and choose 1/8.

This quantizes the start of arpeggiated playback to the following eighth note, keeping it in sync with the project's time grid (bars/beats).

NOTE ▶ The length of each arpeggiated note can be set independently from the speed. You can change note lengths by choosing note durations from the Length parameter's menu. However, this won't have an effect on the Marimba software instrument, as the percussive sound does not sustain very long.

17 Stop playback.

TIP ▶ You can record the output of arpeggiator objects (and others) by first inserting them between the Physical Input and Sequencer object in the Click & Ports layer. If you do this, be aware that *all* input will be arpeggiated until the object is removed from the signal chain.

Using Chord Memorizer Objects

Chord memorizer objects map a single note to a set of up to 12 user-selected notes. This allows you to trigger complex chords by pressing a single key on your MIDI controller.

1 Choose New > Chord Memorizer.

A chord memorizer object appears in the Environment window.

NOTE ▶ You might need to move objects around to get them out of the way of one another throughout this lesson. Generally, signal flow in the Environment should flow from left to right, as cable outputs are on the right side of objects.

2 With the chord memorizer object selected, click a shade of dark blue in the color palette.

The chord memorizer object becomes blue.

3 Cable the output of the chord memorizer object to the monitor object.

4 Double-click the chord memorizer object.

The Chord Memorizer window opens.

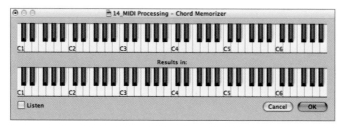

The Chord Memorizer window contains two keyboards. The top keyboard corresponds to the incoming note, and the lower keyboard corresponds to the notes or chords assigned to the incoming note.

5 Click the C4 note on the top keyboard.

C4 is automatically selected in the lower keyboard.

6 In the lower keyboard, click C4 to deselect it.

7 In the lower keyboard, click C3, D3, Eb3, F3, D4, and F4 to select them.

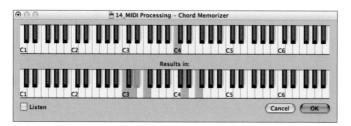

8 Click OK.

In order for the chord memorizer to process the input from your MIDI controller, you need to bring it up in the Arrange track list. Instead of doing this with the MIDI Thru tool as you did before, you can quickly assign objects in the Environment to the selected track using the Library.

9 In the Library, choose Other Objects > (Chord Memorizer).

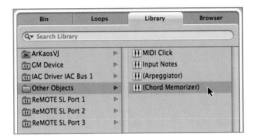

The selected Arrange track (track 1) changes from the arpeggiator object to the chord memorizer object.

Because the chord memorizer is not time based, you don't need to have the project playing in order for it to process MIDI input.

10 Press C4 on your MIDI controller.

A full chord is sounded, outputting the notes you specified within the lower keyboard of the Chord Memorizer window (C3, D3, Eb3, F3, D4, and F4).

Using Delay Line Objects

Delay line objects repeat the MIDI events passing through them, achieving a result similar to that of a delay processor creating echoes from audio signals. The most important difference between the two is that the delay line object creates these echoes with additional generated MIDI notes that mirror the incoming MIDI event, instead of sampling and playing back bits of audio.

1 Choose New > Delay Line.

A delay line object appears in the Environment window.

2   With the delay line object selected, click a shade of yellow in the color palette.

The delay line object becomes yellow.

3   Cable the output of the delay line object to the monitor object.

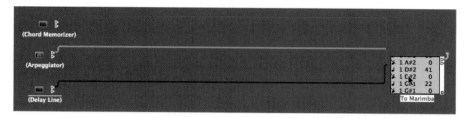

Like the other objects, the delay line needs to be placed in the Arrange track list so it can process the input from your MIDI controller.

4   In the Library, choose Other Objects > (Delay Line).

The selected Arrange track (track 1) changes from the chord memorizer object to the delay line object.

As with the arpeggiator object, the project needs to be playing for you to hear the results of the delay line object's processing.

5   Play the project.

6   While the project is playing, play any note on your MIDI controller, listening to the signal through the delay line object.

The incoming note is echoed by a single repeat.

You can adjust the repeat amount, timing, velocity, and transposition within the Object Parameter box.

7   In the Object Parameter box, double-click the number next to the Repeats parameter and enter *4*. Press Return.

8 While the project is playing, play any note on your MIDI controller, listening to the signal through the delay line object.

The incoming note is repeated four times. This doesn't sound much like natural echoes, where the repetitions trail off in volume. You can simulate this effect by adjusting the Velocity parameter to a negative value. By doing this, each successive repeat will lower in velocity by the selected amount.

9 Double-click the number next to the Velocity parameter and enter *–19*. Press Return.

10 While the project is playing, play any note on your MIDI controller, listening to the signal through the delay line object.

The incoming note is echoed four times, each echo quieter than the previous one.

The speed of the repeats can be set by the Delay parameter. The left value represents divisions, while the right value represents ticks. This allows you to make musical repeats that sync with the tempo of the project.

11 In the Delay parameter fields, double-click either number and enter *240*. Press Return.

NOTE ▶ You need to use tick values when inputting numbers via the computer keyboard for the Delay parameter. A sixteenth note equals 240 ticks.

12 While the project is playing, play any note on your MIDI controller, listening to the signal through the delay line object.

The delay time between the repeats is cut in half.

So far you have emulated the results you'd get from a typical audio delay processor. The delay line also allows you to do something unusual: transpose the pitch of each repetition.

13 Double-click the Transpose parameter and enter *–7*. Press Return.

14 While the project is playing, play any note on your MIDI controller, listening to the signal through the delay line object.

Each successive repetition drops seven semitones (a perfect fifth).

15 Stop playback.

Creating Signal Chains

So far, you've only applied single processors (arpeggiator, chord memorizer, and delay line) to incoming MIDI signals. The Environment starts to show its potential, however, when you cable processors to each other for complex serial and parallel processing.

In this exercise, you will not only learn how to chain processors together in a series but also how to split signals for parallel processing.

1 Click and hold down the topmost cable output from the chord memorizer object and drag the cable to the arpeggiator object (severing the connection to the Monitor object).

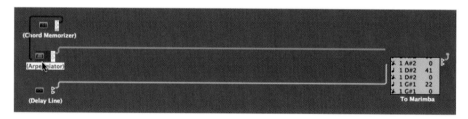

2 In the Library, choose Other Objects > (Chord Memorizer).

The selected Arrange track changes to the chord memorizer object.

The incoming MIDI signal now passes from the chord memorizer object to the arpeggiator object, finally ending up at the Marimba software instrument channel (passing through the monitor object). With these two in series, you can trigger complex arpeggiated chords by pressing a single note on your MIDI controller.

3 Start playback.

4 While the project is playing, play C4 on your MIDI controller (which you earlier set to play back a chord).

The chord generated by the chord memorizer object is arpeggiated.

Let's add to this creation by inserting the delay line object into the signal path.

5   Click and hold down the cable output from the arpeggiator object and drag the cable to the delay line object.

With this arrangement, each note from the arpeggiated chord generated by the chord memorizer and arpeggiator objects will repeat four times, dropping seven semitones each time. All of this is triggered by a single note from a MIDI controller.

6   While the project is playing, play C4 on your MIDI controller.

A whole slew of notes is created, with various pitches and rhythmic durations.

7   Stop playback.

Using Transformer Objects

Now that you've investigated chaining MIDI processors in a series, let's create a parallel processing arrangement in which specified notes will be sent down two different signal paths. You can do this by using the transformer object.

The transformer object is an extremely powerful processor whose main function is to change one type of MIDI data to another. However, that would be barely scratching the surface of its capabilities. It also works equally well as a MIDI filter, track automation splitter, Sysex mapper, condition splitter, and much more. For this exercise you will be using the transformer as a condition splitter, sending data down one of two cable outputs depending on criteria you set.

1   Choose New > Transformer.

A transformer object appears within the Environment window.

2   With the transformer object selected, click a shade of red in the color palette.

The transformer object becomes red.

3   Double-click the transformer object.

The Transformer window opens.

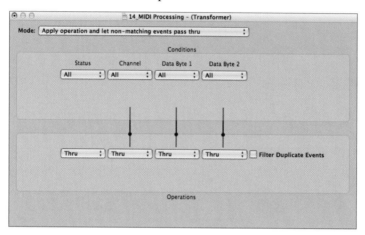

This window is almost identical to the Transform window explored in Lesson 9 in the section "Using Transform Functions." Like the Transform window you used within the MIDI editors to select and edit MIDI data, the Transformer window has places to specify criteria for selection and transformation. Like the Transform window, the Transformer window also has many modes available.

4   Click the Mode menu and choose Condition splitter (true -> top cable).

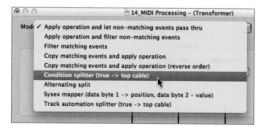

The condition splitter mode sends MIDI data that meets the conditions specified within the top area (Conditions) out the topmost cable output and sends all other MIDI data that does not fit the criteria out the other. In this exercise, you will be using the condition splitter to divide specific notes generated by the chord memorizer object out one of the two cable outlets for separate processing chains.

5   From the Status menu, choose =.

Another pop-up menu displaying Note appears below the Status menu.

6   From the Pitch menu, choose <=.

A value field appears just below the pop-up menu.

7   Double-click in the value field and enter *C4*. Press Return.

With this setup, incoming note values equal to and below C4 will be sent out of the top cable output, and all others will be sent out of the bottom output.

8   Close the Transformer window.

9   Click and hold down the topmost cable output from the chord memorizer object and drag the cable to the transformer object (disconnecting it from the arpeggiator object).

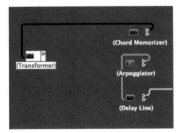

The chord memorizer object will provide the input to the transformer object.

10 Click and hold down the cable output from the transformer object and drag the cable to the arpeggiator object.

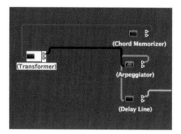

You've now set up one of your signal chains distributed by the transformer object. Now all you need to complete the arrangement is to set up another signal path to process data that does not meet the conditions specified in the transformer object. Begin by creating another monitor object cabled to a different software instrument channel.

11 Choose New > Monitor.

A new monitor object appears.

12 Drag the new monitor object down and to the right, moving it out of the way of the first signal chain.

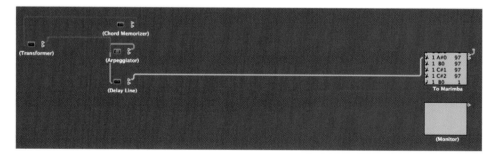

13 Using the Text tool, click the new monitor object and enter *To 8bit Kit*.

14 Using the Pointer tool, Option-click the cable output on the monitor object and choose Mixer > Software Instrument > 8bit Kit.

A cable appears, connecting the objects between the layers of the Environment.

15 Choose New > Arpeggiator.

A new arpeggiator object appears.

16 With the new arpeggiator object selected, click a shade of orange in the color palette.

The arpeggiator object becomes orange.

17 Drag the new arpeggiator object down, moving it out of the way of the first signal chain.

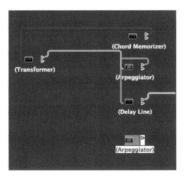

18 In the Object Parameter box, choose Random for the Direction and Velocity parameters, and 1/16 for the Resolution and "Snap to" parameters.

19 Cable the output of the new arpeggiator object to the monitor object labeled To 8bit Kit.

20 Cable the bottommost cable of the transformer object to the new arpeggiator object.

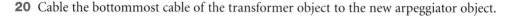
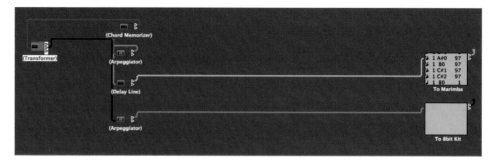

You've now set up two complete signal chains with separate processing. The source events are generated by the chord memorizer object, with the transformer object splitting the data by note range (those equal to or below C4, and those above C4). Now all that's left is to try it out.

21 Start playback.

22 While the project is playing, hold down C4 on your MIDI controller.

What results are pulsating, surging polyrhythms that never repeat twice, activated by a single key on your MIDI controller.

23 Stop playback after you've listened to your creation.

Using Cable Switcher Objects

Like a transformer object, a cable switcher object is used to help direct signal flow. Basically, the cable switcher object is a switch that can be triggered manually to direct the signal flow out of its outputs. The switch can take on different forms, such as a fader button or pop-up menu, allowing you to interact with it in different ways.

In this exercise, you will insert a cable switcher into the signal path, enabling you to switch between two routes at any given time.

1 Choose New > Fader > Specials > Cable Switcher.

A cable switcher object appears.

2 With the cable switcher object selected, click a shade of light blue in the color palette.

The cable switcher object becomes blue.

3 Close the Color window (you won't need it for the rest of the lesson).

4 Drag the cable switcher (by clicking on its name) to the right of the topmost arpeggiator object (the green one connected to the Marimba software instrument channel).

5 Click and hold down the topmost cable output of the green arpeggiator and drag the cable to the cable switcher.

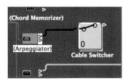

6 Click and hold down the cable output of the cable switcher object and drag the cable to the monitor object labeled To Marimba.

This will form one signal path, directly feeding the Marimba software instrument channel.

7 Click and hold down the bottommost cable output of the cable switcher object and drag the cable to the delay line object.

To make signal flow easier to view, it helps to move the delay line object to the right of the cable switcher object.

8 Drag the delay line object to the right, placing it below and to the right of the cable switcher object.

This will form the other signal path, passing through the delay line object and eventually reaching the Marimba software instrument channel.

9 Try clicking a few times on the cable switcher object itself.

The cable switcher changes configuration, routing the input to a different cable output each time you click.

Notice that there are three output destinations to select, and only two are cabled to signal paths. Like any other Environment object, the cable switcher adds an additional cable output (up to 128) when a new output cable is connected.

In order to have the cable switcher route only to the used outputs, you need to alter its range in the Object Parameter box. The Range parameter is expressed by two numbers, forming the bottom (left number) and top (right number) of a specified range.

10 In the Object Parameter box, drag the rightmost Range parameter (127) down until it reaches a value of 1.

This sets the Range from 0 to 1 (two outputs) and allows the cable switcher object to toggle between the two signal paths connected to its cable outputs.

As mentioned earlier, the cable switcher object's interface can be changed to reflect different types of switches. This is done by choosing an option from the Style menu in the Object Parameter box.

11 Click the Style menu and choose As Text.

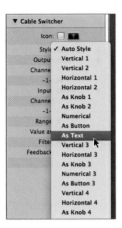

The cable switcher object changes, displaying text. By default, the displayed text corresponds to the numbered cable output (0 or 1), and the number can be toggled by clicking the cable switcher itself. This is not a particularly elegant solution for labeling and accessing the signal paths cabled to the cable switcher's outputs. However, you can enter your own text instead of the default range numbers, allowing clearer labels of the signal paths.

12 Double-click the cable switcher object.

The Cable Switcher window opens.

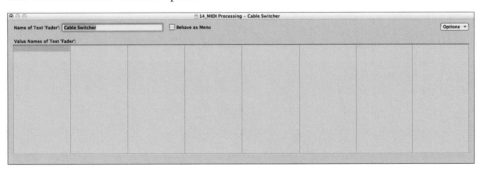

13 Double-click the topmost field of the Value Names of Text 'Fader' column and enter *Bypass*. Press Return.

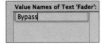

14 In the second field, enter *Delay*. Press Return.

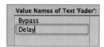

NOTE ▸ There are 128 fields in the Cable Switcher window that can hold text. When using cable switcher objects with large ranges displayed as text, select the "Behave as Menu" checkbox at the top of the Cable Switcher window. This lets you access the entire range via a pop-up menu, instead of clicking the cable switcher itself.

15 Close the Cable Switcher window.

The cable switcher object now displays the text you entered in the Cable Switcher window.

TIP ▸ You can resize any Environment object by dragging its lower-right corner, similar to how you adjust window size. This enables the cable switcher object to display longer text.

Now it's time to try out the cable switcher object while the project is playing. In order to have your hands free to interact with the cable switcher object, you can create a MIDI region with a C4 note held to trigger the rhythmic patterns played on the Marimba and 8bit Kit software instrument channels.

16 In the Arrange area, use the Pencil tool to create a one-measure MIDI region in the Chord Memorizer track (track 1), starting at 1 1 1 1.

17 With the region you just created still selected, choose Window > Piano Roll.

The Piano Roll Editor opens in a separate window.

18 In the Piano Roll Editor, use the Pencil tool to create a C4 note with a velocity of 80 that lasts the entire length of measure 1.

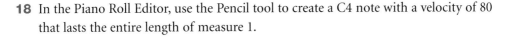

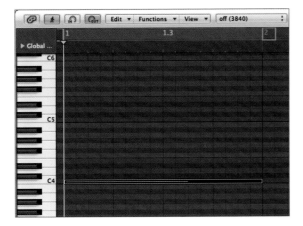

19 Close the Piano Roll Editor.

20 In the Arrange window's Region Parameter box, click the checkbox next to Loop to select it.

The region is now looped and will continually supply a C4 to drive the rhythmic patterns played by the Marimba and 8bit Kit software instruments.

21 Play the project.

22 While the project is playing, click the cable switcher object, switching back and forth between the signal paths (with the delay line object and without).

23 Stop playback.

Using Touch Tracks Objects

Touch tracks objects allow you to trigger MIDI regions or folders by playing single notes. This works especially well in a live performance setting, because you can trigger anything from short passages or phrases to entire songs with a single key from your MIDI controller.

When triggered within a touch tracks object, these MIDI regions or folders play back through the instruments assigned to their tracks, sharing the same track-channel relationship they have in the Arrange window. This means that you can have a single touch tracks object that plays back MIDI regions from different tracks, all through their respective channels (and sound sources).

In this exercise you will be using a touch tracks object to play back the MIDI regions present in the Arrange tracks. Notice that these regions are muted (the track Mute button is active) and have not been sounding when the project is played. However, muted regions will sound when triggered via a touch tracks object. This allows you to create MIDI recordings via normal methods in the Arrange window for import to a touch tracks object, then muting the regions so they don't sound when the project is played.

1 Choose New > Touch Tracks.

A touch tracks object appears in the Environment, and its corresponding Touch Tracks window opens.

In this window you can assign different MIDI regions (or folders) to each key, represented on the far left of the window. Dragging from the Arrange area to the target row in the Region/Folder column will assign a region or folder to a key.

2 Scroll down in the Touch Tracks window until you can see a range of roughly C2 to E3.

3 Drag the first region (Lead 1) on the Analog Lead track to the Touch Tracks window and drop it on the C3 row in the Region/Folder column (the pointer will change to the Pencil tool).

NOTE ▶ You might need to reposition the Touch Tracks window in order to see both it and the Arrange tracks window.

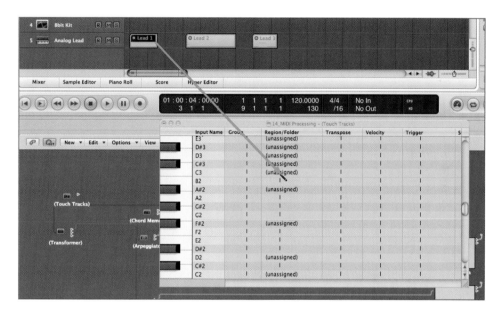

NOTE ▶ If you make a mistake and drop the region in the wrong place, you can delete it by double-clicking on the name (Lead 1) and choosing Delete from the subsequent dialog.

The name of the region now appears in the Region/Folder column for C3.

Input Name	Group	Region/Folder	Transpose	Velocity		Trigger		S
E3		(unassigned)						
D#3		(unassigned)						
D3		(unassigned)						
C#3				Off	⇕	Multi	⇕	
C3		Lead 1		100%	⇕	Gate	⇕	
B2								
A#2		(unassigned)						
A2								
G#2								
G2								
F#2		(unassigned)						
F2								
E2								
D#2								
D2		(unassigned)						
C#2								
C2		(unassigned)						

4 Drag the second region (Lead 2) on the Analog Lead track to the Touch Tracks window and drop it on the D3 row in the Region/Folder column.

The name of the region now appears in the Region/Folder column for D3.

5 Drag the third region (Lead 3) on the Analog Lead track to the Touch Tracks window and drop it on the E3 row in the Region/Folder column.

The name of the region now appears in the Region/Folder column for E3.

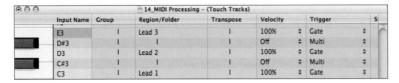

Input Name	Group	Region/Folder	Transpose	Velocity		Trigger		S
E3	I	Lead 3	I	100%	‡	Gate	‡	
D#3	I	I	I	Off	‡	Multi	‡	
D3	I	Lead 2	I	100%	‡	Gate	‡	
C#3	I	I	I	Off	‡	Multi	‡	
C3	I	Lead 1	I	100%	‡	Gate	‡	

Now that you've specified the regions to be played back and assigned them to MIDI notes, you need to place the touch tracks object on a track in order for it to receive MIDI input.

6 In the Arrange track list, select the No Output track (track 2).

7 In the Library, choose Other Objects > (Touch Tracks).

NOTE ▶ In order to work, the touch tracks object must receive MIDI note input. However, it will not pass MIDI events through to its output, so generally it should not be inserted in the signal chain unless it appears at the end.

In order for the touch tracks object to play back the MIDI regions, the project has to be playing.

8 Play the project.

9 With the project playing, try playing the C3, D3, and E3 keys one at a time on your MIDI controller, holding them down for various lengths of time.

The triggered Lead 1, Lead 2, and Lead 3 regions play whenever you press a key, for as long as the key is held or until the regions end. This playback behavior is referred to as the *gate* trigger mode, and is the default mode for any region imported into the Touch Tracks window.

You can change the triggering behavior for any region by changing the setting within the Trigger column in the Touch Tracks window.

10 In the Touch Tracks window, click the Gate setting in the Trigger column for the C3 note (Lead 1) and choose GateLoop.

This setting acts similarly to Gate, except that it will continue to repeat the region for as long as the key is pressed.

11 Change the Trigger setting for D3 (Lead 2) and E3 (Lead 3) to GateLoop.

12 With the project playing, try playing the C3, D3, and E3 keys one at a time on your MIDI controller, holding them down for various lengths of time.

The region playback is looped for as long as you hold down a key.

13 Stop playback.

Using Apple Loops with Touch Tracks

Any type of MIDI region is fair game for use with touch tracks. This means that you can also use imported MIDI regions like Standard MIDI files and software instrument Apple Loops (green Apple Loops). In particular, software instrument Apple Loops consist of MIDI regions paired with a sound source (software instrument and effects settings are instantiated when you drag them to your project) and can be easily dropped into the Touch Tracks window for triggering. In effect, you can use touch tracks to trigger these loops similar to the way a sampler would trigger audio files, mapping individual loops to the keyboard.

In this exercise, you will import a few software instrument Apple Loops for use in the touch tracks object you created earlier.

1 In the Media area, select the Loops tab.

2 In the search field, enter *disco pickbass*. Press Return.

The Loop Browser displays a variety of software instrument Apple Loops with the words *disco pickbass* in their names.

3 Click the Disco Pickbass 03 loop in the Loop Browser, playing it in order to familiarize yourself with the material.

4 Drag the Disco Pickbass 03 loop to the blank area below the existing tracks.

A new track is created with the Disco Pickbass channel strip, and the Apple Loops region (Disco Pickbass 03) appears on the track.

5 In the Loop Browser, click the Disco Pickbass 06 loop (you will need to scroll down the list), playing it in order to familiarize yourself with the material.

6 Drag the Disco Pickbass 06 loop to 6 1 1 1 on the Disco Pickbass track (track 6).

The Apple Loops region (Disco Pickbass 06) appears on the track.

7 Use the Mute tool to mute both Disco Pickbass regions.

8 Drag the Disco Pickbass 03 region to the Touch Tracks window and drop it in the Region/Folder column for C2.

NOTE ▶ You might need to scroll down in the Touch Tracks window. The window will automatically scroll when you drag regions to its upper and lower edges.

9   Drag the Disco Pickbass 06 region to the Touch Tracks window and drop it in the
    Region/Folder column for D2.

Previously, you set up the Lead regions to be triggered when a key was pressed and to
repeat until the key was released (GateLoop). This time, you are going to set up the
triggering a little bit differently, allowing the region to continue looping even after the
key is released, not stopping until a subsequent key is pressed. You can accomplish
this with another Trigger setting, ToggleLoop.

10 In the Touch Tracks window, click the Gate setting in the Trigger column for both the
    C2 and D2 notes (Disco Pickbass 03 and Disco Pickbass 06) and choose ToggleLoop.

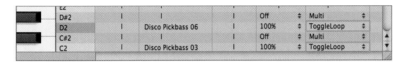

The way we've set things up so far, the regions could be triggered at any part of the
measure, on or off the beat. This is fine for the rubato Lead regions, but the Disco
Pickbass regions could play out of sync with the rhythmic patterns being generated by
the arpeggiator and delay line objects.

For just this sort of situation, the Touch Tracks window provides a way to quantize
the playback start by changing settings in the Start column.

11 Expand the Touch Tracks window in order to view the Start column.

12 In the Start column, click the vertical black line for the C2 note (Disco Pickbass 03)
    and choose Next 1/1.

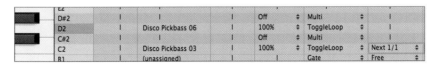

The 1/1 setting quantizes playback to the next whole note, starting the region playback at the beginning of the bar.

13 In the Start column, click the vertical black line for the D2 note (Disco Pickbass 06) and choose Next 1/1.

In addition to the settings discussed earlier in the lesson, the Touch Tracks window also allows you to transpose individual regions by entering an offset in the Transpose column.

14 In the Transpose column, double-click to the left of the vertical black line for the D2 note (Disco Pickbass 06), and enter 5. Press Return.

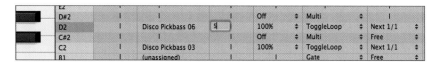

This setting will transpose the Disco Pickbass 06 region up five semitones (a perfect fourth) upon playback.

NOTE ▶ This is different from the typical transposition behavior of samplers, as the length and speed of the region will not be altered, keeping it in perfect time with the project.

15 Play the project.

16 While the project is playing, play the C2 and D2 keys one at a time on your MIDI controller.

NOTE ▶ Remember, because Trigger is set to ToggleLoop for both, you don't need to hold the key down. It will continue sounding until you press the key again.

The Disco Pickbass regions play back in time with the project and are toggled on or off when subsequent keys are pressed. In addition, the Disco Pickbass 06 region plays back a perfect fourth higher, changing the harmonic underpinning of the composition.

17 While one of the Disco Pickbass regions is still playing, try triggering one of the Lead regions (C3, D3, and E3) on top.

You probably noticed that the Disco Pickbass regions stopped playing when you triggered one of the Lead regions, and vice versa. This is because when regions are initially assigned in the Touch Tracks window, they have the same group assignment. When you trigger a region, any other region in the same group will stop playing (similar to a monophonic synthesizer).

This relationship makes sense for the regions of like kind, but not if we want to be able to trigger regions independently from each other without stopping their playback (similar to a polyphonic synthesizer).

18 In the Touch Tracks window, double-click the Group setting for all of the Lead regions (C3, D3, and E3), and enter *1*. Press Return.

19 In the Touch Tracks window, double-click the Group setting for both of the Disco Pickbass regions (C2 and D2), and enter *2*. Press Return. .

Now you are ready to test your creation.

20 While the project is playing, try triggering one of the Disco Pickbass regions (C2 and D2), letting it loop while triggering the Lead regions (C3, D3, and E3) on top.

21 Stop the project and close the Touch Tracks window.

22 Choose File > Save As.

23 Name the project *14_MIDI Processing_Finished* and save it to Music > Advanced Logic 9_Files > Lessons > Completed.

> **TIP** If you have created a useful tool or widget in the Environment, you can import Environment layers from one project to another by choosing Options > Import Environment > Layer.

Lesson Review

1. How are layers used within the Environment?
2. What does the Physical Input object represent?
3. What does the keyboard object do?
4. What does the monitor object do?
5. What does the Sequencer Input object represent?
6. How do you cable an object from one layer to another?
7. What does an arpeggiator object do?
8. What does a chord memorizer object do?
9. What does a delay line object do?
10. What does a transformer object do?
11. What does a cable switcher object do?
12. What does a touch tracks object do?

Answers

1. Layers are used to organize objects of like type or function within the Environment.
2. The Physical Input object represents the ports of your MIDI interface or MIDI controller (with direct MIDI-to-USB connection).
3. The keyboard object displays incoming MIDI notes as well as generating new ones from its output.
4. Monitor objects display MIDI events passing from their input to their output in a list form.
5. The Sequencer Input object represents the connection to Logic's sequencer.
6. Cabling across layers is performed by Option-clicking the output of the object and selecting the input object from the menu.
7. An arpeggiator object arpeggiates harmonic input (chords), outputting each note individually in a selectable pattern.
8. Chord memorizer objects map a single note to a set of up to 12 user-selected notes.
9. Delay line objects repeat MIDI events passing through them, achieving a result similar to that of a delay processor creating echoes from audio signals.

10. Transformer objects primarily change one type of MIDI data to another. They can also act as a MIDI filter, track automation splitter, SysEx mapper, and condition splitter.

11. Cable switcher objects are used to manually direct the signal flow out of multiple outputs.

12. Touch tracks objects allow you to trigger MIDI regions or folders by playing single notes.

15

Lesson Files	Advanced Logic 9_Files > Lessons > 15_Sintra_Start.logic
Media	Advanced Logic 9_Files > Media > Sintra
Time	This lesson takes approximately 90 minutes to complete.
Goals	Enter and edit note data in the Score Editor
	Create note data using step input
	Format notation using staff styles
	Insert text and chord grids into a score
	Transcribe a MIDI performance in score notation
	Create accurately notated percussion parts
	Prepare and print scores and parts

Lesson 15
Working with Notation

Logic was built from the ground up with musical notation as a central part of MIDI sequencing. (In fact, Logic evolved from a 1980s notation application called Notator.) As a result, Logic includes comprehensive notation capabilities for creating and printing parts and scores. You can enter notes directly into the Score Editor or automatically transcribe an existing MIDI recording.

This marriage of notation and MIDI data is integral to Logic. Every note in the score represents a MIDI note event. Logic is often called a notating sequencer because you can access all the powerful arranging and composing functionality of Logic's sequencer within the notation environment of the Score Editor.

In this lesson you will explore Logic's Score Editor, inputting notation and transcribing audio and MIDI regions for the composition "Sintra," a Latin guitar piece with drums, percussion, and bass.

Creating Notation

There are a variety of methods for inputting notation, including graphic input, step input, and real-time transcription. In this exercise you will focus on the first two techniques, entering notes directly into the Score Editor.

Let's start by opening the project file you will be using for this lesson and notating the rhythm guitar part, transcribing the audio file into notation.

> **NOTE** ▶ You will need to set the "Display Middle C as" preference to C3 (Yamaha) to accurately follow the directions within this exercise and others throughout the book. This option can be found in Logic Pro > Preferences > Display > General.

1   Choose File > Open.

2   In the file browser, go to Music > Advanced Logic 9_Files > Lessons and open **15_ Sintra_Start.logic**.

3   Play the song to familiarize yourself with the material.

    As you can see in the Arrange area, the song mainly consists of software instrument tracks outputting to Logic's EXS24 mkII software sampler, mixed with audio record-ings of nylon string guitar. Because the Score Editor interprets MIDI data to create notation, you will be working with a transcription of the main nylon string guitar part (track 3), inputting and adjusting notes where needed.

    > **NOTE** ▶ Guitar notation sounds an octave lower than written. In order to have the Score Editor display the notation correctly and maintain an accurate playback for this project, all regions within the Guitar Score track have a Transposition value of +12 in the Region Parameter box.

4   If the first region (Guitar Score_Intro) in the Guitar Score track (track 3) is not already selected, click to select it.

5   Press the number 3 to recall screenset 3.

    This screenset places the Score Editor in the top half of the screen, Piano Roll Editor in the bottom half, and Transport bar in the middle. Both editors display the contents of the selected Guitar Score track.

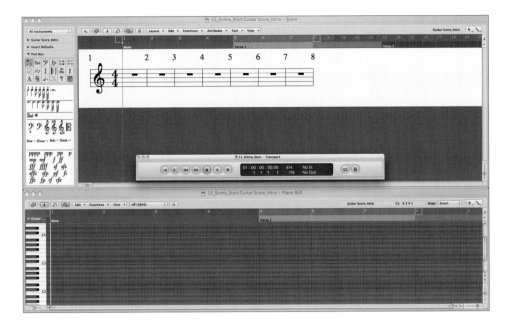

You are viewing a blank region that was created as a place for you to input notational data. Notice that rests are automatically displayed.

NOTE ▶ Like most of Logic's other editors, the Score Editor can be displayed both within the Arrange window and in an independent window. To open the Score Editor in a separate window, choose Window > Score in the main menu bar, or drag the Score button from the bottom of the Arrange window.

Entering Notes Using Graphic Input

You can graphically input notes and other notational elements in the Score Editor by selecting them from the Part box, a palette of notational symbols in the Inspector (at the far left of the Score Editor).

1   In the Part box group menu (the upper section), click each object group button.

The object group is displayed in the panel just below the group menu. The most recently selected object group appears at the top of the panel.

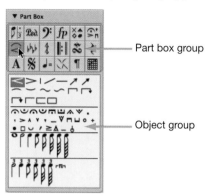

Part box group

Object group

2 In the group menu, click the key signature button.

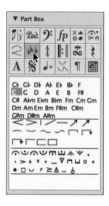

3 Choose the Pencil tool.

4 Since the song is in the key of D major, click D in the key signature object group.

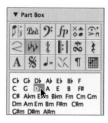

5 Click the staff between the treble clef and the time signature.

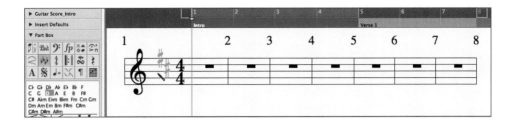

A D major key signature is inserted.

In the Part box, look at the notes group button and you'll see that it contains three areas, represented by an eighth note, a dot, and a triplet symbol. When you click these symbols, you open groups of notes with different rhythmic lengths.

6   Click the triplet, dotted-note, and eighth-note symbols on the notes group button to view those object groups.

Various rhythmic lengths are displayed in each group.

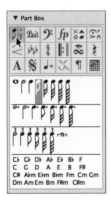

7   If the eighth note is not already selected, select it in the object group.

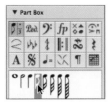

8   Using the Pencil tool in the Score Editor, hold down the B line in the middle of measure 5, using the help tag to position an eighth note at 5 2 3 1. Then release the mouse
button.

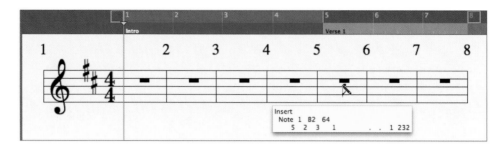

NOTE ▸ When the MIDI Out button is enabled (at the top of the Score Editor), you'll
get aural as well as visual feedback as you drag a note around the staff. The note is
played by the EXS24 mkII plug-in (using a classical guitar sampler instrument) on the
current track.

An eighth note is inserted on the B line at 5 2 3 1.

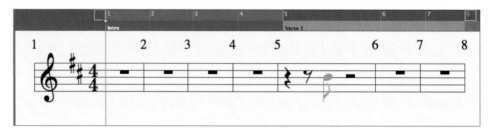

NOTE ▸ The note also appears in the Piano Roll Editor, and it provides a good reference, especially for length.

9   Use the same technique to insert a note on the D line above the first note you created.

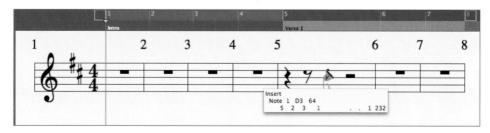

You might find it a little tricky to land on the correct pitch when graphically inserting a note. If your composition falls into a consistent key, you can make input easier by turning on the Diatonic Insert feature. With this feature activated, you are limited to entering only those notes within the current key signature.

10 Choose Edit > Diatonic Insert.

11 Still using the Pencil tool, click anywhere above the D eighth note you created, and then drag up and down while looking at the help tag.

   The pitch choices are limited to diatonic pitches (so in D major, your pitch choices will not include C natural or F natural).

12 Release the mouse button to place an eighth note at E above the eighth-note D you previously created.

   NOTE ▸ The note heads automatically change position, correctly notating adjacent pitches.

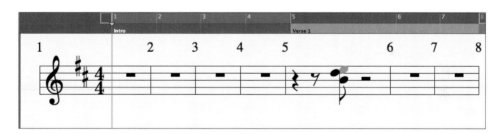

Just as in any of the other MIDI editors in Logic, note data can be copied and pasted.

13 Choose the Pointer tool.

14 In the Score Editor, drag a selection rectangle around the chord you just created.

15 Option-drag the chord to 5 3 1 1.

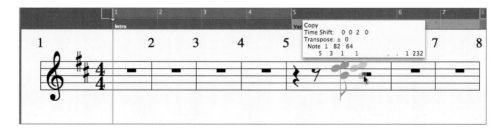

A copy of the chord is created at the new position.

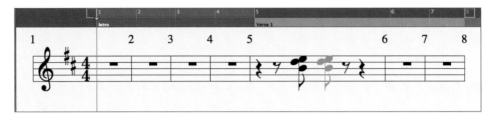

NOTE ▶ When notes are moved and inserted, they automatically snap to the division value set in the Transport bar.

Dragging Notes into the Score

Another way to input notes is to drag them directly from the Part box.

1   Drag a quarter note from the notes object group to the B line at 5 3 3 1.

A quarter note is created where you dropped the note.

Although this can be a good way to input notes with a variety of durations, journeying back and forth across the screen can get tedious. Fortunately, you can open an object group as a floating palette and position it anywhere on the screen.

2   In the group menu, double-click the notes button.

A floating palette opens with all the objects in the group, including the dotted-note and triplet versions.

3   Drag the palette near the measure you are working on.

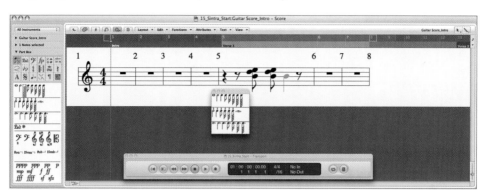

4   Drag two more quarter notes from the floating palette, dropping them on the D and A above the B you just input, to create a chord.

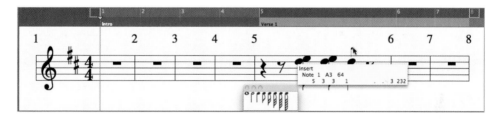

5   Create another chord at 5 4 3 1 by dragging half notes to B (on the same line as the previous B), and to D and F#, above the previous B.

A chord lasting two beats is created, tied across the bar line between measures 5 and 6.

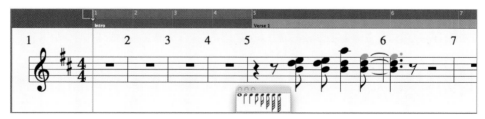

NOTE ▶ Ties cannot be inserted graphically in Logic when using standard notation (they can be with tablature). They are created and displayed automatically according to the length of the MIDI note.

Adjusting Note Length

Musical notation depicts note length using a specific set of symbols (sixteenth notes, eighth notes, and so on). As you can see in the Piano Roll Editor, length is depicted proportionally: The longer the duration, the more space it takes up horizontally. While you can adjust note length in the Score Editor by inputting within the Event Parameter box, new to Logic 9 is the ability to lengthen a note by graphically dragging it directly on the staff.

1   Drag a selection rectangle around the final chord, and then Option-drag it to 6 2 3 1.

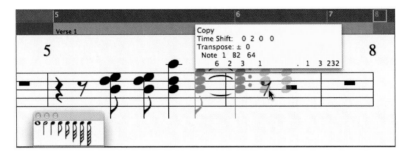

2   In the Inspector, click the disclosure triangle for the selected chord to display the Event Parameter box.

The Event Parameter box displays the parameters for the selected chord, indicated by "3 Notes selected" in the header.

Notice that Logic also supplies a chord analysis of the selected notes (identifying these notes as a B minor chord).

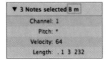

NOTE ▸ When notes are graphically input into the Score Editor, they are given lengths that are slightly less than the full value (hence the high tick numbers) to avoid overlaps in note length.

3   In the Event Parameter box, double-click the numbers next to the Length parameter and enter *0 0 2 0* (with spaces), signifying an eighth note, in the text field. Press
Return.

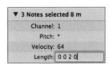

NOTE ▶ When entering numbers into the Event Parameter box, you can also use periods, instead of spaces, to separate the digits.

The lengths of the selected notes change from half notes to eighth notes.

NOTE ▶ The division value setting for a project impacts how you interpret the Length
parameter. In the project file you are using for this lesson, the division value is set for
sixteenth notes (/16), so 0 0 2 0 represents an eighth note value (two sixteenth notes).

4   Option-drag the chord to 6 3 3 1.

A copy of the chord is placed at the new position and is selected, making it ready for
editing.

5   Choose View > Duration Bars > Selected Notes.

The chord you copied now displays duration bars around each selected note.

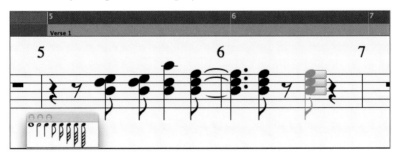

6   Drag one of the selected duration bars to the right, watching the help tag to reach a
duration of 0 1 2 0 (a dotted quarter note).

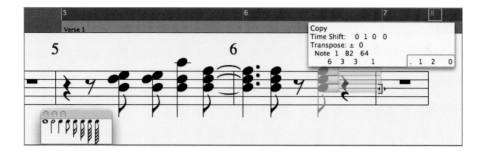

The note lengths of the chord change to dotted quarter notes.

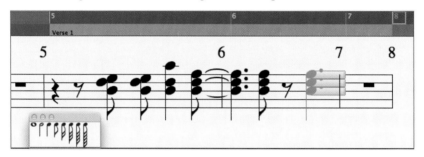

7 Close the floating notes group palette.

Entering Notes Using Step Input

Although graphic input allows the precise entry of notes, it can be slow. A faster technique is step input, which allows you to insert notes at the current playhead position while Logic automatically moves the playhead forward based on the selected rhythmic length. You can set a note's pitch and length by clicking an onscreen piano keyboard, pressing a key on your computer keyboard, or using MIDI input.

To begin step input, you need to place the playhead at the position where you want to begin.

1 Option-click the staff at 5 1 1 1 (use the help tag) to place the playhead at the beginning of measure 5.

> **TIP** ▶ Option-clicking in the staff (not on notes or other symbols) is a quick way to locate the playhead in the Score Editor for playback or editing.

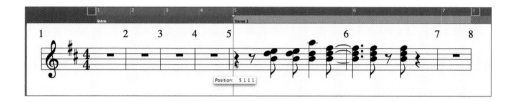

2   In the main menu bar, choose Options > Step Input Keyboard.

The Step Input Keyboard window opens. Buttons in this window can be clicked to set the pitch, length, and dynamics (velocity) of a note.

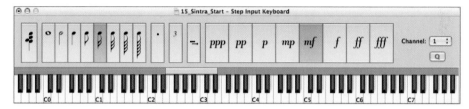

TIP ▶ The Step Input Keyboard can be used in any Logic editor, and it is especially effective when controlled with an extensive set of key commands (including commands for specific note pitches). This allows you to quickly input notes entirely from your computer keyboard for non-real-time purposes such as creating notation.

3   If necessary, reposition the Step Input Keyboard so it does not cover up the score.

4   Click the whole-note button at the left side of the window.

5   On the Step Input Keyboard, click the D2 key.

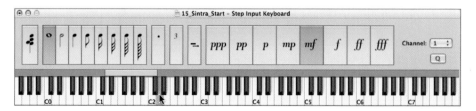

A D note is inserted just below the staff, and the playhead jumps to the end of the inserted whole-note value.

NOTE ▶ Don't panic! The note you just input is displayed as a dotted quarter note for a reason explained in the "Creating a Polyphonic Staff Style" section later in this lesson.

Instead of clicking the note on the Step Input Keyboard, you can also use a MIDI controller to insert notes by clicking the MIDI In button in any editor so that MIDI incoming data can be received. When MIDI In is enabled, Logic "listens" for MIDI note input.

6   While looking at the MIDI Activity display within the Transport bar, find the D2 and A1 keys on your MIDI controller.

7   In the Score Editor, click the MIDI In button to turn it on.

8   On the Step Input Keyboard, click the half-note button.

9   On your MIDI controller, press the D2 key, then the A1 key.

A D note is created at 6 1 1 1 and an A note at 6 3 1 1 (spaced by a half-note interval).

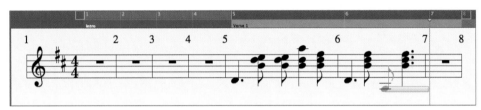

As long as the MIDI In button is on, Logic assumes that you are using step input, and it will create notes based on MIDI input. For this reason, it is necessary to turn off the MIDI In button when you are finished using MIDI for note input.

10   Click the MIDI In button to turn MIDI input off.

11   Close the Step Input Keyboard.

Working with Guitar Notation

Just as text can be formatted depending on the context (such as paragraphs for standard text, stanzas in poetry, and outlines), music notation can be displayed in a variety of formats, depending on the instrument, transposition, number of voices, and so on.

Logic allows you to format notes using staff styles, which incorporate multiple attributes of the notes in a MIDI region, such as clef, staff size, instrument transposition, and various voice-display parameters. A staff style acts like a notation-display filter and can be changed at any time.

In order for Logic to accurately display the guitar part you inputted previously, you must first choose an appropriate score style. There are two distinct schools of guitar notation—tablature and standard—and you will explore them both in the following exercises.

1   In the Inspector, click the Guitar Score_Intro disclosure triangle to show the Display Parameter box.

The Display Parameter box contains parameters that affect the display of the selected MIDI region. The Style parameter designates the staff style assigned to the region.

2   Click and hold the Style pop-up menu.

The staff style options are displayed.

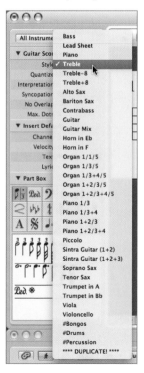

Logic comes with many staff styles that each contain several attributes, such as clef assignment and display transposition.

NOTE ▶ Staff styles are saved in a project file and can be imported from one song to another by choosing File > Project Settings > Import Settings.

3   From the Style menu, choose Guitar.

The notation in the Score Editor changes to display guitar tablature.

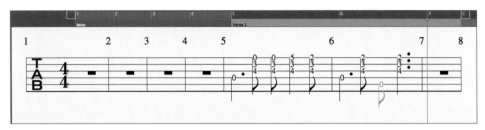

NOTE ▶ Logic has extensive options for creating tablature of all types of string instruments (guitar, bass, banjo, and so on). You can set the string tunings, type of note head, and other appearance options within Project Settings > Score by selecting the Tablature tab. In addition, you can insert tablature-specific symbols like hammer-ons, pull-offs, and palm mutes into your score by selecting the Chord Grid group within the Part box.

As you can see, staff styles are extremely versatile in their displays of note data.

4   From the Style menu, choose Treble, returning the notation to its default setting.

NOTE ▶ Logic automatically assigns a default staff style (Treble, Bass, or Piano) to a MIDI region based on its octave and range.

Creating a Polyphonic Staff Style

You probably noticed that the three bass notes you created by step input are displayed incorrectly in the Score Editor. The notes do not appear to sustain for the full amount of time and are cut off by the notes that follow. However, if you look at the notes in the Piano Roll Editor (in the bottom half of the screen), you'll notice that the lengths of those notes are displayed correctly.

Our guitar part was input as a single voice, and therefore the note lengths are cut off because there is no voice independence. To solve this problem, you need to create a polyphonic staff style that can display multiple independent voices at once.

1   Shift-click to select the three notes you just created via step input (D2, D2, A1).

The corresponding notes are highlighted in the Piano Roll Editor.

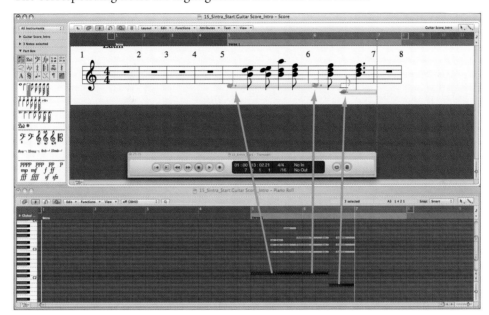

Notice the difference in the representation of the notes in the Piano Roll and Score Editors. The first note is sustained for the entire measure, and should be noted as a whole note instead of a dotted quarter note. The reason for this discrepancy lies in the established system for the notation of a polyphonic instrument. A polyphonic instrument notated on a single staff, such as a guitar, needs to have rhythmically different melodic lines displayed in the same staff. These voices, in turn, must be able to display length, stem direction, and rests independent of each other.

2   In the Score Editor's local menu bar, choose Layout > Staff Styles.

The Staff Style window opens, displaying the contents of the default Treble staff style.

3   If needed, expand the window by dragging the lower-right corner to view all of the parameters.

The data displayed in the Treble staff style represents a single-voice staff with various display attributes.

4 Click the arrow button immediately to the right of the name box, and choose ****DUPLICATE!**** from the menu.

A new staff style is created with the attributes of the Treble staff style. Let's rename it.

5 In the name field, double-click the staff style name and enter *Guitar (1+2)*, and then press Return.

Notice that the new staff style contains a single row of attributes (preceded by the number 1) that represent a single staff. A staff style can have multiple staves with independent settings, each containing as many voices as you need.

In guitar notation, multiple voices are displayed on a single treble staff. Each voice is differentiated by the direction of the stems, ties, and tuplets. Let's continue custom-izing the staff style to reflect these display parameters by first inserting an additional voice.

6 Click the narrow column to the left of and just below the staff number.

Clicking this column enables you to set insertion points for adding new staves and voices. You can also select voices and staves for deletion by clicking within this col-umn, immediately to the left of the number.

The small arrow moves below the staff number, indicating where new staves and voices will be inserted.

7 In the Staff Style window's local menu bar, choose New > Insert Voice.

A new voice is created below the previous staff voice, indicated by the absence of a number at the far left of the line.

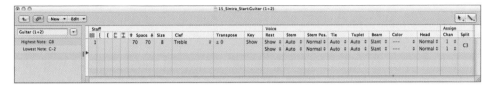

In guitar notation, when more than one voice is displayed at the same time, the stems, ties, and tuplets of the top voice always point upward. You can reflect this in the staff style by modifying the Voice attributes for the top voice.

8   In the top voice, click the Stem parameter menu and choose Up.

9   Do the same for the Tie and Tuplet parameter menus.

10   In the bottom voice, click the Stem, Tie, and Tuplet menus one at a time and choose Down.

By default, each voice in a staff style can display rests. This can create multiple rests in a staff, which are appropriate for divided (divisi) parts but not for a solo part.

11   Click the Rest parameter menu for the bottom voice and choose Hide.

This option hides the rests for the bottom voice.

TIP ▶ Rests can be inserted manually by dragging them into the score from the Part box. These are graphic indicators only and have no effect on the playback of the MIDI region.

The last thing to consider is how to assign individual notes in the region to each voice. By default, a staff style will use a split note to do this. Pitches that fall above the split note are assigned to voice one, and pitches that fall below the split note are assigned to voice two. This split note can be changed in the Assign parameters in the Staff Style window.

However, this technique usually won't work for guitar notation because voices are assigned primarily to represent melody (or bass lines) and the accompaniment, and they can consist of any range of pitches. Instead, voices can be assigned in a staff style using the individual notes' MIDI channel numbers.

NOTE ▶ Each note can have its own MIDI channel in Logic. This setting is applied on input by the MIDI Out channel setting of the MIDI controller, or it can be applied after the fact using Logic's editors.

12 In the Assign columns (far right), click the Chan(nel) menu for the top voice and choose 1.

13 Click the Chan(nel) menu for the bottom voice and choose 2.

With these settings, all notes using MIDI channel 1 will be assigned to the top voice, and all notes using MIDI channel 2 will be assigned to the bottom voice.

Now that you have created the polyphonic Guitar staff style, it's time to apply it to the displayed region.

14 Close the Staff Style window.

15 In the Display Parameter box, click the Style menu and choose Guitar (1+2).

The notation changes slightly, displaying the notes with all stems pointing up. When notes are inserted manually, the same default MIDI channel is assigned to all notes (in this case, channel 1). When you applied the staff style, all the notes in the region were assigned to the top voice.

You don't have to manually change the MIDI channel for each note that you want to assign to the bottom voice. Instead, you can quickly assign notes to adjacent voices by using the Voice Separation tool. This tool works by allowing you to draw a line between voices that need to be separated. Notes below the line are bumped to the adjacent voice below their current assignment, and notes above the line will be bumped up a voice.

16 Choose the Voice Separation tool.

17 Using the Voice Separation tool, draw between the bass notes and the chords in one continuous line.

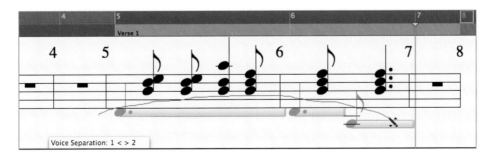

The bass notes are assigned to the bottom voice and are now displayed correctly.

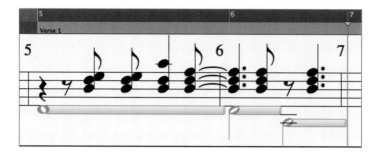

NOTE ▸ You can continually adjust voice assignments with the Voice Separation tool by drawing lines above and below individual notes or entire passages.

Working with Text

Text appears in various ways in a score, supplying everything from lyrics to performance indications. Although specialized text objects (lyrics, chords, song titles, and so on) can only be selected for insertion from the text group within the Part box, standard text can also be added by simply using the Text tool.

To illustrate this, let's create a basic performance indication for the guitar part.

1   Choose the Text tool.

2   Around the first measure, click the area above the staff.

A text insertion point is created.

3   Type *Latin* and press Return.

Inserted text can be formatted in any font or size in the Fonts window.

4   In the Score Editor's local menu bar, choose Text > Fonts.

The Fonts window opens.

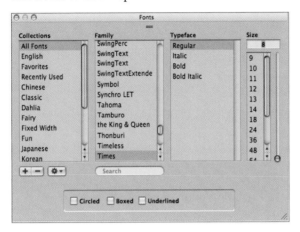

5   In the Size column, click 12.

The selected text increases in size.

6   Close the Fonts window.

Using Text Styles

Just as you can format notes using staff styles, you can also create text styles to format text elements in the Score Editor. Each text style contains attributes, like font and size, that can be applied to specific types of text objects as a group. In this exercise, you will create a new text style that can be assigned to any inserted text in the current score.

1   In the Score Editor's local menu bar, choose Text > Text Styles.

The Text Styles window opens. (You may need to resize the window to view its entire contents.)

2   Click the New menu and choose New Text Style.

A new text style is created at the bottom of the list.

3   Double-click the new text style within the Name column, and then enter *Performance Indications*. Press Return.

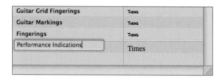

4   In the Example column for the Performance Indications text style, click the selected font (Times).

The Fonts window opens.

5   In the Family column of the Fonts window, choose Arial.

6   In the Typeface column, click Italic.

7   In the Size column, click 10

8   Close the Fonts window.

9   Close the Text Styles window.

Text styles are assigned to a text element in the Event Parameter box.

10 If not done so already, select the performance indication you inputted earlier in the exercise ("Latin").

11 Within the Event Parameter box, click the Style menu and choose Performance Indications.

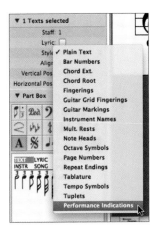

The text you inserted earlier adapts to the specifications you defined for the assigned text style.

TIP ▶ Text styles are useful for creating specialized text formats commonly used in musical notation, such as rehearsal markings. The Fonts window also includes checkboxes for circling or boxing the text (useful for rehearsal markings).

Creating Chord Charts

Let's create some chord symbols in the Guitar score to indicate the accompaniment chords for the guitar solo. Instead of using the Score Editor/Piano Roll Editor screenset, you'll work with the Score Editor in the Arrange window. So far you've been accessing the editors within the Arrange area by clicking the tabs at the bottom of the window. You can speed up workflow considerably by using the various toggle key commands, which both open *and* close an editor within the Arrange area with a single keystroke.

1 Press the number 1 to open Screenset 1.

2 In the Guitar Score track, select the last region (Guitar Score_Chords).

3   Press the N key (Toggle Score Editor) to open the Score Editor within the Arrange area.

The Guitar Score_Chords region is displayed in the Score Editor.

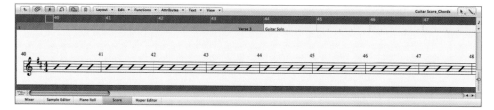

NOTE ▶ The Guitar Score_Chords region doesn't contain any MIDI events or added notational symbols. The chord slashes you see displayed are actually part of the Lead Sheet staff style, which is set for the region. You can display chord slashes for any staff style instead of rests by choosing them in the Staff Style window's Rest parameter menu.

4   In the Part box group menu, click the Chord Grid group button to view its contents.

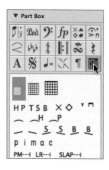

5   Drag the smallest chord grid object to just above the staff at 40 1 1 1.

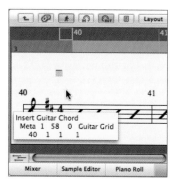

NOTE ▸ You can make chord grids in three sizes, represented by the objects within the Part box. You can always change the size after insertion by Ctrl-clicking the object and choosing one of the scale options (reduced, normal, and enlarged).

The Chord Grid Library window opens.

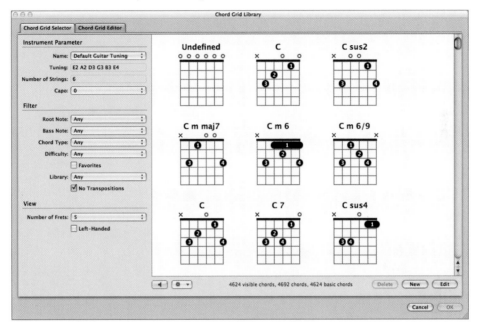

The Chord Grid Library contains a database of more than 4,000 chord grids that you can use in your compositions. Chords are listed by position (fret).

6   Using the scroll bar, take a look at the chord choices in the Chord Grid Library.

Considering the overwhelming number of chords displayed, it is essential to filter your view, enabling you to center in on the chord you want. A good place to start is by specifying the root note, bass note, and chord type within the Filter area.

7   From the Root Note menu, choose D.

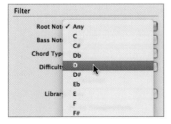

Only chords with D in the root are displayed in the Chord Grid Library.

8   From the Chord Type menu, choose major.

Only major chords with D in the root are displayed in the Chord Grid Library.

9   Click the root position D major chord in the top-left corner of the Chord Grid Library, and click OK.

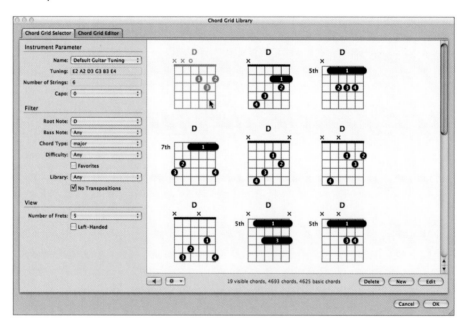

The D major chord grid is added to the score at 40 1 1 1.

> **TIP** ▶ If you need to adjust the position of any inserted score object (including text), you can drag it from one location to another using the Pointer tool. However, when exact positions are required (as they often are), use the Event Parameter box. When an object is selected, you will find parameters there to adjust both the vertical and horizontal positions by single pixels, and to align the object in relation to the page borders.

Creating Chord Grids

You can easily create your own chord grids within the Chord Grid Library. Once created, these chord grids become accessible to any project file.

1   Drag the smallest chord grid object to just above the staff at 44 1 1 1.

2   Select the New button in the lower right corner of the Chord Grid Library. The Chord Library displays an Undefined chord, ready for editing.

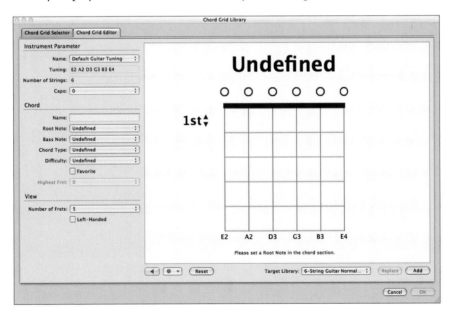

When creating your own chord grids, a good place to start is by specifying the root note, bass note, and chord type.

3   From the Root Note menu, choose C.

4   From the Bass Note menu, choose D.

5   From the Chord Type menu, choose add9.

Now it's time to specify the notes of the chord. This is done by clicking directly on the chord grid at the desired fret and string.

6   Click at the first fret, second string (C4).

A fingering dot is added to the chord grid.

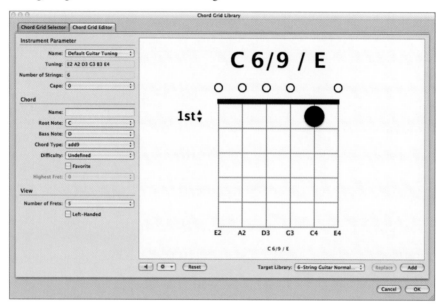

Finger number can be specified for each fingering dot by Control-clicking on it.

7   Control-click the fingering dot you just created, and select 1.

You can indicate whether open strings are played or not by clicking on the area at the top of those strings.

8 Click the area at the top of the low E string (E2) and the area at the top of the A string (A2), indicating that those strings will not be played.

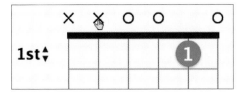

The chord name updates, indicating the harmony (C9/D). Now that you finished creating your chord, you can add it to the Chord Grid Library for future use.

9 Click Add.

The chord grid is added to the library.

The Chord Grid Library window provides a convenient way to audition selected chords, enabling you to hear the result before you add them to your score.

10 Click the Playback button, toggling it on.

The chord plays.

11 Click the Playback button, toggling it off.

12 Click OK.

The chord grid is inserted at 44 1 1 1.

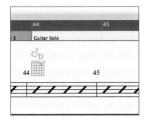

Most likely you will need to adjust the chord grid's position after it is inserted into the score. You can make your job easier by using guides, which allow you to visually align an object's position in relation to the time grid (bars, beats, divisions, and so on).

13 From the View menu, choose Guides > All Objects.

A dotted line extends from the chord grids to the staff below, showing its position in relation to the time grid.

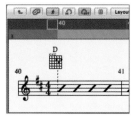

14 Using the guide, option-drag the D chord grid at 40 1 1 1, copying it to 46 1 1 1.

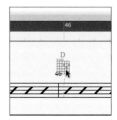

There is no need to worry if your inserted chords are not aligned with each other. This can be easily solved by using the Align Object Positions Vertically command.

15 Drag a selection rectangle around the three chord grids you inserted.

16 Control-click any of the chord grids and choose Align Object Positions Vertically from the shortcut menu.

The chord grid objects align vertically.

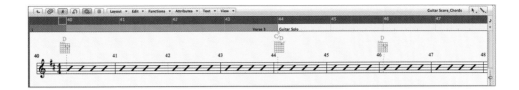

TIP ▶ If you need to create chord charts without the guitar-oriented chord grids, you can use the Chord object within the text group in the Part box.

Transcribing a Performance

Logic's notation engine is designed to preserve the subtleties of an actual performance while organizing the data into cleanly notated scores. With a little finessing, you can create accurate parts and scores based on existing MIDI tracks without sacrificing any of the original "feel" of the sequenced material.

Logic accomplishes this demanding task by using a separate notation display system that allows you to adjust the look of the notation without changing the original MIDI region data.

In this exercise you'll prepare MIDI regions in the Arrange area to aid in the transcription process, and adjust parameters in the Score Editor to correctly notate the parts without modifying the performance data.

Preparing MIDI Regions for Notation

During sequencing, it is commonplace to have tracks made up of noncontiguous regions (that is, regions that have space between them). However, the Score Editor needs regions to display notation and will display nothing (not even a staff) if no region is present.

For the purpose of notation, it is therefore advisable to fill up MIDI tracks with regions by inserting blank regions, or by merging multiple regions into a single composite region. This has no effect on the playback of a part but allows the Score Editor to create staves and fill them with rests.

1 In the Arrange area, scroll down and select the Bongos track (track 6).

   The Bongos track consists of two separate regions.

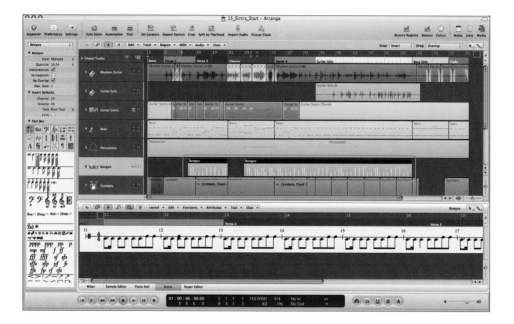

As you can see in the Score Editor, the display starts at measure 11, which corresponds to the start of the first region in the track.

2   In the Arrange area, choose the Pencil tool, and click the beginning of the Bongos track (at 1 1 1 1) to create a blank region.

3   Create another blank region at 81 1 1 1 in the Bongos track.

4   In the track list, click the Bongos track to select all of its regions, including the new ones.

5   In the Arrange area's local menu bar, choose Region > Merge > Regions.

One contiguous region is formed for the Bongos track.

6   Scroll through the Score Editor to view the part. Rests are now displayed for areas with no activity.

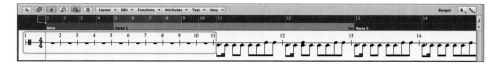

Viewing the Data Accurately

The settings in the Display Parameter box (with the exception of Style) form the basis for the rhythmic interpretation and display of MIDI data. These settings apply only to the score display and do not change the playback of the MIDI regions in any way.

Let's look at how these parameters affect the notation of a selected region.

1   In the Bongos track, click the Solo button to solo the track.

2   Press the "Go to Position" key command (/) to locate to 11 1 1 1.

3   Play the song, listening to the bongo part while watching the notation.

4   When you're familiar with the material, stop the song.

5   Make sure that the Score Editor has key focus by clicking the top part of the score area or by pressing the Tab key.

6   In the upper-left corner, open the Display Parameter box (disclosure triangle next to Bongos), if it's not already opened.

    You can use the Quantize setting (located below the Style parameter) to apply visual quantization to the notes, dictating the shortest value that can be displayed in the selected MIDI region.

7   Click the Quantize menu and choose 8.

The notation changes to display eighth notes as the shortest value.

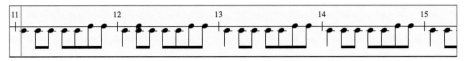

8   Play the song again, listening to the bongo part while watching the notation.

Notice that what you are hearing is not rhythmically the same as what is displayed. This illustrates the independence of display quantization from the actual MIDI performance data.

9   Use the "Go to Position" key command (/) to locate to 11 1 1 1.

10   Click the Quantize menu and choose 16,24.

This default setting works well for the part. It permits sixteenth notes as well as sixteenth-note triplets (indicated by *24*) to appear as the shortest note lengths in the Score Editor.

Let's move on to the Interpretation parameter, which is specifically used to create an easy-to-read score from real-time MIDI recordings. When notes are performed, they generally aren't held for the full length of a given note, rather they are shortened depending on the articulation and the time needed to move to another note on the instrument. With Interpretation turned on, Logic fills in those performance gaps between notes and makes a guess as to the appropriate notation for each note.

11   In the Display Parameter box, deselect the Interpretation checkbox.

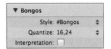

The notes are now displayed as isolated sixteenth notes with rests.

This might be more technically accurate (displaying the actual length of the notes as they are played), but the notation is much harder to read! Considering that the part is a percussive one, it makes sense to have Interpretation turned on (the default setting).

12 Select the Interpretation checkbox to turn Interpretation on.

> **TIP** ▶ Turn off Interpretation when using graphic or step input, because you want the full value of the selected notes to be displayed.

Each note in Logic can have unique display attributes, independent of the region settings in the Display Parameter box. These are set in the Note Attributes dialog.

13 Double-click the first note of measure 11.

The Note Attributes dialog opens.

Here you can make adjustments to individual notes via various menus, including one for Interpretation.

14 Click Cancel to close the Note Attributes dialog.

15 Press the N key to close the Score Editor.

16 In the Bongos track, click the Solo button to turn off soloing.

Working with Drum Notation

Logic has a unique and powerful way of notating drum parts using *mapped instruments*. Traditionally, mapped instruments are created in Logic to represent a drum machine or drum channel in a multi-timbral synthesizer, but they also enable you to assign specific notes to voice groups in the Staff Style window and thereby create drum notation.

In this exercise you will create a mapped instrument to generate a score from the drum tracks used in the song.

Consolidating the Tracks

To create a single drum staff, you first need to consolidate the multiple drum part tracks into a single contiguous region.

1   Press Shift-Command-A to deselect all regions.

2   Shift-click tracks 7 through 11 (Cymbals, Hi Hat, Toms, Rim Shot, and Bass Drum), selecting the regions in each track.

3   In the Arrange area's local menu bar, choose Region > Loops > Convert to Real Copies.

4   In the Arrange area's local menu bar, choose Region > Merge > Regions.

The drum tracks combine into a single region on track 7.

5   Press Command-Shift-A to deselect all regions.

6   In the Arrange track list, delete the tracks left empty by the merge.

7   If it's not selected already, select track 7 (now displays Cymbals as the name).

Creating a Mapped Instrument

Now that everything is consolidated into a single region, you can create the mapped instrument object in the Environment.

1   Choose Window > Environment.

The Environment window opens, displaying the Instruments layer, which has nothing in it yet.

2   In the Environment window's local menu bar, choose New > Mapped Instrument.

A mapped instrument object is created in the Instruments layer, and the Mapped Instrument window appears.

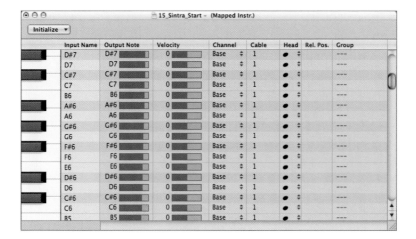

The Mapped Instrument window is used to edit individual notes in a mapped instrument, and it automatically opens when creating a new mapped instrument object.

NOTE ▶ A Mapped Instrument window can also be displayed by double-clicking the mapped instrument object.

3   In the Mapped Instrument window, scroll down until you can see the drum names displayed in the Input Name column (so that Kick 2 is at the bottom of the list).

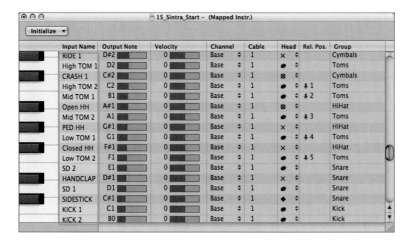

4   Look at the three columns to the right in the Mapped Instrument window: Head, Rel. Pos. (for Relative Position), and Group.

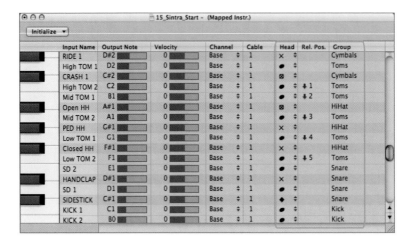

The information in these columns has a direct impact on the drum notation. In these columns you assign note heads and adjust the relative position of the clef for each note. In addition, each note can be assigned to drum groups, which carry common attributes that are interpreted by the staff style in the Score Editor.

NOTE ▶ The default settings in the Mapped Instrument window correspond to the standardized General MIDI (GM) Drum Kit note assignments. This makes it a snap to create drum notation from an EXS24 mkII sampler instrument that also reflects the General MIDI note assignments. If you aren't using a GM-mapped drum sampler instrument to output the part, adjustments can be made in the Output Note column to trigger the appropriate sound.

5   Close the Mapped Instrument window.

6   In the Object Parameter box (for Mapped Instr.), double-click the object's name, enter *Drums*, and press Return.

The mapped instrument object's name changes to Drums.

If the track in the Arrange area is to display the drum notation, you need to assign it to the mapped instrument you created. To ensure that it still outputs to the EXS24 mkII plug-in inserted on the software instrument channel, you need to cable the objects together in the Environment.

7   Option-click the cable output from the Drums object, and choose Audio > Software Instrument > Inst 1(the software instrument with the EXS24 mkII sampled drum kit).

NOTE ▸ Option-clicking a cable output allows you to connect objects in different layers of the Environment.

An alert message appears, asking if you want to remove the port setting for the object.

8   Click Remove.

NOTE ▸ By removing the port and channel settings for the object, you are setting the Drums object to output only to the software instrument object.

A cable appears, connecting the objects between the layers of the Environment.

You're now ready to assign the new mapped instrument to the consolidated drums track (Cymbals) in the Arrange area. Instead of Control-clicking the track in the track list and choosing an object from the shortcut menu, you can quickly assign the selected track to any object in the Environment by using the MIDI Thru tool.

9   Choose the MIDI Thru tool.

10 Move the Environment window to the right, so you can see the Arrange window's Inspector and track list.

11 In the Environment window, click the Drums object while observing the Inspector within the Arrange area (Cymbals).

12 Close the Environment window.

In the Arrange area, the selected drums track (track 7) is now assigned to the Drums mapped instrument. (You can verify the assignment by looking at the Arrange channel strip, which now displays a MIDI fader.)

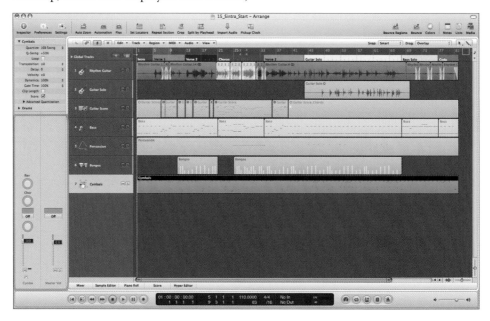

Now all that's left for you to do is assign the staff style in the Score Editor.

13 Press the N key to open the Score Editor.

The Score Editor displays the contents of the drums track but uses the default Bass staff style. In order for the settings in the Mapped Instrument window to be translated into notation, it is necessary to assign a mapped staff style to the region. Mapped staff styles are designated in the staff style list by a # symbol preceding the name.

14 Within the Display Parameter box, click the Style menu and choose #Drums.

The region is now displayed in correct notation.

NOTE ▶ If the display is cut off, you can move the staff by dragging down the clef.

Display the #Drums staff style to see how it affects the settings.

15 In the Score Editor's local menu bar, choose Layout > Staff Styles.

The #Drums staff style is displayed in the Staff Style window.

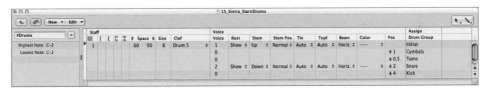

As you can see, this is a polyphonic staff style of sorts, consisting of multiple voices that are assigned to drum groups instead of a split point or MIDI channel. These drum groups correspond to the Group column entries in the Mapped Instrument window.

NOTE ▶ You might need to resize the Staff Style window to see its entire contents.

16 Close the Staff Style window.

Creating Scores and Parts

Logic's Score Editor allows you to use *score sets* to control which instruments will be displayed (and printed) in a score. A score set can include as many (or as few) of the existing track instruments as you want, and instruments can be arranged independently of their order in the Arrange area. In a score set you can also assign instrument names and determine if the group shares bar lines, brackets, or braces.

Multiple user-defined score sets can be created to display everything from a full score to individual parts. In this exercise, you will use score sets to lay out the full score as well as quickly generate individual instrument parts.

Creating a Score Set

1   Click Stop to return the project to 1 1 1 1.

2   Open Screenset 4.

The screenset contains a full-screen Score Editor in page view. Don't worry if the lines appear crowded at this point. You will address this later on in the lesson.

NOTE ▶ Page view can be displayed in any Score Editor window: Choose View > Page View from the Score Editor's local menu bar, or click the turquoise Page View button next to the menu bar.

Prior to the creation of any score sets, Logic displays selected instruments using a default score set named All Instruments, which appears at the top of the Inspector in the Score Set menu.

However, you aren't seeing all the instruments at the moment, because you recently selected the Drums region. To display all the instruments, you need to move up a level (reflecting the Arrange area).

3   Click the Hierarchy button, located in the upper-left corner of the window.

All Arrange area instruments are displayed in the Score Editor.

Although the default All Instruments score set works for the basic display of the instruments, you can refine the score display by creating your own score set.

4   In the Score Editor's local menu bar, choose Layout > Score Sets.

The Score Set window opens. (You might need to resize the Score Set window to see its entire contents.)

5   In the Score Set window's local menu bar, choose New > New Complete Set.

A new score set, made up of all the instruments used in the Arrange area, is created.

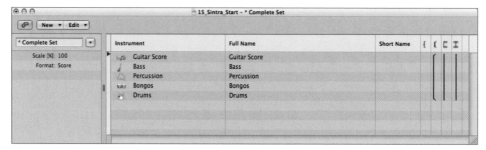

6   Click the score set name and enter *Ensemble* in the text field. Press Return.

NOTE ▶ The instrument names that appear in the score relate directly to the contents of the Full Name column. By default, these contents include the names of the objects within the Environment that are assigned to the tracks (channels, mapped instruments, and so on). You can, however, enter whatever you like in the Full Name and Short Name columns.

A score set also allows you to scale the size of the displayed staves, enabling you to fit more systems on a page. This is especially useful when creating full conductor scores.

7   Double-click the number next to the Scale parameter (below the score set name) and enter *65*. Press Return.

To apply the score set you created, you need to assign it in the Inspector.

8   At the very top of the Inspector area, click and hold the Score Set menu and choose Ensemble.

The score displays at a smaller scale.

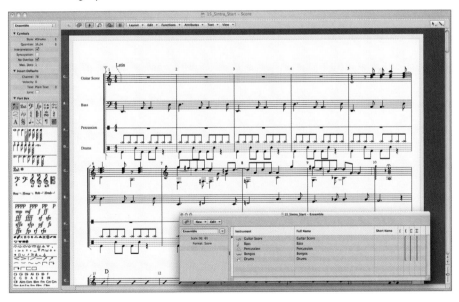

Creating Parts for Printing

Creating individual score sets for each instrumental part in the score is desirable because it allows the most control over naming and other display attributes, and it enables you to print parts by choosing from the Score Set menu.

In this exercise, you will create an individual, printer-ready score set for the guitar part. You will create a new empty score set, and then add the Guitar Score instrument to the set.

1   In the Score Set window, choose New > New Empty Set.

An empty score set is created.

2   Click the score set name and enter *Guitar* in the text field. Press Return.

3   Choose New > Add Instrument Entry.

A single instrument entry is added to the score set. By default, the first instrument in the track list is added, which in this case is the Guitar Score instrument.

To complete the part, it is a simple matter to rename the default instrument as *Guitar* in the Score Set window.

4   Click the Full Name field and enter *Guitar*. Press Return.

Instrumental parts can reflect different layout preferences. To designate a score set as a part, you need to change the Format parameter, which is located below the Scale parameter.

5   Click once on the setting next to the Format parameter (which currently displays Score), toggling it to display Part.

The Format setting changes to Part.

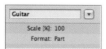

6   Close the Score Set window.

7   In the Inspector, click the Score Set menu and choose Guitar.

The Score Editor displays the guitar part.

Now that you've designated the Guitar score set as a part, you can change its layout settings without affecting the Ensemble score set you created earlier. The layout settings for both scores and parts are located in the Global Score project settings.

8   In the Score Editor's local menu bar, choose Layout > Global Format.

The Project Settings window opens, displaying the Global tab.

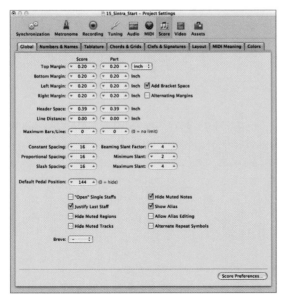

This window includes separate layout settings for scores and parts, designated by the two columns titled (appropriately enough) Score and Part.

The notation in both the guitar part as well as the ensemble score looked at earlier is a bit crowded. You can create more space between the systems by adjusting the Line Distance setting in both the Part and Score column.

9   In the Score column, click the Line Distance field and enter *0.20*. Press Return.

10   In the Part column, click the Line Distance field and enter *0.25*. Press Return.

11   Close the Project Settings window.

The staves for the guitar part are more spread out now, making them easier to read.

Let's finish by comparing the two score sets you have created. The differences can be seen most easily if you view the pages in their entirety. By zooming out in the Score Editor, you can see entire pages side by side.

12   Press Control-Option Up Arrow repeatedly to vertically zoom out until you see two pages.

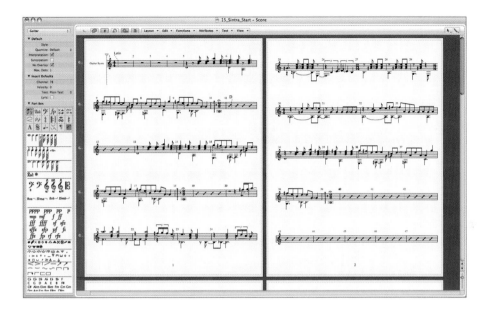

13 From the Score Set menu, choose Ensemble.

The Score Editor displays the full score.

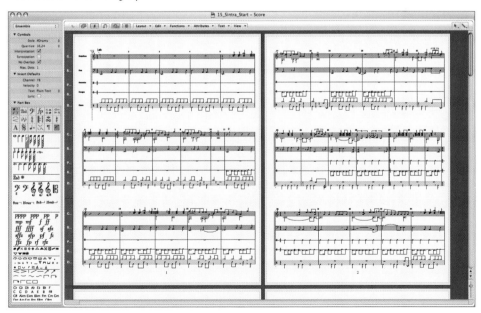

The two score sets display independent scale and line distance settings.

14 Try printing the scores of both the Guitar and Ensemble score sets by selecting them in the Inspector and choosing File > Print.

NOTE ▶ If you don't have a printer connected, you can save the score as a PDF file by choosing File > Print and then verifying the settings and clicking OK in the Page Setup window. Then, within the Print window, click the PDF button and choose Save as PDF.

Lesson Review

1.   In what ways can you enter notation in the Score Editor?

2.   Where do you edit note length?

3.   What do you use to assign display attributes to notation?

4.   How do you assign voices within a score style?

5.   What do you use to assign voices in a part in the Score Editor?

6.   What do text styles do?

7.   Does the Quantize parameter in the Score Editor change both notation and playback?

8.   How do you create drum notation?

9.   What do you use to display and print only selected parts?

10. Can you retain independent formatting for both parts and scores?

Answers

1.   Notation can be entered in the Score Editor using graphic input, step input, and real-time transcription.

2.   Note length is edited in the Event Parameter box or by adjusting the note's duration bar.

3.   Staff styles are used to assign display attributes to notation.

4.   Voices are assigned using a MIDI split note or an individual MIDI channel.

5.   The Voice Separation tool can be used to quickly assign voices in a polyphonic staff style using MIDI channel assignment.

6.   Text styles assign display attributes to text elements in the Score Editor.

7. No. Quantize in the Score Editor changes the notation display but does not affect the performance data.

8. Drum parts can be notated by assigning a mapped instrument and a mapped staff style to a track.

9. Score sets are used to display and print individual parts up to full scores.

10. Yes. You can assign separate format settings for parts and scores in the Global Score project settings.

16

Working with Picture

Scoring to picture is a collaborative effort integrating a variety of media (including digital video and audio) that are often produced by more than one person or facility. As a result, a key skill is the ability to import and work with many media elements in a variety of formats while maintaining the same timing references, especially when the music needs to synchronize with critical moments in the film or video footage. Computer-based music production has greatly facilitated the composition of music for film and video. Computers powerful enough to stream digital video and audio in the same application have simplified the methods for ensuring synchronization between music and picture.

In this lesson you will work with a scene from the television series *Leverage*, walking through the workflow from setting up the project to delivering the soundtrack.

Setting Up Synchronization

It is still entirely appropriate to work with an external video deck synchronized to a DAW using SMPTE time code (converted to MIDI Time Code), but the norm for today's media composers is to work with digital video clips.

Using digital video clips simplifies video-to-music synchronization. You no longer have to add significant pre-roll time at the beginning of a project to provide time for the hardware deck to lock in to sync, and you can instantly locate to any point in the project and the video. What's more, the digital video (along with all the synchronization settings) can be saved in the project folder for easy archiving and retrieval.

Logic leverages the Apple QuickTime engine for video playback and therefore can open a digital video clip (commonly referred to by the single term *movie*) in any format supported by the QuickTime standard.

In this exercise, you will open a digital video clip in a new Logic project, adjusting the synchronization settings to allow for time-locked playback and reference of audio and video.

Let's start by creating a project file around a useful stock project template created for working with video.

1   Choose File > New. The Templates dialog opens.

2   In the Collection column, click the Produce folder.

3   In the Template column, click the Music For Picture button.

     The project template Music For Picture opens, and a Save As dialog appears.

4   Select the Include Assets checkbox, if it's not already selected.

5   Select the "Copy external audio files to project folder" and "Copy movie files to project folder" checkboxes.

     When "Copy movie files to project folder" is selected, a message appears, alerting you that copying a movie file could take up valuable disk space.

NOTE ▶ The file you will be working with for this exercise is fairly small, so it should have minimal impact on your disk space.

6 Click Copy.

7 Enter *Working with Picture* in the Save As field.

8 Set the save location to Music > Advanced Logic 9_Files > Lessons > Completed.

9 Click Save.

Before you begin the lesson, take a minute to explore what the Music For Picture template offers. The Bar ruler is set to display SMPTE time position as well as bars and beats, and a giant SMPTE display is floating in the Arrange area. Both provide easy visual reference to valuable timing information you will use when scoring to picture.

NOTE ▶ You can display SMPTE time in the Bar ruler of any project by clicking the small down arrow located to the right of the Bar ruler and choosing one of the three settings with Time in its name. Displaying the SMPTE ruler also affects what is displayed in the help tags when you're editing regions and events. You can configure the Transport bar to display a large dedicated floating SMPTE time display, which provides easy readability at long distances (especially useful when you're working across the room from your display). Do this by Control-clicking the SMPTE time display in the Transport bar and choosing Open Giant SMPTE Display from the shortcut menu.

10 Close the Media area by clicking the button in the toolbar.

Opening the Movie

You can see that Screenset 1 has been configured to display the global Marker, Signature, Tempo, and Video tracks, as these tracks are commonly used when working with video. The Video track provides many useful functions for importing and working with video.

1   In the Video track, click the Open Movie button.

The Open window appears.

NOTE ▶ You can also open a movie by choosing File > Open Movie.

2   Go to Music > Advanced Logic 9_Files > Lessons > 16_Movie Files and open **Leverage_L215_Act3.mov**.

The video opens in a floating window, and a video thumbnail of the movie is created in the Video track, displaying images at regular intervals.

Working with SMPTE Time Code

You can establish synchronization between the video and Logic just by opening a QuickTime movie in a project, but a few settings should be set so that Logic's time code will match the burn-in time code from the video. These settings are found in the Synchronization project settings.

1   Choose File > Project Settings > Synchronization. The Project Settings window opens, displaying the Synchronization tab.

2   Click the General tab, if it's not already selected.

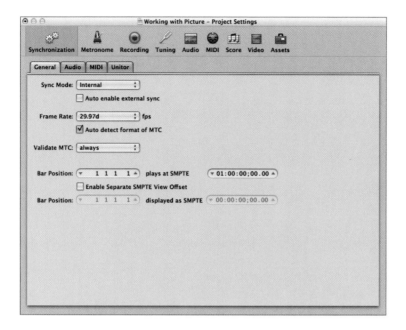

To ensure that the time code display is accurate, the project should reflect the movie's frame rate. This is set in the Frame Rate pop-up menu.

3   Click the Frame Rate menu and choose 23.976. (This is the frame rate of the digital video clip.)

NOTE ▶ The original footage was shot on film at 24 fps and then transferred to video via telecine at 23.976 fps.

The Bar Position setting and Plays at SMPTE setting are used to align the musical timing of the project to the SMPTE start time of the video. With these two settings, you tell Logic where the first bar occurs in relation to absolute SMPTE time. You can find this by locating to the beginning of the video and using the displayed burn-in time code.

As you can see in the Movie window, the time code displays 03:02:50:13.

4 In the Plays at SMPTE field, single-click the number and enter *03:02:50:13*. Press Return.

TIP By default, Logic's SMPTE readout displays subframes, or bits, as its last digit (after frames). You can choose different options for the SMPTE display in the Display Preferences under the Display SMPTE menu.

You might have noticed that the video display changed and is not currently seen in the Video global track. This is because the Movie Start time is now off (it defaults to 01:00:00:00.00). Once the Movie Start time is set, the movie will start when the project starts (03:02:50:13.00), aligning the burn-in time code with Logic's SMPTE readout. This information is entered in the Video project settings.

5 At the top of the Project Settings window, click the Video button to display the Video settings.

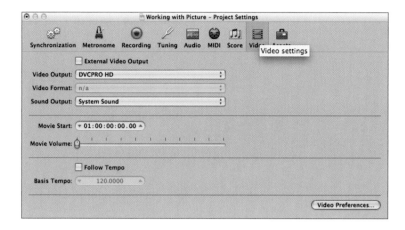

6   In the Movie Start field, single-click the number and enter *03:02:50:13.00*. Press
Return.

The video will now start at the beginning of the project.

7   Play the project from the beginning, observing Logic's SMPTE display in relation to
the burn-in time code of the video.

8   Stop playback after the first 10 or 15 seconds.

TIP ▶ You can resize the QuickTime Player window by dragging the lower-right
corner, or by Control-clicking the video directly and choosing one of the size options
from the shortcut menu.

Configuring Audio

Now that you've configured the video synchronization settings, you need to make sure
that the project's audio settings are optimized to work with video. This includes both the
sample rate setting and soundtrack output routing for the imported video.

1   In the Project Settings window, click the Audio tab.

The audio sample rate of choice when working with digital video is 48 kHz, which is
conveniently set for you by default when using the Music For Picture template.

This video contains an embedded dialog audio track for reference. As mentioned earlier, both audio and video playback are handled by QuickTime, so the audio signal is outputted from whatever device is specified in your system settings (System Preferences > Sound > Output). By default, this output is muted, but you can hear the audio track by turning up the volume in the Movie window controls.

2 At the lower left of the QuickTime Player, click the speaker icon and drag the volume slider up all the way.

3 Play the project to view the scene with which you will be working, listening to the dialog.

You should be hearing the video's dialog track out of the device specified in your system settings.

Navigating with Video

Playback of the movie is controlled by Logic's Transport bar, and it plays in sync with the project.

1 While it's playing, click anywhere in the Bar ruler to locate to another position.

The movie relocates in sync with the project.

2 Drag the playhead in QuickTime Player to the right.

The project relocates in sync with the movie.

3   Stop playback.

NOTE ▸ You can output video via FireWire to an NTSC display (which requires a DV-to-video converter box) as well as to Apple Cinema Display via Digital Cinema Desktop. Choose File > Project Settings > Video and choose a setting from the Video Output pop-up menu. For FireWire video streaming, it is necessary to compensate for the latency in the FireWire setup. This will be a constant amount you can adjust by choosing Logic Pro > Preferences > Video and dragging the External Video to Project slider until the image and sound synchronize.

Using Markers to Spot the Movie

When you're choosing the places where music will enhance your project, you can use Logic during or after the "spotting session" with the director to mark those specific time code locations for the musical cues. Creating markers for this task enables you to place text notes at specific SMPTE positions to use as timing references.

In the scene you are working with in this lesson, the director has specified a change in mood after the male character is inadvertently hung up on while confessing his love for the female character on the phone.

1   Press the Go to Position key command (/). In the Go To Position dialog, single-click in the As SMPTE field, enter *3.4.25.1.10*, and then press Return.

NOTE ▸ When entering SMPTE time code, you can use colons, periods, or spaces to delineate hours, minutes, frames, and subframes.

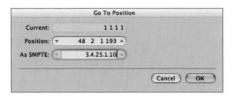

The project locates to 03:04:25.01.10 (as seen in the giant SMPTE display).

2   From the main menu bar, choose Options > Marker > Create Without Rounding, or press Command-Apostrophe. A new marker, Marker 1, is created at the current play-head position.

NOTE ▸ The Create Without Rounding command creates a marker exactly at the playhead's current position on the SMPTE ruler, instead of at the beginning of the nearest bar.

3   Control-click the new marker (Marker 1) and choose Rename Marker from the shortcut menu. Enter *Mood change* for the marker name, and then press Return.

4   Click the Lists button to display the Marker List.

The new marker appears in the list, with position being displayed in bars and beats. Although this is musically useful, it's more relevant to display this list in SMPTE time instead of bars and beats.

5   From the Marker List View menu, choose Event Position and Length in SMPTE Units.

The list is displayed with SMPTE timings. To make sure the new marker won't be affected when changing tempo, you need to lock its SMPTE position. This guarantees that the marker will not move when the project's tempo is changed. You will explore this concept a bit later in the lesson.

6   From the Marker List Options menu, choose Lock SMPTE Position.

A small lock appears by the marker name.

TIP ▸ Markers can be used as the basis for beat mapping, similar to how you used the Beat Mapping track to align both MIDI and audio events to bars and beats in Lesson 2. You can use this technique to align the downbeat of a measure to an exact moment in the movie that is represented by the marker. When the marker is selected, its starting point is displayed in the Beat Mapping track, allowing you to drag nearby bar and beat lines, aligning the two.

Detecting Cuts

Often a director will want musical cues to begin near scene cuts to accentuate the transition from one scene to the next. You can use Logic to identify relevant visual cues in a video with a unique function called Detect Cuts. When this function is activated, Logic analyzes the video information and creates a special marker, called a *scene marker*, at locations where the image changes drastically (such as at scene cuts).

Detecting cuts can be done for isolated areas (in marquee, cycle, or region selections), or for the entire video.

1   Press Command-Shift-A to deselect all markers in the Marker List.

2   In the global Video track, click the Detect Cuts button.

A status bar displays the progress for cut detection.

After the process is completed, scene markers (designated by the movie frame symbol) for the entire movie are created in the Marker track, and they appear in the Marker List.

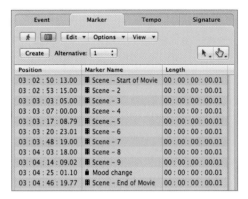

NOTE ▶ Scene markers are automatically locked to SMPTE positions.

3   In the Marker List, use the Finger tool (currently your Command tool) to click the markers in the list.

The movie locates to scene cuts and other points where the video image changes drastically.

NOTE ▶ You can also use the Go to Next Marker and Go to Previous Marker key commands (Control-Command-Right Arrow/Left Arrow) to locate along the scene markers.

4   Click the Go to Beginning button to return to the beginning of the project.

5   Close the Lists area.

TIP ▶ The Marker track can contain multiple alternative tracks, similar to those you looked at in Lesson 2 in the Tempo track. By choosing options in the Alternative pop-up menu, you can create separate markers for marking musical sections and for spotting sound effects or musical cues.

Importing Media

Integration between the editing suites used by video editors, sound designers, engineers, and composers has traditionally proved to be a hurdle when these groups collaborate on media projects. However, integration has been improved with the development of formats that allow you to exchange media with colleagues while maintaining their SMPTE position relevant to the project.

In the following exercises, you will import media in different formats into the current project while retaining the time code information.

Importing XML from Final Cut Pro

Logic supports Extensible Markup Language (XML) files as an interchange format. XML is used by some of the Apple Pro applications, such as the video production application Final Cut Pro, to store relevant information. This information can be exchanged between the supporting applications. For example, XML exchange allows you to import audio files used in a Final Cut Pro project, including their timing and automation information, into Logic's Arrange area.

For this exercise, an XML file has been created from a Final Cut Pro project. This file contains information about the file locations and timing for two tracks of sound effects that the video editor has placed in a Final Cut Pro sequence.

1   Use the Zoom Horizontal Out key command (Control-Option-Left Arrow) to zoom out horizontally, so you can see all of the markers.

2   Click the Global Tracks disclosure triangle to hide the global tracks.

3   Choose File > Import.

4   Go to Music > Advanced Logic 9_Files > Lessons > 16_XML Exports and import **Leverage XML**.

A dialog opens, displaying the sequence information from the original Final Cut Pro project file.

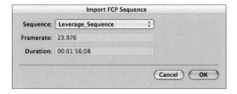

5   Click OK.

A prompt appears, asking you to relink the XML file's associated audio files by choosing the correct file path.

6   Click OK.

7 In the file selector dialog, open the Foley_1.aiff file from Advanced Logic 9_Files > Lessons > 16_FX from FCP.

The audio files associated with the XML file are imported into two new tracks in the Arrange area.

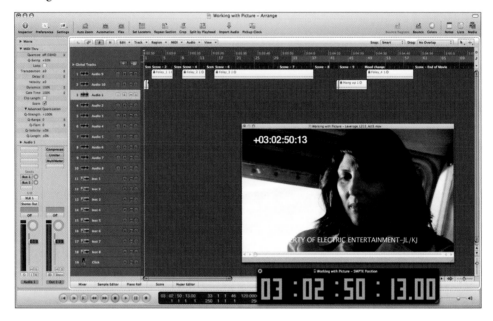

NOTE ▶ Logic creates pairs of mono tracks panned left and right when importing XML. You can always reposition them in the stereo field using the channel's pan knob, or Option-click the pan knob to reset to center position.

8 Play the project, listening to the imported sound effects in relation to the video. Stop playback.

Importing Broadcast WAVE Files

Broadcast WAVE files are similar to files in other PCM audio file formats (such as AIFF), but they also contain time code information in the header of each file that is saved when the file is recorded. That information allows you to import and export these audio files between applications while retaining their absolute position in time.

You can test this by importing a sound effect in the Broadcast WAVE format.

1 Select the Audio 1 track (now track 3).

2   In the Transport bar, click the Go to Beginning button to return to 1 1 1 1.

3   Choose File > Import Audio File.

The Open File dialog appears.

4   Go to Music > Advanced Logic 9_Files > Lessons > 16_FX and open **Static.wav**.

You are prompted by dialogs asking if you want to import tempo and marker information for use in the project.

5   If you are prompted to import tempo and marker information, click No for both dialogs.

The audio file is added to the Audio 1 track at measure 1 1 1 1.

6   With the region highlighted, in the Arrange area's local menu bar, choose Audio > Move Region to Original Record Position.

The Static region locates to the time code position contained in the audio file (03:04:03:18.22).

7   Play the project, observing how the Static audio works with the movie.

> **NOTE** ▶ You can save newly recorded audio files in the Broadcast WAVE format by choosing Logic Pro > Preferences > Audio > General and choosing the format in the Recording File Type menu. When this feature is chosen, all saved audio files will include the region's original record position.

Locking SMPTE Position

Now that you've imported the sound effects, it is a good idea to lock their positions to the SMPTE position so that they cannot be moved by mistake. If you time-lock the effects, you can adjust the music tempo freely without changing the effects' placement in relationship to the movie.

1   Choose Edit > Select All.

2   In the Arrange area's local menu bar, choose Region > Lock SMPTE Position. All regions now display a lock icon in front of their names and cannot be moved.

Now that the regions have been locked, let's see how tempos can be changed without affecting the locked regions' SMPTE positions.

3   Click the background of the Arrange area to deselect all regions.

4   Click the Static region and hold down the mouse button, observing the SMPTE and bar positions displayed in the help tag.

```
Move Regions
4   Static
      37  3   3   83.         4   3   1   70.
 03 : 04 : 03 : 18.22   00 : 00 : 09 : 15.52
```

Note that the SMPTE position is 03:04:03:18.22, which corresponds to the bars and beats position of 37 3 3 83.

5   In the Transport bar, double-click the Tempo display and enter 66. Press Return.

The project tempo changes to 66 bpm.

6   Click the Static region and hold down the mouse button, again observing the SMPTE and bar positions displayed in the movie window.

```
Move Regions
4   Static
      21  1   3   118         2   2   2   123.
 03 : 04 : 03 : 18.21   00 : 00 : 09 : 15.52
```

The region's SMPTE position remains the same as before, but the corresponding bars and beats position is now 21 1 3 118.

When an event is SMPTE locked, it always maintains its time code position, regardless of the tempo.

Importing Audio from the Movie

Listening to the dialog track from the referenced QuickTime movie isn't ideal for most recording studio setups, because the system sound output is most likely not routed to the reference monitors to avoid hearing alert and other system sounds. In order to hear the video's soundtrack through Logic's Mixer, you must extract the audio from a given video file to a new track in Logic. This enables you to easily mute and adjust volume levels for monitoring while you are working on the session.

1   At the lower left of the QuickTime Player, click the speaker icon and drag the volume slider down all the way, muting it.

2   From the File menu, choose Import Audio from Movie.

The soundtrack, named after the video file (Leverage_L215_Act3), is extracted from the video and placed at the top of the track list.

NOTE ▶ Audio imported from movies is always locked to SMPTE position in order to maintain sync.

TIP ▶ Composers are often supplied with a video file possessing a stereo soundtrack that has dialog on the left side and a temp music or sound effects track on the right side. When you import the audio from the video into Logic, you can monitor each of these signals separately by using the Left and Right settings in the input format menu for the channel strip.

Positioning Events on the Timeline

A common task when working with picture is syncing events to specific SMPTE positions. These events could be sound effects referenced from an Edit Decision List (EDL), or musical hits in the arrangement that punctuate visual cues. Being able to quickly and accurately place events on the timeline is a necessity when you're arranging material in a session that has been locked to a SMPTE position.

In this set of exercises, you will learn various techniques for efficiently placing events on the SMPTE timeline.

1   In the toolbar, click the Media button to open the Media area.

2   If needed, reposition the floating movie window and SMPTE display so it doesn't block the Media area.

3   In the Audio Bin, select Audio File > Add Audio File.

The Open File dialog appears.

4   Go to Music > Advanced Logic 9_Files > Lessons > 16_FX and add **Helicopter_1.aif**, **Helicopter_2.aif**, **Helicopter_3.aif**, and **Helicopter_4.aif** to the Audio Bin.

Positioning an Event by Spotting the Video

The simplest technique for positioning an event on the timeline is by manually spotting the video as you drag the event into the arrangement.

1   In the Audio Bin, play the **Helicopter_1.aif** audio file to audition it.

2   Drag the **Helicopter_1.aif** file from the Audio Bin to the Audio 2 track, holding down the mouse button and moving the file back and forth along the timeline while watching the movie. (Continue to hold down the mouse button for step 3.)

     Notice how the movie syncs with the position of the dragged audio file. You can use this visual reference to place cues at specific locations.

3   Position the Helicopter_1 region to sync with measure1. Release the mouse button.

4   Click on the Arrange area background to give it key focus, and use the Play from Selection key command (Shift-Enter) to play the project starting at the selected Helicopter_1 region.

     The helicopter sound effect plays in sync with the video scene.

5   In the Transport bar, click the Stop button to stop the project.

Using Pickup Clock

Let's continue importing audio files into the arrangement, this time aligning the event precisely to the playhead's SMPTE position by using the Pickup Clock command.

NOTE ▶ This function is accessible only via key command or a button added to the toolbar.

1   Use the Go to Previous Marker and Go to Next Marker key commands (Control-Command-Left Arrow/Right Arrow) to locate the playhead to the Scene – 3 marker (03:03:03:05.01).

2   In the Audio Bin tab, drag the **Helicopter_2.aif** file to the same track to which you dragged the previous helicopter sound effect, this time placing it around measure 5.

3   Press the Pickup Clock key command (semicolon).

    The selected region snaps to the playhead position.

4   Click on the Arrange area background to give it key focus. Then use the Play from Selection key command (Shift-Enter) to play the project from the newly positioned region, viewing its placement in relation to the movie image.

5   Stop the project.

6   Using any of the techniques from this or the preceding exercise, place the **Helicopter_3.aif** and **Helicopter_4.aif** files from the Audio Bin onto the same track you have been working with at SMPTE positions 03:03:17:08.79 and 03:04:03:17.79 respectively. They should align with the Scene – 5 and Scene – 8 markers.

7   Play the project, listening to your work.

8   Save the project.

9   Close the project.

    NOTE ▶ When you save the project, a copy of the video file is saved to a newly created Movies folder in the project folder. You set this up earlier in the lesson by selecting "Copy movie files to project folder" in the Include Assets area when you created a new project from the template.

Delivering the Soundtrack

When it comes time to deliver the soundtrack, Logic gives you various options. In addition to performing a standard bounce of the entire mix, you can create a new video file that includes the project's audio, and even create stems, or submixes, that contain isolated material of like kind, such as instrument type or family.

For this exercise, you will be using a finished version of the musical cue for the video with which you have been working.

1   Choose File > Open.

2   Go to Music > Advanced Logic 9_Files > Lessons and open **16_Leverage_Start.logic**.

The project opens.

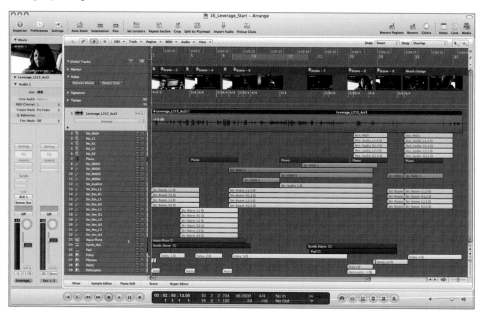

3   Play the project to familiarize yourself with the musical score.

4   Click Stop twice to return to 1 1 1 1.

As you probably noticed, the movie is viewable in its own area at the top of the Inspector. This provides a space-saving alternative to a floating window, which could obscure track material. However, the display might prove too tiny to work with, and it can be displayed in the larger, floating window by double-clicking the movie in the Inspector.

5   Double-click the Movie area in the Inspector. The movie opens in a floating window.

6   If you'd like, play the project again, listening to the soundtrack while you watch the video.

7   Close the movie window. The video returns to the Inspector.

Exporting Audio to Movie

While you are working on a project, you may wish to supply the client or director with a new video that includes your soundtrack in order to solicit feedback. You could conceivably export high quality audio to the video, but you'll more likely want to send a compressed version of your mix, significantly reducing the file size so that it can be easily sent via the Internet.

In this exercise, you will export your soundtrack to the project's video, compressing it with one of the available codecs.

1   Choose File > Export Audio to Movie. The Sound Settings dialog appears.

2   From the Format menu, choose AAC, and then click OK.

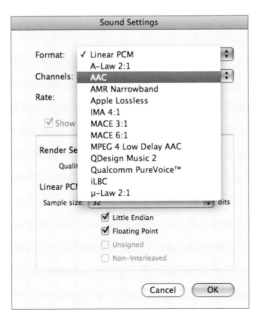

3   In the Save As dialog, name the file *Leverage Mix*, and save it to Music > Advanced Logic 9_Files > Lessons > Completed.

Another dialog appears, allowing you to choose the audio tracks from the project's video file that you want to include in the new movie. In this case, it represents the dialog track that is a part of the video.

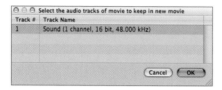

The dialog track has already been imported into the project's Arrange area, so leaving this selected would have the undesirable result of doubling the dialog track.

4   In the dialog, click the background to deselect the original audio track, and then click OK.

Logic bounces the project's mix to the referenced video file, converting the audio to the compressed format you chose.

5   In the Finder, locate the new video, Leverage Mix, located in Music > Advanced Logic 9_Files > Lessons > Completed.

6   Double-click the movie file to play it in QuickTime.

Creating Stems for Dubbing

Stems are highly useful in the final dubbing, or mixing, stage, for the simple fact that they allow the engineer to make last minute adjustments when doing the final mix. These can be created in Logic by first assigning channels of like material to specific busses for sub-mixing, similar to what you did in Lesson 11.

1   Click the Mixer tab to open the Mixer.

2   Drag across the french horn channels (2–6), selecting them.

3 Click the output field on any of the selected channels and choose Bus > Bus 2.

A new aux channel is created in the Mixer (Aux 2), and all selected channel outputs are now assigned to Bus 2.

4 Use the same technique to group tracks by like kind (piano, strings, synths, FX), assigning them to separate busses for output by using the following chart:

Track Number	Track Material	Output Assignment
7	Piano	Bus 3
8–22	Strings	Bus 4
23–25	Synths	Bus 5
26–29	FX	Bus 6

You now have a total of five aux channels in your Mixer devoted to stem groups. In order to record the stems, you need to create five new audio tracks with the inputs set to receive the outputs of the individual stem busses. This way, you can record the outputs of the submixes onto new tracks in the Arrange window.

5 Close the Mixer.

6 Select the last track (track 29, or Helicopter) in the track list.

7 In the Arrange window's submenus, choose Track > New Tracks.

8   Use the New Tracks dialog to create five new stereo audio tracks with Bus 2 selected for Input and both the Ascending and Record Enable options selected.

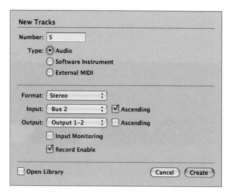

9   Label the new tracks *Horns*, *Piano*, *Strings*, *Synths*, and *FX*, in that order, using the Tab key to go to the next track. These will be the new stem tracks you will record onto.

10 Click the Record button, recording the bus (stem) outputs for the entire length of the project. Click Stop.

Five new tracks are created, containing your stem mixes. Now all that's left to do is to copy them from the Audio Bin or Finder for delivery.

TIP ▶ Having the music, dialog, and effects separated as stems makes creating foreign language versions of the movie easy. All you need to do is to replace the dialog stem, keeping the music and effects (referred to as "M&E") stems the same, saving you the trouble of remixing the entire project.

Lesson Review

1.   What settings govern how a digital video clip is synchronized in Logic?

2.   Where can SMPTE time code be displayed in Logic?

3.   What type of Final Cut Pro exported file format can be imported into Logic?

4.   What audio file format contains timing information and can be imported into Logic?

5.   How can you change the project tempo without changing a region's position?

6.   What kinds of markers are created with the Detect Cuts function?

7.   In what ways can regions be positioned on the timeline?

8. Which command is used to create a new video with your project's soundtrack?

9. What technique is used to create stems?

Answers

1. Digital video clips in a Logic project can be synchronized by setting the SMPTE start times, frame rates, and movie start times.

2. Logic can display SMPTE time code in the SMPTE ruler, Transport, and giant SMPTE display.

3. Final Cut Pro XML files, including automation information, can be imported directly into a Logic timeline.

4. Broadcast WAVE files can be imported directly to a Logic timeline and retain their original recorded positions.

5. SMPTE positions of regions and events can be locked, enabling you to change tempos without changing the SMPTE timing.

6. Detect Cuts creates scene markers that can flag scene cuts and other major visual changes.

7. Regions can be positioned on the timeline by placing them manually, by using the Pickup Clock command to align them with the current playhead position.

8. Logic's Export Audio to Movie command is used to create a new video, marrying the project's mix with the referenced video.

9. Stems are created in Logic by assigning tracks of similar material to a common bus and then recording its output to a new track.

17

Lesson Files	Advanced Logic 9_Files > Lessons > 17_Gibsonia_Start.logic
Media	Advanced Logic 9_Files > Media > Gibsonia
Time	This lesson takes approximately 30 minutes to complete.
Goals	Prepare a Logic session for export to Pro Tools
	Import a project to Pro Tools
	Moving a project back to Logic

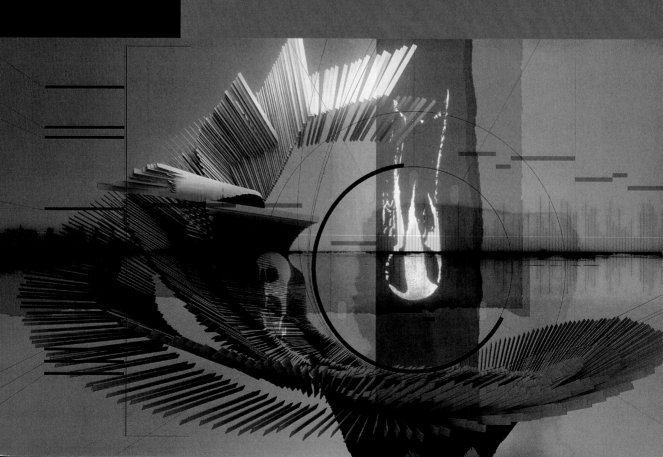

Moving Projects Between Logic and Pro Tools

Most musical projects involve some form of collaboration with other people and/or facilities in order to take advantage of various talent and technical resources. The project you'll work with in this lesson is a perfect example. This singer/songwriter piece is at a point where the vocal, guitar, and bass parts have already been recorded into Logic, and it's now time to add drums. This song's raw acoustic flavor merits recording a live drummer with an acoustic kit. Unless you already have a sonically isolated and treated room with a large microphone collection, it probably makes more sense to rent a recording studio with the proper facilities and an engineer experienced in the art of recording a drum kit.

Moving a project out of the project studio and into a commercial recording studio is a critical step that can be plagued by time-consuming and costly mistakes if you don't understand the technical nuances involved.

When you look at a Logic project's Arrange area, you can see a layout of regions across the tracks in the project. Regions reference sections of audio files and can be placed anywhere along the timeline. This information is contained within a DAW's Edit Decision List (EDL).The problem is that whereas most DAWs can share compatible audio files, the EDLs that DAWs use are not typically compatible, making it a challenge to move multitrack projects between different programs. It's even more challenging when software instruments like the piano track used in this lesson are involved, because it's rare that different DAWs will have the plug-ins necessary to render the MIDI information with the correct sound.

In this lesson you'll learn a workflow that will help you avoid the pitfalls of session compatibility so that you can have seamless collaborative experiences with users of other software. Due to the wide use of Avid's Pro Tools, this lesson will focus on how to quickly move this project into a Pro Tools environment in order to acquire the drum tracks, and later return the recorded material back to Logic for further production.

> **NOTE** ▶ This lesson focuses on a Logic Pro 9/Pro Tools 8 workflow, but you will not need Pro Tools to complete the lesson. The main goal is to understand the concept behind what is happening. Most of the information expressed here will also apply to other digital audio workstations.

Exporting a Project

In order for the session drummer to lay down his or her part, you need to provide the Pro Tools studio with a set of multitracks exported from your Logic project. Because most people like to reference and edit musical bars, you'll also export a tempo map of the song so that the Pro Tools operator can benefit from referencing musical bar lines and section markers.

Exporting Tracks as Audio Files

One of the easiest and most reliable methods of exporting a project for use in another DAW is to deliver a single audio file for each track of the project. These audio files will later be aligned once they get to Pro Tools.

> **NOTE** ▶ Logic supports the ability to import and export projects using standardized project types such as OMF and AAF. These options provide the ability to maintain region positions by using a standardized EDL, but they do not support the sharing of software instrument tracks, nor will they contain channel strip effects. Moreover, Pro Tools requires a costly software option in order to add this support, so many studios do not have this capability.

1   In the file selector dialog, go to Music > Advanced Logic 9_Files > Lessons and open
17_Gibsonia_Start.logic.

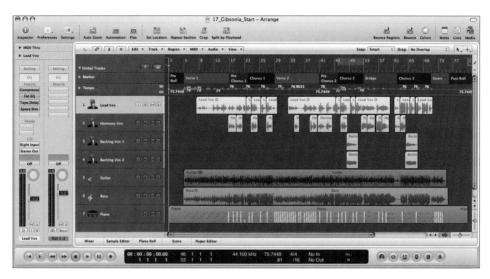

2   Play the project.

Notice that there are four bars of empty space before the song begins. This space will
be included in the audio files you're about to create. Having several bars of space
before the first beat of the song will give the drummer in the studio time to lock onto
the tempo of the project and can also be helpful if additional parts might be recorded
as a lead into the first measure. Although bars of space can be added in the studio,
having this placeholder already in place eliminates confusion when the recorded
drums are brought back to the Logic project.

TIP ▶ You can insert empty bars into the beginning of a project by using the Insert
Silence Between Locators command discussed in Lesson 7.

In Lesson 11 you learned how the Bounce In Place feature can be applied to tracks
and regions. You'll now use a similar command that can be executed for all tracks in
the project at one time.

3   In the main menu bar, choose File > Export > All Tracks as Audio Files.

A dialog opens. You must now choose an audio file type. WAVE files are the most
commonly supported audio file type and work with Pro Tools systems on either the
Mac or PC platform.

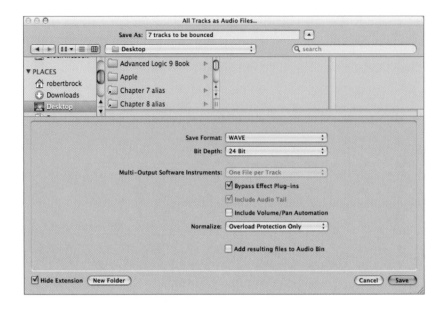

4 From the Save Format pop-up menu, choose WAVE.

Bit resolution impacts sound quality. Although the tracks you're going to export are only going to be used as reference material in the studio, Pro Tools will have to convert the audio file's bit depth if it doesn't match the setting used in the Pro Tools project in the studio. Keep it simple and avoid confusion by setting bit depth to the quality you want the drums to be delivered in. Most professional recording studios will use 24-bit depth.

5 From the Bit Depth pop-up menu, choose 24 Bit.

NOTE ▶ Sample rate of the exported files will be the same as the project's sample rate. This project's sample rate is 44,100 Hz (44.1 kHz). It will be important to know this when the Pro Tools session is created in the studio.

An important consideration is whether or not to include channel strip effects in the exported tracks. Including the effects limits what the studio engineer can do to tailor sounds to the liking of the musicians in the studio, but in some cases effects are a critical part of how a track is musically perceived. In this case effects like the reverb on the Lead Vox track can be recreated in the studio without too much trouble.

NOTE ▶ Effects applied using sends will not be included in the exported audio files.

6 Select the Bypass Effect Plug-ins checkbox.

Now you must choose where you want to save the track audio files you're about to export. In this case you'll create a folder on the desktop as your destination.

> **TIP** ▶ If you want to include effects on some tracks but not others, first bypass the undesired effects in channel strips and do not select the Bypass Effect Plug-ins option in this dialog.

7 Press Command-D to change the directory to the desktop, and then click the New Folder Button in the lower-left corner.

8 Enter *Gibsonia Reference Tracks* as the folder name and click Create.

9 Click Save.

Onscreen you'll see progress indicators as Logic renders each track as an individual audio file. The playhead will move across the Arrange area showing the progress as well. This process will vary in the time it takes depending on the project length and track count.

10 In the Finder, navigate to the desktop and look inside the Gibsonia Reference Tracks folder.

All the audio filenames include the track name with the extension _bip (bounce in place).

Name	Date Modified	Size	Kind
Backing Vox 1_bip.wav	Today, 6:52 PM	26.3 MB	WAVE Audio File
Backing Vox 2_bip.wav	Today, 6:52 PM	34.9 MB	WAVE Audio File
Bass_bip.wav	Today, 6:52 PM	29.4 MB	WAVE Audio File
Guitar_bip.wav	Today, 6:52 PM	78 MB	WAVE Audio File
Harmony Vox_bip.wav	Today, 6:52 PM	33.3 MB	WAVE Audio File
Lead Vox_bip.wav	Today, 6:52 PM	74 MB	WAVE Audio File
Piano_bip.wav	Today, 6:52 PM	78.3 MB	WAVE Audio File

/Users/robertbrock/Desktop/Gibsonia Reference Tracks

Notice that all the files are not the same size. There are two reasons for this. In this example, stereo tracks such as the piano require twice as much space as mono tracks such as the bass. In addition the files are rendered from the beginning of the song, to the point where the track last produces audio material, resulting in files of different lengths.

Exporting a Tempo-Marker Map

When producing music, it makes sense to have the timeline expressed as bars and beats when making edits, generating click tracks and referencing specific points in the song. If your project has a constant tempo, this is as simple as entering the same tempo and time signature into Pro Tools. However, if there are tempo or meter changes throughout the song, this becomes a much more complex process. In order to make the Pro Tools time-line match the bars and beats of the Logic session, every tempo or time signature change must be reflected in the Pro Tools tempo list.

Displayed in the Global Tempo track, the current project has a complex tempo map because the song was originally recorded without a click track and later beat mapped, which created numerous tempo changes. There is also a Global Marker track with song sections clearly identified.

Rather than trying to re-enter all the tempo and marker information into Pro Tools, you can use a standard MIDI file to communicate all of this information in a few easy steps. To export a standard MIDI file, you need at least one MIDI region in your project.

1   Return to the Gibsonia Logic project and select the Piano region.

Notice that the Piano region starts at bar 1 and extends through the end of the project. It's important that the MIDI region is as long as the entire song because only tempo and marker events that are within the boundaries of time covered by the region will be exported.

TIP ▸ If your song doesn't contain any MIDI sequences, you'll need to create a new track and record at least one MIDI event into that track. Change its region length to start at bar 1 and extend through the end of the project so that all tempo and marker events will be included in the exported file.

2   In the main menu bar, choose File > Export > Selection as MIDI File.

The "Save MIDI File as" dialog window appears.

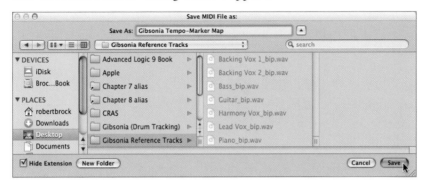

3   In the dialog's Save As field, enter *Gibsonia Tempo-Marker Map*.

4   Navigate to the Gibsonia Reference Tracks folder you created on the desktop and click Save.

The Gibsonia Reference Tracks folder is ready to be transferred to a portable drive or burned to an optical disc for transfer to Pro Tools.

Importing Projects into Pro Tools

Now you are ready to import your prepared reference tracks into Pro Tools. This section is designed to help you see the collaborative process from the Pro Tools perspective. Although you won't be working through detailed lesson steps, reading through this section will give you better insight to the technical considerations of exchanging files. You'll be able to better communicate the specifics of what you want to take away from the session.

> **NOTE ▶** Although general Pro Tools operation will not be covered, this section will highlight steps that are important to understanding and navigating the collaborative process.

Setting Up the Session

Upon creating a new Pro Tools session, a New Session dialog appears, containing session parameters. What is chosen here directly impacts session compatibility.

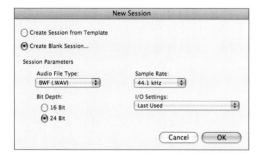

▶ Choose BWF (.WAV) to match the reference files.

NOTE ▶ The audio file type used in the Pro Tools session is not critical—it can be converted without impacting quality at a later time.

▶ Select 24 Bit to match the reference files.

▶ Match the Sample Rate to your exported reference files (in this case 44.1 kHz).

Importing the Audio Files

Because all your audio files were bounced starting at the beginning of bar 1, all imported audio files need to placed at the beginning of the project.

▶ Import the reference audio files you created with Logic as new tracks.

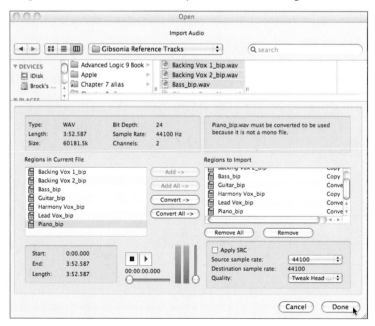

NOTE ▸ The Import Audio dialog will indicate that some files must be converted. This is because Pro Tools is unable to play the stereo interleaved files Logic exports. Conversion will copy stereo interleaved files and store them as two mono files (one for each channel).

▸ Choose Session Start in order to place the audio files at the beginning.

The audio files are imported, and Pro Tools displays the audio files you exported from Logic.

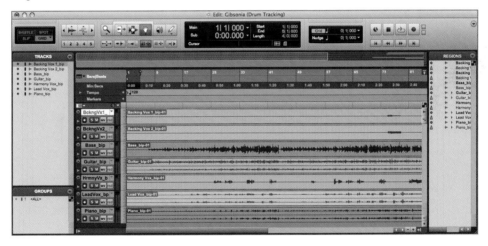

Importing the Tempo-Marker Map

You can see that the Bar/Beat ruler is not accurate because the Logic project file ended at bar 81, where in the Pro Tools session the regions extend beyond that measure. This is because Pro Tools is set to a default tempo of 120 beats per measure. Because you saved a standard MIDI file with tempo and marker information, it is only necessary to import the MIDI file to quickly create a map of the song's tempo and sections.

NOTE ▶ It is important that the Elastic Audio feature (similar to Logic's Flex Time) is disabled on all tracks before importing a tempo map to prevent time compression/expansion of the audio in the project.

▶ Import the MIDI file you created in Logic.

▶ Select "Import tempo map from MIDI File" in order to extract the tempo and marker events.

The Tempo and Marker rulers now show the imported events, and the audio regions now correctly align with the bar lines.

Recording New Tracks

Once the reference tracks are imported, new tracks for the drums will need to be created.

▶ Use stereo tracks instead of two mono tracks for anything that uses stereo microphone techniques such as drum overheads.

NOTE ▶ Although stereo tracks are not recorded as interleaved audio files, having recorded with stereo tracks will make it easier to export stereo interleaved files later.

At this stage Pro Tools is configured to record the drums, and the session can proceed without further consideration of compatibility until the recording process is finished.

Consolidating Tracks

In the process of recording it's possible that the drummer might be punched in and out at different parts of the song, or that edits might be made to the recorded audio files. This will result in numerous regions that begin and end at different times in the track. In order to successfully return the recordings to Logic while maintaining the proper timing relationships, you need to render each track as a single audio file, much like you did when exporting the tracks from Logic. Unfortunately Pro Tools doesn't have an Export All Tracks as Audio File feature, but you can create a similar result by consolidating (merging) the regions together in each of the respective tracks.

▶   Smooth edit transitions.

▶   For each track, consolidate all regions to the beginning of bar 1.

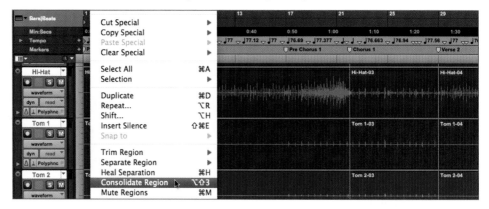

After consolidation, each track will contain a single region that is ready to be exported.

Exporting Audio Files

The consolidated audio files are stored in the Audio folder inside the Pro Tools project folder. Although it's possible to dig these files out of this location, exporting the files from within the Pro Tools session provides options for converting sample rate, bit resolution, and file type. Most importantly, exporting will provide an option for turning any material recorded on stereo tracks, such as the overheads, into a stereo interleaved file that is preferred in Logic.

▶   Select the drum regions in the region list.

▶   Export the regions as 24-bit, 44.1 kHz WAV files.

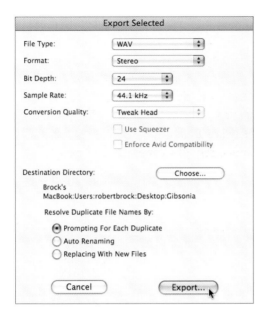

After a few moments, the exported files will appear in their destination folder, and they're ready to be introduced to the original Logic version of the Gibsonia project.

Importing Audio Files into Logic

The drums recorded for Gibsonia were prepared for you in advance and are in the Media folder included on the DVD that came with this book. You'll now import the drums into the Gibsonia project.

1   Select the Piano track header.

The files you're about to import will be added to tracks below the selected Piano track.

2   In the Finder, navigate to Advanced Logic 9_Files > Media > Gibsonia > Gibsonia Drums.

To import the drum tracks, simply drag the entire Gibsonia Drums folder to where you want the tracks to appear.

3   Drag the Gibsonia Drums folder from the Finder into Logic's Arrange area while using the help tag to position the folder at 1 1 1 1.

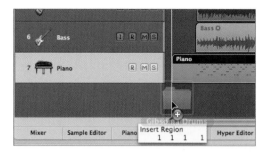

When you let go of the mouse, a dialog appears, asking you to specify the track placement for the imported audio files.

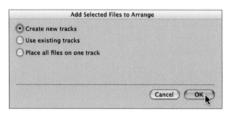

4   Select "Create new tracks" and click OK.

The drum audio files are imported onto new tracks starting at bar 1 and located just below the piano track.

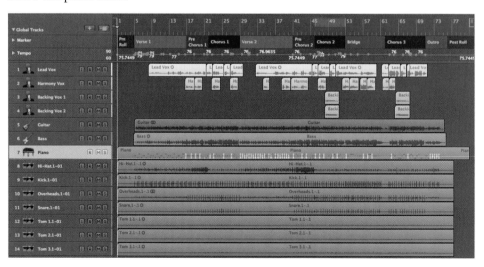

5   Drag the track headers to rearrange the track list into the order you prefer.

6   Play the song with the newly imported drums.

Lesson Review

1. In Logic, how can you export audio tracks in a way that will be compatible with most other DAWs?

2. How can Logic's tempo, meter, and marker lists be exported for use in other DAWs?

3. How can you insure that tracks recorded in Pro Tools will work properly when they are imported into Logic?

4. How can you import audio files recorded elsewhere?

Answers

1. Use the "Export All Tracks as Audio Files" command to render both audio and software instrument tracks as unique audio files.

2. Export any MIDI region from the project as a standard MIDI file. Be sure the MIDI region extends through the entire length of the project.

3. Consolidate each recorded track before exporting. Be sure that the sample rate matches the original Logic session, and stereo files should be interleaved.

4. Drag them from the Finder into Logic's Arrange window, and then reorder them as necessary.

Index

Apple Certification
Fuel your mind.
Reach your potential.

Stand out from the crowd. Differentiate yourself and gain recognition for your expertise by earning Apple Certified Pro status to validate your Logic Pro skills.

How to Earn Apple Certified Pro Status

This book prepares you to earn Apple Certified Pro – Logic Pro Level Two. Level One certification attests to essential operational knowledge of the application. Level Two certification demonstrates mastery of advanced features and a deeper understanding of the application. Please note that Level Two exams can be taken only after Level One certification is earned. Take it one step further and earn Master Pro certification in Logic Studio.

Three Steps to Certification

1 Choose your certification path.
   More info: training.apple.com/certification.

2 Select a location:

   Apple Authorized Training Centers (AATCs) offer all exams (Mac OS X, Pro Apps, iLife, iWork, and Xsan). Please note that all AATCs offer all exams, even if they don't offer the associated course. AATC locations: training.apple.com/locations

   Prometric Testing Centers (1-888-275-3926) offer all Mac OS X exams, and the Final Cut Pro Level One exam. Prometric centers: www.prometric.com/apple

3 Register for and take your exam(s).

Reasons to Become an Apple Certified Pro

- **Raise your earning potential.** Studies show that certified professionals can earn more than their non-certified peers.

- **Distinguish yourself from others in your industry.** Proven mastery of an application helps you stand out from the crowd.

- **Publicize your Apple Certifications.** Each certification provides a logo to display on business cards, resumes and websites. In addition, you can publish your certifications on the Apple Certified Professionals Registry to connect with schools, clients and employers.

Training Options

Apple's comprehensive curriculum addresses your needs, whether you're an IT or creative professional, educator, or service technician. Hands-on training is available through a worldwide network of Apple Authorized Training Centers (AATCs) or in a self-paced format through the Apple Training Series and Apple Pro Training Series. Learn more about Apple's curriculum and find an AATC near you at training.apple.com.

training.apple.com/certification

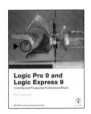

Alchemy

The Ultimate Sample Manipulation Synthesizer

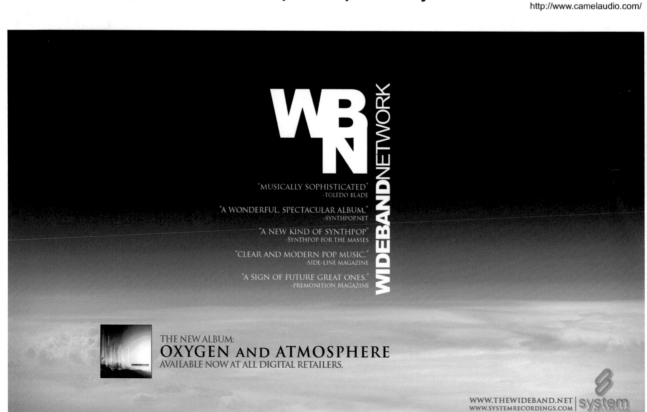

Brandon Jaehne

acoustic rock

nashville, tn

for more music, visit
www.myspace.com/brandonjaehne
for booking info, contact
brandon.jaehne@gmail.com